Amidst the Fray

Amidst the Fray

My Life in Politics, Culture, and Mississippi

WILLIAM D. MOUNGER
WITH JOE MAXWELL

Wm D Mounger

Glenn, be nice to your baby sister.

Billy

QUAIL RIDGE PRESS • MMVI

First Edition
Manufactured in the United States of America

Design by John Langston

Library of Congress Cataloging-in-Publication Data

Mounger, William D.
   Amidst the fray : my life in politics, culture, and Mississippi / William D. Mounger ;
with Joe Maxwell.
     p. cm.
   ISBN-13: 978-1-893062-97-9
   ISBN-10: 1-893062-97-X
     1. Mounger, William D. 2. Politicians--Mississippi--Biography. 3. Republican Party
   (Miss.)--Biography. 4. Mississippi--Politics and government--1951- 5. Fund raisers
   (Persons)--Mississippi--Biography. 6. Businessmen--Mississippi--Biography. 7. Art
   patrons--Mississippi--Biography. 8. Jackson (Miss.)--Biography. 9. United States
   Military Academy--Biography. 10. United States--Politics and government--20th
   century. I. Maxwell, Joe, 1962- II. Title.
   F330.3.M68A3 2006
   976.2'063092--dc22
   [B]   2006021407

QUAIL RIDGE PRESS

P. O. Box 123 • Brandon, MS 39047
1-800-343-1583 • info@quailridge.com • www.quailridge.com

CONTENTS

PART THREE. THE GOP STORM

PART FOUR. DAYS OF FAME (AND SHAME)

ACKNOWLEDMENTS

Consummate procrastinator that I am, this book would not have evolved if my son Billy, about two and a half years ago, had not stated that "I am fed up with your intention to write a memoir, I am going to make it happen." As a consequence, he contracted with his friend, experienced writer and fellow Christian activist, Joe Maxwell, to work with me to compile this depiction of my life. Without the prodding and insistence from Billy together with his substantial monetary expenditures, this project would have died aborning.

It has been immeasurably pleasing to work with Joe Maxwell, with his writing expertise together with his knowledge of the necessary requisites to publish such a book. It has been a great pleasure to have worked with someone of such a good moral, family, and Christian background.

Fortuitously, Dr. Orley Caudill interviewed me in 1977 for approximately forty hours which was transposed into 359 written pages for "The Mississippi Oral History Program of the University of Southern Mississippi," which served as the initial genesis for this written outpouring. Without these interviews the earliest material would have been much more difficult to recall correctly. "Southern's" oral history program is of utmost importance for future generations.

Many people have incessantly urged me to write a memoir, but my friend Craig Castle, (deceased) was the most goadingly insistent. Also, I am very appreciative of the contributions of Fox Garraway, Jim Furrh, Billy Powell, Bill Spell, Wirt Yerger Jr., Nat Rogers, Herman Hines, Clarke Reed, Senator Thad Cochran, Senator Trent

Lott, Governor Haley Barbour, my son Bobby, my wife Jan, and my incomparable assistant for 44 years, Peggy Mize, plus many others who are not herein enumerated.

William D. Mounger

WRITER'S NOTE

By Joe Maxwell

William Donald Mounger, now 80, voraciously reads biographies. Hundreds of them line his home's bookshelves. "Why read a novel," he quips, "when true life is infinitely more entertaining?"

To read Mr. Mounger's biography is to read the history of that "greatest generation"—of many in Mississippi and nationally who dared challenge "evil empires" abroad and the stateside status quo. Beyond its political and cultural accounts, this book's rendering aims to be an enjoyable and factual story—a tale full of moral and material consequence and contrast.

Poet Ralph Waldo Emerson is said to have written, "To be great is to be misunderstood." Mr. Mounger and key compatriots are great and, doubtless, often misunderstood. A few young bucks took on and defeated a stagnant state one-party political system that was a national embarrassment, ushering in the modern Mississippi Republican Party. For years, as well, Mr. Mounger out-fundraised every other GOP state party in America!

Yet lost in such obvious accomplishments are Mr. Mounger's love of language and his commitment to excruciating self-examination. For instance, Mr. Mounger insisted that this book include, as much as possible, interviews and opinions from key rivals—an acknowledgement that life is a complex web. Some may protest at Mr. Mounger's full disclosure of certain episodes, but this book is merely the reflection of a man who does not hedge.

My thanks to Mr. Mounger for allowing me to work at his side. I have learned so much from him and had fun, too. I am grateful to his son, and my friend, William M. "Billy" Mounger, who invited me to partner on this excursion. I am inspired to know this superbly successful businessman who is more conversant in theology than most ministers. Billy is sought-after by many, yet sold out to his family. He is the closest I know to a truly humble man.

Thanks to my wife, Rosanne, and our five children for their love and support. I am grateful to my colleagues at Belhaven College for stimulating friendships and expressions of interest. Finally, as all of the aforementioned would no doubt agree, praise to God, who uses passionate men like Mr. Mounger for his great purposes in this world. Along with Mr. Mounger, a lover of biographies, I hope you will find his life story as entertaining and provocative as a good novel. I sure have!

Joe Maxwell
Journalist-in-Residence
Belhaven College
Jackson, Mississippi
Summer 2006

INTRODUCTION

By William M. Mounger, II

If the LORD delights in a man's way, he makes his steps firm; though he stumbles, he will not fall, for the LORD upholds him with His hand. I was young and now I am old, yet I have never seen the righteous forsaken or their children begging bread.

They are always generous and lend freely; their children will be blessed. Turn from evil and do good; then you will dwell in the land forever for the LORD loves the just and will not forsake His faithful ones. Psalm 37:23–28 NIV

From an eternal perspective, the impact of one individual on human history seems small and insignificant. Upon closer examination, however, God creates each individual human being in his image with the qualities to make good contributions to human society and history is the sum of individual interactions. Yet most never reach their potential and are content to exist as part of mass culture, living and dying without any real effort to have a meaningful impact on human society.

This book is the story of an individual who has tried to make a difference in every endeavor in which he has participated. He has always had the perspective of a great battle between two philosophical camps of history. The first camp consists of those who believe that human nature is perfectible and that with correct education, cultural influences, and social engineering human society can reach the utopian ideals articulated in ideals of liberalism, humanism, enlightenment philosophy, Marxist socialism, and Post-

Modern atheism. The second camp consists of those who hold that we live in a fallen world where human nature is not perfectible, and only through dependence on the Creator God and his principles can human society maximize its potential. This camp most often recognizes that a free enterprise economy is the best system to harness sinful human nature, and an open, competitive political system allows human creativity to flourish while restraining the negative aspects of human nature. It is "amidst this fray" that my father charged as a young man and he has never wavered from any of his beliefs throughout his battles.

As a young man growing up, I remember my father imparting to me a simple quote that his father inculcated in him: "Be honest and pay your debts." My father added to that simple yet profound saying the concept that "we are put on this earth for a purpose beyond a mere existence like that of animals." As such, he taught me the value of doing our best at everything, whether it be education, sports, business, politics or philanthropic pursuits. My father understood that real significance is found in character, integrity, leadership and unselfish giving to others.

My father, "WD," as I call him now, has the exceptional gift of being able to convince people to give their hard-earned money to various worthy causes. I remember going to his office as a young boy and playing with his "coffin bank," a small, plastic coffin-shaped toy on which you could place a coin and a plastic skeleton hand would reach out and rake the coin into the coffin. The true point that he would make with this toy is that "you can't take it with you." Over the years this gift of fund-raising helped establish the Republican Party and a two-party political system in the South and led to the election of governors, congressmen, senators and perhaps even the president of the United States. As such, one individual from the poorest state in the United States, with the help of others for sure, has in some way affected human history in a meaningful way.

It is ironic that it was not until mid-life that he realized the principles for which he was fighting were based on a biblical world-and-life view. Though he has fought hard for good government and other causes, he has always understood that ultimately all politicians, governments, nations and cultures will pass away. Furthermore, in the midst of all his various battles, through good times and difficult ones, WD has been a loyal and sincere friend to his contemporaries and a loving husband, father and grandfather to his family.

In the process of creating this book we have tried to present events in a complete and balanced way, yet WD is quite outspoken, so his presuppositions and opinions are quite evident. Whether you agree with him or not at least you know where he stands. With this warning, read on if you dare. It is my sincere hope that the stories and experiences recounted in this book will entertain you, inspire you, and encourage you as you carry forward your own life "Amidst the Fray."

PREFACE

By William D. Mounger

[Author's note: This preface was written approximately eighteen years ago, in one of my abortive efforts to write this autobiography; and it is just as pertinent today as it was then.]

Is it the height of vanity to assume that others are interested in an agglomeration of experiences and events from one's own life? Perhaps? In justification for plunging ahead, hundreds of people have stated that I should write a book.

Every person lives a unique life; consequently, each could convey some beneficial message to mankind if he were sufficiently motivated. What do I have to convey? More, or less, than the norm? Certainly, I have been in the maelstrom of many activities, particularly those pertaining to politics. Are people interested in these activities? Can I describe them in an interesting and readable fashion? Can I delve into my own psyche to explain my evolution through so many controversial involvements?

How does a person develop into what he ultimately becomes? The very serendipity of creation is mind-boggling. Why the Good Lord chose the proper elements to unite the appropriate split second is beyond our human comprehension. He knows, for he has a plan for each of us on earth; and this compilation is an attempt to depict his plan as it pertains to my life.

My growth, development, and education are possibly sufficiently abnormal to merit a modest amount of interest; but my Republican political activities are, to say the least, unique. Leavening the politics with tennis tournaments, governmental commissions, the Channel 3

TV settlement, West Point, numerous nationally recognized cultural exhibitions such as the Palaces of St. Petersburg, and the U.S.A. International Ballet Competitions brings additional spices to the table.

What has caused me to become so controversial and to participate in so many convoluted situations? Am I an iconoclast who wants to tear down and destroy, a conservative in the Edmund Burke tradition, or am I an atavistic reincarnation of my fourth great-grandfather, General Elijah Clark, a truly individualistic and recalcitrant character?

Oh, well! Here it goes; but it also may die here, too.

Part One:

Mississippi Made

CHAPTER 1

1976: The Political
Storm before the Calm

Magnolia State delegates were ensconced at an old Ramada Inn in Independence, Missouri, home of Harry S. Truman, the only U.S. president to drop the atom bomb. Now a figurative atom bomb hurled through political space at this suddenly powerful Mississippi entourage. NBC, ABC, and CBS network crews crowded our every move. *New York Times, Washington Post,* and *Los Angeles Times* writers greeted us in the lounge at breakfast. News-hungry correspondents would avidly listen to glean comments.

Clarke Reed—a Delta political dealer and the state Republican Party chairman—and I, the state party finance chairman, led Mississippi's bicentennial-year delegation into history-making, heartbreaking territory at the 1976 Republican presidential convention in nearby Kansas City. Mississippians in 1976 commanded the nation's attention, after a mere twenty-two years of modern Republican Party-growth efforts in our state. Forget New Hampshire or Iowa; Mississippi, as much as any other state, would plot America and its Republican Party's future in 1976 and, arguably, for years to come.

You couldn't eat or breathe for reporters. Everybody wanted a story from us. Every second they wanted to learn what was going on, which made it very hard to operate. All us Mississippians were in a fish bowl. We couldn't think. We almost felt that if one of us took a shower, a TV camera would be peering at us. The press continuously knocked on my door in the middle of the night while I was trying to sleep. Everyone from Mississippi had to deal with this constant attention.

Satellite trucks sporting space-age dishes surrounded our Ramada, beaming worldwide the latest Mississippi chirp. A relatively tiny but flamboyant group, Mississippi's mere thirty delegates to the Kansas City convention suddenly held GOP center stage. In years to come, our new Republican Party in Mississippi would place two of our own among the top four most powerful U.S. senators in the nation; two Mississippians would co-chair the Republican National Committee; two of Mississippi's four congressmen would be prominent Republicans; two of our three most recent Mississippi governors and lieutenant governors would be Republicans, the first since Reconstruction. Perhaps no other state would experience such gargantuan political shifts at the end of the twentieth century.

How we Mississippi Republicans gained such power is a true American success story. I feel blessed to have been part of it, an entrepreneur who did what he could to lend his fund-raising skills and old football tenacity to an increasingly high-tech and savvy political landscape.

This book tells many stories. There are the sickening stories about former Mississippi governor Bill Allain, sad stories of former United States congressmen Jon Hinson and Mike Parker, happier stories about Haley Barbour, Thad Cochran, and Trent Lott, and a bevy of other recollections. There are stories of me living at West Point, flying bombers, and saving the U.S.A. International Ballet Competition. There are stories of black transsexual prostitutes and of princes. In countless battles spanning more than four decades, I've offered my opinions to others and the media, and my course will not change in this book.

Old South honor with a New South vision might describe my hopes for our state. I was greatly influenced by my years growing up in Jackson, by the privilege of attending the United States Military Academy, and by decades of political and entrepreneurial challenges.

Nothing, however, could prepare me fully for that 1976 Republican National Convention, which proved to be a coming of age for the state party apparatus. It was unique. Rarely in Mississippi history have the national media centered on our state. The exception would be the times of racial strife or natural disaster. Of course, the 1976 spotlight was really more than some of my Mississippi colleagues could, in truth, handle. Perhaps that was one of the reasons that some didn't act appropriately during the 1976 convention in Kansas City.

But on the other hand, it is absolutely amazing that twenty-eight of sixty delegates and alternates at the convention held their ground amid so much turmoil and the currying of favor from a sitting president of the United States, Gerald Ford. These brave twenty-eight delegates and alternates did so with nothing personal to gain, only a hope for good government, service to the cause, building the Mississippi Republican Party, staying compatible with the people, and following their conservative instincts. All of those are ethereal things. They're not like a job or a contract. They're not like an invitation to the White House, appointments for kin folks, or personal perks.

Politics attracts various people for sundry reasons. I hope that I have represented most Mississippians' propensity for principle over persona or power; yet every principle eventually leads to a defining precipice. History was at stake in 1976—Mississippi's, the nation's, and the world's. The Republican National Convention of 1976 danced on the razor's edge with the potential for altering lives. It ultimately led to four years of Jimmy Carter as president, years conservatives—and even some liberals—have deemed disastrous. Ironically, in truth, those Carter years paved the way for Ronald Reagan to succeed in the 1980s.

The 1976 convention played out in the shadow of the recent Watergate scandal that caused President Richard Nixon to resign. Vice President Gerald Ford—who had earlier replaced a disgraced Vice President Spiro Agnew—eventually filled Nixon's Oval Office vacancy. Ford's field generals came to Kansas City's Republican National Convention to seek four more years for Ford, after Ford initially said he would not run for a full term of office. Ford now pursued a presidential popular election and an attempted resuscitation of northern Republicanism prominence.

Ford's cabinet had a residue of Richard Nixon's choices. Nixon had won the South four years earlier in his 1972 reelection, but had long since disillusioned many of us southern leaders with an aloof, unapproachable staff. Southern Republicans had called Nixon's team the "mafia" long before Watergate made these miscreants into water-cooler chitchat.

Now the nation's bicentennial celebration—1776 to 1976—was on. It couldn't have come at a more important time for our deflated United States of America. After Nixon's fall and the debacle of Vietnam, the bicentennial was a chance for fireworks, patriotism, and renewed hope. The nation embraced the bicentennial year like lemonade in a sultry southern August! And as if by script, a rising star came out of Hollywood—a California governor with a clear vision contrasted to Ford's muddled ideas. Ronald Reagan was the anti-Ford—approachable, affable, and pristinely conservative. Ronald Reagan, a patriot and personal friend, was a true speech-maker to counter Ford's stultifying intonations.

Reagan's charisma was known and loved in the South long before 1976. His type of true conservatism had been spawning a modern Republican revival since at least the early 1960s. During the 1964 presidential campaign of Arizona senator Barry Goldwater, conservative Republicanism had filled the South; one of Goldwater's greatest cheerleaders was Ronald Reagan. Reagan made a half-hour nationally televised speech in 1964 on behalf of Goldwater; that speech was re-aired by the National Republican Party using excess Mississippi GOP state funds of about $140,000 raised almost exclusively by me. Reagan's "Goldwater Speech" invigorates true southern conservatism to this day.

This book is the story of how my peers and I jumped on board the national Republican machine to ride for all it was worth. In many ways, our story is original; in some ways it parallels hundreds of leaders nationally in my generation who felt a tug to pursue our beliefs through public means. Several of us got into the fray in the early 1960s to change the balance of political power not only in Mississippi, but also nationally. My good friend, Senator Trent Lott, kindly recognizes the efforts of our generation. I am happy to say that I am the only senatorial campaign fund-raising chairman that Trent has ever had. Says Senator Lott: "I consider myself one of the first generations of progeny of Billy Mounger's Republican generation. [His generation] were the ones who did the organizing and raised the money. But then they went out and got candidates. That's one of the things I like about Billy Mounger. Billy's not involved because he wants to be invited to the White House or because he wants to go the Republican National Convention; no, he wants to win elections and put men and women in office who will make a difference."

By the time Ronald Reagan threw his trademark cowboy hat into the ring against Ford before the 1976 convention, we were seeing a new brand of conservatism growing nationally; it was replacing a stale, southern Democrat conservatism tied to segregation and party patronage. We new Republicans had made our mark by the time Reagan finished two terms in office. Everyone had to recognize that the Republican Party nationally and in Mississippi was suddenly a dominant force.

Anyone can note all the "red" states on the political maps during election night coverage in recent years. We Mississippians now exert political power disproportionate to our citizenry's numbers. Thad Cochran, whom I personally recruited in 1972 to run as a Republican in the state's Fourth Congressional District, now heads the all-powerful Senate Appropriations Committee. When Thad first ran, we believed that he met the criteria we needed to be successful in electing Republicans to Washington—someone educated and thoughtful, who was also in touch with the rural part of the state. Thad offers these kind words regarding my political instincts: "For Billy to have figured that out [concerning the kind of person Mississippians would elect], he really was kind of a genius, really quite impressive."

Ideas have power. This fact makes our story of southern Republicanism go. And it is no surprise that as the nation celebrated its two-hundredth birthday in 1976, the ideas that sweltered into bright hope in Mississippi caused the nation's neon lights to shine curiously back our state's hot, humid way.

In the mid-1950s, the state's fledgling Republican Party was inert, almost invisible in the face of a heaping Democrat machine.

(In this book, I choose always to call the rival party of the GOP the "Democrat" Party, versus the "Democratic" Party; thus, also, the "Democrat" machine; this is due to my conviction that all good Americans are "Democratic!") Rising from turn-of-the-twentieth-century Reconstruction, the Mississippi Republican Party eventually became known as the Black and Tan Party, a largely inept, invisible group led up to the fifties and sixties by Perry Howard, a black Mississippian in name who resided in Washington, D.C. No real party apparatus existed at the midpoint of the twentieth century. However, by the 1950s, national Democrats began to mock and dismiss the brand of largely racist conservatism maintained by southern Democrats, who held onto power by flaunting patronage and years of service in the United States House of Representatives and Senate. These southern Democrats—led in Mississippi by United States senators James O. Eastland and John C. Stennis—did what they could to insure that Mississippi stayed a one-party state. In so doing, they had to trade votes with liberal northern Democrats, often supporting liberal laws that Mississippi conservatives disliked.

But a new conservative taproot—informed by a desire to achieve a two-party system in Mississippi—started in the 1950s and fed life into a host of upstart hopefuls; ideas of strong defense, greater states' rights versus federal intrusion, and lower taxes watered a collective soul. By the 1960s, with the rise of Arizona senator Barry Goldwater's conservative Republicanism, Mississippi's GOP was newly constituted and gaining steam.

Spiro Agnew (before resigning the U.S. vice presidency) came to the state on October 20, 1969, to speak to one of the earliest significant gatherings of Republican Mississippians (itself the largest political fundraiser in the history of Mississippi). Agnew told the crowd that national Republican leaders were convinced that "Mississippi should become a strong state in the Republican column." Agnew further joked regarding the gargantuan 2,600-person audience of Mississippi conservatives—both Republicans and Democrats—listening to his speech: "From what I was led to believe, Republican dinners in the Deep South attracted the party loyal from ten counties and there was still room for the rest of the state's

Republicans—in a phone booth. . . . I think this turn-out proves some of Washington's political pundits wrong."[1]

Party leaders were cheered by Agnew's words. We even saw him as an emerging, strong conservative whom we might happily support once President Nixon finished his second term in the White House. Then Agnew ignominiously fell and was replaced by a much more moderate Michigan congressman, Gerald Ford.

This shift, along with the accompanying Watergate scandal, was terribly timed as young Republicans in Mississippi struggled for in-state validation; nonetheless, we did not cease. We wanted a clean break not only from Watergate, but also from the antique Reconstruction-era state Republicanism and the sycophantic Mississippi Democrats who told voters one thing but then kowtowed to their party's liberal majority.

Mississippi's new Republicans had achieved autonomy and national respect by the mid-1970s. We managed this by voting consistently as a bloc (via a system known as a "unit rule") at the Republican National Conventions, a practice that now has ceased. Bloc voting galvanized our limited political power until the last second at the national convention; early on, it was a good political strategy. Mississippi's new Republicans had built our party ranks while remaining mostly undetected by the national media's radar in the 1960s and early 1970s. The light now glared on us as Ford's and Reagan's campaign staffs scrapped for votes in the summer of 1976 leading into Kansas City. Our Gulf Coast state's thirty delegate votes resembled a school of fecund fish for the political sharks.

Clarke Reed, our state GOP chairman in 1976, and I, the state GOP delegation vice chairman and state finance chairman, were to keep those delegate votes together, as the Mississippi bloc had done in 1968 and 1972. Safety and strength in numbers would be key at the 1976 convention. Any strays were potential dead meat for hardened political hacks from the Ford or Reagan camps. The moment was fraught with important implications, but it also was what Mississippi Republicans had worked for—a chance to play at "the table." Mississippi and Clarke Reed were "in the catbird seat," Ford southern political strategist Harry Dent cawed.[2]

Seeing the chance to pick off some Magnolia State votes—or at least to bust up the tightly schooled political guppies—President

Ford dispatched Dent to work our Mississippi delegation. Dent wanted to break up our delegation's commitment to vote as a unit-rule bloc for Reagan. Any break could topple Reagan's election chances and seal the national deal for Ford. As summer yielded to fall in 1976, the "catbird seat" suddenly became a hot seat. Extreme political maneuverings and pressure by the Ford campaign staff, coupled with 180-degree turns by some key Mississippi party leaders prior to the national convention, blew this ember into a blaze, and I was consumed with trying to hold together our group in its stated commitment to Reagan.

Mississippi's thirty delegates plus thirty alternates (one delegate and one alternate equaled a total of one actual vote, for a total of thirty delegate votes) were, indeed, suddenly the "kingmaker of this convention," as Dent predicted.[3] Many of our delegates had never attended a national convention, but now held potential glory in their hands; they also knew they could become national scapegoats, something we state party leaders adamantly had hoped to avoid. What would the average, Reagan-loving Mississippian back home think if we didn't keep our intention to vote for Reagan?

Never had Mississippi Republicans' favor been so curried; Mississippi Democrats at their national conventions were mocked and ignored by their national leaders, something that had not escaped the notice of average Mississippians. The national press at Kansas City showed the nation a new sight as they reported on the emerging importance of Mississippi's Republican bicentennial delegation. Viewers around the nation could surely sense the Democratic vice-grip loosening in Dixie. A West Point graduate and a high-school All Big-8 football lineman, I knew something about teamwork and staying the course. But in 1976, just trying to hold the delegates in line would tax me to the core for several weeks. The magnitude of the moment began to overwhelm all of us.

Kingmakers? Sitting in the catbird seat? Mississippi's movements during that 1976 convention would decide much. Whom would the Republicans choose to oppose Georgia's Jimmy Carter? A litany of repercussions followed: the nation's teetering economy, a troubling nuclear arms race, Islamic strife, and a disheartened populace stung by Watergate and Vietnam. Suddenly Mississippi seemed the potter and its delegation like magical clay. As went our Magnolia State, so went history.

A political convention resembles an unfolding battle. You do things in the heat of the campaign and a lot of times the best things you do just occur at the moment, taking advantage wherever the opportunities are. I always have approached political conventions like war or football. I have a fighter's nose, which has taken many a hit; and, no doubt, I have a no-nonsense oilman's defiance in me. I've tried to hold unflinching ideals of duty, honor, and country, and to keep my promises. My nickname was "Bull" in my youth, and I admit to hitting the opposition hard; but I've always tried to play by the rules. I want the ball when the pressure is on, but in 1976, the Republican convention eroded my soul; it was almost like a combat zone.

During the convention, Ford's staff wore signature red caps on the convention floor. Red seemed to pop up everywhere. Ford's staff had stacked the deck allowing very few Reaganites easy floor access. The breakdown of Ford-to-Reagan floor workers seemed at least 150 to 5. Ford's red caps exploited weakness like a wolf pack, using the story-hungry media to create confusion. Both the media and the Ford camp began spouting that my GOP partner, state chairman Clarke Reed, was imminently vulnerable.

Starting in the mid-1960s, Reed and I had worked together to build the Mississippi Republican Party. We were a strong team, but were actually polar opposites. Reed has always been more hip than hardnosed, a posh dresser and sound-bite factory known for testing the wind before taking a step. For years he had chaired the Southern Association of Republican State Chairmen as well as the Mississippi Republican Party. He planned to cede his state office after Kansas City to a rising young conservative star—state senator Charles Pickering.[4] Reed clung to the state chairman title through the Kansas City convention as a token nod, insisting that his experience at prior conventions would help prevent any problems with the 1976 delegation and the convention voting allocation process. Keeping Reed as our chairman through the convention all but insured an eventual battle of wills between some of us whose idealism told us to do the honorable thing, and those heeding Reed's emerging pragmatism that indicated an opportunistic jump from Reagan to Ford. "[Reed] liked to think and say that he acted out of ideological conviction," wrote long-time Washington correspondent Jules Witcover in his acclaimed book, *Marathon: The Pursuit of the Presidency, 1972–76*. Witcover added: "But the truth was that Clarke Reed's strongest ideological conviction was that the causes in which he believed were best served if he ran with a winner, if he could retain power."[5]

To me, however, if you have given your word to back Reagan, then you must do so; honor and principle are preeminent. Mississippi Governor Haley Barbour, who attended the 1976 GOP convention as the cub executive director of the Mississippi Republican Party, knows that I've participated in my share of arguments in which I felt the honorable path was threatened. Barbour in 1976 was charged with the unenviable job of keeping consensus among our Republican delegates, and he watched those groundbreaking days at the convention—no doubt learning a few things!

Barbour says that I am "representative of the [West Point] long gray line and the beliefs they teach at the academy."[6] I hope so. I believe that the values instilled at West Point are right, and along with those of the Bible, they guide my conduct. Governor Barbour continues: "[Billy] didn't care if it was politically popular or not; he was going to be for what he thought was right. And he was going to be for whom he thought was right. I have said this a zillion times to people about Billy Mounger: If Billy Mounger tells you something, he believes it's true. It may not always be right but he believes it's true. He is a straight shooter if there ever was one. And his politics are that way, and I'm sure it rubbed some people the wrong way, because he's blunt and he's outspoken, but you always know where he is because he's a straight shooter if there ever was one."[7]

Adds Barbour:

Interestingly, we don't think about Mississippi being an entrepreneurial state, but when [Mounger] was coming along after the war in the fifties and sixties, one of the centers of entrepreneurship in Mississippi was the oil-and-gas industry. We didn't have the big oil companies in state. We had these "little guys" who were independent businessmen. They called themselves "independent operators" or "independent producers," but they were small business people, family business people. They were the ultimate entrepreneurs and it is no coincidence that the Republican Party in Mississippi and nationally is the entrepreneurial party and that these guys would be leaders in the entrepreneurial party. One thing I've learned about entrepreneurs—they're for what they're for. They are not going to support some politician to get access. They're not going to pay the cannibals to eat them last. They give to what they're for and they give to the candidate they're for. And, if the guy gets 30 percent of the vote, well they know that they gave to the person they believed in.[8]

The governor's words are kind. I hope that to some extent those words are true. I try to decide what is right and then stand behind it. I saw in 1976 that we were in danger of abandoning the clear mandate of the Mississippians who sent us to the convention! The world watched as some of us strived to keep our promises. That is always the pattern for me. Whether it has been fighting for Ronald Reagan in 1976, fighting to elect a young Thad Cochran to the United States Congress in 1972, or helping Trent Lott win the United States Senate in 1988—whatever the challenge, I've always gone all out to achieve principled goals. My story, however, begins not in lofty adulthood, but in a simpler time of childhood—living in a joyful place called "Jackson."

CHAPTER 2

The 1930s: Big Bill and Little Billy

"**B**uckalew."

The name inspired thoughts of shootouts and bad guys and courage. And it inspired me as a young boy. Buckalew represented real manhood, with his stocky build, ready smile, and the motorcycle he rode. Plus, Buckalew wore a star—he was a policeman. Buckalew bravely stood down traffic outside Power Elementary School, which I attended as a five-year-old. The world bent to this officer's beckoning. Cars stopped, turned, and started again. A whirl of his wrist was all that was required. As Buckalew stood daily in his police blues, I sometimes dreamed of becoming a cop like Buckalew one day.

Our Mounger family lived away from the better part of town in an unpretentious house on Keener Avenue, off of Northwest Street and west of Millsaps College. As a five-year-old I roamed our neighborhood's rolling hills. Trains sounded nightly to the west along the Illinois Central railroad. Feral woods once full of Indians led eastward to the Pearl River. Knobby hills to the east of Millsaps College eventually were leveled to construct Bailey Junior High School, an architectural feat featured in *Life Magazine*. Jackson's downtown unfolded southward in a line of homes that yielded to the old charity hospital, then to the Baptist Hospital and down to Capitol Street and the Mississippi State Capitol.

Every day, my dad bummed a ride to this downtown land of adulthood. He was important. People called Bill Mounger, my father, a "man's man."[1] His astounding banking career had barely begun. It eventually would take him to the presidency of the state's largest bank, Deposit Guaranty. Leland Speed Jr.—currently the executive director of the Mississippi Development Authority; a major real estate developer; and an R.E.I.T. entrepreneur (Parkway and Eastover corporations)—grew up down St. Ann Street from me. He recalls how his father, Leland Speed Sr., admired my dad. "My father used to just laugh at Mr. Mounger Sr.," recalls Speed. "He said, 'You've got every damn S.O.B. in the state of Mississippi as a customer.'"[2]

Each school day my mother or a friend drove me from our tiny home, past the Jewish Cemetery at North State Street and Pinehurst, to Power School. There, I watched morning and afternoon for Buckalew to direct me across the street. I relished walking by Buckalew. Power School was the best elementary education Jackson had to offer. Most of the children came from the prominent Belhaven neighborhood on the east side of North State Street. My schoolmates were a "Who's Who" of those-who-would-become-something in the capital city.

Each afternoon I exited Power's school door to the playground (where most of First Presbyterian Church now sits to the north). Iron stars held the decrepit school building together, and westward across the street, Stars of David speckled the Jewish graveyard. My buddies prowled Power's playgrounds while Model T and Model A Fords bounded over North State Street. Cars pulled over on Pinehurst and picked up school children. Buckalew calmly directed motorcars. No one—no one—crossed North State Street without Buckalew's permission.

Then one day . . .

For whatever reason, the traffic cop was gone this day. Everyone seemed gone—all my kindergarten buddies were already picked up. "Heck," I thought, "there isn't anything to crossing this street. I'll just do it myself and then walk the mile-or-so home on my own. That's better than waiting for no one to come for me." I dashed for the other side. Skidding tires shrieked. A thud. I lay like a wounded deer in North State Street. Mrs. Morrison popped from her Model A to my woozy side. Someone scooped me up and conveyed me up the hill to the Baptist Hospital. My leg was set in a full-length cast. A broken fibula. A scraped head. Missing teeth.

Mrs. Morrison thoughtfully came to visit. Other family and friends regularly checked on me. The *Daily Clarion-Ledger* newspaper took a photo of me on my crutches a few days later and ran a neat article. And Buckalew came to the Baptist Hospital. The policeman felt at fault that he had not been there for my safety. The stocky cop produced a present. My five-year-old hands opened the package revealing a two-in-one screwdriver/hammer with variable settings. That trusty tool from Buckalew became my faithful companion—a badge of courage.

Outpourings of sympathy flooded the mail to my parents. Mr. W. A. Shipman of the State of Mississippi Department of Justice wrote: "I was inexpressibly shocked to learn of the accident by which your little son was hurt." My Aunt Lanna wrote from Oklahoma City to my mother that she "got [my mother's] letter late last night telling me of little Billie [sic] getting run over. It does seem that we all are headed for the hardest luck that can be imagined and that 1931 is our peak year," adding that her husband was scrounging for work in that Depression-marred time and that they would offer to help monetarily but "money is something 'we ain't got' and can't get as long as we have no income." The Great Depression was hitting everywhere, and no doubt my aunt was sad she could offer us no assistance.

Mrs. Morrison's insurance company paid a thousand dollars to me. My father held it in trust.[3] Misfortune seemed prevalent when my paternal grandfather died shortly after my accident. This October 28, 1931, letter of sympathy from Bill Mounger's pastor at Galloway Memorial Methodist Episcopal Church, South—the Reverend Lawrence Ludlow Cowen—stated:

> Owing to my absence out of the city for the past week, I did not
> learn until yesterday of the serious accident that happened to your
> young son, and when I called to express my personal sympathy for
> you and yours in the serious illness of your fine boy, I was deeply
> shocked to learn through your inestimable good wife, of the sudden
> death of your beloved father. I cannot begin to convey to you in

words my keen sense of condolence for you and the members of your family in this added grief that has come into your life.

It does seem at times that it "never rains, but that it pours down." Sorrows have a way of coming in bundles, and testing the faith and courage of us all. Learning that you would be out of the city, and in order that you may know of how deeply all of us sympathize with you, I am using this means of conveying to you our most tender feelings to you. . . .

Faithfully your pastor,

Lawrence L. Cowen

Football consumed my later elementary years. When we Power School guys weren't playing pickup softball down below the old charity hospital (the only ground close to level in the area!) or where the First Presbyterian Church is located today, we were playing football about anywhere. Our little sixth-grade football team played one game a year against Davis School. The boys at Davis bragged: "We have a player named Jerry Tiblier who can't be stopped!" When the teams finally met, Power won 20–0. I scored all twenty points.

The *Clarion Ledger* reported on another game, "Bailey Juniors Win Opening Game 26–0 From Greenwood," stating that "Billy Mounger, husky fullback, shifted this year from the line, counted" for one touchdown. Another report stated that I "bucked the ball over center for five yards and a touchdown." The big rivalry was with Enochs Junior High, and in that game, I scored on fourth down from the six-yard-line to win 6–0.

Girls started looking pretty, too. These were beautiful girls: Polly Wells, Jane Ross, Dorothy Lee Crum, Doris Johns, and Deanie Wallace. All of them married local boys. All of them were eye-catchers. Polly Wells ended up "Most Beautiful" at Central High School and at Ole Miss, and most of the others were "beauties" at Central and Ole Miss.

We boys ogled as much at anthills, squirrels, and thunderstorms as at the girls. Jackson's future leadership was maturing. Leigh Watkins would later found a top electrical engineering firm; Sam Sanders became a prominent oral surgeon; John Countiss was named a federal judge; Fox Garraway, my lifelong close friend, owned an insurance agency; Eddie Guillot owned a dental supply company and a real estate agency; Harold Caver became a dentist; Dick Deaver became a scientist. Curiously, for my sixth birthday, the preponderance of invitees were girls, according to the following report in the *Clarion Ledger/Jackson Daily News*:

> William Donald Mounger, son of Mr. and Mrs. William Mounger, celebrated his sixth birthday with a party in their home on Keener Street. The guests were greeted at the door by the honoree, who presented them with paper caps and candy suckers dressed like dolls. After a number of games and contests were enjoyed on the lawn, ice cream and cake were served by Selby Watkins and Marjorie Mounger. The guests were Adine Terrell Wallace, Patty Grayson, Julia Goodman, Selby Watkins, Miriam Mary Marceline, and Asa Warren Hersey, Eva Hart, Billy Hollingsworth, Betty Jean Garner, Emily Winters, Betty Jane Varnado, Henry Phelps Jr., Helen and Dorothy Macharon, Mary LaVerne Gosley, N. E. Gozley, Dickey Russell, and Anabel Holiday, and Majorie and Olivia Rosalma Mounger.

We Jackson boys often traipsed to the Pearl River, through lush woods rolling east of the Belhaven neighborhood, past where Eudora Welty would eventually write classics. The Jackson waterworks emerged over the crest of one hill. The hill later became part of LeFleur's Bluff State Park; however, in the 1940s Indians still visited the bluffs once a year, where they built a bamboo tepee and sold wares to the intrigued. This hill and its gullies had been their home earlier. The deep, water-hewn gullies possessed names like "Dead Man's Gulch." A boy could die plummeting into a thirty-foot hole. Fossils adorned the caves and gullies. We boys found our share.

A mile or so farther into the woods, the Pearl River's soap-white sandbars beckoned. Sam Sanders and I skinny-dipped whenever possible. By the end of our sixth-grade year we had notched a record: We swam in the river every month of the calendar year; February was jump-in-and-jump-out month, but it counted.

Great bluffs pushed up along the Pearl River, where Jackson's business district lay. Anchored by the old state capitol building at the intersection of Capitol and North State streets, fortunes were being made and lost. My father inhabited this world. Mr. William M. Mounger, or "Bill," was a handsome man. His six-foot frame sported a bowtie and suit with polished confidence. His staid demeanor and quick mind won the respect of his fellow men, who never underestimated him. A graduate of Mississippi State College, the Collins, Mississippi, native had married his high-school sweetheart, the prettiest girl in Covington County, Veronica Robertson, shortly after his college graduation, and they moved to Jackson from Hattiesburg.

Veronica was the last of nine children—five boys and four girls—and this made her the most pampered member of her family. Her father, James Robertson, was reputed to be the most popular man in Covington County. He was elected sheriff, but he was killed in 1905 before Veronica turned two. A fugitive shot and killed him while my grandfather was in hot pursuit. The following report from a local paper circulating in Covington County indicates both how beloved a man he was and how different those days in Mississippi were:

Sheriff Robertson Murdered by Two Soulless Negro Brutes

Will Robertson [sic] and Tom Fifer shoot him near Collins, killing Mr. Robertson instantly. Fifer has been caught, but Robinson is still at large, heavily armed, and his capture is only a question of a few hours.

If caught will never see prison

Tuesday night about 7 o'clock our dearly beloved sheriff, J. A. Robertson, was shot and killed about one mile from Collins on the Williamsburg Road, by a negro named Will Robinson, whom he was trying to arrest.

The following are the particulars as we get them:

It seems that several parties were in Collins Monday afternoon, under the influence of liquor. It appears they left Collins and the next heard of them was at the negro house where the killing occurred. A dispute arose between the negroes and white men, which resulted in either Fifer or Robinson hitting one of the men on the jaw with his pistol, breaking it in two places. After the melee, the white men left the negro shack, and told the negroes they would see them later. This was Monday evening. One of the parties went to Williamsburg and conveyed the intelligence to Sheriff Robertson, and Tuesday afternoon in company with the man in question, proceeded to the negro house. Before they went to the negro house to make the arrest they thought best to go to Collins and get a deputy, A. I. Walker. The sheriff, the man in question and Mr. Walker proceeded back to the negro house and demanded the surrender of the occupants. The sheriff went in at the front door and the two negroes ran out the back door. The sheriff demanded their surrender, (and reports say he shot one time at the fleeing brutes) but they kept on running and when about 25 or 35 yards off, Will Robinson raised his Winchester and commenced firing promiscuously at the posse. One of the deadly missils [sic] hitting Mr. Robertson in the mouth. He fell on his face and was dead by the time he hit the ground. Mr. Walker the deputy, and the other party seeing Mr. Robertson fall, went to him, but he was dead. The negro brutes kept on firing at Walker and the other party and as they had exhausted their ammunition nothing was left for them to do, only to get out of the battle the best way they could. They went to Collins and posses were organized to scour the country. Fifer was soon caught; Robinson was also caught, but during the excitement made his escape.

The report that Sheriff Robertson had been murdered by two negroes soon spread over the entire county and the people of Covington County were aroused and were anxious to avenge his death.

Fifer was hidden by special deputies, a fact the negro may well be proud. Had he been caugh, [sic] "business would have been picked up" and there would have been one more negro less in this world.

The dead sheriff, Mr. Robertson, was universally popular over the entire county, and had the reputation of being one of the best officers not only in the county, but the state. He knew the people; he mingled with them; he was one of them. He knows [sic] their thoughts, their wishes and their aspirations. He sympathized with them in their joys and their sorrows, and in the name of the people of this county "he was a man, take him all in all, But we shall not look upon him again."

But he is gone. In the plentitude of his fame as an officer, a citizen and a friend to one and all. Like ripened grain, he has fallen before the reaper. We deplore our loss, but our grief is not unmixed with joy. His aim is done. His record is clear. No detraction can ever dim the glory of his life. His future is in the hands of Him who is able to do for His children exceedingly abundantly above all that we, poor creatures can ask or think, or anywise worthy to receive. He believed in God and Jesus Christ, His Son. He stayed his hope of eternal life upon the word of Him who hung upon the cross; and such hope can never be disappointed.

Verily, he was to his people—A pillow [sic] of cloud by day, and a pillow [sic] of fire by night.

But he is gone! No more will we see his congenial face; no more will we grasp his benevolent hand. God knoweth best and why should we mourn? A kind father, a devout husband, a noble friend is gone. The family fireside, the community and church give silent evidence that he is gone, never again to mingle with us. Such principals [sic] as were born to him will never die. The mortal may depart. That which made him great was immortal; it was the soul, and it does not die.

Cold in dust the perished heart may life [sic], but that which warmed it once can never die.

Mr. Robertson was 45 years of age, and was serving his third year as sheriff. He has held many positions of trust. He served as treasurer and assessor of this county, positions which he filled with marked ability. He was a prominent Mason, a devout member of Williamsburg Baptist church, and by his death this county has suffered an irreparable loss.

He leaves a large family, five brothers and many relatives, all of whom have the sympathy of every man, woman and child in the county.

Funeral services were held Wednesday at Collins, by Rev. T. Dale. Late Wednesday evening his remains were consigned to mother earth in the family grave yard at Williamsburg, where they will repose in refreshing slumber, until a just and Alwise [sic] God shall proclaim that time shall be no more.

His life was like the day, more beautiful in the evening; like the summer, aglow with promises, and like the autumn, rich with the golden sheaves, where good words and deeds have ripened the field.

My mother, Veronica, never really knew her father. Her mother, being left essentially destitute upon her husband's death, converted their large home on the square in Seminary, Mississippi, into a boarding house to survive.

My paternal grandfather, Mr. Milton Uriah Mounger of Covington County, was born near Heidelberg, Mississippi, on September 13, 1867. An attorney and a "prominent member of the county bar," according to the *Clarion Ledger*, M.U. Mounger had served two terms in the Mississippi House of Representatives and four terms in the Mississippi Senate. He was a Mason and a Methodist. My father's childhood home was shared with his parents and three siblings in Collins, the county seat five miles north of Seminary, Mississippi. There he had grown up with his brothers Dwyn (who became a Presbyterian minister) and Carlton (a Millsaps graduate), and sister Marion (who attended French Camp Academy, graduated from Belhaven College, and became a school teacher and Presbyterian missionary).

My father, Bill Mounger, married Louise Veronica Robertson of Seminary in September of 1923, "amid hundreds of friends," according to a newspaper account, adding, "One of the most beautiful weddings ever witnessed in Collins was solemnized" in a "lavishly decorated" Baptist church. That led to the unremarkable day on which I was born at the Baptist Hospital in Jackson, Mississippi, March 31, 1926. My parents first lived in Hattiesburg, Mississippi, where my father was employed as a bank teller. They then moved in 1924 to Jackson where he worked as a bookkeeper for the Merchants Bank and Trust Company, located on the southwest corner of State and Capitol streets across from the Old Capitol, where BancorpSouth currently has its Jackson headquarters.

Mother was the youngest of nine children and everyone in her family pampered this little sister. Her pictures depict a beautiful girl, who was obviously very popular, especially with the boys. Several photos show her traveling and enjoying life in Model T Fords, indicating she was the belle of Covington County; thus it is easily understandable why my father fell in love with her. She attended Mississippi Woman's College in Hattiesburg, Mississippi, where she earned enough credits to qualify as a teacher. Upon graduation she taught for a year or two in south Louisiana; and, according to her, she taught some mature Cajuns to whom she had to be alert, defending herself.[4]

My mother and father were valiantly struggling economically to survive together with my sister, Marjorie Lynn (eighteen months older than I), in a small nondescript apartment in a green two-story wood frame house at 307 North Street in Jackson. The house was torn down long ago; the Eudora Welty Public Library now occupies the site. Shortly after my birth the family moved a few blocks north into a house at 816 North Jefferson Street, which has been replaced. I have only extremely vague memories about that house, one being the memory of catching the back of my head on a nail on the back porch of the house, and the other of an old up-ended black pot in the weeds of the backyard that I imagined to be a monster. I also remember a very nice house a couple of doors down the street owned by the Blands, a prominent banking family in town, who, I believe, lost most of their money during the Depression. My parents in 1928 or '29 bought a small two-bedroom one-story white wood frame house at 328 Keener Street (my father often said that the street's name was changed from "Keen" to "Keener" after we moved there) from which my first real memories emanate. I particularly remember the first car we owned, a used Essex. It was a substantially larger car than a Ford or Chevrolet, and I recall that we kept that car for a number of years. We even traveled to Arkansas in that old Essex.

My father worked very hard, and others were suitably impressed. "Other men flocked to him," recalls Nat Rogers, who worked closely with my dad.[5] With time, Rogers himself would serve as president of two banks and of the American Bankers Association. Herman Hines, another subsequent president of the bank that later became Deposit Guaranty National Bank, recalls how my father started "from scratch." His ability and presence opened doors.

Early on, my father caught the eye of Major George L. Donald, the president of the small Deposit Guaranty Bank, located next door to the Merchants Bank and Trust. The Merchants Bank and

Trust built its office building at the site of the current AmSouth building, where I have kept my office for more than thirty-five years. In 1927, the building rose in Jackson to eighteen stories, a spectacle of accomplishment admired by local citizens. Then the Great Depression hit with the "bankers' holiday" of 1933. Big banks collapsed like soufflés. Some small banks, including the Deposit Guaranty, eked through. "The Merchants Bank, the largest bank in Mississippi at the time, quit in 1933," recalls Hines. "They had their assets tied up in mortgage loans, which couldn't be easily liquidated, so they just didn't have enough liquid assets. They could have gone and borrowed them. But they got to fighting among themselves and just quit. . . . Bill Mounger joined Deposit Guaranty as a trust officer and brought the entire trust department of the Merchants Bank with him. He was a par-excellence trust man, a lawyer, a man of great breadth of understanding, great mental capacity.[6] And he loved the trust department."[7]

Meanwhile, my father's good friend, Leland Speed Sr., also from outside Collins, lost his Merchants Bank job in 1933.[8] He became self-employed in the bond business, and soon my father and Mr. Speed began a long and mutually productive business association.

Dad had been offered jobs at the larger Capitol National and the Jackson State National banks, which were both about $7 million banks. He related to me shortly before dying that the Capitol National was controlled by the Lampton family and the Jackson State was controlled by the Gaddis family, adding, "I was not a Lampton or a Gaddis, so I figured I could never be president of either bank. The Deposit Guaranty Bank was controlled by no family; therefore, I calculated that I had an excellent chance to be its president."

Within four years of going with the Deposit Guaranty, he was effectively running the bank; within eight, he was outright elected president. Bill Mounger, working on behalf of the bank and in relationship with Leland Speed Sr., cornered the market on several issues of Mississippi State Bonds. Speed decided in the height of the Depression to go into the bond business. These two young men arranged credit with the Guaranty Trust Company in New York City and proceeded to bid and win several bond issues, Speed for himself and my father for the bank. My father probably made a larger profit for Deposit Guaranty than it had made cumulatively up to that time. Dad often stated that his bond transactions made him president of the bank and made Leland Speed rich. "Mr. Mounger Sr. banked the entrepreneurs of Jackson," recalls Leland Speed Jr.[9]

Shortly after Dad went with Deposit Guaranty, the bank purchased the eighteen-story Merchants Bank building, moving its headquarters to that spectacular location. I didn't visit the bank much. The world of men and boys was kept separate in those days. The first three people seen upon entering the bank were bank president, Major Donald, his executive vice president, Mr. Myer A. Lewis, and my father, Bill, who was inveterately smoking a cigarette and eyeing the bank entrance through his black horn-rimmed glasses. Tellers behind the golden bars lined the bank's perimeter. Two or three loan officers held desks on the main floor. On the mezzanine, the guts of the bank, credit officers and money counters buzzed.

Nothing escaped the sight of Major Donald and my dad. The bank had approximately $3 million in assets in the mid-thirties (about $1 million when my father had first joined), which was relatively small. From his perch, Dad drew on a cigarette, observed his world, and fashioned the finest loan agreements ever in the state of Mississippi. He wrote a loan simply and comprehensively, perhaps better than any, recalls Nat Rogers.[10] He took risks, but never foolish ones, says Hines.[11] He exuded integrity and expected the same from clients and employees. At night, Dad studied law, eventually earning his degree. Major Donald kept handing more bank business to my father, who always produced. He earned about two-hundred dollars a month when he started working at Deposit Guaranty in 1933.

Dad may have seemed quiet, but he was no introvert, rather more forceful and to the point, recall both Rogers and Hines. Newspaper clippings from the 1930s show a youthful Bill Mounger being "elevated to the position of vice president and trust officer," stating that "Mounger is a valued official of the bank and has been connected with them for a number of years." About the same time, Bill Mounger's photo appeared with three other men wearing trademark Shriners hats with red fez. Dad led more than one-thousand "nobles and novices of Wahabi Temple" at the "Spring Ceremonial," stated the May 27, 1936, edition of the *Daily Clarion-Ledger*. His Shriner's position at the time was "chief rabban," the second in command. He eventually became "potentate," the top nabob.

The bank would grow under Dad's leadership from less than twenty employees to hundreds; from $3 million in assets to more than $200 million in the 1950s. It was the largest bank in the state, outdistancing even the First National Bank, which had been formed from the merger of Capitol National and Jackson State National banks. Dad was firmly in charge as president of the Deposit Guaranty by the time my four siblings and I reached our teen years. Major Donald died, though for several years Dad already had effectively run the bank. Bill Mounger at age thirty-nine became the state's youngest bank president. The April 16, 1941, edition of the *Daily Clarion-Ledger* ran several important headlines: "Latest Reports Indicate Nazis Scourge Allies"; "FDR Says Armed Protection Goes with U.S. Ships"; "Nazis Boast of New Gain"; and others about the escalating World War II. In the center of the front page ran this headline: "W. M. Mounger Is Named by Directors to Head Deposit Guaranty Bank." Under the headline was Bill Mounger's photo, the only one on the page.

The article began, "At a meeting of the board of directors of the Deposit Guaranty and Trust company here yesterday, William M. Mounger was elevated to the presidency of the state's largest financial institution succeeding the late Major George L. Donald." It continued:

> Mr. Mounger, previously vice-president, climaxes eight years connection with the bank and 21 years in the banking business, with the ascension to the president of the 18-million dollar bank.
>
> Action of the board, composed of some of the leading businessmen of Jackson and vicinity, was announced in a simple statement by Myer A. Lewis, Sr., executive vice-president.[12]

In the post-Depression and post-WW II era, there was money to be made for the savvy individual who possessed a strong work ethic. That was my dad. Other banks died or merged, yet for him, opportunity abounded. Dad spent his days making strategic loans which began or boosted the careers of Leland Speed Sr., Dumas Milner,

Warren Hood, and others. His eagle eye spotted entrepreneurial opportunities like they were mice in high grass. Chevrolet car dealerships, the Tinsley Oil Fields, Reed Construction Company, bonding companies—all began with money loaned by my father. He surrounded himself with men upon whom he relied for years afterward. Herman Hines and Nat Rogers, both of whom served as president of Deposit Guaranty National Bank after Dad died, were among them.

Herman Hines at age eighty-nine in the year 2003 still kept an office on the second floor of AmSouth National Bank (the eventual buyer of Deposit Guaranty): "I had been going to the Jackson School of Law at night. I was hustling soda water in the daytime for Morris Ice Company down on Commerce Street. One of my friends said, 'You are about finished with law school. What are you going to do?'

"And I said, 'I don't know, but I'm not going to hustle soda water on the street!'

"So he said, 'They are looking for people down at Deposit Guaranty Bank and Trust Company. Why don't you go down and see Major Donald and see if you can get a job? Well I thought that was a pretty good idea. That was about the first of July of 1936. So I came down, spoke to Major Donald, gave him a review of my education, so forth. I didn't have a degree, and he gave me a job—two weeks from then. So I had to go back to tell my boss, and he didn't like it at all. He tried to tell me he'd get me a job. And he also told me, 'You don't want to go work for that Jew bank.' There was a lot of Jewish ownership at Deposit Guaranty. I said, 'Look, I got a job there, so I'm going to take it.'

"The first day, I walked in, . . . there was Bill Mounger. Bill Mounger was a top officer. That was July 20, 1936. It was a little bitty old bank at the time, right on the corner of the street."[13]

On that street corner, Bill Mounger created the future for many Mississippians.

CHAPTER 3

The 1930s: A Father's Son

Our family moved to the Belhaven neighborhood in 1935. When Leland Speed Sr. learned that the Moungers were about to buy the lot adjoining his new Belhaven home, he told my dad that he wanted to remain good friends but there was a limit! "In those days with no air conditioning on sixty-foot lots, you got to know each other *real well*," recalls Leland Speed Jr. "And so my dad thought this was a little closer than he really would prefer. So he found that there was a lot down the street for sale, on the next block. And he said, 'Bill, this is a neat lot. It's a bigger lot.' So he got him to buy that other lot!"[1]

Our new house afforded us a third bedroom and a second bathroom. With four children in the house, I slept in the "sun room" for starters. After my sister Veronica was born in 1942, I was ceded the concrete basement for my bedroom. Along with it came a personal sink that drained straight into an adjacent vacant lot. The room lacked direct access to the rest of the house, so I relieved myself outside at night.

Not long after moving to St. Ann Street, five-year-old Leland Speed Jr. and I, age ten, started a cold drink stand in the Speeds' side yard. We bought ice from an ice truck and chilled and sold Cokes, Royal Crown Colas (RC Colas), grape sodas, strawberry sodas, cream sodas, and such to people in the cars and buses passing by. The Number 4 bus ended its run in front of the Speeds' home, and many workers and maids lingered there. It was 1936, recalls Speed, "And all the yard men and maids and everything from the whole area congregated out there on that corner waiting for the bus. And it occurred to me that this was a great spot for a soft drink stand. And so I decided that we needed to have a business there. But I had one problem—I didn't know how to make change. I couldn't tell a nickel from a quarter. But I knew I had a good location. So I decided I had to get an older partner who knew about these things. And, of course, we needed somebody to man the stand all the time. I needed to have somebody to trade off with. And so I went up to see Billy. I can still remember it. . . . Here I am, a little squirt, coming up to see Billy. And I'm making this proposal to him. And he accepted. And so we went in business together. And we built a stand; and we had big old metal stands— RC Cola. We built the whole thing. And we had a soft drink box, one with a sliding top on it. And we put ice in there. And so we had soft drinks that came from the bottling company. The truck came and delivered it by the case. And then the ice company would come and deliver the ice. We did volume. Today they wouldn't have let you do something like this. It would have violated zoning."[2]

Continues Speed: "This was a business. . . . We really did a lot of volume. . . . We made a little over five dollars a piece for our whole summer's efforts. But we got a lot of free drinks. . . . Billy and I basically have been in business together from that day until this."

Leland and I, however, soon were confronted by a neighbor in Business 101: the boy across the street, Billy Howard, whose father owned an ice company, upped the ante. His ice was free from his dad; his markup was lower. His drink stand was built by the ice company and swamped ours in size! The bus drivers began stopping across the street at Billy Howard's stand. Howard forced us out of business. It was our first experience with "unfair subsidized competition." I sucked up my pride, crossed the street, and went to work for Howard for a pittance a week.

I learned from the experience.

My oldest-boy's sense of "right" was strong. I held cheaters and punks in growing contempt. My fire for leadership fomented. Our small house provided little privacy for reading. Still, I loved history books—about cavemen, the Nile Valley, the Phoenicians, and the Lewis and Clark expedition. Great men. My father never dedicated much time to me, owing to his busy work schedule; but, when I was five or six years old, we created one unforgettable memory: Dad took me to meet Babe Ruth, the famous homerun hitter. Ruth was doing a clinic in Jackson for kids and I was able to meet him and receive batting instructions from him. The Babe signed a baseball for me, but over the years, with no personal place to keep any memorabilia, it somehow disappeared.

Like other folks of that day, my family listened to the radio. Franklin D. Roosevelt's speeches were common fare. Everyone loved Roosevelt, it seemed. Infrequently, someone calling himself a "Republican" would speak; I assumed they were a northern monster as strange as a warthog or wildebeest.

It is clear that my friends back then regarded my opinions as strong; however, even then they tended to be on target. For example, I did not drink, nor did I believe we boys ought to be smoking; the health risks were already obviously sufficient to cause me to take a stand with my buddies. I hated cigarettes. Smoking eventually cost my father one lung, which was removed in 1950. Some reports already linked smoking to cancer. That was enough for me. My lifelong friend, Fox Garraway, recalls how I used to jump on him and others: "Yeah, Bull Mounger has always been kind of up front, you know. I could tell you a few things. Well, when we were in the high-school fraternity, there were ten or twelve of us in the same class that joined TKO at the same time. Just two or three of us smoked and Mounger used to sprout these tusks and let us hear about it. He'd ride hard. He'd say, 'You sorry jackass, you know we'd have the best fraternity in town if it wasn't for you smokers.'"[3]

In the late 1930s, as my dad climbed in prominence to become president of the state's largest bank, I was taking my place among my peers as well. If I had a combative or rough edge, my friends seemed to appreciate it; they would sometimes call me to their aid. Once the girls' high school Cotillion Club held a big downtown dance in the Green Room of the Heidelberg Hotel, located on East Capitol Street. I had a date with Dorothy Lee Crum (now Mrs. Leslie Lampton), who was a beauty at Central High School and Ole

Miss. While inside the Green Room, I heard that some thugs had chased some Central High boys from a rival fraternity back to the dance and were about to fight. I walked through the lobby and sat on a car fender outside on Capitol Street to watch the fight. A crowd had formed across the street when someone informed me that one of the gang was about to fight Fellow Kirst, a close friend of mine. Kirst was smaller than normal due to an illness at birth. I burst through the crowd, pushed Fellow Kirst aside, and told the thug that he had to fight me, not Fellow! The thug wanted no part of me!

The crowd dispersed. As we all returned to the dance, a six-foot-plus thug challenged Bill Phelps, who was walking ahead of me, having mistaken Phelps for me; so I confronted the aggressor. "I'm the one you're looking for," I said. We headed in back of the hotel, to an area timbered over our local Town Creek. A tumultuous fight ensued. The twenty-one-year-old taxi driver landed one good hit on me, but then I tore into him. He was doubled over and almost "out" when the police arrived. The cops grabbed the thug around the neck and, quickly, I gave the guy one more swat. We both were hauled to the police station near City Hall, where Jackson's chief of police asked my name and then he asked whether my father was president of the bank.

I said, "Yes sir."

"Call your father immediately," the chief ordered.

The chief made me go into a private room and make the call. It was about 11:30 at night when Dad answered. "Daddy," I said, "guess where I'm calling you from."

"Where?" asked my father.

"The Police Station."

"What for?"

"For fighting."

"Did you win?"

"Yes sir," I replied.

"Fine," Dad said, "I'll see you in the morning."

It was like *Brer Rabbit in the Briar Patch.* I bemoaned to the chief that he had caused me immeasurable trouble with my father, when the reality was otherwise. The truth is that I was in many fights through high school, with almost every one of them strummed up by someone else or caused by my standing up for someone who couldn't defend himself.

Another fight, similar to the one at the Heidelberg, occurred at another party. Between my eighth and ninth grades at Bailey Junior High, the mothers of Dorothy Lee Crum, Martha Lynn Kenna, Deanie Wallace, Polly Wells, and other girls invited a gaggle of youth to a picnic outing at Legion Lake in Rankin County. A number of the boys decided to throw a much older and very tough "Cotton" Caldwell Jr. into the lake. Cotton roared and thrashed, knocking everyone down and standing there as if a king. I felt compelled to save the day and pushed Caldwell into the lake. Cotton charged from the water like a roaring bull with fists flying. Jerry Tiblier snuck on his knees behind Cotton, and I toppled Cotton reeling over Jerry's back. Cotton thundered back even more ferociously. Several blows were thrown, but inflicted no great damage. About that time the severely distraught mothers halted the imbroglio. Cotton and I agreed to continue the battle three days later, at nine o'clock on Saturday morning at the prearranged corner of Fortification and Whitworth streets. I pedaled my bicycle from my St. Ann Street house to rendezvous with Cotton, but by that time, our ardors had abated and we shook hands and called it off. Thank the Lord, because he probably would have smushed me!

Another fight pitted me amid two competing high school fraternities—TKO and SPO. One night, during the tenth grade, Eddie Guillot and other TKOs were riding in Guillot's car. They passed some rival SPOs, who they believed demeaned them. They showed up at my house and pled with me to stand up for the TKO fraternity and demand an SPO apology. I dressed in a brand new shirt and trousers that I had purchased that very day—not thinking a fight would occur—and rode with Guillot's crew to Cain's Drug Store, the main neighborhood hangout, on the corner of North Jefferson and Fortification streets and two blocks north at North Jefferson and Manship streets, where I spotted the offenders and demanded an apology. Leon Cruise immediately backed away; but Gere Woodward, who played football for Central and whose father was a bond dealer and friend of my father, stepped up and refused to apologize. That was the most difficult fight of all for me and left both of us battered. I received a long gash above my right eye;

Gere's nose was bludgeoned. Bystanders broke it up. I required several stitches.

Summers were magic. When it was hot, we guys walked down to Belhaven College's lake and splashed buck-naked. Old Man Mack, the college's groundskeeper, caught us there a time or two. We Belhaven boys would disappear before the cops arrived. I do remember clinging to the back bumper of our getaway car one time to cover the license plate from the policeman's view. My basement room became a gathering place for fun, as my old friend Fox Garraway recalls. "Eighteen-sixteen St. Ann Street. That house wasn't too bad. It had a basement to it and we'd go over there . . . probably six or eight of us, spend the night, play a little poker, shoot a little dice, spend the night. Mrs. Mounger would feed us the next morning. She was quite a fine lady. She really enjoyed looking out for Billy and his friends and did a good job of it. She had this gadget. I don't know what you call that thing—a clacker or something—a little toy, a little racket maker. She had a big one—an antique—made out of wood. It made some kind of racket! She'd catch us not quite awake and she'd come down there and clack that thing. Boy it really got our attention!"[4]

"Billy's room in the basement," recalls another friend, Leland Speed Jr., ". . . was so neat. He had his own little place down there. . . . He had a rare collection. People used to swipe all the numbers off all the city buses. There were these little U-shaped places where they would slip the number of the bus in; it was metal sheet with a number four or number two or whatever it was on there—Billy had a complete collection."[5]

We were growing up and having a good time. I was also hoping to take my place as a leader. One newspaper article reported the recent officer elections by the ninth grade at Bailey Junior High: "For president, Jerry Tiblier and Bill Mounger were nominated; they ran a close race with the victory in Bill Mounger's favor." Jerry was later voted the most handsome in the class and was a better athlete than I. But while I may have been assuming some natural leadership roles, I really knew nothing of that leadership factory called "West Point." Football and fraternity filled my life.

My high-school yearbook said it this way: "Another one of our

'Big Eighters' in football, Bill is one of the best-liked boys at Central. He is frank and quick to express his opinion on any subject, but don't let that fool you—underneath, there is a heart of gold. Bill says that in the future he'll confine himself to football—basketball is just too rough a sport." I broke my leg when I kicked a guy too hard while playing rough-house basketball.

Adults sometimes looked my way when in need of a teen's assistance. Mr. McEwen, the principal of Central High School, once asked for help. A teen from Central was to speak before the Downtown Jackson Kiwanis Club at the Edwards Hotel (predecessor to the King Edward Hotel). Would I be so kind as to introduce the youth? A tenth-grader at the time, I enjoyed jawing. Speeches, however, weren't my thing. But my father was a prominent member of Kiwanis, so I agreed to make the introduction. I prevailed upon my older sister, Marjorie, to write a speech about this student, whom I only vaguely knew from Junior ROTC.

Marjorie wrote the speech; I attempted to memorize it. I remember thinking that it was a bunch of gobbledy gook! She rambled about how nice this guy was, *ad nauseam*. Her words sounded foreign and fake. The day eventually arose. The city's top men convened and I ate a fine meal while seated at the head table with my father watching from the audience. Minutes seemed to stretch like taffy. The bank president was always center stage. Now I, his son, was, too. Finally, in front of the city's finest, I rose to introduce a boy whom I didn't know, attempting to speak words that were not mine. My name was announced. I ascended the dais; stood behind the podium, and . . .

The crowd. The faces—I was melting. And . . .

No words.

Marjorie's inane speech sunk like a marble in my gut. I stood there for what seemed an eternity. The only thing I remember saying was, "He belongs to the Junior ROTC." I immediately sat down, totally embarrassed and chagrined. I consequently committed: *Never again would I script a speech.* I've since become known for saying the most impromptu things in front of very important people—heads of state, United States presidents, even. But my words are sincere, and they are my very own.

A few months after my dad was named Deposit Guaranty's president in 1941, he, my two sisters, my brother Henry, and I—along with four other men and their children—made the cover of the society page of the *Clarion-Ledger*'s June 15, 1941 edition, in a Father's Day article. The five photos were each five inches by seven inches, and each featured one of the Jackson men with his children. Our photo showed father Bill with Marjorie, age seventeen, seated to his left; Henry, age six, in my father's lap; and Libby, age nine, seated by Henry. At age fifteen, I stood alone behind my siblings.

To the world, our family was picture perfect; but my mother, Veronica, was troubled. She was, frankly, a woman-child who wanted to remain the pampered little sister and always hankered to have children and babies around. In reality, she craved children and would constantly play with them, and she was the happiest when she could be involved with children and the black help, who were always employed at the house; however, she went out of her way to care for me. Yet during the spring and summer of 1940, when I was beginning my high-school years, she took the two younger children—Henry and Libby—to Oklahoma to visit her sister, Mrs. M. A. Weaver. Mother had recently delivered a stillborn child while my father had been away on a banking trip to New York City. The traumatic incident seemed to have strained their marriage. I stayed for months caring for myself in Jackson. Mother needed her sister's support a great deal.

I wrote my mother, who received the following letter postdated June 7, 1940, while she was in Yukon, Oklahoma:

Wednesday

Dear Mother,

Don't worry about me and my parties because I have been having fun.

I think I may go to a few others, but not many more. I am going to a picture show thing tomorrow and it will be the first I have seen in over a month.

I haven't played any golf lately because it's so hard to get to the club, but I am going to play Friday.

I have been swimming all day at Livingston. I am very sleepy right now and am not doing anything tonight. I finally made an A in English and Daddy liked it.

I am going to play tennis with Sam in the morning. And I hope to play golf better this summer than I did last summer.

I haven't tried to be lifeguard but they already have somebody and they won't let members work.

I have done some funny things lately. I got in a fight . . . the other day and knocked [him] silly. The last day of school I played hooky in gym class and went to the drug store but coach caught us but I didn't do anything.

I almost jitterbugged myself to death the other night but I had a wonderful time. I've been having fun at parties but I have been to a few that weren't any good.

I got your letter the other day and was certainly glad to hear from you.

I hope you are getting better and will be well again when you come back home.

Your loving son,
Billy

P.S. I am a little bit too lazy to write Libby and Henry but I will try to.

My older sister, Marjorie Lynn, also faced troubled emotions. She was only eighteen months older than I; as a consequence, she never had the personal attention from my parents that she needed in the nascence of her life. She had many psychological problems in later years, and I believe my usurping her babyhood was a strong contributing factor. The fact that I was a boy pleased my father tremendously—and frankly, my mother also—and added as well to my sister's insufficiency of affection.

One evening in 1942 my father, the banker, arrived home as usual. Yet it was no usual evening. Bill Mounger—city leader and banker extraordinaire—had great news for his oldest son. I was now a strapping sixteen-year-old. "I've secured you an appointment to West Point!" he said.

I stood there, stunned. Up to that point, my life was going just fine. My sophomore year I'd made the Central High football team. In my junior year, I made third team All Big 8. Football. High-school fraternity. Good grades. More football. My life was a neat circle.

But this West Point announcement threw me for a big loop, and I told my father as much.

"I'm not going!" I replied. "And if you try to make me go, I'll join the Marines instead. I know I'm in shape enough to pass the physical." World War II was in full swing at the time and I could not see the appeal of a West Point education. That night in 1942 on Belhaven's St. Ann Street was difficult. Few words were exchanged.

My dad had actually wanted to attend West Point himself and had been accepted, but he broke his leg playing baseball his freshman year at Mississippi State—just before transferring to the Point—and resultantly had failed to pass the Army physical.

Now he hoped I would go there, instead.

I met my friends at the TKO fraternity house at 1028 Quinn Street in Jackson. As cars purred by in the night, we played records and shot the bull. I mused about Dad's end run—West Point? I just had no sense of the place. It was fifty miles north of New York City.

How could my dad want me to move so far . . . *North*?

CHAPTER 4

The 1940s: Big 8 Football and West Point

Central High School was a wonderful place. My senior year at Central was full of great memories. But my tenth grade didn't start off that way. My fraternity lined up candidates for sophomore class officers, and I was a shoe-in for president. I had been class president in the ninth grade at Bailey Junior High and I was a football star. In my own fraternity, TKO, no one rushed underclassmen harder or did more work than I.

There were two sororities and, counting the Demolay group, which was really a Shriners club, there were four fraternities. These clubs made political alignments—"Your group runs Mounger for president and we'll run so-and-so for secretary/treasurer." SPO was the main competition for my fraternity, TKO. SPO wanted to run Ernest Allen, whose father owned the barbershop in the old Lamar Life building. Ernest grew up in West Jackson and attended Enoch's Junior High School and we were friends.

Ernest's SPO buddies wanted to nominate him for president, but he wouldn't let them because he knew that I deserved the position.

"You and I are friends," Ernest told me, adding, "I'm not running against you."

Ernest was the only person with a chance to beat me, so I conjectured, "I've got to be automatic because essentially there is no real competition." Nomination time came at the sophomore class meeting. Some West Jackson guys in my TKO fraternity tossed a curve ball, nominating Ed Harlan, who had been their ninth grade president at Enoch's Junior High.

I was floored—my own fraternity nominated another guy. I glanced at Ernest Allen, my buddy in the rival SBO frat. In a split-second decision I motioned to Ernest to take his frat's nomination as president. I ended up not running at all, avoiding a stinky inter-fraternity spat.

Allen won president. I got nothing.

The same story repeated itself when my TKO fraternity elected its own officers. I had worked harder and spent more time getting good people in the fraternity than anyone else. I could not imagine the members voting for my good friend Sam Sanders over me. But they did! Some members seemed to resent my tough stand about smoking and drinking, and they wanted to take me down a notch. I was shattered.

I learned: I would not make the same mistakes in future years. You don't get something in life just because you deserve it over everybody else. You may deserve it, but you also attain it because you make everybody of importance understand that you are the one who has all the qualifications. You don't leave it to chance; you don't assume.

I probably loved football because the lines determining who won and who lost were clearer than in politics—grit, muscle, and guts usually won in football. Eleven guys worked together; no surprises; the ball moved down the field; the opposition got whipped. Straightforward. Honest. Hardnosed. My senior season at pulling guard was a big success. I made All Big 8 along with my buddy, "Jarrin" Jerry Tiblier, albeit on a Central High Team that the *Jackson Daily News* called "mediocre." Yet sports writer Gene Wirth lavished praise on me as a guard and blocking back: "He is the man to fill the bill," Wirth wrote in anticipation of the Central Tigers' impending clash with Canton. "Strong, fast, and a hard blocker, Mounger will make his presence to the opponents well-known."

Meridian High School's team dominated that season, going 10–0 behind the running of "Shorty" McWilliams. I chased Shorty down the field all night when Central played Meridian, saving innumerable touchdowns. Looking back I was gaining rough-and-tumble life lessons through my football pursuits. It didn't matter if the other members of my team fell down, as long as I did everything I could possibly do and played to the maximum of my ability. Once I made three straight tackles on the one-yard line, stopping Shorty from scoring. I corralled Shorty in sheer open field more than once. Still, Shorty McWilliams made six touchdowns in that game!

In those days, helmets were leather with no facemasks. I blocked one place kick . . . with my nose—*smash!* My nose is pliable to this day. When the season ended, the *Jackson Daily News* wrote: "Mounger of Jackson missed by one vote being unanimous choice for one of the guard spots. He was regarded as one of the finest blocking linemen the Big Eight has seen in several seasons."

Yet it all went too fast. Football is that way. Central High football was over and I couldn't fathom it ending. Class officers and fraternities were nice. Girls were great. But football had been my life! Now, at age eighteen, I faced losing my first love. The rest of the year was fun, but with summer approaching, I had no hope for football next fall. Then my father received a phone call. It was Doug Kenna Sr., the father of Doug Jr., who was already attending West Point. At Central High just three years ahead of me, Kenna had dominated at running back, making All-South in football and basketball and winning the state tennis championship. He held a four-point GPA at Central and also at West Point. Kenna was a brown-haired, blue-eyed Irish photo-op. He was famed at West Point as Coach Blaik's go-to guy, despite recurring injuries; he made All America in football and basketball and he graced the cover of national sports magazines. Jackson, Mississippi, was proud of Doug Kenna.

So when Kenna's father—a prominent man himself—had stopped to visit with Mississippi Fourth District U.S. Congressman Dan McGehee in Washington, D.C., McGehee listened to Mr. Kenna promote a Central High football prospect. "You know," Mr. Kenna said, "you ought to give that Mounger youth an appointment to West Point to play football."

"I already did last year," the congressman replied, "and he turned it down!"

Mr. Kenna was unfazed. "You give him another appointment

and I'll get Doug this summer when he's home from West Point to talk to him." It was a deal.

Mr. Kenna called me to say that Doug would be in town to visit. I met with my idol in the summer of 1943. We talked about Central, about leaving Jackson, about how the Army was the football team to beat nationally, and about the famed Coach Blaik. I was impressed. West Point meant one thing for me at that moment—a chance to play more football.

Shortly after my senior football season, I broke my leg playing basketball. I had to reassess my life. Then Coach Blaik mailed me a recruiting letter. It got my attention. Navy also made a quick, last-second pitch from its Coach Hamilton for me to play there; but I soon announced to my father—"I'm going to West Point." The deal was sealed. I would be a cadet. I would play more football.

The Point. A major peninsula of granite thrusting into the Hudson River, West Point is starkly glorious and intimidating. Revolutionary War Patriots in 1777 established a fort there due to its strategic and defensible position, which prevented the British from using the Hudson River to sever the colonies. Since 1802, the United States Military Academy has been fixed there—a privilege to visit, an honor to attend. President George Washington conceived of the academy and President Thomas Jefferson founded it.

On the Illinois Central's Panama Limited train from Jackson to Chicago en route to West Point, I spent the night in Al Capone's city. This was the farthest I had been from home; up to this point, I had traveled no farther than Shreveport, Louisiana. The next day I rode the New York Central train to New York City, where Mr. Cavanaugh—the vice president of the Guaranty Trust Company in New York City and a friend of my father's—met me and M. T. Reed Jr. of Belzoni, also entering West Point. Cavanaugh took us to Jack Dempsey's restaurant, my first musical, *Hayride*, and, afterwards, Reed and I visited a barbershop and had our heads shaved to pre-empt the West Point shearers. Then we joined hundreds of prospective cadets on the Weehawken Ferry to Hoboken, New Jersey, boarding the West Shore Line for destiny. When the train groaned to a halt, I stepped off and looked up. A cliff grimaced down over the Hudson River, like nothing I'd ever seen. My life was about to change—forever.

Upon disembarking from the train, my group toted a motley assortment of bags up that cliff to the Central Area Barracks. The sound was thick as molasses with First Classmen yelling "Beasts!" at new freshmen. We all were running, bracing, and reporting for equipment, company, and room assignments. We soon gained our roommate "wives." The first day of West Point remains a blur to me to this day, but "Beast Barracks" were unmitigated hell. We were considered "beasts" until transformed into cadets.

A few days later a "Firstie" (a first classman, or senior) asked my name. I stated, "New cadet MOUNGER, Sir!" I sweated profusely while "bracing" (shoulder blades squeezed together, chin pulled in until I almost choked, standing stiffly straight). The Firstie said, "Dumbguard MOUNGER [most words describing plebes had "dumb" appended to them], I have a name for you!"

I replied, "YES, SIR!"

"I am going to name you 'Curly' because you look like Curly of *The Three Stooges*. From now on when asked to state your name, state it as 'Curly Mounger.'"

When classes started on September 1, a "yearling" (sophomore) braced me: "Dumbsquat, what is your name?"

"'Curly' Mounger, SIR!"

"'MOUNGER' sounds like '*MONJAY*' in French," the yearling proclaimed, adding that *monjay* means "to eat." "You are thick so you must like meat, which is '*lavione*' in French. From now on, your name is 'Curly Monjay Lavione Mounger.'" That was my moniker all my plebe year. Upperclassmen laughed and I avoided a lot of hazing because I accepted it good-naturedly. "Curly" proudly remains my moniker among my classmates to this day.

There is a "point" to the Point—it is for you to abandon your former life. Plebes are stripped of all earthly goods, their heads are shaved, and hazing is begun. Initiation is severe, even today. The goal is an outright transformation. Living in Beast Barracks, I was assigned to a company of taller cadets (in those days companies were sized by height from the shortest ["runts"] to the tallest ["flankers"]). After Beast, I was assigned to the H-1 Company, the shortest in the First Regiment. Strangely, my two H-1 roommates

were also from Mississippi: Ashby "Polecat" Foote Jr. from Hattiesburg, and Eugene "Flick" Fleming from Meridian. Ashby had attended Marion Military Institute in Marion, Alabama, a preparatory
school for West Point, then had served in the Army. Fleming went
to West Point, as had I, directly from high school.

Flick's natural recalcitrance and built-in snarl decidedly irked
the upper classmen, motivating them to overly scrutinize his personal appearance, demeanor, and equipment. This treatment of
him overflowed into inspecting the condition of Flick's, Polecat's,
and my room, and demerits rained on us. Each plebe was allowed
sixteen demerits a month. All cadets had to walk at attention with
rifle an hour at a time for each demerit in excess of sixteen. Two
hours could be "walked off" on Wednesday and three hours on Saturday—the only free time that cadets had all week.

September of 1944 was the first month demerits counted for the
new plebes. In that month alone Flick Fleming amassed fifty-six;
Polecat, thirty-nine; and I, forty-two. Our Mississippi threesome
earned demerits the old-fashioned way: one at a time. Our room
possibly outstripped any in West Point history with a total of one-
hundred-thirty-seven, exceeded only by those nailed by big
"slugs"—major infractions.

"Duty, Honor, Country" is West Point's motto. "Yes, Sir," "No,
Sir," "No excuse, Sir," "Sir, I do not understand," or "Sir, may I
make a statement?"—these were the only words freshmen
"plebes" could use to address an older cadet. Period. I missed my
South terribly.

Then came a cataclysmic football experience.

As I have stated, the game of football had been my solace, where
the scales had always balanced. Hitting was allowed. Putting up or
shutting up was the universal language. My plebe football class
sparkled with ability. Of the twenty-seven signees, seven became
college All-Americans; two won the Heisman Trophy. Practice was
intense.

Whenever coaches called for a team, I leaped to the guard spot.
"Okay, let's have a team!" Coach Blaik once called, and I scurried
up alongside fellow Mississippian, Barney Poole, who became All
American at Army and at Ole Miss. Poole's shadow dwarfed me.

DeWitt Coulter, an All American and NFL tackle, could unscrew my head with his massive hands. Still, I stayed at it.

After a few weeks, Blaik asked, "Who's that guy out there?" I saw the coach gesture my way. A thrill shot through me—the recognition of all my hard work was about to come. I jogged over to Blaik, the man Green Bay Packer coaching legend Vince Lombardi credited with teaching him the most about football.

"What's your name?" Blaik asked.

"MOUNGER, Sir!" I replied.

My mind darted through how our conversation would go—"I've read all your clippings!" "You're a great blocker!" "Keep up the hard work!"

As future greats Doc Blanchard (Mr. Inside) and Glenn Davis (Mr. Outside) continued working out, Coach Blaik mumbled toward me: "You're kind of small, aren't you?"

My heart ruptured. I had never thought of myself as small. If my five-seven frame could move 240 pounders, who cared about my size? No one had to tell me I wasn't the fastest. Determination and grit were my aces. Now Blaik burst those balloons—and my self confidence. I skulked away.

Still, I did not fully comprehend the devastating meaning behind Blaik's words. A few days later, however, when the notices were sent for football players to get their equipment, I combed the list, and my name was not there. A disemboweling blow! That one statement—"You're kind of small"—is the most devastating thing that has happened to me in my life.

My whole existence had been centered around football—I mean I lived, thought, slept, and ate football. I didn't give a damn about anything else but football. And then I went to West Point and I could not make the team. I had to reconcile, "Okay, I'm here, and no matter how hard, I'll be damned if I'm going to have the people in Jackson, Mississippi, say that I couldn't make it through West Point."

So a shift occurred in my mindset. As a first-year cadet, I thankfully could not go home for a year—a West Point rule—so I focused on being a cadet. Time soothed the sharpness of my rejection, and I made corporal my second year and sergeant by my last year. I survived West Point without overly exerting myself. In hindsight,

I am too individualistic for the military system. The more I advanced, the more freedom I accrued; the more I roamed enjoying my liberties, the less I achieved. This cycle insured West Point middle-of-the-road. Still, fellow cadets remembered my southern accent and unreconstructable attitude. The academy magazine, *The Pointer*, noted one brazen request I made to a first classman in the dining hall: "Mr. Mounger, the only plebe at Kohler's table, popped off—'Suh, may the fourth classmen sit at ease for this evening's meal?'

"Kohler: 'What's the reason?'

"Mounger: 'Suh, today is Abraham Lincoln's Birthday.'

"Kohler: 'Where from, Mr. Mounger?'

"Mounger: 'Mississippi, suh!'

"Kohler: 'Seems to me that's a strange request from a man from deep in the South, but I'll make a deal with you. Do you know *Marching Through Georgia*?'

"Silence . . . then hesitatingly . . . 'No Suh.'

"'Well, how about *Yankee Doodle Dandy*?'

"More silence . . . 'Yes Suh.'

"'Okay, Mr. Mounger, if you'll entertain us with a chorus of *Yankee Doodle* you may fall out.' . . .

"More silence . . .

"'Suh, may I make a statement?' . . .

"'Yes.' . . .

"'Suh, I'd rather "sit up" than sing *Yankee Doodle*'!" ["Sit up" meant that I would brace and not eat another morsel of food.]

Anticlimactically, I still got to sit at ease. My adamancy had triumphed without sacrificing principle.

I no longer could eat at the plebe football training table as of the beginning of 1945; therefore, I was assigned to an H-1 Company table. There I constantly was asked to sing. I could not sing a lick, but being a so-called "personality plebe" (an upper classmen's title of endearment) I seemed always to find ways to entertain. The only song I could remember was Cab Callaway's "Minnie the Moocher," conjuring "Hydie-Hydie-Hey" and "Ho-De-Ho-De-Hay" with great élan. All the tables within earshot chimed in and added to the din. My table often was allowed to sit "at ease." My "Minnie the Moocher" rendition became a regular dining hall din; and all my fellow plebes at the surrounding tables loved it because all were allowed to sit at ease afterwards.

My antics earned this tribute in the *Howitzer*, the West Point annual:

> A promising football prospect, Curly matriculated at the Academy expecting a spot on a Squad. Because of keen competition, he early realized that his gridiron aspirations would take a definite intramural twist. Recovering from this minor egotistical reverse, Bill was the rare personality Plebe who enjoyed every laugh he doled out to the upper classes. The Munge cultivated his deep devotion to constructive bull sessions and never failed to flavor them with his staunch, adamant Southern viewpoints. A semi-radical at heart, Bill plodded the glory road in a path all his own.

During my third year—in the fall of 1946—I wrote my father, saying that though I was not playing football, I nonetheless had hopes for my future:

22 October 1946

Dear Daddy,

Well, Army set another undefeated down this past weekend. Every team we played was undefeated till we whipped them. Davis is even better this year than ever before and that goes for Blanchard and Fulcher, too. Miss. State didn't do badly either. They seem to have finally found themselves and started to click. Everybody seems to have scored except Shorty Mac. What was the matter?

Ashby's folks were up from Hattiesburg this past weekend. I went to dinner with them and had a very enjoyable time. His parents certainly are nice people. Daddy, Mrs. Foote said that most of Miss. held it against Shorty for doing what he did. She also said that the boys on State's team were griped so much that they would not block for him. Is that right? It doesn't seem as if it could be. She is an Ole Miss fan and it is probably all wishful thinking on her part.

We are going . . . for the Duke game this weekend. It should be a fair game; at least Davis' running is enough to make any game good.

I am not going to do much; just go to see *Oklahoma*, that's all. It will be a break from the dreary monotony of old 'Hell on the Hudson' though.

Daddy it is certainly surprising how good I am doing in academics this year. I am sick and tired of studying so therefore I can do only slightly more than nothing yet I still do better. It will all catch up with me soon and I will nosedive, but I just feel as if I will burst if I attempt to cram any more knowledge down myself.

I don't know whether you have lined up any Navy tickets or not, so last night I signed up for four of them and wrote a check. You said you wanted to see that game so I figured you would come and bring someone. The only catch is that you will have to bring people that I know in order to use my tickets because if someone that I did not know used my tickets, it would cause me to violate my honor.

Daddy, here is some news that you will be very sorry to hear. We cadets can now wear civilian clothes, so it looks as though I am going to have to buy some. I am so damn sick of this grey that I can't see straight and it would surely be good to wear a good suit. You said I did the wrong thing in giving my clothes away, didn't you. [sic]

This place can certainly get a person down most of the time. It seems as if the best years of my life are flying by with me standing still. This West Point reputation may be something to have but believe you me, it ain't just handed to you. It is ruthlessly rammed down your throat with many miserable hours of toil. If this place doesn't do me some good I will be one of the most bitter persons there is. [sic] It had better pay off, that is all I can say.

Well, Dad, you are one of the luckiest persons in the country getting to see the Army-Notre Dame game. Undoubtedly they are the two best teams in the country. I would love to see Army trounce them not only because I am an Army man but also because I hate to see that papist school trouncing over other schools. I certainly do not want them to dethrone Army and take over first place.

Well, Dad, that is about all for now. How about dropping me a line. You haven't answered my last letter yet. Well, so long, take care of everything at home and I am still looking forward to seeing you at the Notre Dame game.

Your loving son,
Billy

Dad missed that famous 1946 Army/Notre Dame game, which ended in a 0–0 tie. Army and Notre Dame were tied for first in the end-of-the-year national polls. A year earlier, my father actually attended the 1945 Army/Navy game at Philadelphia's Memorial Stadium. He sat with several business friends on the civilian side of the field as I marched with the Corps of Cadets. At that moment, I was very proud. Army defeated Navy 32–13. At the end of the game, I had prearranged to meet my father under Army's goalposts. I maneuvered through the crowds to our meeting place. As the masses receded I stood in my dress grays, combing the stadium for my father. Dad never showed.

We never discussed that day; obviously, my father preferred his business associates. To assuage my disappointment, I charged some new clothes on my dad's line of credit at a Madison Avenue, New York City clothier. West Point had been his dream, yet he skipped out on me at the big game. I have remembered that moment my whole life and have consequently tried to attend my sons' or grandchildren's events—whatever they may be—making them a definite priority.

The Point was changing me forever, perhaps without my knowledge. Some worlds were closing and others opening. The country's future leaders—young, smart men from all strata—came there from all forty-eight states to achieve. They came from orphanages and opulence, and as a consequence, I met first-generation Czechs, Poles, and sincere Catholics, which were a novelty to a young Southerner. We studied the world's great ideas and heroes and together we laid our presuppositions at the Army's altar and became cognitive men.

My upbringing had been only mildly political. Dad, as a banker, played political affiliations below the radar. Still, Mississippi was a one-party state; but now, from my northern perch, I started seeing the sheer absurdity of the South's one-party system. Mississippi served the whims of national Democrats as a one-horse Democratic state, whether or not in ideological agreement, and I began hearing West Point friends talk of Republicanism—even if it were the northeastern brand of Republicanism, it provided an option.

A Republican in Mississippi in my youth was like a chicken in a snake pit—it didn't live long. Republican ideas were aired and considered at the Point. Republicanism had begun as Abraham Lincoln's party and had forced the issue of abolition of slavery, and thus had alienated a great many southern whites. Blacks were able to vote upon passage of the Fifteenth Amendment to the United States Constitution in 1870; however, a series of local voting laws in the South, including literacy tests and poll taxes, made many blacks ineligible to vote until the Voting Rights Act of 1965 was passed. Southern Democrats began to fall out with their national party after World War II. The Democrat Party of the State of Mississippi was "whites only, made possible because legally the Democratic Party was a private organization rather than a government agency, and thus was not required to obey the provisions of the Fourteenth Amendment. Even registered black voters in Mississippi could not vote in the Democratic primaries which, for all intents and purposes, decided who won the general election."[1] The Republican Party's base was in the more moderate North and West, but the Democrat Party, which enjoyed unprecedented congressional and presidential power under Roosevelt and Truman, developed schizophrenia. As the 1950s gave way to the 1960s, southern Democrats felt pressure from within their party to include black leadership and voters; but a set of new white voices outside the Democrat Party believed that more was at stake than black voting rights. This group began feeling ashamed of how southern Democrat senators and congressmen deferred to their national Democrat leadership's lessening of support on issues of maintaining national defense, opposing communism, and sliding toward socialism.

I studiously read the *New York Times*, straining for news from home. I read of Mississippi Democrats like Theodore Bilbo and John E. Rankin and sometimes my stomach turned at the image of white racist ignorance and the hatred they projected nationally about our state. My father was called to testify during the Bilbo hearings regarding certain checking transactions and contracts pertaining to his close personal friends and business partners, M. T. and Tom Reed of Belzoni—large wartime contractors who had strong ties to Bilbo, a vocal racist. Dad was eventually the chief financial advisor to a Bilbo opponent, Governor Fielding Wright. Wright later ran on the national Dixiecrat ticket as the vice presidential candidate to Strom Thurmond, the presidential candidate.[2]

Over the May Day weekend of 1948, I joined West Point class-mates Sid Berry from Hattiesburg, Mississippi—a future lieutenant general and West Point superintendent—and Bill Byers in traveling to observe New York City's May Day Parade. The First of May for Communists was comparable to America's Fourth of July at that time; and we knew a large number of Communists and sympathiz-ers would show. We three became incensed at so many Commu-nists marching, wearing military uniforms or articles of military clothing, causing us to yell, "Why don't you move to Russia?" and other derisory phrases. Our threesome gravitated to Union Square, a notorious Communist gathering place.

We misfit West Pointers entered the Square as antagonists, who stood out with our crew cuts. We fended off all comers in three separate large crowds for more than an hour, eventually breaking free and driving back to West Point. Henry Wallace was then run-ning for president with Communist support, and I felt real concern about such anti-American antagonism to our military.

Spoiled by all the beautiful Jackson girls from my youth, I dated only occasionally during my West Point years. For June Week 1947, (the week leading up to the First Class's Graduation) of my junior (cow) year, I invited Dorothy Snow of Jackson to be my date. Doro-thy was three years younger and a beautiful girl. Her father was Charles Snow, a prominent, wealthy lawyer and one of my father's closest friends. Dorothy, a beautiful, pampered only child, arrived with her mother and a completely new wardrobe of evening dresses and everyday outfits. She was by far the best dressed, most beauti-ful, and best dancer of all the females there. For the "hops," each girl carried a Hop Card that named her partner for each separate dance. I took most of Dorothy's dances, allocating others to bud-dies and those most clamorous. I told my friends that all the Jack-son girls were like Dorothy, thus my disinterest in "Yankee girls." The next year Dorothy married my kindergarten friend, Eddie Gu-illot, and their picture appeared in magazines as the "Woodbury Soap Bride and Groom for 1948."

Academically I was middle-of-the-road, seeking the best grade for the least possible effort. Yet achieving a West Point degree—no matter the rank—molds a man for life. My father recognized my anticipated West Point graduation with a promised automobile. A huge shortage of automobiles existed in 1947 in the aftermath of World War II, but Dad nonetheless kept his word, giving me the exact car that I desired—a Chrysler Highlander convertible. It was silver with a black top and a red Scotch plaid interior—the finest car in my 1948 West Point class. My convertible arrived in Jackson during the Christmas holidays of 1947.

On my last night in Jackson, I had partied all night long at Parham Bridges Jr.'s house, delaying my departure for West Point until about 11 A.M. I was so exhausted that I had to sleep a couple of hours in Birmingham, Alabama, and then drove continuously, dozing at the wheel and picking up hitchhikers to help keep me awake. Upon arriving in Washington, D.C., I was so sleepy that I could not drive another foot. I dumped my car in a parking garage, then caught the train to New York City and the bus to West Point, eventually stumbling into the academy just before the 9 P.M. reporting deadline.

Two weeks later after retrieving my automobile, I joined some classmates, including Warren "Gravey" Graves, and headed for the Barclay Hotel in New York City for the weekend. Graves was dating an Argentinean girl who lived in Kew Gardens, Long Island, and whose father was the Argentinean Consul for New York City. After carousing before a roaring fire, about ten of us piled into my Highlander and set out for New York City. It was a windy, sleety, snowy night with severely icy roads when we left Kew Gardens. Due to my ineptitude at cold-weather driving combined with my inebriation, I smashed into the back of a pickup truck. The Chrysler's grill crumbled, the hood twisting into a V shape. I stood in the snow and dejectedly dropped pieces of the car's front grille through my fingers. Steam spewed from the radiator.

We abandoned the car at a filling station, trudged a mile or so through deep snow to a subway stop, and returned to the Barclay Hotel. The next morning I was too ill to move; therefore Chuck Wurster and Herb Barineau volunteered to find my car. After several hours of searching without locating it, they asked that I pack all of our bags and meet them at the bus station to return to "Woopoo Tech," our nickname for West Point. The next day, Graves called his girlfriend and asked if her father could find my car and have it hauled to the nearest Chrysler dealership. Her father had difficulty locating the car, because I had wrongly turned north instead of south on Queens Boulevard, heading away from the city, not toward it. That obviously was why Wurster and Barineau could not find it.

I contacted the Long Island Chrysler place, which estimated the repairs to be $375, which seemed excessive because the car's original price was $2,700.[3] I told the dealership to fix the radiator for $85 and retrieved it the next weekend. I drove all the way through congested New York City traffic to Highland Falls (just outside the south gate of West Point) by leaning to my right side and peering below the bent hood and over the exposed engine. A garage in Highland Falls agreed to repair my car for $300, which was essentially what the other Chrysler place had quoted! Somehow I scrounged for $300 from my secreted stockpile of cash along with writing checks on my father. (It was against regulations for a cadet to possess money, ostensibly because all cadets were supposed to be equal in status.) Ironically, later, my class began a short course on insurance, and it occurred to me that my father must have procured automobile insurance for me. I wrote him several times stating that I needed my insurance policy so that I could analyze it in conjunction with the short course. Belatedly, the policy arrived and, lo and behold, it contained a $50 deductible clause; however, another clause stated that a claim had to be reported in sixty days. I looked at the calendar and it was the sixty-first day.

Immediately I called Mr. Dan Bottrell in Jackson who had sold the USF&G policy on the car. I elicited Mr. Bottrell's promise not to inform my father about the wreck. Mr. Bottrell then prevailed on USF&G for an exception to the reporting rule, and the company sent an appraiser to West Point. After talking to the repairman at the Highland Falls garage, he reimbursed me $250 for repairs! This contorted fiasco made old Curly—already a renowned individualist at West Point—fit for folklore amid the Class of '48 as the first to wreck—and the only one to misplace—his car.

Nearing graduation, I considered how I would spend my minimum of five years of mandatory service. The Air Force Academy had not yet been authorized, so flying in the Air Force was thought to be the luxury path. I took it. If I had to be in the military, the best deal was to be a pilot. I would receive more money and could go to more places and sleep in a clean bed each night. I passed all the strict flight standards, jumping ahead of some of my higher-ranking West Pointers.

My father, mother, and two sisters arrived for my graduation, and I put them in a very rustic inn in Fort Montgomery. On graduation day, I shipped my things home, loaded my car, picked up my family, and headed for Jackson. We were traveling through Secaucus, New Jersey, when a large truck turned and cut my Highlander off, smashing it again. The police arrived, and I realized I had no driver's license; I had packed it in the bags that I had mailed home. The truck driver tried to shift blame onto me, but Providence smiled on me when I told the policeman that I had just graduated from West Point. One of my classmates was Jack Doody, whose father was the police physician and a close friend of Boss Haig, the dictatorial boss of the Jersey City area. The police ordered the truck driver to shut up, took my family to a hotel (my father immediately flew back to Jackson), and arranged for a Chrysler dealership to fix the car for an equitable price. The police then offered to drive us wherever we needed. Interestingly, the World Middleweight Boxing Championship second rematch between Rocky Graziano and Tony Zale was in Trenton, New Jersey, on the second night of our New Jersey stay. Graziano won. I attended that historic and classic fight.

Meanwhile, as the Korean situation simmered. I completed tiers of training, earning my pilot's wings at Randolph Field (San Antonio) and Barksdale Field (Shreveport), from which I traveled back to Jackson each weekend. Ultimately I reached the pilot rank of "aircraft commander." My airplane's precious cargo required steady nerves and physical endurance.

The cargo was atom bombs.

A few days after the Korean War started, I was on temporary duty at Tampa, Florida's McDill Field attending Lead Crew School as a member of a "number one select crew." Top secret, top personnel, best of the best—bombardiers, radar operators, pilots. Each of us by order wore a .45 caliber pistol and stayed in close contact. When I first came to the squadron, I made sure I kept one piece of gear hidden—my West Point ring. Many non–West Point officers branded academy graduates "trade-schoolers." I wanted to be one of the boys; therefore, the ring remained out of sight at that time.

I had met Mike Diaz, who lived on Davis Island in Tampa, while on a previous trip to McDill Field. His father was the Seagram's liquor distributor for the Tampa area. Diaz invited me home one Friday for dates and fun. Mission accomplished! "We're having such a good time, don't go back to the base," urged Diaz at the end of Friday night. "Why don't you just spend the night?" I agreed. The next day (Saturday) we went to Mike's private beach club in St. Petersburg. I decided to spend Saturday night with Mike, also. When Sunday arrived, we returned to Mike's beach club. I returned on Sunday to McDill Field at around 10 P.M. The bachelor officers' quarters were dreadfully dark and quiet for a Sunday night; I arrived somewhat tipsy, searching for my crew.

No one!

I groped for my bunk, grasping a note from my aircraft commander, Lt. Col. Ray Gottner: "Meet us at the plane right away. We have emergency orders to leave." I was an A.W.O.L. pilot, and I knew no protocol for this blunder. Suddenly I'd plummeted to the nadir of a military existence, failing to be ready when called upon. I phoned the tower. "I have a note that says my aircraft must leave right away."

The officer in charge answered: "What's the matter with you? Your plane left Saturday morning without you!"

My mental ticker tape was running . . . *"I'm going to be court-martialed. Terrible. Just terrible."*

Monday morning a C-47 flew this befuddled Mississippian to El Paso, Texas. There was plenty of time in the air for me to contemplate my probable court marshal. "What's going to happen to me?" I couldn't help but wonder what the urgent mission was— "Something horrible must be happening in the world." Arriving at midnight amid scrambling troops at Biggs Field, El Paso, Texas— golf clubs and duffel bag in hand—I'm sure I was a sight for my crew members! Planes were loaded with parts, records, and .50-caliber ammunition. I felt both sick and excited as I reported to my aircraft commander. "Go to your quarters, pack up, and get back up here," my aircraft commander said. "We'll fill you in." The next day I learned our mission: Fly an atom bomb to England, and be prepared to drop it on Russia. Meanwhile, my mates got a hoot out of my foibles. "Yeah," they crowed, "you were having a good time partying and drinking with dates, and we had to stay up for three nights in a row, working our fannies off. You're the smartest guy in the whole squadron!" I put my West Point ring back on. Now I was accepted!

I had stayed abreast of home news during flight training in San Antonio. The year was 1948, and the Dixiecrat Party was stirring. I was especially intrigued since Senator Strom Thurmond of South Carolina, the Dixiecrat national presidential candidate, invited Mississippi governor Fielding Wright—my father's good friend—to be his vice presidential candidate. Television and radio news lampooned Mississippi.

I saw my home state in a different light. I remember wondering: "Why do we have to be subservient to the Democrat Party? Why do we have to take this? There is an alternative: get out!" To me the problem had started years ago—back when prominent Mississippian Pat Harrison, a United States senator from 1918 to 1941, undermined the South. Harrison ambitiously sought to secure a vice presidential bid from the Democrat Party and thus supported eliminating the highly important "Two-Thirds" rule from the Democrat convention. The two-thirds majority vote rule had always been a firewall of protection for the South from impositions of the more populous northern Democrats. Our own great senator did in the very precepts of philosophy, ideology, individual freedom, and southern politics that we are supposed to stand for. The Mississippi Democrats looked worse and worse.

Meanwhile, my flight crew members were becoming fast friends. Using Europe as our aerial playground, our wing and another wing (from Merced, California) flew the first A-bombs to Europe. On the flight from Waco, Texas, to England with our A-bomb aboard, I glanced down at one point from the plane and there below was Jackson, Mississippi! None of my family or friends would know for years how I had lugged an atom bomb through the air over our home turf. But I called to give our plane's location to the local Jackson airport control. "How are things down in my old home town of Jackson?" I asked.

A strangely familiar voice answered from the ground: "Looking fine. I've been around here a long time. What's your name?"

"Mounger," I said.

Ground: *"My name is Mounger, too!"*

It was my own Uncle Carleton, on duty as the air traffic control officer.

Our B-50 crew cleared Jackson and headed to Bermuda on our way to England. About forty B-50s landed in Bermuda, each with an A-Bomb. All crew members were toting .45-caliber pistols, and each airplane maintained armed guards at all times. The Bermuda airport was for both civilian and military traffic. As we walked through the passenger area, I overheard two little old ladies say, "Look at all these armed military people and all those airplanes. I wonder if they have any A-Bombs on them." I laughed to myself, "Little ole ladies, if you only knew, every plane out there has an A-Bomb on it, and you would probably faint if you knew."

During this secret mission to base A-Bombs in Europe, our wing of B-50s divided, following two routes—most flew the southern route over Jackson; others took a northern route over the Midwest through Keflavik, Iceland. One B-50 flying the northern route developed difficulties and crashed in rural Ohio. Its atomic bomb was not yet armed for nuclear destruction, but the 10,000 pounds of TNT detonated, blasting a huge crater. Somehow the event was concealed, though none of the sixteen crew members survived.

My 97th Bomb Wing of SAC—Strategic Air Command—stayed on alert for eight months should we need to bomb Russia if that country entered the Korean War. Our crew practiced a war plan that included striking several cities from two different routes, one northern and one southern, with air refueling done over Scandinavia or Greece. Each route had designated landing destinations if the planes survived. Only 10 percent of us were ever expected to complete our missions alive.

My squadron of fifteen B-50s was assigned to Waddington, an RAF Base just south of the city of Lincoln, England, where being single benefited me. I enjoyed my tour, impressed with Britain's parliamentary system and the country's numerous historical sites. I once spent three days visiting Copenhagen, Denmark, where the beautiful blonde females were much more attractive than the English girls, who were drab and deprived due to the effects of World War II.

Our crew experienced one particular flight that was anything but drab. Our plane was assigned to fly home through Keflavik, Iceland, in February of 1951. My plane was fully loaded with wing tanks filled and a bomb bay tank installed to hold extra fuel. After several hours of flying, it was determined that Keflavik was closed due to clouds and fog, so the flight continued. One-hundred to one-hundred-and-fifty mile-per-hour head winds were experienced, and when we sighted the cliffs of Greenland, it seemed as if the plane was just crawling. After finally reaching Canada, the aircraft commander, Lt. Col. Gottner, decided to attempt landing in Presque Isle, Maine, rather than in Labrador. Upon approaching Presque Isle, the crew discovered it was also shut down due to bad weather. The only alternative was our final destination, Westover, Massachusetts. After we violated route procedures by heading directly towards Westover, our fuel reserves became extremely low and our crew made preparations to bail out in the middle of the night. When all seemed lost, Westover came into view directly below in a valley and we prepared to land. Fuel was so short that the plane could barely be banked because the fuel would flow to the side of the tank. After we finally landed, two engines quit while taxiing due to lack of fuel. God had protected us!

About this time, I experienced a resurgent feeling of being trapped in a military rut. Every day that our crew languished, quartered from real fighting in Korea, I grew restless. The Army had invested too much in me as a bomber pilot to switch me to another field position, yet my bomber team simply did little. I was bored.

I found myself back in Biggs Field, El Paso, Texas, and then returned on temporary duty to McDill Field for more training. Later, I attended the Air Force Atom Bomb School at Sandia Base in Albuquerque, New Mexico, and then was assigned to be an aircraft commander of a new ten-man B-50 crew; but, ridiculously, we were without an airplane, which proved to be very frustrating. Every time someone of superior ability was assigned to my crew, that person was soon reassigned to a senior crew. Bumming B-50s in order to train my crew was so dissatisfactory that I became very disillusioned with continuing an Air Force career.

I gained invaluable experience during my military career—especially the opportunity to live outside Mississippi. I also learned a great deal about democracy, governments, personal responsibility, and much more; and my love of history and craving for personal success was enhanced; but inevitably I was drawn towards home after my father had a cancerous lung removed. Irritatingly, I was belatedly notified of Dad's illness weeks after his operation, while I was in England, which helped spur my first attempt at resigning from the Air Force in mid-1952. My resignation was perfunctorily rejected, however, and I was transferred to Randolph Field in San Antonio, Texas, where I immediately filed another resignation. It was accepted in February 1953, at Bolling Field, Virginia, with the impetus of United States Senator John Stennis, then-chairman of the Senate Armed Services Committee.

I was constantly thinking about the South and voraciously reading during my military days. I had made sufficient grades in engineering at West Point, but could never effectively use a screwdriver. Books and ideas were my love. The Point's history classes set me on a lifetime journey of reading and, the more I read, the more Roosevelt's government-solves-everything policies festered in my mind. I thought like a small-government Republican. The Democrat Party had increasingly alienated those of us who believed that private enterprise did more to spur local economies than government; but in the 1950s there was no strong support for private enterprise's role in building a better United States; the New Deal's emphasis had increased the role of government. I noticed that even England had two strong parties! The southern political landscape was monochrome, and upon returning home, I discerned change in the wind. Mississippi's one-party system was un-American and Mississippians needed a political choice. I longed to bring my new analysis of the situation home.

CHAPTER 5

The 1950s and '60s: Finding Oil, a Wife, and a Life

My father was tiring back in Mississippi. Bill Mounger had taken charge of Deposit Guaranty in 1941. He made the right moves. Nat Rogers became his personal assistant. Herman Hines ran the first branch bank in Mississippi on South State Street. Business opportunities expanded for my father. When he saw a good deal, he spread the opportunity around; he included friends like Leland Speed Sr. and the Reed brothers of Belzoni in the possibilities. The Reeds after World War II saw a need for a concrete operation. They included my father, and he invited Leland Speed Sr. to join them. "That is the day that Delta Industries began," recalls Speed Jr. "It started off with a bunch of old war surplus equipment."[1] Often Dad also asked employees like Rogers to take a piece of the pie. Oil fields. Bonds. Land. The very principles that I and others were beginning to strongly embrace—of free enterprise as the best route to job creation and decreasing poverty— were manifest in the fruit of my father's efforts. As Dad's Deposit Guaranty expanded, so did new business in Jackson, Mississippi, and beyond.

Bill Mounger's standards were cloud-high and made an indelible mark in Mississippi banking. "We are a receptacle for their wealth," he preached to his officers.[2] He would add: "Now what are you *going to do with their wealth*? Are you going to sit on it like some other banks do, or are you going to buy bonds and lend money out and push the community, which pushes the people? Creating wealth. Take this wealth, lend it out, use it to the benefit of the community, and generate more wealth and a better community."

Dad embodied the very spirit of private enterprise, self-help, and capitalism that I was beginning to comprehend. The idea of creating jobs and new capital, versus recycling them via government programs, was something that my father exhibited to a younger generation who sought to carry the torch after him as many of us moved into the Republican Party to shape its business-growth policies.

As for me, I had sent home my Air Force savings of $5,000-plus to Dad, who matched it dollar-for-dollar as he had earlier promised.[3] He invested that $10,000 in oil and other investments for me. Also, the $1,000 from the insurance settlement when a car struck me at age five had ballooned and I had my own funds waiting and compounding when I returned home. Some of the Colorado royalties grew so much that my father actually split it with my younger brother, Henry; next Dad took some of my money and bought one half of a Brookhaven Pontiac dealership from one of the bank's biggest customers—Dumas Milner, another noted Mississippi business baron. Milner would become the nation's largest owner of General Motors dealerships and the owner of National Car Rental.[4]

For all of Dad's financial genius, chain-smoking had debilitated him. In 1950, he had a cancerous lung removed. Dad's surgery by doctors Harvey Johnson and George Twente of Jackson was a success. Though continuously sick thereafter, he survived another seven years, conquering the cancer.

Adds Nat Rogers of his former boss: "He was a truly great man. I don't know of anyone I've ever known that I admired any more. I can tell you many aspects of his life that I think would help characterize what kind of person he was. He was certainly an entrepreneur. He started some businesses himself and he assisted many other people who were in the process of forming businesses. He had a dynamic personality. He was extremely popular and attracted friends from all sectors and sources. He was a man of vision who was a risk taker but only if there was proven character in the person with whom he was dealing. He attracted friends like a magnet. He was one of the most popular persons I've known. He helped such friends."[5]

"He had a very forceful presence," Rogers continues. "He was easy to get along with but he was ready and willing to assert himself whenever he was confronted with negative thinking on the part of his associates or with whomever he had contact. If he thought the proposed action of some person in the bank was wrong, not beneficial to the bank, he would take on whatever the issue was and he, not only because he was president, but because he was the leader, would prevail. On the board were one or two that I would describe as reactionary and, when they opposed him, he took them on and could cope with any situation of that sort."

Rogers, as my father's executive assistant, witnessed his management creativity. It was nothing more than an exercise in Dad's belief in personal responsibility; government could not motivate change in a man's morals nearly as much as appealing to his pocketbook! A very talented officer from a prominent Jackson family had a drinking problem. No one, including Rogers, could make him stop. My father, who was the end of the line, summoned him. "You know, you can't continue on this way," Bill Mounger told him, adding, "I want your resignation."

The man wrote it out and handed it to Dad, who opened the top drawer in his desk and inserted the note. He looked at the man: "I'm going to lock this desk drawer. I'm not going to give it to the board unless I see you drunk again." From that time, the employee remained sober and productive.[6]

My father's shoes were big and still growing, but his life would be short.

The Mounger paterfamilias and my mother moved one last time— from Belhaven's St. Ann Street to a large two-story house on Jackson's premier Old Canton Road. The white-brick Georgian two-story rested on two-and-a-half acres of green lawn with magnolias and shady oaks. Dad's strength was waning. His "boys"—Hines and Rogers, et al—tended to his needs. Hines brought slabs of fine steak cut from Dennery's and fresh buttermilk churned by Hines's mother, who lived in south Jackson. The two men sat in our front yard as Dad drank buttermilk. Fast friends, they talked of life.

My older sister suffered from schizophrenia, so I effectively became the oldest child. With Dad's health failing badly, I had continued seeking release from the military. Dad's influence had kept Herman Hines out of the military draft twice when his number was called for World War II before Dad finally acquiesced a third time to placate Hines's desire to serve. He'd prized Hines's help at the bank. Dad did finally pull a string or two with Senator John Stennis for me. I returned home, aided by Stennis, with just four months left on my five-year military service obligation.

Immediately upon returning to Jackson, I started studying the ins and outs of my father's affairs. An ocean away, I had worried that Dad needed me. I realized that my fears were slightly premature, once I returned home and analyzed the situation. Dad exhibited a slight comeback, thus my presence was not as necessary as I had thought.

So with no real new course set, I discarded the chains of nine years of discipline. I had missed many good times with my Ole Miss buddies because I attended four years at West Point and almost five years in the USAF. My good friend Parham Bridges Jr. had the answer. Parham's father owned a fifty-five-foot boat, and Parham owned an airplane and a thirty-foot boat. So we tripped to the Gulf Coast, roaming the ocean from Gulfport to Destin. Sometimes we invited pretty girls on board. Another buddy, Fred LaRue, owned a forty-five-foot Norseman on which we once crossed the Gulf of Mexico from Naples, Florida, to Cozumel, Mexico. Fred's father (one of my father's closest friends) was a highly successful oil-and-gas transplant from Athens, Texas.

I definitely enjoyed some crazy outings with Parham and Fred. We were once in Mexico and looked up from our boat, having heard gunfire. As Fred recalled it, Mexican bandits fired at us for intruding on their waters. Fred continued in an interview before he died in August 2004.[7] "They made us dock and they scared the living daylights out of us," Fred cracked. After some well-placed phone calls, we were released to fish once more.

Parham and I once buzzed some girls at 5 A.M. (while guzzling straight gin) at the Allison Wells Hotel out of Canton; then we flew at tree-top level all the way to Pascagoula to enjoy the Gulf water and breezes, before returning to Parham's woods-shrouded cabin abutting the north side of River Hills Tennis Club. My father became justifiably irritated with me after learning of that excursion.

All was not fun and games, however. As every young man eventually must, I began to contemplate my future. I dabbled in the oil business, using the money that I had saved. One particular deal irked my father: I had purchased an oil lease and some oil-and-gas royalty near the Lincoln and Pike county line in south Mississippi. I quickly found out that I had paid top dollar—two-hundred-dollars per acre for fifteen acres of royalty—somewhat above what Dad would have paid. I admit to having felt stupid. I also bought three-sixteenths of a 387.5 acre Covington lease for twenty-five dollars per acre, which I tried to sell, with no takers. Dad paid me three-hundred dollars per acre for ten acres of royalty, clearing five for me.

I had to live with that lack of financial acumen. Meanwhile, I did begin working for Yazoo Manufacturing Company, producing the famed Yazoo Mowers, as well as working on a road construction project near Grenada Lake. But the budding bourgeois class of oil entrepreneurs in the South—from Texas to Louisiana to Mississippi—captivated my imagination. Oil men were, at once, fiercely competitive and uncontrollably independent. That suited my personality. Plus, if God or fate (whatever the oilman's personal convictions!) smiled your way, there were great sums of money to be made.

On this matter, both my father and I agreed—the oilmen who did business with Deposit Guaranty were the most respected entrepreneurs. They would become with the passing years almost completely Republican, and I certainly aided and abetted that development.

Dad and I voted in 1952 for Republican Dwight Eisenhower, though I felt more akin to Senator Robert A. Taft's philosophical leanings. The Party of Lincoln had largely ceded its mantle as the party of the average man to the Democrats during the Depression years and thus opened the door for Democrat Franklin Roosevelt's ascendancy. Northern and western Democrats had worked deals with their more conservative southern Democrats thereafter to keep a vise-like grip on national politics. World War II and the ensuing popularity of General Dwight Eisenhower finally enabled the Republican Party to win twice.

Dad was strongly for Eisenhower, as were many of his generation. After all, Eisenhower's great leadership helped win World War II and later revived America's economy. Those facts trumped issues of politics or philosophy. Bill Mounger had worked long and hard to keep his bank up and running during the Second World War; he'd seen some of his best men, including Herman Hines, leave for battle. Some, including Hines, were blessed to return. The war had spurred local lending to big contractors like Belzoni's Reed brothers and also clothing manufacturer Bob Sanders, who was the wealthiest man in Mississippi for a long time (making his money initially in Mississippi-based textile mills), and jumpstarted the economy. The Deposit Guaranty Bank suddenly exploded with the capital of new entrepreneurs, the capital of many future Republicans.

National Democrats that year proved how far out of touch with American reality they were, nominating a religious Unitarian and avid political liberal, Adlai Stevenson of Illinois, to run against "Ike," who was Republicanism's overnight sensation. With Stevenson as a national candidate, Mississippi Democrats were starting to look pretty foolish and out-of-step with their mostly white, conservative electorate. Mississippi governor Hugh White led the state's Democrat convention delegation. Northern and western liberals mocked the Magnolia State's Democrat Party leaders, who were hectored in public on issues of race.

About this time, Mississippi's next generation of conservative leaders—the Wirt Yergers, the B. B. McClendons, the Clarke Reeds, and Charles Pickerings, along with me—had had enough. Northern Democrats showed great disdain for our racial predicament, but lacked any real understanding of the social pressures weighing down the southern states. Twenty-five-year-old Yerger, a Jackson native just returning home from insurance school in New York City, fumed about the quagmire; I did, too. In time, Wirt and I would forge a friendship and long political partnership.

For now, the cobwebs of youthful whims were clearing from my young head and I yearned to be productive. I wanted to build. After

I took some geology classes at Jackson's Millsaps College, Dad and I agreed that I should attend the University of Oklahoma in the fall of 1954.[8] At this time I met a beautiful recent graduate of H. Sophie Newcomb College (then the adjunct female school to Tulane University)—Jan Gore. We began dating and, on December 17, 1955, the Gores hosted an announcement party at a friend's Peachtree Street home in Jackson. We were married in Jackson's historic First Presbyterian Church on January 21, 1956. Jan then joined me as I finished my petroleum engineering studies at the University of Oklahoma.

Oklahoma's rigorous program was very easy in comparison to West Point. I acquired a second bachelor's of science degree (in petroleum engineering) and then a master's of science in petroleum engineering attaining a grade point average of 3.85. This positive traction earned a valuable fellowship from Standard Oil Company of Indiana. While in Norman, Oklahoma, I registered as a Republican for the first and only time. I did so to vote against Mike Monroney, an Oklahoma Democrat who represented two things I had come to despise—Roosevelt's New Deal giveaways and government's growing intrusion into the business community.

Jan and I lived in a $55-per-month school-subsidized apartment. We drove a paid-for Pontiac Catalina from my Brookhaven, Mississippi dealership, and lived on $160 a month from the "GI Bill of Rights" and $150 a month from Standard Oil, Indiana, with tuition and books also paid for by Standard Oil. Life was good. I wrote my father a letter dated October 24, 1956, to tell him so: "Jan has been doing extremely well and has had almost no trouble. We have made some very good and enjoyable friendships up here so that we are enjoying a very pleasant life here."

The letter added: "The oil companies are really flocking in to interview the engineers." I was considering going to work for one of two companies, Humble Oil or Gulf Oil. I ended my letter with an expression of concern for Dad's health and welfare:

I hope that your facial pains [Dad suffered from *tic delaroux*, a form of multiple sclerosis] have about entirely cleared up now and that you are comfortable again. I trust that the bank and all your other interests are doing well. By the way, it appears to me that your Tuscaloosa sand is not being credited to your William's well in Soso.[9] Was it considered asphaltic or what? Tell Mother and the rest of the family hello. I'll be in touch with you later about the job situation and would appreciate what advice you might be able to give me.

Your loving son,
Billy

After earning my master's in March of 1957, I took a job with Humble Oil and Refining Company, a wholly owned subsidiary of Standard Oil of New Jersey, eventually Exxon. I fortunately attended the company's reservoir engineering school in New Orleans only six months after joining the company. At age thirty-one in 1957, I was working math problems about oil flow for forty hours a week; however, I quickly began to chafe at the oil company's bureaucracy, which (déjà vu) was like a military bureaucracy. There was one difference. The oil bureaucracy had sent me to roughneck amid a swamp on a bug-ridden oilrig! The rig was located outside of Paradis, Louisiana, in Lake Des Allemands, where I worked the 4 P.M. to midnight shift. My driller boss was a Cajun appropriately nicknamed "Coonie" who hated educated roughnecks. A medical student from Tulane and I were assigned the demeaning job of scraping putrescent decomposing bugs off the rig. The bugs' oil-filled bellies splat gooey, black blotches all over everything. Misery set in with every bug I scraped from that rig. I commiserated, "What would my classmates from West Point think of how low I have progressed to the job of cleaning stinking bugs off an oilrig?"

Bug busting and snapping to attention in military style at Humble's district meetings and reservoir engineering schools almost motivated me to say, "Enough!" After working on the drilling rig, however, I was at least able to do some more creative work at Humble's Paradis office, analyzing wells for latent reserves or outright abandonment. Once I showed scientific proof that the company should rework a well using newly developed techniques instead of simply abandoning it. Proudly, I submitted the findings to my boss.

He screamed, "What are you trying to do to me?"

"What do you mean?" I asked.

"I was the engineer on that well when we couldn't make a completion out of it. Do you want me to look bad?"

He ordered me to alter my report to recommend its abandonment. Later, another astute petroleum engineer in the New Orleans office recognized the same potential and returned it for reanalysis. The signature on the original instrument declaring abandonment was mine, the one-and-only time I ever knowingly failed to do right. My boss had scuttled my good work and left me looking inept. I concluded that I could not continue to work under such conditions and pledged that, at the first opportunity, I would have to leave Humble and work for myself—period.

My father's health suddenly slipped again. Lung surgery had led to the fatal deterioration of his heart. I drove from Louisiana to Jackson to visit and discuss business with him as much as possible. Then, on October 26, 1957, a few days into his fifty-sixth year, Dad suffered a fatal heart attack. The funeral at Galloway Memorial Methodist Church was a Who's Who of Jackson and the South. Dad had ceded daily bank duties by this time to others, though still serving as vice chairman of the board of directors and chief executive officer. After Dad's death, Pat McMullan Sr. took Dad's post as chief executive officer and Nat Rogers became the bank's president. Shortly before dying, Dad had told his protégé, Herman Hines, to wait patiently and his turn at the helm could come. "I think you are going to be president of the bank one day, and I want to tell you one thing," Bill said to Herman. "Whenever you get to be the president of the bank, don't you ever forget the people who helped you along the way. You can see that I haven't forgotten and I want you to be that way."[10]

My father left his family in excellent financial shape. More than that, he left Mississippi stronger. From his perch as the state's most prestigious banker and head of the largest bank in Mississippi—the Deposit Guaranty National Bank—he'd managed a postwar recovery and boom in Jackson and beyond. He'd developed jobs statewide; funded men of vision and integrity; sealed deals with a handshake. Men watched him, mimicked him, and there was no better example than my father's: "I loved him dearly," recalls

Hines, with tears in his eyes one day in 2003 as he offered his personal reflections. "He set the predicate for this bank and my future was in this bank and I became almost like a son to him. It was that close a relationship."

Herman Hines did, in time, become Deposit Guaranty CEO, after Nat Rogers (who took the job as president and CEO of a much larger Texas bank, and who became president of the National Bankers Association). Nat Rogers recalls with affection my father's influence: "I worked with a lot of people, was president and chairman of a major bank in Texas, but I never worked with anybody that I thought was smarter and more capable and more effective. He's been my role model. He's been my ideal for fifty years."[11]

Bill Mounger believed wealth was a trust carrying a responsibility to give back. I now took the reins of our family's estate, and the task was heavy, made harder because initially I remained with Humble Oil in Louisiana, flicking bugs and fighting heat. Dad's death devastated me. Jan and I looked to friends for encouragement. It was football season in the late fall of 1957, and friends and football offered an outlet. The Petroleum Club of Jackson often took special trains from Jackson to New Orleans for Ole Miss or Saints games. On one particular weekend, a bunch of our friends were making the train ride to the Sugar Bowl, where Ole Miss would meet LSU. Jan and I met the group as they got off the bus at the Tulane stadium. I was smiling big, because I had exciting news. Parham Bridges recalls how I approached him: "Billy met us when we arrived, walked up and smiled. He said, 'You remember that bum oil lease I bought? Well, it hit!'"[12]

Only four months after Dad died, Shell Oil Company drilled the discovery well for Little Creek Field, a fifty-million-barrel oil field. It was near the land that I had purchased "for top dollar" (twenty-five dollars per acre) years earlier. My father had berated me for paying so much, leaving me feeling like the oil-business neophyte that I truly was. Quite honestly, that purchase had been the primary reason I decided to acquire an additional oil-and-gas education at the University of Oklahoma.

Now my "bad purchase" turned out to be only a forty-acre drilling unit away from the Shell Oil discovery well. Had I never inherited a dollar, that discovery of oil at Little Creek alone would have made me wealthy for life.

Oil men started calling me while I was still with Humble, trying to make a deal on that lease, but I stood pat. Finally, after much pressure from highly experienced and much older oil producers, I joined some others to drill.[13] In April of 1958 the big drilling day arrived, and I drove my Pontiac from New Orleans to Pike County to observe the coring of the first well on the Covington lease. Drilling a core is like taking a biscuit cutter sample of the hoped-for oil sand. All day long the driller ran the drill pipe to 10,000 feet, with the core barrel attached to cut a fifty-foot core. Upon removal, the core was laid down for examination around dusk. Everyone knew upon seeing it just how porous it was, with the emanating smell of oil, proof that it contained oil. To this day I have a piece of that core at my office in the AmSouth building.

At the well, an oil man looked at me—a bug-scraping engineer neophyte from Paradis, Louisiana—and chuckled, "I know one guy who's not going to be a petroleum engineer with Humble much longer!" That night, after pulling the core, I drove back through Covington, Louisiana, around midnight, just dying to tell my news to someone. So I awoke my friend, Bill Huls, and thrust the piece of core under his nose. I said, "Smell this!" A couple of months later, I received my first check from the well and it exceeded my yearly income from Humble as a master's-degreed petroleum engineer. I knew that my career with Humble would soon end. I said a silent prayer of thanks for J. B. Halstead, who brokered that lease, and for Melvin Campbell, who sold it to me. Little Creek would soon become a famous oil field.

Jan and I traveled to New York in May of 1958, immediately before I left Humble, to attend my tenth West Point class reunion, my first trip there since graduation. It turned out to be wonderful timing, coming just after my big oil discovery. Before going to West Point, we stayed in New York City, a thrill to Jan, who had never been there. Mr. Cavanaugh, my father's old banker friend, took us to eat at Les Marmiton. He also arranged for us to see *My Fair Lady*, the number one Broadway musical at the time. Jan and I unappreciatively snoozed constantly through the musical—possibly due to the Martinis we drank at Les Marmiton.

Mr. Cavanaugh also organized a meeting with the president of Morgan Guaranty Trust Company and its top executives. The bankers discussed a $400-million off-shore loan to Humble during the meeting. I have often wondered if those New York executives ever mentioned my name to any major Humble officials, who surely would have asked, "Mounger Who?"

The New York City trip culminated as Jan and I attended *The Ed Sullivan Show*, the most popular TV show at the time. Afterwards, as lagniappe, Sullivan called us on stage and posed for a picture. From New York City, we traveled fifty miles up the Hudson River to the United States Military Academy, and Jan finally saw this beautiful, historic school. That West Point reunion engendered a heartfelt revelation of what my education truly had meant, and I vowed someday to repay the debt.[14]

Not long after receiving my first check from the Little Creek Field, I received a call from Mr. Pat McMullan, Deposit Guaranty's new CEO. My father had serviced the lion's share of the state's oil business for years, and now, desiring to initiate the first petroleum department in Mississippi, Mr. McMullan stated: "I want you to come to Deposit Guaranty and establish an oil department."

"Well, I've only accumulated a year-and-a-half of experience," I replied.

"Yes, but we want you now. And we will also bring in a prestigious oilman, Mr. W. M. Vaughey. He is the most renowned oilman in Mississippi."

I certainly recognized the name. Mr. Bill Vaughey had been a good friend of my father's and was, no doubt, the state's most respected oilman. He had served as president of the Independent Petroleum Association of America, and later of the National Mid-Continent Oil and Gas Association (the only person ever to do so), and had been a member of the National Petroleum Council for years. [Later, President George H. W. Bush appointed me to the National Petroleum Council.] I recognized the potential of this new petroleum department and readily accepted.

Jan and I packed our things in July of 1958 and said goodbye, waving "adios" to Paradis, Louisiana, and New Orleans. No more bug busting. No more formal education. No more improper orders! I didn't fully appreciate the important implications at the time, but I was about to take my place among Mississippi's conservative leaders.

Upon my arrival at the bank, I had to be—or at least I felt I had to appear to be—an authority on areas of oil-and-gas production even though I had limited experience with Humble. Everyone in oil and banking statewide sought my advice. The department grew from about $2 million at its start to about $60 million in oil-and-gas loan volume. The bank's customers believed that my personal oil production was due to my engineering degrees and savvy, but I knew it had much more to do with being blessed by God.

Nonetheless, my own oil investments were mounting. I enjoyed my position as head of Deposit Guaranty's petroleum department, where I could make decisions and where I was the boss. Even though I now had three engineering degrees, I didn't spend a lot of my time with technical matters. I delegated the details. If I had a forte, it was the West Point mindset of making the final, big decisions. If you make a bad decision, you lose; if you make good decisions, you can keep making loans or replenishing your oil-and-gas production, and then you really don't have to do much with it.

I soon developed a saying—"I'm making money while I'm sleeping!"

Sun Oil Company, together with J. Willis Hughes, in 1959 opened another oil field—the McComb Field—also a winner for the bank and me. An opportunity arose for me to buy 205 acres of leases, with the closest portion being two miles from the McComb discovery well. I asked J. Willis Hughes what he thought about the leases, and Hughes said, "All of these leases are out of the area that will produce and my advice is that you not purchase them." Notwithstanding that advice, I personally financed the purchase, taking one half and splitting the other half between Howard Stover and Rodney Jeffreys. All but four acres of the leases produced in the field. Additionally, Little Creek kept exploring and the whole 387.5-acre Covington lease produced, along with all fifteen acres of the royalty I had purchased. Finally, I bought interests in other fields that produced big for me and additionally produced large loan volumes for the bank.

By 1960, I was earning almost $14,000 a month from Little Creek and McComb alone, a sum today (at sixty dollars per barrel of oil) that would be about $300,000 a month. My bank salary never amounted to more than 5 percent of my yearly gross income. I nonetheless remained in my bank position until 1970, building the petroleum department and working with the bank president, Nat Rogers.

For me, oil meant independence, something that I dearly valued, and something that has freed me to advance the ideals I cherish for my state and country. I've always preferred to travel and enjoy going to lots of different places, rather than being tied substantially to one. Jan and I have traveled a great bit, and for years we enjoyed our friends in Jackson, especially at the Petroleum Club, Mississippi's number one private club, which up through the seventies was dry in name but not in reality.[15]

With my financial and social life in good standing, the stage was now set for my best-known years—the political days. I could never have foreseen what was about to occur!

CHAPTER 6

The Early 1960s: Goldwater Rush!

T he average black or white Mississippian in the 1950s would have been surprised to learn that Mississippi Republicans actually had existed for decades. In fact, the ringleader of the Black and Tan Republicans—an enterprising African-American wheeler dealer named Perry Howard—did not even live in Mississippi. He had latched onto the Republican leadership in 1924, at the tail end of the Reconstruction years, which came following the Civil War. Howard, who made his home in Washington, D.C., held his power for nearly four decades. Northern Republicans had long used Howard to secure whatever "Republican" votes that were allocated to Mississippi for Republican nominations; Howard then was reputed for a price to pay friends or contacts to be Republican delegates from Mississippi. In essence, this meant that blacks in Mississippi, who could not turn to the state Democrat machine at that time—for it was a whites-only club—were also cut out of levying any real political protest by joining a second party via the Republicans—Howard's private purview for making money and wielding personal power.

In the spring of 1968 Nelson Rockefeller visited with several top southern leaders—including me—for breakfast in the Roosevelt Hotel in New Orleans. Rockefeller was accompanied by a perennial political operative named Leonard Hall, who had engineered

Thomas Dewey's two nominations for president and was the lynchpin in Eisenhower's agreeing to run and to win the presidency as a Republican in 1952. Hall essentially controlled the moderate-to-liberal northeastern establishment Republicans, and he explained to us how they bought and controlled the Black and Tan delegates all over the South who would attend each Republican National Convention. When the time arose for a Mississippi delegation, perhaps totaling ten votes, they would call Perry Howard in Washington, D.C., and inform him that they needed ten delegates. He would calculate what it would cost—for instance $20,000—then he would contact nine others and give them whatever he could negotiate, perhaps $1,000 each, and then Howard would keep the remainder for himself. They did something similar for each of the other southern states amounting to a substantial number of delegates, thereby insuring that they would control the national Republican Party.

As the 1950s wound down, Howard's dominance over Mississippi Republicanism was eroding. At the 1956 Republican convention, a group of mostly young Ole Miss alumnae led by a twenty-six-year-old self-described "ideologue," Wirt Yerger, made a bid to oust Howard from state party control. These were my friends, although I was not yet a part of their efforts. They strove to rid the state GOP of its "delegate-for-hire" status and the resulting noninfluence in Republican circles, as well as to overcome Mississippi's one-party Democrat system.

They eschewed patronizing Democrat powerhouse Senator James O. Eastland. Wirt Yerger's longtime friend Tom Crockett met Charles McWhorter, then head of the national Young Republicans, and Tom recommended that McWhorter meet with Yerger. A new Mississippi Republicanism was thereby hatched—creating an organization called the Mississippi Young Republican Federation—which was separate from both Perry Howard's Black and Tan faction and another faction of Republicans, called the "Lily-Whites."

The new Republicans first attended the 1956 national convention, where Wirt made news by refusing initially in a compromise to be seated on the convention floor in conjunction with the state's Black and Tan delegates; but later Wirt did agree to split the seating fifty-fifty. Then, in the 1960 convention, where Richard Nixon won the Republican nomination, Mississippi's new Republican delegation controlled all the convention floor seats.

Soon after that 1960 convention, Wirt walked into my office in the petroleum department to discuss the future of the Mississippi Republican Party. He described a plan to solicit numerous $100-, $25-, or $10-a-month donors to build a financial base for the state Republican Party. I signed on at $25 a month. Then the new local Republicans began anticipating the 1963 upcoming state elections. Soon thereafter, I began raising money for Republican events in Mississippi, and my office began to show the signs that my Republican affinities were growing along with my distaste for national Democrats. People who sat at my desk to get a loan would look down under the glass cover of my desk and see the following sign: KENNEDY IS A RAT FINK. An Irish Catholic—Tom Glennon, originally from Philadelphia, Pennsylvania—once visited my office to secure an oil-and-gas loan. Seeing the Kennedy sign, he exclaimed, "How can you have a sign like this so demeaning to the president of the United States?" I replied, "Well, Tom, if this offends you, just slide this piece of paper over it. If you really don't like it, and thus you want to seek your loan some place else, fine." He replied, "I believe I'll just slip this paper over it." In 1968, during the Nixon-Humphrey presidential contest, I also played a game with those seeking loans: anyone who wanted a loan had to take a dart and throw it at a dart board composed of Hubert Humphrey's picture—they at least had to give it a try! Today, such behavior would be viewed unfavorably, but standards were different in those days, and I never worked at the bank for the money.

By 1962 the party invited Barry Goldwater to Mississippi for a major fundraiser, a hundred-dollar-a-plate function. I thought, "Here's the opportunity. Here's the chance to really turn this country around and change it in the proper direction." We all loved Barry Goldwater's articulate, Republican conservatism. So I bought and sold several thousand dollars worth of tickets, attended the function, and was mesmerized by Goldwater.

I was hooked.

Others were aware of my great energy if given the right cause. Fred LaRue, son of "Big" Ike LaRue (who had taken my mother and father at times to visit and fish at the "Koon Kreek Klub," haunt of multimillionaire oil men, near Athens, Texas) also became enthralled by Republican politics. Fred LaRue and I knew each other through our parents and many mutual friends. We both had attended the University of Oklahoma, LaRue in geology and I in petroleum engineering, as had others, including Howard Stover. Fred also was a groomsman in my wedding, and he was deeply involved with Goldwater and ready to plunge full force into Republican politics, even though his own father was close to Senator Eastland.[1] Fred unfortunately was eventually convicted of being the "bag man" who delivered hush money as a part of the Nixon administration's attempted cover-up of the Watergate scandal.

The LaRues enjoyed great wealth and Fred had plenty of time. Wirt Yerger prevailed upon the Republican National Committeeman from Mississippi to resign so that LaRue could fill that spot. Money and influence were accruing. Almost imperceptibly, I joined Mississippi's new Republican inner circle.

The newly energized state Republican Party in 1963 ran Rubel Phillips as governor, propelled by the funds raised from Goldwater's visit. Born in Alcorn County, the Mississippi Public Service Commissioner was an attractive individual, as was his wife, Margaret. Rubel was virtually aphilosophical, but when he observed the bankroll ready to support a Republican candidate, he announced: "I believe I'll run as a Republican!" Paul Johnson Jr. won that gubernatorial race as the Democrat. But Rubel received about 39 percent of the vote—the first real Republican to run for statewide office in Mississippi since Reconstruction.

I had given Johnson a thousand dollars at the request of a mutual friend, Herb Shortridge; however, I also gave Phillips a thousand dollars. Disconcerted after that campaign, I resolved never again to split my money between a Democrat and Republican. Give to the person you want to win—period. I started looking at the political map. Sitting in my petroleum department office, I contemplated, "Well, maybe we can do something statewide. We're on the road!"

Then came 1964. Not only was Arizona senator Barry Goldwater running for president as the Republican nominee, but he also was advancing a conservative national philosophy. Goldwater's 1960 book, *Conscience of a Conservative*, had sold 3.5 million copies.

Grassroots, common-sense Americans—of which I considered myself one—had hope. During that campaign a California actor named Ronald Reagan recorded a nationally televised speech supporting Goldwater, thereby enhancing both of their reputations.

The 1964 Republican Convention was to take place in the Cow Palace in San Francisco and Fred LaRue offered me his two spectator tickets. Fred recalls how he called me two weeks before the big event: "[Fred] said, 'Look, do you want to go? I've got two national committeeman seats, and I've got a place to stay in the Richelieu along with the Mississippi delegation.'"[2]

"Well, I'd like to," I replied. I hung up that phone and went to see Nat Rogers, Deposit Guaranty's president and my boss. "Nat, I've got to go!" I said. Rogers naturally gave me the thumbs up.

I knew the Lord had a plan that involved me politically, because he kept giving me these opportunities. Jan and I flew to San Francisco several days early. Fred had already been there as a committeeman for more than a week. We attended all the Mississippi meetings and participated in the political process. We also participated in the demonstrations against Rockefeller, whose big-money, liberal days of party control were terminating. Nonetheless, northeastern Republicans littered San Francisco with disinformation. Pennsylvania governor William W. Scranton released an infamous letter decrying Goldwater's conservatism and so-called extremism. A copy was slipped under Jan's and my door; we read it and became more supportive of Goldwater.[3]

The night when Rockefeller arrived to speak, the chorus of "boos" was so cacophonous that the nabob probably couldn't hear himself speak. It became one of the most poignant moments in twentieth-century American politics. Jan (she doesn't like to admit it) and I stood on our chairs and booed our hearts out. Years later, after Rockefeller became vice president, I told him: "I don't know whether you know it or not, but several of us in this room in 1964 booed you at the Cow Palace."

At the San Francisco convention, Communist agitators seemed omnipresent. Some were protesting the notorious recent deaths of the three civil rights activists in Philadelphia, Mississippi, deaths that Wirt Yerger, I, and any other sane Mississippian abhorred. Some protestors even let the air out of the tires of our Mississippi delegation's buses, forcing us to catch a ride with the Texas delegation.

While driving to the Cow Palace with Fred LaRue, Wirt Yerger, and Charlie Klumb on the last day of the convention, Klumb told me, "We want you to be active for Goldwater in Mississippi."

Klumb, from Crystal Springs, was at that time my predecessor as the Republican state finance chairman.

"I'll do anything you want me to do," I said. I was now sensing that there was a place for me in this new Mississippi GOP movement. "What do you want me to do?"

Klumb issued an invitation that would open the door for years of influence and trips to the White House: Klumb asked me to become an official Republican fundraiser.

"We want you to be Hinds County finance chairman," Klumb asserted.

"Well, I've never really done anything like that on a substantial basis. If that's what you want me to do, okay. I will do whatever ya'll think will be most beneficial."

Yerger, Klumb, and LaRue asked: "How much money do you think you can raise?"

I had no actual experience, and Klumb and Yerger indicated low expectations, yet I was competitive and possessed a hardnosed energy. "I don't know what anybody else has done," I told them. "I never really have raised much money before. But I don't see why I can't raise at least $150,000 from Hinds County."

"Are you crazy?" the threesome laughed. Yerger, Klumb, and LaRue bet me a steak dinner that I couldn't come close. "We've never gotten as much as fifteen-thousand dollars out of Hinds County before." I won that steak dinner, raising more than $160,000.

In the last two weeks of the Goldwater campaign, Wirt Yerger took $140,000 in funds from our state GOP treasury—funds mostly raised by me—and boarded the Goldwater Campaign airplane in Washington, D.C. While in the air, Wirt stated to Goldwater's people that the Mississippi GOP would donate the money to the Goldwater campaign with a proviso. The campaign badly needed an infusion of life because the Johnson Democrat campaign was bashing away in national advertising, confronting Goldwater with his own sound bites. Johnson had convinced Goldwater's staff that he should ameliorate his rhetoric, when, to the contrary, Barry's clear-spoken, tough language was his greatest strength. Wirt told Goldwater's staff that the Mississippi money was theirs if they would use it to rerun the very effective famous Reagan speech for Goldwater. Wirt stipulated that the speech must be re-aired nationally on television. It was agreed, and the inimitable Reagan speech was rerun using Mississippi's money. (The airing of this speech has been credited with further rocketing Reagan's popularity turning him into a prominent national political phenomenon.)

After the campaign was over, Mississippi had led the nation raising money for Goldwater, with the state raising 1,800 percent of its quota set by the Republican National Committee. We had stepped up to the plate and hit a grand slam.

Wirt Yerger resigned as the chairman of the state GOP in 1966, just two years after Goldwater had ignited the conservative base of the Republican Party with his principled but failed bid for the White House. "After serving as state chairman for ten years and seeing the development of Mississippi as a two-party system, I feel that I owe it to my family and my insurance business to devote more time to them," he said in the *Jackson Daily News*.[4] The state was ripening for Republicans. "Soon," predicted Yerger, "we will be the dominant party in the state."[5]

Wirt had already engineered my election to the Mississippi Republican Party executive committee in January of 1965. He also attempted to get me to be state finance chairman; now, with Wirt retiring, and with my again refusing his request that I succeed him as state chairman, Greenville's Clarke Reed volunteered for the position and asked me to become the GOP state finance chairman. Reed averred: "I'll be state chairman, but it's going to be contingent upon Mounger being finance chairman."

In my oral history interview with University of Southern Mississippi professor Orley Caudill, I recalled how Reed essentially crowed, "I'll pull 'duty, honor, and country' on him [Mounger]."[6] Clarke in an interview admitted to using that very approach to solicit me.[7] "Look," I recall Reed saying, "you owe this to the country. . . . You've got to do it because of your West Point motto: 'duty, honor, and country.' I know you too well, that you're not going to let this thing fall down and you're not going to let me down when I step up and do something that you refused to do."[8]

Reed's well-aimed pitch struck my sense of responsibility. I guess in a way we all find our role in life. And I think my role in life has been to be the perpetual guard, blocking and making the way via my fundraising for others to run into the spotlight. For many years, Clarke and I worked well together. "We ran together all the time," Reed recalls of our early days working together. "We were good friends. And then things really started happening in all kinds of ways."[9]

Clarke was voguish—one-part Washington, D.C., one-part fraternity boy, one-part Delta statesman. "Colorful and eminently pleasurable."[10] "Excitable."[11] He used the latest clichés to accent his clothes with some conservative consciousness. Words like "Cat" peppered his chatter.[12] He had a "look-my-way" sort of foppishness. He was a great quote, though I would soon nickname him "Mumbles" because he talked like he was chewing a mouthful of marbles.

David Keene, whom I worked with when he was the southern coordinator for Ronald Reagan, characterized Clarke thusly in the 1976 book, *Marathon*: "Clark is not an evil guy. He's weak. He's a guy whose reputation was made in part out of a whole cloth. He's brighter than most of the people on the [Republican National Committee]; he is good at maneuvering to some extent, although not as good as he thinks he is."[13]

Clarke eventually became, in my mind, a bad sort of Republican insider. Yet he insisted in a personal interview that he never really meant to stay as long as he did as the GOP state party chairman, a notion I do not believe. "I didn't want to do it," he said. "It was the last thing I wanted. . . . I planned to stay through [a second Lyndon Johnson term] and then quietly go away. And then Nixon gets elected and nobody dreamed that, see? . . . So I never expected to see him become the president. Hoped someday [it would happen,] but not in my time."[14]

Whatever the case, Clarke and I began running the Mississippi Republican Party together in 1966; immediately we faced the task of completely replenishing our fund base. Then, just about the time that I took over as the state's Republican fundraiser, our sole Republican congressman Prentiss Walker decided to run for the U.S. Senate against Senator Eastland. The problem was that he had not consulted Yerger, Reed, or myself! Walker saddled Clarke Reed and me with his candidacy. In desperation, we invited Goldwater back to the state, creating a prime opportunity to raise big money.

I desired a hundred-dollar-per-person fundraiser, but Walker and others protested so vehemently that I reluctantly acquiesced to only ten dollars per person and vowed that if they could not make it succeed, I would never again allow another low-figure fundraiser. I traveled the state seeking donors. In the end, I made sure the Goldwater event was a success, by purchasing the last two hundred ten-dollar tickets myself and by selling them in two-hundred- to two-thousand-dollar blocks. That event reinforced a valuable axiom: *Don't waste time nickel-and-diming toward fund-raising goals.* Don't ask for ten dollars when people will give you a hundred. There is a degree of snob appeal to high-priced events. Some donors, if charged small amounts, actually feel it isn't worth their time to attend—just not exclusive enough. I knew there were many who simply love to attend silk-stocking gatherings, and from then on, I was determined that I would not allow politics and fundraising to be mixed in the future. That may sound incongruous, but I mean simply this: If you want a large political crowd, make it free; if you want to raise money, make it an exclusive big-dollar affair. In other words, separate popular politics from fundraising.

Meanwhile, lifelong Mississippi Citizen's Council members— mostly old-style conservatives who were Democrats—began to note our fund-raising successes and to vilify our newly emerging Republican aplomb, especially any of our attempts that seemed to challenge Jim Eastland's power. One minister, Delmar Dennis of Meridian, lumped Clarke Reed and me into a most unlikely group in a letter to the editor of the *Clarion-Ledger*. "I will be unable to join with you [the *Clarion-Ledger*], Marvel Lang, Martin Luther King, Lawrence Guyot, Phil Lapsonsky, W. D. Mounger, and Clarke Reed in your efforts to unseat my lifelong friend Jim Eastland," Dennis stated. He said that to do so was to promote every "Civil Rights law that has been passed since 1952."[15]

Despite our newly raised (but insufficient amount of) money,

Prentiss Walker lost predictably badly to Eastland. Even worse for the GOP, Walker had vacated his seat in the U.S. House of Representatives, and Sonny Montgomery, a Democrat (and my distant cousin!), ran and won Walker's place there.[16] Yet despite Walker's 1966 loss, our successful fund-raising efforts and the growing Mississippi GOP had been impossible to ignore. The *Atlanta Journal Constitution* on Sunday, April 24, 1966, further reported, "W. D. Mounger, vice president of Deposit Guaranty National Bank and Republican finance chairman, has been designated chairman of a May 6 'Conservative Unity Dinner' to be held in Jackson." People even in Georgia were starting to notice what we were doing in Mississippi.

In 1967 we recruited Rubel Phillips to run again for governor. Phillips, one of the more progressive early new Republicans in Mississippi, had gained valuable name recognition in his failed 1963 gubernatorial run. Phillips really did not want to run against John Bell Williams, a conservative Democrat holding the Fourth District U.S. Congressional post. National Democrats had stripped Williams of his committee chairmanship after Williams backed Goldwater for president in Mississippi, and appreciative Mississippians rallied to their mistreated underdog, John Bell, who was a good man. I comprehended why Rubel didn't really want to challenge him, but his running was crucial to the development of the GOP in the state; we needed a candidate.

Richard Nixon—former vice president under Dwight Eisenhower—came to the state in 1966 to help stock the GOP coffers, but the funds could not elect Phillips, who ran an admirable but doomed campaign. Yet Phillips gave a landmark speech that helped adjust Mississippi Republicans' future views of race. Against the counsel of most of his advisors, Rubel gave a speech that may, in part, have been written by his brother, Hal, an award-winning novelist. The speech tackled race directly, urging moderation and cooperation among the races whose fates always have been and will be inextricably linked in our state. Some rank-and-filers squawked, but I realized the speech could prove immensely forward-thinking and might ultimately be helpful to the state party. Though a lopsided loss (67 percent to 33 percent), Phillips's second campaign had kept our Republican growth alive and it helped preempt the inevitable race issue, offering an alternative conservative point of view to counter the stereotypical racist one that had been advocated by Democrats and some conservatives in the past.

Nixon spoke at the 1966 GOP fundraiser at Jackson's Heidelberg Hotel, and I was the dinner's master of ceremonies before an audience of more than a thousand. The ROTC color guard marched into the festive event with their flags. The flag bearers reached the front table with Nixon standing next to me. The National Anthem played and, immediately afterward, I invited the designated minister to give the invocation, just as the ROTC sergeant simultaneously barked the order for his team to march out. Billy Mounger, the West Pointer, had forgotten to allow time for the color guard's recession before the prayer!

The highly formal crowd erupted in laughter and I joined them. In his ensuing speech, Nixon joked about my gaff. Later he wrote me a note recalling the humorous occurrence, something to the effect of "a West Pointer actually fumbling a flag ceremony!" Nixon's path would cross mine several more times in the not-too-distant future. In particular, two years later, 1968 would prove eventful as I helped deliver Mississippi's GOP delegation to secure Nixon's nomination as the Republican presidential candidate. In the process, Mississippi's GOP received the first hints that our unit rule system was flawed; the state caught its first glimpses of Nixon's fatal flaws as well.

CHAPTER 7

The 1960s: Taking the
Bull by the Horns

ississippi's unit rule had given the state's young Republican
Party rapid recognition and multiplied power in the late
1950s and early 1960s. The Republican National Committee had discontinued recognizing unit rule votes on a national
basis, but Wirt Yerger rightly convinced the state GOP that a voluntary unit rule vote would give our new party more political
muscle.

Unit rule dictated that the national presidential candidate who
won the most Mississippi delegate votes was awarded all our
state's delegate votes. This provided a big slice of political pie that
no real national presidential contender could ignore. What made
Mississippi's bloc vote especially enticing in the 1960s was that
the Mississippi delegation waited until actually walking onto the
national convention floor to broadcast our bloc vote. No presidential candidate could be certain how our bloc would go until the
final minute. No candidate, therefore, could afford to ignore us.[1]

In 1968, Mississippi had twenty delegates (with twenty alternates) to the national convention.[2] When the delegation actually
voted, one delegate plus one alternate equaled one actual Mississippi vote (for a total of twenty votes). Whichever presidential candidate won the largest number of our delegate votes received all of
our final votes. The unit voted as one.

Our Mississippi Republican team was not in the best of spirits after Rubel Phillips's 1967 gubernatorial loss. Yet Clarke Reed, myself, and other state GOP leaders organized precinct meetings, county conventions, and the state Republican convention for the 1968 presidential race. I was deeply involved in the delegate selection process.

I must admit that our Mississippi version of unit rule was unique. Time showed that it worked, provided genuinely honorable delegates were chosen. It had been a formula for success, but it proved to be fraught with future catastrophe. Clarke Reed is quick to say now that the concept was Wirt Yerger's, adding that it served the state party well early on. "Wirt had the idea and we went along with it because, you know, unit rule, which was pretty silly, . . . you've got a small delegation so we'll all vote together and have a big impact for the majority candidate and go with that. . . . I thought it was a good idea [at the time]. At that time we [as a state party] were sewed up and we were playing every angle we could trying to—it's all smoke and mirrors."[3]

Mississippians inclined toward Richard Nixon in 1968 because, on the heels of the various civil rights controversies, he had been willing to visit the state in 1966 when others such as Ronald Reagan would not. So in 1968 Reed and I began moving our state delegation's majority toward Nixon.

Prior to the local and state conventions, Reed, who ultimately engineered his own reelection as state party chairman in 1968, called a meeting in New Orleans of some of the Southern Association of Republican State Chairmen to meet with potential presidential candidates. The SARSC consisted of the old Confederacy states, plus Kentucky and Oklahoma. Ronald Reagan and Nelson Rockefeller came to New Orleans, while Richard Nixon scheduled his own personal meeting with SARSC's leaders soon afterward in Atlanta.

Reed and I were influencing our state GOP toward Nixon, but I inherently leaned toward Reagan. A year earlier, in 1967, Winthrop Rockefeller—then governor of Arkansas and the less-liberal brother of Nelson—had loaned the state party his private jet to fly Rubel Phillips to California. There, we three, with some others, met Reagan in his Sacramento governor's office, and Reagan cut a

TV spot endorsing Phillips. When Governor Reagan emerged into the room to greet us, his magnetism overwhelmed me as no one else's has ever done.

In New Orleans, those attending dined with Reagan in his personal suite; he signaled a desire to run for president but had not yet committed due to the existing overwhelming support for Nixon. Reagan knew the South was becoming the key to gaining a Republican victory, as evidenced by Goldwater's popularity.

The liberal northeasterner, Rockefeller, knew that our group's inclinations were conservative, but he angled for our votes anyway. All of us southern leaders enjoyed meeting him for a breakfast buffet. I stood next to this chiseled-faced, bespectacled New Yorker in the buffet line as he helped himself to eggs, but passed up the grits.

"Whup! Whup! Governor!" I said, with no reason to be coy around the politically liberal tycoon. I pointed at the grits. "Governor, those are grits there. You've got to have them."

Rockefeller spooned up a big ole dollop of grits on to his plate. Therefore, I make the claim to fame that I made Rockefeller eat grits! Peter O'Donnell from Dallas introduced Rockefeller to the group: "Well, I guess Governor Rockefeller really is serious," O'Donnell joked. "Governor Rockefeller not only ate those grits, but he actually put salt and pepper on them, not sugar as most Yankees do!"

The New York governor was skewered with polite questions from us southerners, and we procured promises from him—should he win the nomination—concerning the direction of the Supreme Court, not as to specific appointments, but about eliminating the activist role of the Supreme Court. We inquired whether the South was to be influential in the affairs of the party and prospective government, and whether a reasonable proportion of southerners would be appointed. I especially desired an adamant anticommunist, pro-national defense stance.

The bottom line was our desire to gain national recognition and clout and, in so doing, convince our fellow southerners—the rank-and-file voter—that we, not the Democrat counterparts, actually held the keys to the new southern influence nationally.

Nixon's later Atlanta meeting, by mistake, had been scheduled to overlap with our state convention. So Reed and I asked Wirt

Yerger and GOP stalwart Jim Furrh to meet with Nixon in Atlanta and push the same key southern questions that we had asked of Reagan and Rockefeller in New Orleans.

Our state party leaders faced two significant problems as we sought to build: First, Senator Eastland was proving to be an insurmountable roadblock as we tried to build a party; second, many national figures steered clear of visiting the state for fear of appearing racist. In 1968, Reagan had spoken in Memphis, rubbing salt in Mississippi's festering wounds by declining to cross the state line. In truth, he snubbed us.

So when Yerger and Furrh contacted Clarke and me with a satisfactory report of their Nixon visit in Atlanta, the Mississippi GOP convention proceeded with our delegate election. We gave each national candidate one last shot to woo the Mississippi delegates after the state convention. Governor Reagan sent Cliff White, a former Goldwater election whiz. Richard Kleindienst attended as Nixon's representative, and even Rockefeller had a spokesman.

White did well. Kleindienst, who years later became prominent during Watergate as Nixon's U.S. attorney general, flopped. Before a group of daring and proud new Mississippi Republicans—those willing to take on the Eastland machine to their own detriment in hopes of national party recognition and pull—Kleindienst suggested that Nixon needed 576 delegates to win the Republican nomination; then he boasted: "We have it cinched!" implying Mississippi's delegate vote didn't matter.

The aftermath required some crisis management. Mississippi delegates buzzed that "if Nixon doesn't need us, if he's got it all sewed up, then to heck with him." A Harvard man, Kleindienst came over like warm beer.

Later that same night, Fred LaRue, who was already strongly for Nixon, took Kleindienst to his family's Jacksonian Motel. I never had cared for Kleindienst, and my wife Jan could not stand the man. But after we had finished dining at Primos Northgate, LaRue's wife, Joyce, told us that Fred and Kleindienst were caucusing at the Jacksonian. Several of us delegates made tracks there.

I knocked on the door. Immediately, I discerned that something was amiss—my wife and Fred LaRue's wife were with us—for no one would answer the knock.

I finally convinced the crowd to leave, but they still kept asking, "What's going on?" It eventuated that Kleindienst had become drunk thereby making an ass of himself, cursing and more. Fred and those inside did not want delegates to see Kleindienst acting in that disreputable manner. His misbehavior could have been harmful to the Nixon effort.

The Mississippi delegation consisted of a commanding majority for Nixon with a smattering of holdouts for Rockefeller and Reagan. At the state convention, a minor skirmish occurred while voting on the wording of the state party platform; a Pike County delegate suggested removing the word "sovereign" from the description of Mississippi in the party platform. Many felt it implied a bent against national civil rights, but I retorted that, though the word might conjure certain stereotypes, pragmatically "if you take out the word 'sovereign,' the people of Mississippi are going to believe we're not for state's rights."[4]

I prevailed and "sovereign" remained.

Soon after the Mississippi convention delegates were chosen, I received the following note from Richard Nixon, dated August 8, 1968:

> Pat and I are grateful to you, and to all Republicans, for the confidence that you have just demonstrated.
>
> We will try to repay your faith in us by hard campaigning in a manner to unify our Party and our Nation. This must be a team effort. We need your help.
>
> Please resolve now to rededicate your efforts for a Republican victory on November 5th.
>
> With best regards.
>
> Sincerely,
> Richard Nixon (personal signature)

Reed and I headed early to Miami for the 1968 national convention, armed with our mandate for Nixon. There we gathered with other key southern Republicans hoping to fashion a larger bloc of seventy-four votes (Florida, Mississippi, and South Carolina) and to use that power to advance the concerns of southern conservatives. We worked with Florida's Bill Murfin and South Carolina's Harry Dent—and, more importantly, the former Dixiecrat presidential candidate, South Carolina senator Strom Thurmond. Dent had served on Thurmond's staff since the mid-1950s and had moved with Strom from the Democrat to Republican Party.

Our states shared common concerns: if Nixon didn't win, Rockefeller might. That would sabotage any hopes of attracting any more southern conservatives to the southern Republican fold. Likewise, if Reagan received too much support, it could create a stalemate, stopping Nixon and allowing Rockefeller to eke out the nomination.

I understood this political math, yet felt unsettled after we southern states leaders met with Nixon campaign chairman John Mitchell. I felt something was fishy, but John Mitchell made all the right promises, and the others prevailed upon me. I looked Mitchell in the eye and stated: "Well, I just don't feel right about all of this, but I know that you can't put this kind of thing in writing. . . . There comes a time when you have to accept a person on his word. John, I guess I've just got to take your word.'"

What concerned me were two prior commitments Nixon had made: to choose an acceptable vice president and to exercise party patronage, together with making good judgeship appointments. An issue paramount to me was Mississippi's patronage; however, I agreed to Mitchell's assurance, and we instigated our southern coalition.

Later, after the Watergate fiasco with Mitchell in the middle, I contemplated the role I'd played in the chain of events creating the Nixon White House. There is no doubt that if I had not been for Nixon, we would not have had the unit rule; it would have been voted out in some fashion. While some believe that Reagan may have had a chance to defeat Nixon and preempt any Watergate, I believe that there easily could have been a catastrophic Rockefeller nomination.

We traveled to Miami, accumulating a total of about ten hours' sleep while staying in a miserable hotel (The Shore Club) within walking distance of the convention hall. I experienced my first up-close-and-personal taste of how easy it might be for a unit rule vote to backfire. Nixon and Strom Thurman met with some Mississippi delegates who seemed to be weakening on their bloc-vote commitment to Nixon. In the heat of the national convention a delegate is rushed as if for a fraternity. Rockefeller's camp attempted to convince Mississippi delegates that Nixon was reneging on promises to them, particularly as to who would be vice president. Reagan's camp promised perks to former Mississippi congressman Prentiss Walker, and another Mississippi delegate, Dr. Ray Lee, to break the unit rule and vote for Reagan on the convention floor.

Prentiss had decided he was going to run again for U.S. Congress after he lost his post while running for the United States Senate in 1966. Oh, he wanted to break unit rule!

Clarke and I visited with him and he looked me straight in the eye and averred, "Why should I worry about breaking the unit rule? The Republican Party has never done anything for me." I stared him down and said, "Prentiss, what are you talking about? I was your largest contributor; and, furthermore, fundraising for you was the hardest that I have ever done. Admittedly it wasn't a huge amount, but it was a hundred times harder for me to come up with a dollar for you than for any other campaign. Virtually all the money you received came through me and you are sitting here looking me in the eye and telling me that the Republican Party has *never* done anything for you? Frankly, the biggest mistake I ever made in my life was *ever* doing anything for you. You are probably the most unappreciative soul I have ever seen." This was prior to Clarke Reed's, Gil Carmichael's, and Doug Shanks's tergiversations. (More about these three later.)

Ray Lee and Prentiss Walker threatened right up to the floor nomination vote to break the unit rule, which was surely a portent for future national conventions. I just couldn't conceive of such backtracking once a delegate had given his word; he had to keep it. People have always bothered me who seem to be unwilling to keep their word; but politics, I have learned, breeds such. Personally I require appreciation and loyalty, which appears to be too high a price from some politicians. As the old adage goes, if you want gratitude and appreciation, get a dog!

Another Mississippi delegate, Dr. Charlie Pruitt, "sat on Walker and got him back in line," recalls Clarke Reed. Reed added: "It was a pretty clear question for me at the time. Reagan was too new on the scene and Rockefeller was running. Nixon was in the middle; he was going to get it. He was going to get it from the South or from the Northeast side, see?"[5]

Mississippians at the Miami convention started appearing on national TV, as well as at impromptu convention parties. Crazy things were beginning to occur as bigger fish tried to proselytize our tight school of delegates. One of the wildest schemes involved then-Florida governor Claude Kirk. Clarke and I were telephoned from Kirk's office. The caller said: "We want you two to visit with Governor Kirk." He was on a yacht moored in the canal. Clarke turned to me: "You want to go see Claude Kirk?"

I said, "Well, what the heck? We're not doing anything right now, let's go see Claude."

We had dubbed him "Claudius Maximus" because of his unbridled attempts to pontificate. So Kirk's highway patrolmen escorted us from our flea-bitten hotel to his sumptuous yacht.

The crew had vacated with the only ones on board being "Claudius Maximus" and a very prominent industrialist, a builder of refineries and chemical plants.

After some socializing, Kirk finally divulged his mission. "Well, I wanted to talk to you two. I want y'all to support Rockefeller for president."

"My Lord, Governor Kirk, we can't do that!" we told him. "If we did, we could not return to Mississippi." We could not have swung the delegation to Rockefeller, even if we had tried. Mississippi's residents would have torn us apart like piranha.

Governor Kirk desired to secure the nomination for Rockefeller in the vain hope that Rockefeller would designate him as his vice president. In desperation, he finally said, "If you can't do it for Rockefeller, then get the delegation to support me for vice president."

We said, "Nobody does that!"

This event was highly embarrassing.

The day before the final Miami convention votes were announced, Reagan spoke to our delegation, but our bloc of twenty remained solid. The final straw poll before walking to actually cast our vote didn't go exactly as planned; Lee Brent, a Greenville delegate whose family owned Brent Towing Company, had toyed with backing Rockefeller. I had warned him, "You're going to be in trouble back in Mississippi if you do." Now Brent was teetering again.

Meanwhile, alternate delegate Clarissa McNair's unknown original propensity for Rockefeller was reignited by the convention lights. The native Pennsylvanian's family was old-line northern Republican; she told me she could not vote for Nixon.

"Well," I replied, "that's all right, Clarissa, we don't really need your vote. Go ahead and do what you want to do." I mistakenly believed she was pro-Reagan.

Alternate delegates had no vote, but they had one-half vote under unit rule, but McNair (an alternate) and Brent (an actual delegate) both raised their hands for Rockefeller in the final poll of delegates. If the unit rule had not been in effect, there would have been one actual vote for the New Yorker! From Mississippi, of all states!

Clarke and I were shocked. Mississippi's final straw vote yielded one vote for Rockefeller, three votes for Reagan, and sixteen votes for Nixon. Everyone—including Brent and McNair—honored the unit rule, however; so on the final convention count we delivered all twenty votes for Nixon as a unit.

One last-minute moment of confusion ensued when Reagan's campaign called Clarke on our convention floor telephone, urging him to bring the entire delegation to Reagan's personal trailer outside the convention hall.

"Reagan wants us to go to his trailer!" Clarke told me.

I was the vice chairman for the convention while Clarke was the chairman and I had to put my foot down. "Clarke, the delegation is in line," I said. "At this late date, leave it alone."

Clarke was too weak to say "no," and never developed any backbone. He told me that he was worried hard-core Reaganites would become upset if he declined Reagan's last-second invitation.

"They're already upset!" I growled.

I was more concerned that national TV cameras were pointed our way. How would the nation interpret a last-second exodus to the Reagan trailer? I told Clarke to take half the delegation off the floor to the Reagan trailer, while I kept the other half on the floor. I have never forgotten Clarke's ambivalence; it was my first indication of Clarke Reed's instability.

The evacuation of one-half of Mississippi's delegation was observed by the national press, especially by NBC reporter John Chancellor. He sought me out for an interview, wondering what was occurring. The following is a full transcript of that interview:

J.C. I'm standing in the Mississippi delegation with a member of that delegation, Mr. W. D. Mounger of Jackson, Mississippi. There are a bunch of you here on the floor. Are these the Nixon delegates in the Mississippi delegation?

Mounger: No, not necessarily. These are split up in both ways. We have approximately twenty out here. I believe we have twenty on the floor, and we think there are approximately twenty in the meeting.

JC: Now you are wearing the biggest Nixon button I've seen tonight. How many total votes would be cast as of the last time you checked in the Mississippi delegation for Governor Reagan, not just counting the bodies, but the votes.

Mounger: Well, we have twenty votes that can be cast for president from Mississippi. And we have a unique way of voting by allowing our alternate delegates to vote. And then we vote the unit rule and go by the majority. This morning we had a vote and thirty-two out of the forty votes went for Nixon; six went for Governor Reagan; and two went for Governor Rockefeller.

JC: So in our vote tallies for people keeping it at home, the way you stand now is three votes for Reagan, the way it is normally computed, out of the twenty votes in the delegation. Is that right?

Mounger: Well, that is right, except we vote the unit rule, so that the majority controls and all twenty of our votes go at this time for Nixon. And as of this morning it was thirty-two out of forty.

JC: Now Mr. Mounger, Governor Reagan has made a rather dramatic attempt here in the early hours of Thursday morning to wean away from the Nixon supporters in this delegation some votes.

Mounger: That's correct.

JC: You know these people in the delegation. How well do you think he is going to do?

Mounger: Well, he spoke to us once before. He has already appeared before us, and the most votes he got out of that was six votes. He's not the only one trying to wean them away, because he and Governor Rockefeller have the same purposes in this. We have been getting rumors all day long about the vice presidency, and most of which were designed to upset the southern delegates.

JC: We have a story today on NBC that says that, in talking to some Alabama delegates tonight, Governor Reagan said that he now has evidence that Mr. Nixon wants Mark Hatfield of Oregon as his vice president. Have you heard that?

Mounger: Oh, the rumor has been floating around all day, but we in our delegation—at least I have met with some of the higher people in the Nixon organization, and Senator Thumond has met all the way with Mr. Nixon himself on these issues, and we do not believe from what we know and understand that Mr. Hatfield would be the vice president.

JC: You don't believe that.

Mounger: We don't believe that.

JC: So you don't think, to sum up, some of your people have gone in to give Governor Reagan a hearing in the caucus room here in convention hall. And you don't think that he is going to get very far with them?

Mounger: Well, it would be hard for me to see that he could turn around enough delegates, when we got a vote of thirty-two out of forty, to turn them around so that he would have a majority in the delegation.

JC: So as far as we can tell now, you expect Mississippi to stand firm for Nixon.

Mounger: At this moment I do. Now, these people that are on the floor will probably go in and meet later with Governor Reagan, and then we will appraise the situation after they all get back out.

JC: Alright. Thank you very much, Mr. Mounger. Mr. W. D. Mounger of Jackson, Mississippi, indicating that as far as we can tell here on the floor, Governor Reagan probably won't be too successful with those delegates, although Mr. Mounger, wouldn't you say that this is, I hate to say "eleventh hour," because it is one o'clock in the morning in the east, that this is kind of a dramatic attempt on his part to get support in the South? What would you say about that?

Mounger: Well, it is certainly dramatic because we have been staying firm all day, and we've been bombarded by a great number of Reagan people and a great number of Rockefeller people, including Bill Miller himself, telling us the same stories, because they know that it is designed to bother us. Now most of us in the delegation haven't paid any attention to it because they are really, in our idea, mostly rumors just to upset us. And I have offered to bet several of the people who tell me it is going to be Hatfield two-to-one and I can't get any takers. And I know that the South Carolina delegation has offered to bet them three-to-one and they can't get any takers, so I think the whole thing is designed to upset us. And then Governor Reagan is coming over here to try to capitalize on that, because the only hope that he has, or Governor Rockefeller, is to stop the Nixon voting surge.

JC: That is very interesting. Thank you, Mr. Mounger. Very nice.

Moments after my long interview, the podium began announcing states, which then pronounced their votes to thunderous applause. Another state, more applause; another state, more applause!

My heart beat faster as Mississippi's turn approached; at the last second, Clarke and the remaining delegates returned before I had to cast the Mississippi vote in place of Clarke. The meeting with Reagan had not changed any votes; it had only made Mississippi look stupid. The unit rule had held.

Nixon won Miami in 1968 with a majority of fifty-six votes. Florida delivered thirty-one out of thirty-two (Claude Kirk was the sole dissenter), South Carolina twenty-two, and Mississippi twenty, for a total of seventy-three. Our southern states had nominated Nixon; if we three southern states had not done so, Nixon would have been beholden to states like Ohio and New Jersey, who would have nominated him on the second ballot. The now-famous, much-studied and maligned "southern strategy" had worked.

The next task was to name Nixon's vice presidential running mate. His choice was Maryland Governor Spiro Agnew, who had sat directly in front of me in the Maryland delegation all week. His selection seemed sound to us, although we had not considered him for the job. The *Jackson Daily News* quoted Clarke as saying of Agnew, "He's more liberal, perhaps, than we would like, but hell, that's part of the game." The paper quoted me saying I was "definitely pleased" with Agnew. Prentiss Walker, on the other hand, left the convention in protest that Ronald Reagan had not been chosen and, said the *Jackson Daily News*, "departed for his chicken farm in Mize."[6]

The Mississippi GOP earned a tremendous amount of credit with Nixon. Newspapers reported that the Mississippi Republicans' use of unit rule had provided the state's delegation with disproportionate attention and pull. Dr. Charles Pruitt of Magee (a great country doctor and high quality person) and several other delegates agreed that Mississippi had drawn more attention because of this unique setup.

I told one paper that the contention of "a few delegates . . . that the state GOP leaders had committed the delegation" to Nixon was wrong. "We didn't do that at all. The only thing we did was to hold to the unit rule as we had previously agreed we would do."

Parties and celebrations ensued after the nomination, and Clarke and I were vociferously thanked by Nixon. "Every time I turned around I saw you guys from Mississippi on TV and you really did great and I really did appreciate it," the soon-to-be president chortled. "I want to let you know how much I appreciate it; and just anything you want, I will do!"

A few weeks after the national convention, I began receiving letters from friends and thankful supporters around the state like this one from State Women's Foundation Chairman Marijo Denson of Newton, Mississippi: "T.V. personalities are always the recipients of praise, so I will not attempt a flow of adjectives, but will confine my remarks to a simple 'thank you.' Thank you for your leadership ability in making Mississippi's role in the Republican convention the most rewarding of any party in recent history."

City editor Charles Smith of the *Clarion-Ledger* recalled my satisfaction in an August 12, 1968 column, saying that Nixon told me that he had watched the Mississippi leaders on TV. Smith said that Fred LaRue, Clarke Reed, and I were on a first-name basis with Nixon, who also "knows several others in the delegation by name. State GOP leaders have worked closely with him for a number of years. Nixon, who has an exceptional memory for names, also has staffers who feed the information to him. Familiarity with his people, as any good politician knows, is one of his best tools."[7]

Our annual hundred-dollar-per-plate fundraiser, which I emceed, occurred shortly after the nomination, where Senator John Tower of Texas added his two cents: "Look, you guys really played a role in that convention. Don't you worry about Richard Nixon and the people knowing it. We know how key you were." It seemed that we conservative southerners had achieved our goal—national respect.

Yet one of Reagan's top men, Lyn Nofziger, played the harbinger. He knew that Clarke and I had said all along, "Our hearts are with Reagan, but our heads are with Nixon." Nofziger predicted to us: "I'm not going to be one of these people who say, 'I told you so,' but you just wait and see. You are going to regret it!"

As a confirming omen, a major disappointment occurred marring our otherwise good relationship with the Nixon administration. A few weeks after Nixon's inauguration, during a National Committee meeting, Bo Callaway (a 1949 West Point graduate who became Secretary of the Army and who had been southern coordinator for the Nixon nomination) scheduled a meeting with Attorney General John Mitchell to confirm the promises made before and during the Republican National Convention. Callaway, Reed, and I showed up as scheduled for the meeting. John Mitchell let us cool our heels for two hours in his lobby and finally sent a lackey to say he could not see us. This was the first indication of deficiency of character in Mitchell, who was inextricably responsible for the Watergate fiasco. The specific reason he would not see us was that he was reneging on his patronage commitment to us. Later, it was learned that Senator Eastland had introduced Mitchell so abruptly to realpolitik that he had no choice.

Asserts Clarke in a personal interview: "They needed Jim Eastland so badly. . . . I remember I had promised [Laurel, Mississippi, native] Charles Pickering he'd be U.S. Attorney. And Eastland said, 'What are ya'll doing fooling with my turkey?' Sure enough, we didn't get to name 'em. Charles has gotten bad news all along for things like that. He's a good man, I'm sorry . . . he should have had all those things."[8]

Eastland, as chairman of the Senate Judiciary Committee, had informed Mitchell that he was going to control all federal judicial appointments in Mississippi—judges, district attorneys, marshals, and other appointments—period! Eastland said he would cause immeasurable difficulties with judicial appointments in the other forty-nine states if Mitchell contested Mississippi appointments with him. In reality, Mitchell had no other choice and if he had possessed one iota of integrity and decency, he would have told Callaway, Reed, and me that story, and it would have been understood and accepted. He could have easily made it up to us in many other ways. Mitchell ultimately lacked the character to confront us *mano a mano*.

Miami 1968 taught us some hard lessons. The unit rule had cracked but not broken. I glimpsed the state party's potential weaknesses, but also remained a believer in the efficacy of the unit rule's ultimate goals. I believed that Miami proved the unit rule's ability to help attain greater clout for Mississippi.

I went on to raise 270 percent of the quota set by the Republican National Committee for Mississippi during the upcoming Nixon campaign, causing us to lead the nation once again in presidential fundraising as a percentage of quota. Mississippi's inauguration attendees enjoyed the best seats at Nixon's inauguration. We built the best state float for the inaugural parade (for which I raised all the money). We had the best of everything!

For all his faults, Nixon had tapped anew the voting power of southern conservatives and had reached out to our leadership. For the first several months after his presidential election, the honeymoon was aglow.

In 1969, I was invited by President Nixon to a stag dinner at the White House honoring Prince Philip of England, the husband of Queen Elizabeth. It was a black-tie affair where everyone sat at a

U-shaped dining table. Immediately preceding the state dinner, I had attended the annual meeting of the Independent Petroleum Association of America in Houston, Texas. The president of the association was Dave True of Casper, Wyoming, a prominent oil-and-gas producer. I told True that I was headed for the White House to dine with the president and Prince Philip. True stated, "Prince Philip is currently hunting on my Wyoming spread (True owned about a hundred-thousand acres of mountainous land) and will be departing Casper for Washington, D.C."

So during the cocktail portion of the White House gala, I approached the president and Prince Philip and asked the prince: "How was your hunting in Wyoming?" The prince and the president were both startled, and the prince asked: "How did you know where I was?" I stated that Dave True was a very good friend and that I had just left him in Houston, Texas. President Nixon was somewhat miffed that I one-upped him.

We Mississippi Republicans were in high cotton. We had learned the political ropes faster than anyone, and we tugged them often and well. We enjoyed a continuity of leadership in our growing apparatus while other states—prone to infighting—did not. Others couldn't understand how we did everything we did; we just knew how to outmaneuver everybody else. We were the best-funded state GOP party in the nation due to our successful fund-raising efforts. We also were the best organized owing to the Machiavellian machinations and maneuvers of our talented and brilliant Mississippi Republican Party executive director, Bill Wilkins.

Clarke and I spent as much time in Washington as any nonresident during the first two years after Nixon's election. Fred LaRue, one of our own, had an office in the White House, although never a title. He and fellow southerner, Harry Dent, an assistant to the president, were Mississippi's White House contacts. A red carpet was laid out for us when we Mississippi brass desired to visit. Clarke enjoyed unprecedented notoriety as a political player in the national GOP; and he was reelected as the chairman of the Southern Association of Republican State Chairmen (SARSC). Within the state, he held court in his lustrous office in Greenville's downtown, talking in his cliché lingo to visitors. As the chairman of SARSC, he began to exert some influence on the GOP's national level. One thing that started concerning him greatly was an emerging effort by liberal Republicans to change the way the number of delegates were allotted per state for voting at the Republican National Convention. The liberals, seeing the growth of the southern GOP, were hoping to take advantage of their more populous Northern and Midwestern GOP states. They wanted the number of state delegates to be determined by the popular vote for president, and took their plea to the United States Supreme Court. Meanwhile, the states of Wyoming and Mississippi countersued alleging that such a system would unfairly over represent states with bigger populations. Clarke began to argue at RNC meetings that such a move would make Republicans like the Democrats. "That helped me win this thing because people had seen what the Democrats had done to themselves," Reed recalls.[9]

When the 1972 Republican Convention came around, Clarke felt that he couldn't trust Nixon's people to leave the delegate apportionment rules alone, and, he says, he told our state executive director, Bill Wilkins, to go early to Miami. Recalls Clarke: "[Wilkins told me], 'Well why? You've got Nixon in your pocket.'" Clarke told Wilkins, "I know, but I don't trust them and they don't trust me and that's the way it should be. . . . I think, by seeing us set up by the [Miami convention] ballroom, [it] . . . will make them behave, but, if they don't, we need to be in business, you know."[10]

Ten days before the start of the 1972 convention, which was again in Miami, Reed played host to Nixon, Jeb Magruder, and many others, seeking to stave off a change in convention voting rules. "I lost ten pounds," Clarke recalls. "I didn't sleep for ten days. . . . We were meeting all night and this kind of stuff. . . . So we held it pretty good on the rules until the other [1976] convention."[11]

For all Clarke's maneuverings, I had observed the Greenville resident in a true pinch at the 1968 convention and had begun to wonder. I had detected friction between us at the 1968 convention. Clarke is a very egocentric person. All of us are to a degree. Certainly we are human beings and the Lord created us to think of ourselves and to protect ourselves. Clarke needed the limelight, needed the adulation, needed the excess credit and such, more than the norm. He was also appointed to the prestigious 1976 Bicentennial Commission, a plum that allowed him to rub shoulders with the *crème de la crème*. I received an appointment from Nixon to a relatively new commission, the National Review Board for the Center for Cultural and Technical Interchange between East and West based in Honolulu, Hawaii. This was a State Department–funded group led by *Time Magazine* baroness Clare Booth Luce; another notable member was Otto Miller, chairman of the board of Standard Oil of California. We worked for years to effectively educate students from the Pacific Rim in every subject from animal husbandry to PhDs. Over the years, many high-ranking government officials and business executives from countries around the Pacific earned degrees at the East-West Center. Jan and I met a large number of important people in Hawaii and made many new friends. We enjoyed fourteen or fifteen trips to Hawaii and I felt that I was helping to bring business principles to bear on this governmental board.

This previous Lyndon Johnson–appointed board had allowed $25 million of federal money to be expended on buildings, but had not acquired title to them. The University of Hawaii immediately expropriated the Eisenhower Auditorium and a dormitory, a situation which our board spent its entire eight years rectifying. Before ending our term, we succeeded in having the East-West Center deeded forty acres by the State of Hawaii, and their legislature appropriated sufficient funds to build a replacement dormitory; the university also vacated the Eisenhower Auditorium.

The committee reconstituted itself in 1976, at the end of my service on the board, becoming separate from the State Department, supported by other government and business interests. This was one of the few instances of the self-dissolution of a governmental board. This appointment was not as prestigious as Clarke's, but it suited me greatly and lasted for seven years.[12]

By the time Nixon took the White House, Clarke and I had both learned that politics requires taking credit for accomplishments to ensure that you aren't overlooked in the future.[13] Ultimately, we knew that the twenty votes we delivered for Nixon in 1968 had been a foregone conclusion, even if there were some tight moments. When it comes to receiving credit with Nixon or the national party, we wanted to say, "Yes! We did that."

It was hard for anyone to miss the massive financial numbers that we were racking up. They were unprecedented not only for Mississippi, but nationally, as the Mississippi Republican Party's newsletter, *Eagle*, stated: "State GOP Finance Chairman W. D. Mounger has set a fundraising record that is getting increasing attention in both Mississippi and Washington." Clarke persuaded Vice President Agnew to speak at a Mississippi Republican fundraiser in 1969 that suddenly exploded the party's previous fundraising records and caught everyone's attention, locally and nationally. A total of 2,600 people paid a hundred dollars a plate to attend the vice president's event. I oversaw this feat, which required shifting from a smaller venue to the Mississippi Coliseum. An October 20, 1969, issue of the *Eagle* ran the headline "Mounger Tops Record." The article stated:

> It took the largest seating facility in the state to hold the over 2,600 persons who crowded into the Mississippi Coliseum Oct. 20 to hear Vice President Agnew. The Agnew fundraiser was the largest in the history of the state and the South. Mounger came into the Agnew Dinner with a performance rating that is rare. In 1964, as Hinds County finance chairman, he raised more money for presidential candidate Barry Goldwater than any other county finance chairman in the nation in a single-handed effort. And more recently, while Mounger served as state finance chairman for the 1968 Nixon campaign, Mississippi was recognized for raising over 300 percent of the national campaign quota.

People were showing up at the door for that event purchasing hundred-dollar tickets, as if they were peanuts—even paying out a thousand dollars for a table of ten. It was unbelievable! Agnew had appeared on the Gulf Coast after Hurricane Camille and was very supportive of the people. By way of contrast, Teddy Kennedy had berated the locals concerning the issue of integration, offering no real assistance. Consequently, Mississippians showed up in droves to support Agnew and the Mississippi Republican Party. Also, Agnew had recently given a speech in New Orleans in which he coined the phrase, "pusillanimous prostitutes of pragmatism," thereby enticing people even more. The Lord must have intervened because the caterer, Morrison's Cafeteria, arrived with a refrigerated trailer full of food and was able to serve the entire, overflow crowd.

I felt my presence was making a difference to thousands of Mississippians, even if some of the rank-and-file didn't know it. I toured the state, giving speeches urging local conservatives to unhitch their wagons from a one-party system and become Republicans. At the Sardis Rotary Club, at the Capital City Kiwanis Club, at the Canton Rotary Club—my rhetoric for new Republicanism was fiery. One paper quoted me, "Mississippi now has a front row seat in the National Republican Party. Never in my lifetime has Mississippi played such a vital role in any national convention as it did in Miami."

I noted in a speech to the Capital City Kiwanis Club (the same club where I froze as a youth!) how poorly Mississippi Democrats were treated by their national constituents, and how poorly they represented the state at the 1968 Chicago convention, in contrast to the way Republicans looked on camera in Miami when nominating Nixon. "The Mississippi Democrats have been caught 'eating off both sides of the hog' too often," I was quoted as saying. "They have somehow been saying that they are Mississippi Democrats and not National Democrats; but have continued to take their seat in Congress as National Democrats." I noted that Mississippi's governor, lieutenant governor, senators, and congressmen were not seen on TV representing their state at the Democrat National Convention in Chicago. Then I rhetorically interjected: "They are the first team. Why are they not fighting for their party and Mississippi before the TV cameras? If [Ole Miss football coach] Johnny Vaught sent his scrubs in before national TV to play in the Sugar Bowl, we would disown him. Why do we let our elected politicians get away with it?"

Now I had a bit of clout and was getting a hearing, and I felt a responsibility to use it to the benefit of our state when I could. For instance, I served on the board of Jackson Academy, when it was a small private school teaching phonics. Eventually some of us southern conservatives stood up strongly when the Internal Revenue Service under Nixon's administration considered removing

private schools' nonprofit tax exemption. That fight helped to preserve our excellent private school system in Mississippi.

I stood up to Nixon on several occasions when his positions on
issues worried me. One example is a December 6, 1970, Western
Union Telegram to "The honorable Richard Nixon."

> In Miami, I vice-chaired the Miss. Delegation and instrumentally
> guided its twenty votes to you. In 1968, Miss. lead [sic] the states in
> fundraising as a percentage of quota predominately because of my
> efforts. When you retreated from your Houston commitment on the
> oil depletion allowance, I stayed with you. Your reneging on your
> Atlanta and Miami commitments regarding schools was unpalat-
> able; but I continued my support. And I stood by you when your
> strongly biased oil import committee recommended an ill-consid-
> ered tariff on oil imports. Your IRS ruling to Gestapo-like police pri-
> vate schools was intolerable, politically idiotic, and totally
> inexplicable; but I still remained a supporter. Now, your disembow-
> elment of the oil industry may have exceeded the limits of my
> tolerability. . . . Have you sold out totally on the Ripon Society; or
> are Kennedy, Muskie, and Proxmire running this government? . . .
> My disillusionment and evisceration are overwhelming.

> William D. Mounger, Republican Finance Chairman of Miss.

We had worked hard to earn the right for Mississippi to be heard
by the national circles of the Republican Party. I now strove to
make sure my voice represented Mississippi's voice, and that we
were heard. Whether I was always on target or not, one thing was
now certain: Mississippi's Republican Party was a national player.

Part Two:

A State of Change

CHAPTER 8

The Early 1970s: State Coffers, Candidates, and Hurricane Camille Explode

A black coffin-shaped box, about half the size of a cigar box (given to me by Joe Sims), sits on my desk in my office in the AmSouth Building (the former Deposit Guaranty building). Drop a penny on the top of the box, and a spring-driven skeleton rises out of the box, clasps the coin, and retreats back inside the coffin. The message on the side of the box: "You can't take it with you, but you can try." It also symbolizes that even after my death, I'll still come back and raise money, so you better go on and give now.

This adage was one of my pitches to visitors. Money has no soul or afterlife. And as the early seventies rolled in, I sought to collect as much as possible for the GOP and other good causes this side of eternity. I also accumulated other GOP responsibilities, perhaps more than I wanted.

In 1970 our state party fielded a well-funded list of candidates for every congressional district, though none won. The fact that every race had a decent GOP contender in it evinced progress.

Mississippi's Republican Party was now developing its own stable of leaders from within, rather than transplants: W. T. "Bill" Wilkins—the best administrator that I have ever seen—and Haley

Barbour, one of the finest political minds I would ever encounter, both came into the state party apparatus straight out of Ole Miss. Both men served stints as the state party's executive director over the next two decades. Meanwhile, Clarke continued to chair the SARSC, while Wilkins also served as that group's executive director.

Monthly pledges to the state GOP now exceeded twelve thousand dollars, the fruition of Wirt Yerger's initial URF pledge system and my incessant soliciting. Some of my friends learned to sidle away when they eyed me walking down the street, but I did not take it personally when I cleared the street like a snow plow. They never were able to avoid me; eventually I cornered them and they came through. I also took in large contributions from our annual hundred-dollar-per-plate and thousand-dollar-per-table events, where I raised enough additional money to make us the best-funded state political party in the country.

Trent Lott says that he learned a few tricks about picking the money tree from me: "He's not shy about asking. I came to realize early on that just an average guy, or academic, or a lawyer are not good fundraisers. To be a good fundraiser you have to have money yourself, and you must give it; then you have to be willing to ask for it from others. But when you ask for it, you have to ask like Billy does. I'd go in and say, 'Could you help with five-hundred dollars?' and Billy would go in and say, 'Hey, your share is five thousand.' And who's going to tell him no, because he'd argue with you and give you lots of reason why that would be a reasonable commitment? Now that's a unique talent."[1]

Trent is pretty much correct. I felt that if I kept at someone, they would yield. My childhood friends received no free passes. Leland Speed today occupies a third-floor office in the Woolfolk Building across the street from the Mississippi State Capitol. As the unpaid executive director of the Mississippi Development Authority, he entertains any and every kind of pitchman. They come asking for advice and for state support for major new business endeavors. Speed notes: "I've never turned down one request Billy's ever made of me. He's been a very expensive friend. . . . And Billy is that rare person who likes to ask people for money. And he's so damn good at it."[2]

I do enjoy asking others for money, especially because I always feel deeply about the cause, or I wouldn't ask in the first place. Billy Powell, a Texan, arrived in Jackson in 1969 to assume some of my old duties in the petroleum department. Billy is an ex-Mississippi GOP chairman and obviously one of the most influential Republican leaders in the state. He had no real political affinity when he arrived in Jackson, but I would quickly change that. Powell recalls the first time he and I met in 1969: "[Billy Mounger] was still head of the petroleum department. He handed me a form. He said, 'Billy, you're a Texas A&M graduate and you're a petroleum engineer, so you must be conservative.' And I said, 'Well, yeah.' 'Here,' he said, 'take this and fill it out. You must be a Republican.'"[3]

The form said "United Republican Fund," the organization Wirt Yerger and Buddy Klumb had founded to collect donations for the party. I asked for ten dollars or more a month from about everyone who came in my office to do business. "At that stage of the game," recalls Powell, "I didn't know if I was a Republican or a Democrat or what. I just voted for whoever I thought was the best candidate. I knew one thing, that Billy Mounger was still in charge of the petroleum department. I was not about to do anything to start off on bad footing with him."[4]

I smile a bit sheepishly thinking back on those times with Powell. I admit that certain of my "techniques" from back then would be questioned by some people today. I didn't feel like it was anything at all out of the ordinary as a banker to encourage customers to make gifts to the Republican Party. Powell, a self-described "naïve redneck country fellow from the backwoods of Texas," tells everyone now that he knew who buttered his bread. "I understood that he [Billy Mounger] was the boss. So I guess he just sort of stamped me right on the back of my red neck at that stage of the game, 'Another Republican made in Mississippi by Mounger.'"[5]

Getting Billy Powell involved was one of the greatest contributions I made to the party. Powell continues: "He [Billy Mounger] obviously was lending to the oil people. And every time they got ready to complete a well, they then had to come in to borrow the money to complete it. So the poor fellow who had to have money to complete a well at the same time there was a Republican event going on, knew good and well that he better borrow enough money to go ahead and pay for a table, because he was going to be asked to come to that event. Many a person did just that, thinking, 'Boy, he's selling tables. I've got to either avoid him or get caught for a table.' If Mounger was walking down the street, he was going to ask you for money."[6]

We were making our mark among the top brass in our state, that's for sure. Conservative Democrat Congressman Sonny Montgomery (my distant cousin) and the powerful Democrat Senator John C. Stennis cooperated with us young Republican gurus. On top of all this, the state GOP's newfound status with a Republican president, Richard Nixon, permitted unprecedented influence on national governmental departments that mattered for Mississippians: for instance, the Farmers Home Administration, to which we named Buford Yerger Sr. as state director, became more amenable to Republican concerns.

President Richard Nixon himself, however, was a mounting disappointment. His White House staff was insular and insolent. Mississippi Republicans were among the many who felt more than managed. Fred LaRue answered Clarke Reed's and my phone calls to the White House, but we questioned whether Fred ever delivered our messages effectively. Fred seemed to be a token presence; at best, he was John Mitchell's toady and, disastrously, Fred's greatest usefulness to Nixon turned out to be Fred's close friendship with U.S. Senator Jim Eastland.

Nixon rightly understood that he needed Eastland's support for just about anything he hoped to accomplish in the United States Senate. He wouldn't cross Eastland, even if it proved a detriment in the short haul to Mississippi Republicans. The big powerful Deltan guarded the Magnolia "good ole boys' club" with Fred LaRue, who was his White House Uncle Tom.

Republican insiders in Mississippi knew that Eastland kept the GOP from unfettered navigation of the state's future, not to mention from full influence with Washington, D.C., powers. No candidate breathing the humid hot air of Mississippi was capable of grappling with Ruleville's giant.

Even Senator Eastland, however, couldn't control the forces of nature, and the political weather turned our way amid the most unusual—even catastrophic—circumstances, including a major hurricane.

August 17, 1969. Winds gusting more than two-hundred miles per hour and a storm surge in excess of twenty feet smashed the Mississippi Gulf Coast. Hurricane Camille was the worst hurricane to hit the United States mainland prior to Hurricane Katrina in 2005. Camille wreaked unprecedented damage. Nixon sent LaRue to his home turf on the Mississippi coast to coordinate relief efforts. The president also visited the coast, promising generous national aid, thereby earning favor with the desperate Mississippians. They would repay in 1972 with their votes.

In Camille's undertow, another Mississippian edged further into politics as a member of the Governor's Emergency Council. Gil Carmichael's white-haired visage and name for the first time really became noticed, and I also seriously mulled running for Congress after John Bell Williams vacated his congressional seat to become governor. I enjoyed oratory, as well as writing letters to the editor. I contemplated, "I do like to be persuasive about which way the government should go and what we should be accomplishing for the nation and Mississippi."

West Point had taught me to lead, and my heart tugged in that direction. I felt that I measured well next to other elected officials whom I had met on the national political scene.

But life has more than a political side. The ballpark lights shone in the summer at the Lakeland Drive fields in Jackson, Mississippi. I loved sharing the red-dirt infield with my sons—Billy and Bobby—coaching them and their buddies to step to the plate and swing, teaching a new generation about life. Bobby also was competing in tennis tournaments and we traveled a lot. Furthermore, I wanted to enjoy a private life with my wonderful wife, Jan. As perfervid as I was for politics, my greatest passion has always been Jan, our sons, and their families. I made it a priority to be better than my own father was to his children—to be present in their lives, sharing their joys and sorrows.

Still, running for a high political office seemed almost a duty to be met.

I told myself, "If I'm trying to tell these other people to run, should I not consider it myself?"

True leadership meant not asking anyone else to do something I wasn't willing to attempt myself. To persuade someone else to run, I had to consider whether I ought to venture into the public political arena. Thus, I scribbled on a yellow legal pad a list of pros and cons about a possible run for office.[7]

Scrapping for candidates was getting hard. The ones who were running, frankly, seemed weak. Throwing money at bad political products irked me. Bill Wilkins in 1970 surfaced local television personality, Hagen Thompson. Hagen had strong name recognition and was an Ole Miss graduate—another plus. Thompson was also a regular ten-dollar-a-month party contributor—a good sign.

"Hot dog!" I told Wilkins, "here is someone where we start out with some strengths."

Hagen proved, however, to be a case of throwing money down the political drain. A pattern emerged as I canvassed contacts to financially support Hagen. "I'll give you money because you are the one asking," people kept telling me, "but I know Thompson and I don't like him."

Raising money for Hagen was like pulling ticks off a cornered possum. I learned another political lesson: Name recognition certainly is good, but not if the name is recognized in a negative way.

Candidates are really the name of the political game, and electing candidates is the *sine qua non* of a viable party. The logic: a strong political campaign requires respectable money, but even more so, appealing candidates. The paradox: to have appealing candidates is that they must feel comfortable there will be sufficient funding. How do you break through this circle with no entry point? Nevertheless, I had simply continued to fill the money bags. Eventually, this funding helped secure and maintain the state office in the early 1970s with a $150,000 annual budget, insuring top-paid employees. The state GOP's fundraising in those days soared above its RNC-set quota, outstripping all other states. I hated to send more of our surplus funds than necessary to national headquarters. So we figured out ways to swell the local coffers by skirting most of the national requests. This allowed the 1970s Mississippi GOP to experience unprecedented in-state expansion.[8]

Mississippi, for all these funds, still could not best the Democrat machine. Deciding to switch to Republican, as did Dr. Tommy Davis, the incumbent Hinds County Democrat coroner, invited a voluntary death sentence. Davis's case showed just how absurd the political field of the time was: an incumbent, medical doctor was beaten for coroner by a used car salesman who ran as a Democrat. "Well," I told the press after Davis's loss, "I hope when somebody's kinfolks die they realize their coroner may know how a carburetor works but not how to conduct an autopsy as would a medical doctor."

The "coattail effect" was a political notion we Mississippi Republicans had never enjoyed—until 1972. For all our frustrations with Richard Nixon's presidency (and they were only about to begin), state GOP leaders in 1972 had a unique opportunity to run statewide races on the coattails of Richard Nixon's run for reelection as president of the United States. Hurricane Camille's aftermath rippled concentrically statewide; Nixon's strong response earned Republicans clout. But then, in 1972, federal courts forced the Magnolia State into a series of permanent steps known familiarly as "desegregation." Whites and blacks statewide swapped schools in a bureaucrat-driven mess. President Nixon's Public Education Advisory Committee gave free advice but little real assistance. Nixon looked the other way, angering state GOP leaders.

Gil Carmichael stepped into the limelight again, helping Nixon secure the civil rights measures within Mississippi. In so doing, Carmichael's name recognition grew amid his work on the twin cataclysms of Camille and desegregation—two epic struggles that rocked all Mississippians in one way or another. By 1972, recalls Carmichael, "I had gotten some visibility."[9]

Amid the fury of Camille and desegregation, we Mississippi Republicans prepared to travel for a second straight Republican National Convention in Miami to renominate Richard Nixon for a return to the White House. I still was state finance chairman and a member of the state GOP executive committee. My eyes were on the tremendous first-in-a-century opportunity emerging for Republicans to win the Fourth Congressional District seat (at this time Mississippi still had five congressional districts). If we had good candidates, we would have a good opportunity to win. I had decided, once and for all, not to run for Congress. Yet I was more energized and motivated than ever for Republicans to recruit a Fourth District candidate that could make history by winning as a Republican.

Meanwhile, Rep. Bill Colmer (Democrat, Fifth District) was retiring on the coast, leaving his district seat up for grabs. He decided to endorse his assistant, thirty-year-old Trent Lott, who chose to switch to the Republican Party. That race looked extremely bright. Closer home, Fourth District U.S. Congressman Charles Griffin also was retiring. Hinds County was the heart of the Fourth District. I was scavenging for a strong Republican candidate.

The iron was hot. Now was the time!

Initially when looking for a Fourth District candidate, I eyed Gray Jackson, a young, local stockbroker who had been very successful in campus politics at Ole Miss and was highly recommended by my good friend, Homer Best Jr. After discussions, Jackson said he would not run. I had been waiting for Jackson's reply but simply couldn't afford to sit still. So I kept testing the water seeking other potential candidates. When Jackson declined, I replied to him: "Well, okay, then. We've got to have candidates so I'm going to go find some other people."

At home one evening after Jackson had declined, I received a call from Mike Allred, a product of Ole Miss's Young Republicans and the legal council to the state party.

"Well," Allred asked, "when are we going to have a candidate?"

"When we can come up with one," I joked. "I just cannot come up with the right person."

Mike said, "I've got some ideas. Would you visit with them if I come up with them?"

"Of course. Anyone in particular?"

Allred listed three names, among them a young lawyer from the Watkins and Eager law firm, Thad Cochran. "Well, all right, look, Thad Cochran is not going to run," I plainly predicted.

I knew of Cochran and considered him attractive and intelligent. Yet I remember telling Allred that Tom Watkins was the main partner at that firm and quite possibly the number-one supporter of former governors Ross Barnett, Paul Johnson Sr., Paul Johnson Jr., and others. I predicted to Allred: "All that will happen if Thad Cochran even thinks about running is that Tom Watkins is going to say, 'Over my dead body is a young member of my firm going to run as a Republican.'"

Still, I felt the same about recruiting candidates as I did about raising money: if you don't ask, you don't get!

Allred asked Cochran to come to my office, and he sat before me and listened to my spiel. I laid out the possibilities for a Republican winning the Fourth Congressional District. Thad was a *cum laude* graduate of the Ole Miss Law School, a straight-A student in high school; his father was the superintendent of education in Hinds County and his mother was a schoolteacher. He had graduated from high school in Byram, politically advantageous because we could then say that Thad hailed from Byram and not Jackson. Being from Jackson was a negative with most country voters in the Fourth District, with almost every previous congressman hailing from the rural southern part of the district. Thad was the recipient of a Rotary Fellowship and had spent a year studying international law at Trinity University of Dublin, Ireland. He also had been a cheerleader and vice president of the student body at Ole Miss. His father-in-law's first cousin was a federal judge and his father-in-law was former president of the Mississippi State Bar with many lawyer connections and also had been the former Democrat National Committeeman, as well as a close friend of ex-governor J. P. Coleman. In 1968 Thad had been executive director of Citizens for Nixon in Mississippi.

At that time, little did I know that Thad Cochran was beginning to consider just where his political affinities should be. Like so many growing up in Mississippi, he had thought there were a limited number of ways to have a political career in Mississippi. Thad explains in his own words: "Either you were a Democrat or you weren't a Democrat—you couldn't be a 'Mississippi Democrat' and think that that was any different from being a 'National Democrat.' So I just thought the whole thing was crazy. And my wife's father was the Democratic National Committeeman. . . . The first time I would have voted, I voted for John Kennedy. It was in 1960. I was twenty-one years old. I was in the Navy, a naval officer aboard a ship. . . . All through my undergraduate years at Ole Miss, I identified with the people who were young and different from the old leadership. But I didn't think of myself as a partisan anything."[10]

Once Thad returned from his military service to Jackson, he began considering his political leanings more seriously. He actually heard me speak one time at a local Jackson men's group. He recalls: "I think I heard him [Billy Mounger] speak at a civic club. I was a member of something called the 'Jackson Men's Y Club.' It was a group that met every Monday night at the Jackson Y. And we had dinner and we'd have a speaker. He came to talk about the Republican Party and how he was excited about the Republican Party. I was impressed with the fact that he was so sincere, and so committed, and so sure that it was right for Mississippi to realign with the Republican Party nationally to get ourselves more of a political voice and influence, that we were sort of a joke—the laughing stock of the nation. . . . He persuaded me. I was listening to him and I thought, 'He's absolutely right.' He made abundantly good sense."[11]

Having gotten to know Thad a little, I felt that he clearly would be a very attractive young candidate; he had a lot of friends and was electable as a Republican. Frankly, over the years I've learned that we can't take an average Mississippian—slightly rural, slightly country type—and elect him as a Republican. On the other hand, we Republicans in Mississippi are criticized for being the country-club set; but the electorate wants as a Republican a young, well-educated person who is able to speak well and who presents himself well on TV. That's the image they want as a Republican candidate. When we deviate, they won't vote Republican.

Notes Thad: "That was very insightful that [Billy Mounger] had that kind of an insight in that environment and in that era."[12]

The next day, after our meeting in my office on Monday, I was at a Republican meeting in Clarksdale concerning the Farmers Home Administration.[13] I thought that Thad would be a whale of a candidate, but I didn't truly believe he would run. That day, Thad located me through my assistant, Peggy, and said we needed to get together. On Monday, he had returned to his law firm with comprehension of all the possibilities I had conveyed to him. He had talked to Tom Watkins, and Tom Watkins agreed with him and confirmed that it was a good idea.

Normally, the main problem with a candidate is that, if he were working for a bank, was a lawyer, or whatever, he would not have a livelihood while campaigning. But Thad was a partner of the prestigious law firm of Watkins and Eager, and Tom Watkins said, "Okay, if you choose to run, that's fine with us. All of the time you're campaigning you will continue to receive your proportionate part of the partnership in the law firm."

So over the phone Thad told me, "Look, I want to talk to you more about this thing."

"Well," I replied, "I'll come on home tonight and we'll get together tomorrow."

Wednesday morning Thad came to my office and told me that he thought he would run. I took him on a tour of the state Republican headquarters in Jackson and then introduced him to Bill Wilkins. The impression was favorable both ways.

Thad told me, "I am thinking very seriously about this but, you know, I've never done anything Republican. I don't really know the leaders. I don't know who comprises the party. I lose a number of good close contacts within the Democratic Party who, if I don't lose totally, obviously they can't do anything for me."

Thad and Brad Dye were good friends; Brad at the time was state treasurer and would eventually become a very powerful multiple-term lieutenant governor and would not be able to support him. "And," said Thad, "I don't really have any connections with you all and your Republican Party."

"Well, okay," I said, "You don't really have to know them. I know them and I won't have any problems in taking you and selling you to any of the leadership. I know you would be a good candidate. I'm convinced that we can win with you. If you will run, I will make you this pledge: I will give you my number-one priority in fundraising. I will not guarantee you that I'll raise you ten dollars, ten-thousand dollars, or a hundred-thousand dollars, but I will give you my first-priority efforts over anything else that I do. I won't do anything else as it relates to any other candidates or the party, either national or local, until I feel that your campaign is sufficiently funded and financed. Even though I won't guarantee you anything, I have never committed to anything that I have not delivered on."

"Well, if you will do that," replied Thad, "I don't have to talk to another soul. I'm the candidate."

That Wednesday afternoon in the Walthall Hotel, I saw Gray Jackson, who asked how the search for a candidate was progressing. I mentioned Thad Cochran had committed to run. "Oh, I know Thad Cochran real well," Jackson said. "Great."

I told Gray, "With Thad I'm going to do the things that I was going to do for you, and I want you to get out and totally commit yourself and give some money and raise money and get workers."

"I'll do anything in the world," Jackson told me.

I went home that night satisfied that a tremendous Republican candidate had surfaced. The next morning, Thursday, I received a shocking report: Gray Jackson was calling a press conference Friday to announce his intention to run for the United States House of Representatives. That floored me. I said, "Good gosh, what is Thad going to do now?"

The matter of a potential primary per se did not bother me; rather it was pitting these two young North Jackson men against each other, who shared the same friends and many of the same connections and who lived within two blocks of each other; both even belonged to the Jackson Country Club. Their battle might divide key members of the district's Republican Party. We were being accused of being a country club set party and this particular primary would be red meat to the Democrats. I worked the phones, effectively sabotaging Gray's prospective supporters, as well as calling six to eight key district Republicans to solidify their support for Cochran. I then met with some of Jackson's closest friends and told them that he, in truth, had reneged on me and that his candidacy was divisive.

After a verbal screed, many from this group along with Thad and me met with Jackson in the Republican headquarters. One of Jackson's closest friends, Gerry Lauman, was considering being Jackson's finance chairman; he told Gray not to count on him. A few others joined in and told Jackson to expect no help from them. Everyone was on board with Thad, including Hinds County chairman Jack Breed.

Gray Jackson withdrew his candidacy on the following Monday.

Then, before we were able to get organized and do anything for Thad, we became involved in a massive and horrible Hinds County political battle that substantially split the normal party activists. That's when I organized the old hands who had originally started the new Republican Party, including Wirt Yerger. Some of those who had come in since and had been involved in the last few years on the other side also joined me. It was very sticky because the opposition had control of the Hinds County Republican Party apparatus, and I had to fabricate a new group. (The next chapter is all about this serious but necessary political battle in the heart of Mississippi.)

Understandably, the sudden storm that brewed confused Thad. He probably thought, "Here I am and Mounger has talked me into doing this and I'm not close to the Republican structure. And now they are in this massive fight! Mounger's the guy that recruits me and he leads the fight."

I know Thad was saying as much, and I later teased him about it. I said, "I know you thought that we really had conned you into doing something not in your best interest."

CHAPTER 9

Hinds County's
Historic Shakeup

The luxury of infighting is a sure sign of an organization's success. That's easy to say now. The emerging GOP factions in Mississippi demonstrated the outward strength of a growing, prosperous party which started wrestling internally over how to take the party to the next level. Our adolescent Mississippi Republican Party was about to sprout some of its first public pimples.

Clarke Reed was a presence on the national party scene. Bill Wilkins was state executive director and ran a tight ship; yet his administrative bent was accented by what seemed to some to be a cold personality. The most efficient people tend to be the coldest. They don't let their emotions get a hold on them at all. They keep their eyes totally on the immediate goal, and as a consequence, they tend to step on toes and irritate constituents.

Local Democrats paled in strategic creativity to our smoothly honed Republican state office. Our state GOP office, financed by my efforts, was the most proficient nationally, run by Wilkins and later Haley Barbour. Even though the party hadn't cracked the state Democrat stranglehold on big-state elected positions, our party frustrated Democrat counterparts by continuing to grow nonetheless. They could not understand. We just would never go away. It didn't make any difference how badly we were defeated in an election, we regrouped and grew.

The reason we were able to continually grow is that we were adequately financed, thereby keeping a competent staff in operation as an efficient nucleus.

So when I heard that national committeeman James Moye of Laurel—who had run a solid Fifth District race for Republican congressman in 1966 against Bill Colmer—along with Hinds County Republican chairman Jack Breed were planning a coup d'état, it was not altogether surprising. Breed and Moye felt Clarke Reed was hurting the state party as its state party chairman. They believed that he was too oriented towards Washington, D.C., and was only concerned with gratifying his own ego, thereby neglecting the local party and candidates. They felt (with justification) that Reed was diluting the party's true conservative base.

These two men planned to oust Reed as state chairman. They teamed with up-and-comer Charles Pickering of Laurel to secure votes at the GOP state convention. Moye and Breed would deliver their two congressional districts. They hoped to persuade Victor Mavar of Mavar Shrimp and Oyster Company to help deliver voting delegates from the coast's district.

The idea was that Clarke Reed would be left with delegate majorities in only two congressional districts—the two in North Mississippi. I listened with interest to Moye and Breed, thinking, "Well, either way I'll end up being a delegate to the national convention. Nobody wants my dumb ole finance chairman's job anyway." But in a later meeting Breed crowed to me, "Well, we've got this thing all under control. I just want to tell you that because you are aligned with Clarke Reed, we can't let you be on the executive committee; but after we get it all done and everything, we might let you be finance chairman."

I couldn't believe what I was hearing Jack Breed say—"Might *let* me be finance chairman?"

Well, they were stomping on my toes! The news of the planned coup was well known to Clarke Reed and Bill Wilkins, who approached me with a counter-coup: "The only solution for this coup is for you to become Hinds County chairman," they told me. If Breed could be unseated as Hinds County chairman at his own county convention, it would control the district, torpedoing the Moye-Breed effort.

I replied to Reed and Wilkins, "The last thing I need is to be county chairman. I've done all these other things, and I just don't want to get involved in all of the nitty-gritty precinct work in conflict with these other jobs."

I had turned down being state chairman years ago, which was my worst political mistake. Why run a hard race for Hinds County chairman now?

But Reed and Wilkins convinced me that I was the only person who could unseat Breed and thus deliver the central Mississippi congressional district for Clarke Reed, keeping him and Wilkins and myself in power. Only two weeks were left before precinct elections, to be followed by county elections, where delegates were chosen to the GOP state convention. Wilkins and I had to work fast while keeping below Breed's radar. It was a very clandestine operation.

We assembled in two weeks an alternative group of precinct leaders and voters throughout Hinds County. Johnny Palmer, who eventually served as United States ambassador to Portugal for U.S. President George W. Bush from November 9, 2001, to November 30, 2004, loaned us space at his CPA firm office building on the southeast corner of President and Capitol streets, across from the State Republican Party Headquarters.[1]

All of the clandestine operations that culminated in my taking over Hinds County's GOP reins were coordinated from Palmer's office, with Johnny being on the other side because of his closeness to Rubel Phillips. We had to find new people to attend precinct meetings since most of the rank-and-file local Republican activists were committed to Moye-Breed. A complex web of new faces emerged, including Billy Powell and other oil-and-gas and banking people. Associates of mine from years of business and social friendships stepped up to help. African-American support was enlisted, especially in predominately African-American precincts that had sometimes been overlooked. I must admit that I sneaked monies to the black community to turn out black precinct support.

The net effect was that the GOP's base of motivated workers in Hinds County virtually doubled overnight! We structured it exactly the way political organizations are structured. Bill Wilkins, the artful machinator, was organizing it. We Hinds County Republicans held our convention on Saturday to make it more available for working people to attend the precinct meetings. We also held them in the morning and the county convention that afternoon, so there would be limited time to politic between the caucuses.

An unprecedented melee of a county convention swept Hinds County Republicanism. It was like a mini-national convention! From seemingly nowhere, suddenly fifteen-hundred people from Hinds County attended precinct meetings and the county convention. Democrats never really bothered to attend their precinct meetings; but, again, we were traveling a different path than they.

The battle ensued between Jack Breed's people and mine. Breed, the sitting county chairman, had appointed the credentials committee and refused to seat my delegates. But B. B. McClendon, Jr. fought them for me, forcing the recognition of my delegates.

Immediately at the county convention, the main battle ensued over the selection of the presiding officer of the Hinds County GOP.

What was normally a mere matter of protocol resulted in verbal parrying. My people showed up with red and silver "Mounger" lapel stickers—unprecedented for a county convention in Mississippi, not only among Republicans, but also among Democrats, who often picked such leaders over a beer and cigar. Everyone could see the Mounger people were out in force and it was intimidating. It encouraged any uncommitteds to move my way.

The vote between Breed and me for Hinds County chairman was close. I won 98–88.

The essential key was one precinct. Our large Republican precincts in northeast Jackson were allocated many votes. My own precinct, for instance, had five votes, and I was awarded all of them. Other North Jackson precincts weren't so easily corralled. The swing precinct was where Wirt Yerger lived. Yerger and his brother, Swan, worked for me and supported me at their precinct, which had seven votes. Three people projected to vote for me weren't there when the time arrived to vote at their precinct. So Wirt stalled until a Mounger majority was in place. The three finally showed, Wirt called for the vote, and I carried that crucial precinct 37–35, with Wirt, Mary (Wirt's wife), and Swan Yerger's votes making the difference!

In another five-vote North Jackson precinct, Fred LaRue along with Rubel Phillips and Dr. Tommy Davis spoke against me and disallowed a secret ballot. By doing so, they caused friends and neighbors to vote publicly between Jack Breed—who was standing there watching them—and myself, who was not present. I lost that precinct by one or two votes with many, including my good friend, Gus Primos, disgustedly sitting down and not voting because of LaRue's and Rubel's maneuvering. This also infuriated my brother Henry, who voted in that precinct. Even though we won the overall Hinds County vote, that crazy race shows how friends can divide over such heated matters. It becomes a very terrible, fratricidal contest.

Notwithstanding the heavy political air of that day, some humor emerged. One of the black delegates participating was supposed to vote for me. When the time came for him to declare his vote, he cast it for Breed, though he was wearing one of my Mounger stickers. He stood and said, "I votes for Breed!" My supporters shouted, "What do you mean voting for him? You're wearing a Mounger sticker!" So he reversed course and said, "I means, I votes for Mongo! Mongo! Mongo!" It was riotously funny.

I had prevailed in what was to go down as an historically significant moment; while the vote chose only the Hinds County chairmanship, it effectively dictated control of the Fourth District and, thereby, the state. My victory saved Reed, keeping him in statewide power.[2] The vote also introduced hundreds of new, important Jacksonians into the GOP local process, activating "elephant" power in our state like no other single event and energizing further presidential interest in our party.

I hosted a party that night at my house for those who helped achieve my election. Clarke Reed traveled down from Greenville, worked the crowd, and congratulated me. He told me something that would be tested in the future: "You are the greatest person in the world. Every time I have ever asked you, you have stepped up and you have been counted, particularly when I had to have a finance chairman, but especially on this election. If there's anything *in the world* you ever want from me, you've got it."

"Well," I replied, "Clarke, I don't need anything. But a time may come, so remember what you told me."

"You just name it, whenever the time comes," said Reed.

Later I realized the validity of the complaints that James Moye and others had leveled against Reed, culminating with his dastardly tergiversation during the 1976 nomination fight. Afterwards, I began to ally myself more and more with Pickering, Moye, and Rubel Phillips.

In a relatively brief period of time, I had gone from becoming state GOP finance chairman, to recruiting Thad Cochran, to becoming the chairman of the biggest GOP county in the state. I placed several members of the opposition on the county executive committee, and I named to it three members of the black community—Ruth Mosley, James Johnson, and Howard Moman—when the Democrat committee contained zero. I even named Jack Breed as a delegate to the state convention. Everyone's efforts were needed to continue to build the party. I had enticed Thad Cochran into the GOP with the goal of winning the Fourth Congressional District. Now I found myself with unanticipated new influence to use not only for Thad, but also for Trent Lott and the reelection of Nixon.

I was still the effective blocking guard, opening gaping holes in the Democrat line for our new Republican superstars to run through.

CHAPTER 10

1972: The Year of the Rising Republicans (Lott, Cochran, Carmichael)

T had Cochran must have looked at the Hinds County imbroglio of 1972 and wondered whether running as a Republican was a good idea. Still, after the Hinds County melee ended, I convinced Thad that it all couldn't have worked out any better for him. "This is the best thing that could happen," I told Cochran, now the powerful Appropriations Committee chairman in the United States Senate.

The Hinds County fight had boomeranged positively by bringing hundreds of new people into the Republican process. Fifteen-hundred people had participated in the Hinds County convention battle. We had excited those folks to work for Thad's election. We were ready for the Fourth District race, for the 1972 campaigns, for the 1972 Miami Republican Convention.

Then came James Meredith, the man who won national fame for integrating Ole Miss. He had gone north and received a law degree from Columbia University in 1968.[1] Now he returned home and filed as a Republican candidate for the United States Senate against Jim Eastland. Becoming a candidate was that easy in Mississippi, where any person could declare any party affiliation at any time by filing with the secretary of the party's executive committee and paying a filing fee.

We in the GOP hierarchy considered Meredith's move and said, "If we sit back, then James Meredith is automatically our nominee, therefore he will be our party's candidate to run against Eastland." We decided to oppose him, not because he was black, but just because he was simply a sensation seeker. The things he had done evidenced as much; he had filed for almost every office and advocated almost every kind of ridiculous proposition imaginable. Democrat or Republican, black or white, Meredith was not the person that either party wanted as their nominee.

Clarke Reed, Gil Carmichael, Bill Wilkins, Tommy Giordano (of Brandon), Dr. Charles Pruitt (of Mendenhall), and other party leaders including me began searching for a prospect better than Meredith. Attorney John Arthur Eaves—with his George Wallace look-alike slicked hair, white suit, Confederate flag pin, and heavy southern drawl—was suggested by Jack Breed. Eaves, however, demanded assurances of a large sum of money up front, and that didn't sit well with me.

I never say that I am going to raise you a hundred-thousand dollars, and I certainly never say I am going to write you a check for a hundred-thousand dollars; but I do say that I will give you my best effort. Eaves's demand for up-front money was absurd.

Eventually a group (I was out of town) gathered at Jackson's Thompson Field in a private conference room to talk with Eaves again. After this meeting with Eaves, the group was uncomfortable with him but they also felt inordinate pressure to contest Meredith. Gil then plunged into the void, announcing, "I'll run."

Carmichael had toyed in 1971 with running for lieutenant governor, but eventually withdrew. The Meridian native and automobile dealer had faithfully pledged ten dollars a month to the party from the time that Wirt Yerger and Buddy Klumb founded the United Republican Fund. Carmichael was personally ambitious but also desired to crack the Democrat's vise grip on major state offices. He had felt frustrated trying to sell his credentials because, as he once said, he "had gone to a foreign college—Texas A&M—implying that I couldn't be trusted."[2]

"Governor Ross Barnett had made us look foolish nationally," said Carmichael. "His successor, John Bell Williams, was leaving the Democrats and leaning Republican. I thought the power structure was now vulnerable. One could sense the death of the old Democratic Party, whose black and white factions were coming apart."[3]

Carmichael felt hopeful about both Thad Cochran's and Trent Lott's 1972 candidacies; but Gil was never fully in touch with reality. He was not unaware of Senator Eastland's power, although in certain recent speeches Carmichael has plainly articulated the very real and powerful alliances that the state GOP faced when we ran him for governor. "At the top of the Democrat ticket stood Jim Eastland, one of the most powerful members of the U.S. Senate, who had represented Mississippi since 1943. . . . He was wired with the national Republican Party and the Nixon Administration. He would cooperate with the president on judges and on administration bills. In turn, they would look the other way while others quietly killed civil rights and voting rights measures."[4]

Carmichael claims that the group at Thompson Field rushed him to run. "State Chairman Clarke Reed and his predecessor, Wirt Yerger, both put pressure on me," Carmichael claimed.[5] Wirt denies that was the case.[6] Clarke Reed, however, said, "I was for his running. I don't think that is terribly inaccurate."[7]

Whatever the case, when I returned to Jackson from my trip, Clarke Reed phoned me, urging me to encourage Carmichael, which I did. There was no other choice. The car salesman turned full-time politician had the backing of all the party leadership. In the words of Carmichael himself: "I gave in."[8] That, of course, is quite an interesting statement; the reality was that Gil wanted to run for just about anything, and he didn't give in, he plunged in.

I do not really believe we would have run someone against Eastland in 1972 if the Meredith situation had not forced the choice on us. Personally, I had no desire to confront Eastland, because I felt my primary obligation was Thad Cochran's race in my congressional Fourth District, and next, Trent Lott's race.

But now we had to support Carmichael, as well.

Six main tasks remained ahead for me in 1972: 1) to keep my word to fully finance Thad Cochran in his Fourth District race; 2) to aid Gil Carmichael in his historic race against Jim Eastland; 3) to help elect Trent Lott in the Fifth District; 4) to help Clarke Reed lead the state Republican delegation to the 1972 Republican National Convention, which was being held for the second straight time in Miami; 5) to insure sufficient funds for our state party and our national GOP quota, and; 6) to be number one in raising money for President Nixon.

CHAPTER 11

1972: Miami's Vice:
The Nixon Renomination

The 1972 Miami convention prepared to renominate Richard Nixon. U.S. Attorney General John Mitchell ran CREEP—the Committee to Reelect the President.

Clarke and I had clearly seen early in Nixon's first term that Mitchell, et al, kept only convenient campaign promises. Appointments of South-friendly federal marshals, judges, and the likes burned to ashes in CREEP's fiery desire to gain four more years of presidential power. We had become wary of Mitchell.

Once at a southern Republican party function in Washington, D.C., Mitchell had seemed a bit tipsy. Fred LaRue was there bolstering Mitchell in case he had drunk too much. There were only about fifteen people remaining when Mitchell approached Clarke and me. "You two are anti-Nixon!" Mitchell barked.

"My gosh," I thought, "how could he think we are anti-Nixon? We certainly have not uttered anything publicly and certainly plan to support him very strongly for 1972 reelection."

"That's ridiculous," Clarke and I replied. "What are you talking about?"

Mitchell slurred his speech: "You two are anti-Nixon. You're against Nixon because you're against Jim Eastland."

"My goodness!" we replied. "What's that got to do with it? Jim Eastland is a Democrat. We are Republicans. We have been fighting

Jim Eastland all of these years trying to build a Republican Party in Mississippi."

We Mississippi Republicans always had known that we must eventually overcome the "Eastland Machine" to be competitive; however, we had no desire for a head-to-head confrontation with such a powerful local Democrat who held some conservative ideas. We would much rather have bided our time. Eastland was old; sooner or later his day would pass. CREEP would much rather sacrifice a local person in order to get a few more votes for Nixon. Clarke and I contended with this skewed playing field as we headed to Miami in 1972 to renominate Richard Nixon for a second term.

Our 1972 Mississippi Republican Party delegation decided to stay in the same flea-bitten hotel, the Shore Club, as we had during the 1968 Miami National Convention. It was within walking distance of the civic center, and we were not cognizant that in four years' time it had become so grossly seedy. That fact, coupled with the heated Vietnam Veterans Against War protesters who showed up in 1972 in Miami, made that Republican National Convention immeasurably worse than the one in 1968.

Clarke and I arrived more than a week early, ready for a lot of work but also to participate in some of the same fun we had enjoyed at other conventions. We rented a car with an attached siren, as Fred LaRue had done in 1964 and Clarke and I had done in 1968. We would screech it and everyone would scatter, thinking we were the president of the United States. It was fun, but the fun had its comeuppance.

As chairman of the SARCS, Clarke continued with Bill Wilkins's brilliant stratagems to fight for the small states to keep their fair share of delegate votes at conventions. Clarke Reed: "Everybody wanted more delegates. . . . I wanted a small convention like we had" but, at the same time, Clarke also was lobbying, saying, "Look, I've got to have more delegates [too]."[1] To his credit, Clarke won that fight.

The fight that Clarke waged was essentially about how to decide delegate totals for each state in 1972 and at future national GOP conventions; the battle was rife with national Republican Party ramifications, which remain to this very day. In a nutshell, the more populous northeastern and midwestern states wanted each state's delegate numbers to national conventions to be allocated based upon how many Republican votes residents of each state had cast during the most recent presidential contest. Smaller, mostly southern and western states wanted a system that rewarded states for delivering a Republican majority for president; states also should receive extra delegates for electing Republican U.S. senators, representatives, governors, and majorities in their state legislatures.

Prior to the 1972 convention, several state delegations filed a lawsuit in the federal court system to enjoin the Republican party from deviating very much from an allocation based substantially upon numbers of voters. Immediately before the start of the 1972 convention, the national party was enjoined from acting contrary to the petition and a motion to set aside the injunction was filed by state chairman David B. Kennedy of Wyoming, the smallest state population-wise and the most Republican state in the nation; Wyoming would be damaged the most by the percent system. Kennedy hired a Washington, D.C. attorney named Robinson to seek a stay of the injunction so that the convention could work its free will without the onus of a federal injunction coloring its every move.

Mississippi also had much at stake and thus joined with Wyoming in financing the hiring of Robinson (with excess funds I had raised). Additionally, Clarke served on the GOP national rules committee and concomitantly on the rules committee of the 1972 national convention. From his position on both rules committees he served as the point man for the effort to preserve the small, mostly conservative states' advantages. Bill Wilkins, our brilliant Machiavellian executive director, was the brains of the operation and was the very effective covert operator. The group, substantially with Mississippi funding, paid for a suite of rooms in the Nixon headquarters in Miami. The suite was staffed by Mississippians, David Keene, the *Human Events* and *National Review* magazines crowd, Howie Phillips, and many other movement conservatives.

With the ensuing contest proceeding, nip and tuck, under the pressure of the federal court injunction, the liberal Ripon Society with the tacit support of national party chairman George H. W.

Bush (my first realization of his ingrained, eastern establishment, liberal weaknesses) was persuading many pliable and moderate members of the rules committee to support its position. Reed reminded Bush that he owed Wyoming and Mississippi for carrying the ball with the lawsuit earlier. Reed said, "George, how about paying us? We defended your party. How about repaying us?"

Recalls Reed: "He said, 'No.' . . . George had a blind spot for leftists that had backed him in the past. So they put a couple of feminists, all kinds of people who didn't have any business on the committee. It was their committee and we'd meet twice a year."

At the "eleventh hour," our attorney lurked until he cornered the newly appointed Supreme Court justice, William Rehnquist, who at the last second issued a stay on the injunction thereby relieving the rules committee of the suffocating pressure of the injunction. The committee then voted for our delegate selection process, which was later confirmed by a vote of 910 to 434 before the whole convention.

The approved formula set out the following allotment of delegates for every state: 1) three delegates for each GOP senator; 2) three delegates for each GOP U.S. representative; 3) 4.5 plus .6 of each state's vote in the electoral college, provided the state was carried by the Republican presidential nominee in the last election and if not, at least one delegate for each senator, governor, or a majority of the state's U.S. representatives elected since the last election.

For example: Mississippi had 14 delegates in 1972, and Wyoming had 12 for a total of 26, and New York had 88; consequently, the ratio of New York to Mississippi and Wyoming was 3.38. The ratio became 3.28 in 1976, 3.00 in 1980, and 2.83 in 1984, each year giving a progressively additional comparative edge to Wyoming and Mississippi. And for the latest convention in 2004, the ratio had improved tremendously to 1.55!

The historic consequences of this delegate selection process continued to increase the strength of the South and West because we much more consistently vote for a Republican president and we are electing more and more Republican senators, governors, and U.S. representatives.

The role that we Mississippians played in this consequential battle can not be overestimated. Clarke's leadership role on the committee was crucial, Wilkins's guidance and maneuverings were essential, and the funds available through me to pay for the lawsuit and to procure the headquarters suite were immeasurably important. Certainly, I am proud of all that we Mississippians did to culminate in this conservative triumph.

The Mississippi party delegation was also watching the Vietnam War protests outside the preconvention meetings. The protesters were marching down the streets and were throwing rocks, sabotaging cars—doing everything conceivably obstructive. The main group concerned was a group called Vietnam Veterans Against the War. It was a really cruddy, scrofulous, mangy-looking group of people—ultra radicals and leftists—they hated us! They hated Nixon, and they hated us, because we represented American middle-class patriotism. Ironically, the delegates who had attended the Democrat convention were substantially that same demographic, but their convention was a fiasco. The anti-Vietnam attention that hounded and debased the 1968 Chicago Democrat convention was also in Miami, but the press typically only presented the protesters' side. Lost were reports about how people like Clarke and me and our wives were attacked, mobbed, and robbed. One night as the Reeds exited our siren-car, a crud grabbed Clarke's medals (those designating Reed's position and place at the convention) from his coat and dashed off. The attacker also absconded with Reed's tickets. Before I could exit the car, Clarke—and I'll certainly give him credit for this because it demonstrated courage—chased the guy. It was dark and dangerous with all of those mangy people milling around, and my wife, Jan, was particularly scared.

Reed disappeared into the darkness as I tried to escort our wives toward the civic center out of the melee. The crowd of protesters harassed us every step of the way for two blocks and the next day even greater numbers of protesters came out. They had decided, if they could, to prevent the delegates from getting into the convention center. For those in buses and for those who stayed on the northern part of Miami Beach, a route remained available, cordoned and barricaded by police with unused, empty buses and police escorts.

However, because of the Mississippi delegation's location, we could not take advantage of this protected route. We were isolated because the rioters had blocked all traffic. Rioters had stopped cars, ripped off their distributor caps, and broken windows. Really, the police were derelict and did nothing. The Miami police chief was afraid of hurting a rioter and thereby suffering the media's wrath.[2]

We were told to get to the convention hall early that day—the earlier the better. Bill Wilkins and I led our group—about eighty people—and left for the civic center about 5:30 P.M. We heeded police warnings to avoid certain blocks and were doing fine until we arrived at the street that intersected with the one that circled the convention center. Protesters had locked arms, forming a human wall blocking our route. We were walking with approximately eighty people behind us—delegates, children, and spouses—moving towards the convention center. When I got within a yard of those protesters, I inwardly vowed, "There is no way I am going to stop! I don't give a darn what those people do, I am not going to stop."

I reverted to my old football days, lowered my shoulder, and smashed a guy with everything I had. Even though I was older, I still had a substantial degree of my football prowess left. I must have knocked that guy ten feet and blasted a hole through there. Our people poured through their disintegrating blockade.

People were yelling every cuss word at us and calling us every name in the book. They were throwing urine, excrement, red paint, and other repulsive things on the delegates. They were trying to trip and intimidate us, causing me to fear that I might be knifed or shot.

Dr. J.D. Boyd of Lorman, an African-American and a leader at Alcorn State University, was a Mississippi delegate. He was accompanied by his wife and their teenage daughter. A photograph of Boyd stomping one of the protesters made the *Miami Herald* and the *New York Times*. Boyd's being a black delegate made the picture more poignant.

With no police in sight, everyone was fending for himself. Jan was clinging to my arm with a death grip. When we finally made it through the fence surrounding the convention hall, with the police inside, I vociferously cussed them. "Who in the hell do you think is paying you guys?" I said. "We have just put our lives in jeopardy just by walking down a public street and you police hide behind this fence!" Of course, the poor policemen were in sympathy with us, but they were under orders from the cowardly chief of police.

Jan began sobbing as soon as we all made it to safety. Another young man who had just earned his teaching certificate—Dennis Williams—had bought a new suit for the convention week. He said, "This is the nicest suit I've ever had in my life, and look at it."

I thought, "Those cruds out there, half of them probably come from rich parents and they don't have anything better to do than intimidate people." I presume they considered all of us to be upper-middle-class or rich. Of course, most delegates weren't. There were all gradations of people from various economic strata; a broad combination of people were at the convention. But what sticks out in my mind was that Dennis Williams kept moaning, "This is the best suit I have ever owned."

The media avoided showing the true situation. The people of this country never did understand how bad that was. That evening, one of the protesters—using a stolen ticket—ended up sitting near Jan and Julia Reed, screaming cuss words. That night, also, a man in a wheelchair interrupted the convention proceedings and was thrown out. Conservatives don't get up and raise Cain and prevent a liberal from speaking. It's the liberals who prevent conservatives from speaking.

The business inside the 1972 convention might have seemed routine given that Richard Nixon was a shoe-in for nomination for a second term, but the cameras did not show the constant moves and shuffling going on. You could not inform the average person about all the deals and agreements. The average Mississippian was strongly pro-Nixon, yet the Republican state leadership saw the way former U.S. attorney general and current Nixon campaign director John Mitchell iced Gil Carmichael from the beginning of the convention. He assigned fellow Mississippian Fred LaRue to watch the senatorial candidate and block any opportunity for notice. Gil assiduously sought publicity—and he's the biggest publicity hound I ever saw. He had stark white hair and he stood virtually the whole convention near the Mississippi microphone so that anytime a camera panned us, it could not miss him.

All our Republicans who were running for major offices needed publicity. Thad Cochran and Trent Lott were allowed access to the main convention microphone and podium; Carmichael was studiously blocked. Frankly, Senator Eastland was very worried in that particular 1972 race against Carmichael, much more worried than I ever thought that he would be. All through the campaign he used his influence with John Mitchell and others in the Republican national ranks so that no administration person at that convention or thereafter would have anything to do with Carmichael. The Nixon forces did not want to cross Eastland.

Fred LaRue and another Nixon aide, Jeb Magruder, met with Reed, Carmichael, and me, along with some other delegates, and I stated that I expected the Committee to Reelect the President (CREEP) to support—or, at least not to do anything negative regarding—our campaign for Carmichael. I told the Nixon people that we did not appreciate CREEP's plan to send Nixon's current attorney general, Richard Kleindienst, to the Mississippi Delta to make a campaign speech for Eastland.

When the meeting broke up, Fred LaRue toured us through the Nixon convention offices. "Now Fred," I said, "you know that a lot of party people in Mississippi are not happy with the role you play in Washington. There is a lot of deep-seated ill feeling there, but you can offset that. You are close to Kleindienst and to John Mitchell, so tell them, 'Don't come down to Mississippi! Come another time after the election, but don't come during the election because that is a slap in the face to the Mississippi Republican Party and to our candidate.' Fred, this is something you can do. Do not give me any rigmarole."

LaRue mumbled and hedged in his response.

Meanwhile, the convention played out as the Nixon team had planned. When it came time for Spiro Agnew, Nixon's running mate, to be presented to the convention delegates, Clarke Reed was invited to stand on the podium in the Agnew entourage—a sign of friendship between the South and Agnew. Clarke wore my convention medals, since his were stolen, and I was left in charge of the state's delegation as vice chairman. The last thing Clarke told me before he went to appear on stage with Agnew was, "Look, don't let anybody pull any hanky-panky with the microphone, especially Carmichael."

I agreed. "This microphone is to make our Mississippi report, period. That's it."

But after Clarke departed, Carmichael's people began to goad me and would not let up. "Why don't you just introduce Carmichael and let Carmichael give the report?" they asked. The pressure kept coming. Finally, truly believing that Carmichael had been maltreated, I acquiesced.

At reporting time, I stood at the Mississippi mike on national T.V. and said something to the effect of, "To give the Mississippi report, I want to present a tremendous Republican who is going to be the next Republican U.S. Senator from Mississippi, Gil Carmichael." Carmichael stepped to the mike and got his moment in the sun.

That was a bad decision. Immediately, I wanted to crawl in a hole of abysmal depth. I wanted to disappear because I was indeed embarrassed. It was against my nature to do such a flamboyant thing. Typically, Carmichael demonstrated a complete lack of gratitude.

CHAPTER 12

1972: Mississippi's Historic Statewide Elections

A fter Miami 1972, the run for the November national and statewide elections burned hot. I raised more than 75 percent of Cochran's money, led all the state parties in the nation raising money for Nixon, and I still raised all of the funds for our state party. We blew away our quota again to be number one nationally. I made clear to Carmichael that my primary commitment was to Cochran, but nonetheless I was Carmichael's largest individual giver, plus raising more than 25 percent of his funds.

Despite my talk with Fred LaRue, Kleindienst came to the Mississippi Delta and spoke in support of Eastland. That infuriated everyone in the state party; however, a brighter note was a commitment that Spiro Agnew had made to Clarke Reed during the Miami convention that he would come to Jackson to campaign for Mississippi's Republican slate of candidates.

Agnew invited Clarke to a party in Miami after we had successfully won the delegate selection process for future conventions. Reed: "We won it and he [Agnew] asked me to come out and eat dinner with him and I did."[1]

The phone rang at the Miami hotel room where Reed and I were staying. Reed answered and recognized the voice on the other end. "[Agnew] said, 'Look, a friend wants to talk to you.'" Reed recognized the next voice, too. Reed: "I said, 'Hello, Jack.' It was Jack

Benny." Reed enjoyed the company of several superstars when visiting with Agnew, among them Frank Sinatra, Zsa Zsa Gabor, and Jonathan Winters. "All them old Hollywood types," laughs Reed.[2]

Reed was working the big wigs of the RNC and I was raising the money, and Agnew began to see how strategic Mississippi might be for his potential 1976 presidential run. I was impressed with Agnew, as well. He had a good mind, made a great speech, and tended to say what we liked to hear.

Mississippi Republicans enthusiastically anticipated Agnew's arrival. The event was planned in cooperation with Agnew's personal staff, not CREEP, which fumed when it learned that Agnew was headed into Eastland territory. They told Agnew, "You just can't come down to Mississippi. You just can't go."

Agnew bucked CREEP and came anyway; nevertheless, CREEP made one inviolable demand: "All right, you can go to Mississippi. But you cannot have Gil Carmichael appear with you at any place where the public would know anything about it."

The Mississippi GOP faced a dilemma: to cancel Agnew's visit would be disastrous; to force our own U.S. senatorial candidate to go into hiding would be equally devastating. It was sickening to me, truthfully, and it was just a pathetic experience when we informed Gil Carmichael, "The vice president of the United States, a Republican whom you have supported, is coming, but you as a U.S. senatorial candidate may not be seen with him."

It was simply Jim Eastland's longstanding influence. Eastland, who chaired the powerful Senate Judiciary Committee, held immense sway over federal judicial appointments. Eastland probably was the man more responsible for how the courts have turned out than anyone else. Eastland stymied judicial appointments during the Eisenhower years until John Kennedy took office; then he opened the floodgates for Kennedy to name numerous liberals. As soon as Jack Kennedy was elected president, Democrats produced a bill creating a large number of new judgeships, enabling Kennedy to appoint vastly more judges than any other president. Jim Eastland thereby assisted the expansion of the national eastern liberal establishment.

Such knowledge made it harder for Clarke and me to break the news to the Carmichael people. Clarke believed as I that CREEP was totally wrong. In time, though, Clarke also felt the same as I did about Carmichael's politics. Says Reed, recently, concerning Carmichael, "He's not a liberal but he's sure not a conservative; you know, he's just there."[3]

The news hit hard when Clarke and I met with Carmichael and Wayne Weidie, who was Carmichael's campaign chairman and a Moss Point newspaperman. I thought Weidie and Clarke were going to come to blows. It looked as if we were sabotaging Carmichael, but we absolutely were not. There was no way Clarke was selling out, nor was I, but it was a horrible situation. Agnew's visit, however, was essential for us to promote both Cochran and Lott running to be United States representatives.

Gil accepted the situation surprisingly well. A short time later, Agnew came to Mississippi. A grand stage was set for him in front of the Old State Capitol at North State and Capitol streets in Jackson. Across the street was the state Republican Party headquarters, which occupied a fifth-story view of the Capitol steps. Bands played, girls danced, and Lott, Cochran, and other Republicans enjoyed sharing the light of Agnew's appearance. While Reed was meeting Agnew at the airport, I spoke impromptu to the boisterous crowd. I looked up from the stage to the fifth-story window of the party offices, where, framed in a small window, was Gil Carmichael's white mane. The Republican senatorial candidate was peering out that little old window. How demeaning!

I said exactly what I felt as I spoke to the crowd by expressing my true feelings and making an intrinsically anti-Eastland speech. Many Eastland people were in the crowd, including his son, Woods Eastland. I told the pro-Nixon crowd that everyone should vote straight Republican, including for Carmichael. I was disgusted with the injustice of that disgraceful situation.

Trent Lott spoke from the podium that day and he now recalls when I spoke up for Carmichael: "Even though he may have had reservations about some of the philosophical positions of Gil Carmichael—Gil was clearly more moderate in his philosophy than Billy—still Billy also has a very strong sense of fairness, which I think comes out of his West Point days and who he is, and to him that was unfair."[4]

A few years later, Weidie remembered my comments in a tribute article he wrote: "They couldn't put a lid on Mounger. When he made his brief talk, he urged that 'all' Republican candidates should receive strong support. You could see Agnew, Reed, and others on the speaker's stand swallow hard." Weidie added: "Politics needs to be cleaned up of special interest groups on both sides of the fence and of the 'fat-cats' who expect to buy candidates and their campaigns. But such purity isn't forthcoming and the Billy Moungers represent the best among those who give their strong financial support to candidates and political parties of their choice."[5]

Many have told me that it was one of my finest speeches. But none reveled over it more than Carmichael, who effusively thanked me: "Oh man! I owe you everything! You were the greatest," Carmichael said.

The press began to notice Carmichael's outsider status, played it up, and, in the end, Eastland's icing of Carmichael cost the Democrat more votes than if he had left well enough alone. Though Eastland spent about $750,000 campaigning compared to Carmichael's $150,000, Carmichael garnered immense coverage with a positive Mississippi message and a martyr-like visage. This also helped Lott and Cochran, since Eastland was so tied up opposing Carmichael that he could do very little campaigning for the Democrat congressional candidates. I raised about $85,000 for Cochran's campaign—at least 75 percent of his total money. For Carmichael, I raised 25 percent of his funds and was his largest contributor.

Carmichael carried the then-heavily conservative city of Jackson and some other counties. Nixon took the state with 78 percent of the vote. Cochran won with 45 percent of the vote, garnering five-thousand more votes than Ellis Bodron, who was blind and a very a good man. We had copied an idea from a campaign in North Carolina, that of the St. Louis Cardinals baseball player, U.S. Congressman "Vinegar Bend" Mizell (who was born in Mississippi, and received his mail in Vinegar Bend, Alabama, but actually lived across the line in Mississippi and played baseball for St. Louis). "Vinegar Bend" was elected to Congress in North Carolina. In his election to Congress, he developed a campaign technique of having young people go out into shopping centers with windshield cleaning equipment and wash windshields. They would wipe a windshield and leave a little note saying, "Your windshield has been cleaned by a young worker for 'Vinegar Bend' Mizell. We hope you see your way clear to vote for Mizell."

We in Cochran's camp loved the Mizell idea. I recruited my own children to be a part of Cochran's windshield-wiping crew. The Bodron people turned it around and said that when Cochran's people said, "We hope you *see your way clear*," they were being invidious because Bodron was blind. Cochran had made it a point to run an almost issueless campaign, but now he had to do damage control. We handled it in such a way that it turned the tables on Bodron. Nobody campaigns against a fellow because he is blind. Thad, incensed at such an accusation, was energized to campaign more forcefully and positively.

Cochran did not always do what we campaign officers suggested, but I felt he always listened to us. Meanwhile, Carmichael made people feel that their opinions didn't matter because he believed he had all-superior ideas.

On election night in 1972, Grady Jolly (now a U.S. Court of Appeals judge), Thad Cochran, Jim Keenan, and I, among others, listened to the 1972 election returns at Keenan's house. Thad was behind and losing most precincts, and Keenan was distraught, believing Thad could not win. I continuously assured him that our good precincts, particularly in Hinds County, were not in and that Thad would be elected. After all the votes were counted, Cochran carried Hinds by fifteen-thousand votes and also carried Adams (Natchez) and Lincoln (Brookhaven) counties, thereby winning a plurality of about five-thousand votes. The national CREEP organization had ordered that no local candidates could be involved with any campaigning for the reelection of Nixon for president; however, in my capacity as Nixon's state finance chairman, Hinds County chairman, and state finance chairman, I ordered the Hinds County Nixon telephone banks to piggyback Thad Cochran's name with Nixon's when they called Hinds County citizens to solicit their votes.

Cochran and Lott were elected that day giving Mississippi its first two Republican U.S. representatives since Reconstruction, excepting the Goldwater aberration of Prentiss Walker. Richard Nixon that night also won a second term as president of the United

States, carrying Mississippi with 78 percent of the vote.[6] The Republican power struggle in Hinds County between Jack Breed and myself ultimately had energized many new people for Carmichael and Cochran. As a result, the first two modern Republican congressmen from Mississippi took office—Thad Cochran and Trent Lott.

When the vote was done, I couldn't help taking a jab at our then-governor, Bill Waller, who had held an October 28, 1972, "statewide rally" at the Jackson City Auditorium in hopes of getting out the Democrat vote. I wrote a Hinds County Republican Party press release dated November 22, 1972, that stated, in part:

> When will our Governor learn that he should be using his minimal talents to attempt to govern this state instead of trying to dictate how the people vote? He, along with our two powerful Senators, the Lt. Governor, and almost all major State Officials, held a statewide rally at the City Auditorium on October 28th to intimidate the people to vote Democrat. Out of a Jackson Metropolitan population of 250,350 people, 250,000 stayed home that night. I could get more people in my yard to watch a cat fight than the whole leadership of the so-called Mississippi Democrat leaders did that night."

Meanwhile, Gil Carmichael had received about 38 percent of the vote while capturing the hearts of many Mississippians because of his underdog campaigning. That would prove a strength and weakness in the future. Gil thrives on martyrdom. There's nothing better than martyrdom for him. He glows as a martyr, but utterly fails in practicality.

CHAPTER 13

1973: WLBT Station
and I Make History

Civil rights was the major domestic issue in the United States as the 1950s crept into the 1960s and '70s. For many nationally, that meant turning their eyes upon Mississippi, deemed to be a major violator of the rights of African-Americans. One area garnering a great deal of attention was the lack of coverage of blacks by local television stations in the South. WLBT (NBC) was the largest FCC-regulated broadcaster in the state of Mississippi. It had to reapply regularly to keep its license to operate by federal law. WLBT was owned by Lamar Life Insurance Company, which also owned the state's largest radio station, WJDX.

Everett Parker was head of the New York City-based Office of Communications of the United Church of Christ, which does not represent my definition of Christianity. He had long felt that the time was nigh for a major suit to be brought against a key southern TV station to force the FCC to toughen its standards on equal racial rights in broadcasting. He solicited the help of many liberal activists in the Jackson area to begin to monitor twenty-four hours a day the broadcasting patterns of WLBT. People were kept in a room—both the office's physical location and the people's names working there were kept secret—where they took copious notes about every show and news program WLBT aired. They made notes that correctly demonstrated a pronounced lack of equitable local coverage of African-American people.[1]

Armed with this information, the United Church of Christ, which also sponsors Jackson's Tougaloo College, challenged the FCC to revoke Lamar Life's permit to operate WLBT.

Lamar Life responded by arguing that it had been progressively airing increasing African-American content, even firing key employees and hiring new progressive ones. Still, the U.S. Appeals Court for Washington, D.C., led by Judge Warren Berger, stripped Lamar Life of its FCC license. That opened the door for others, including me in 1969, to become a part of the WLBT story when Lamar Life did not appeal to the U.S. Supreme Court, which would have been futile because Warren Berger had just taken over as Chief Justice.

The FCC named an interim group chosen by the United Church of Christ to run WLBT until a new license could be awarded; then the FCC in February of 1970 invited new groups to apply for ownership of the WLBT license. Five groups launched efforts to win the FCC's license for WLBT, which was worth millions and, perhaps more importantly, was sure to give an inestimable amount of influence to the license holder.

Five groups applied: Lamar Life Broadcasting Company, which was allowed to reapply, but had to go through presenting the same massive amounts of new documentation as other new applicants in hopes of gaining the license; Civic Communications Corporation, formed of liberals including Greenville media mogul Hodding Carter III and Charles Evers, brother of slain civil rights leader Medgar Evers; Dixie National Broadcasting Corporation, with me as its CEO, along with a mix of black and white leadership including famed African-American novelist Margaret Walker Alexander, author of *Jubilee*, the black community's equivalent of *Gone with the Wind*, and Talmadge Portis, who was to be my chief executive assistant; Jackson Television, Inc.; and Channel 3, Inc.

An immense amount of suing and countersuing then followed, as each group tried to discredit the principal members of the other groups. Charles Evers had just published his biography, admitting in his book that he had once been a gambler, bootlegger, and dabbler in pimping prostitutes. The FCC judge said Evers's actions since those less admirable days had demonstrated "rehabilitation," and "outweigh[ed] his unlawful conduct."[2] But some questionable tax practices by Mr. Evers, coupled with his failure to produce requested tax records, caused the FCC judge to rule that because of this, "Civic must be given a significant comparative demerit."[3]

Meanwhile, the United Church of Christ-endorsed group, Channel 3, Inc., was sponsored by a wealthy Texas lawyer and banker with seemingly unlimited funds and an unbridled passion to take over WLBT. The lawyers for the United Church of Christ—which had been in charge of the company temporarily running WLBT—attacked Dixie Broadcasting, whose principal stockholders were as follows: myself with 40 percent; Rubel Phillips, 6 percent; Talmadge Portis, 1 percent; Roland Powell, 1 percent; John N. Palmer, 2 percent; Margaret Walker Alexander, 2 percent; Owen Cooper, 2 percent; Rev. Dudley Wilson, 1 percent; Elaine Crystal, 1 percent; Dixie National Life Insurance Company, 40 percent; and others who made up the difference.[4]

Channel 3, Inc., after myriad investigations, finally latched onto an apparent discrepancy in Rubel Phillips's filing data for our FCC application. Although Rubel had a fine reputation for integrity as an attorney in Jackson, the UCC lawyers argued that he had forged a certain signature regarding a $15-million request for construction loans from the Farmers Home Administration to finance pre-fab housing produced by the Sterling Homex Corp.

Ironically, Rubel and his brother were two of the more progressive conservatives in Mississippi concerning treatment of blacks. Hal, Rubel Phillips's brother, was a nationally respected novelist (an O'Neil Award winner). Rubel helped register blacks in Alcorn County in 1951 after being elected county clerk fresh out of law school. He defied the state's existing law that said that to be registered a person had to be able to read and interpret a portion of the U.S. Constitution. "Rubel Phillips did not apply either requirement to any voter, black or white. He appeared before a committee of the state legislature urging the committee to abolish these requirements and was told to mind his business. He told the committee that he was going to ignore these requirements, and he did."[5] He was general counsel of Dixie National Broadcasting Company and its board chairman.

The FCC judge considered all the following and decided in a 135-page decision that Dixie should receive the license, adding that, "Based upon his testimony and his demeanor, it is concluded that Mr. Phillips was telling the truth when he explained that he certainly would not have chosen willfully to withhold matters from the Commission, . . . the facts do not support a finding of deliberate misrepresentation or of a deliberate intent to withhold information from the Commission."[6]

Our brilliant Washington attorney, Joe Hennessee, outsmarted the opposition. We structured the organization with myself as 40 percent owner, to be CEO assisted by Talmadge Portis as executive assistant, avoiding a jaded TV person aboard who might be loaded with negatives. Additionally, Margaret Walker Alexander and Hal Phillips originated our very distinctive programming, greatly influencing the administrative law judge. We had only 4 percent black ownership, and the other competitors never fathomed that the judge would render a 135-page, very pro decision for us while at the same time derogating all the other applicants.

After Dixie National Broadcasting Company in 1973 was awarded the FCC license, the United Church of Christ would not relent. They kept challenging the makeup of our Dixie ownership. Their northern-based liberal leadership would not accept the FCC judge's statement that Dixie's local ownership and strong local leadership could do a respectable job of further racially integrating the station's programming.

Things began to heat up all the more. I was punctiliously scrutinized as the CEO of the new WLBT ownership. The UCC improperly influenced the FBI to investigate my Republican activities, but the FBI inevitably came up empty-handed. Then they attempted to use the race card on me because I had served on the Board of Jackson Academy since 1961 and at that time was vice president and had been instrumental in JA's financing its original building on Ridgewood Road. Jackson Academy's *raison d'etre* was to teach phonics, which led to its organization in 1959 five years prior to integration; thus there was no racism involved. JA moved to Ridgewood Road at a cost of $120,000. Our board was able to secure a $100,000 loan from the now-defunct First Federal Savings and Loan, with the endorsement of several of us board members. Jackson Academy was then still $20,000 short in financing the original construction that still forms the front structure of today's sprawling school. As a banker with Deposit Guaranty, I decided to make the final $20,000 loan with nineteen men's individual endorsements of $1,000 a piece, and with one board member endorsing for $2,000, of which I guaranteed $1,000. Making such a loan is an absolute banking no-no with such limited endorsements. Any bank would prefer to charge off such a loan than have to dun twenty different customers. Today, I am quite proud that I bent the rules, as the immense success of Jackson Academy is self-evident.

I testified before the FCC that JA had no racial exclusion policy, that no African-American had ever applied or been rejected, and that if a black applied with the proper academic credentials, provided there was a vacancy, the child would be accepted. The final FCC decision absolved me of the racial bias allegations. Later events vindicated my statement. Today, there are numerous black students enrolled in Jackson Academy.

Thwarted in their assault on me, the opponents of Dixie decided that we were most vulnerable through Rubel Phillips, Dixie's chairman of the board. As stated before, this charge proved to be our Achilles' Heel. Though the Securities Exchange Commission said that Phillips had done nothing wrong, the UCC proceeded with the complicity of the district attorney's Manhattan office in New York City to sue, alleging fraud against the Sterling Brothers, the major officers, and the owners of Sterling Homex. A New York assistant U.S. district attorney was a friend of Marty Firestone, the Channel 3, Inc. lawyer, and was prevailed upon to cooperate by indicting Rubel along with the Sterlings if Firestone could arrange to incriminate Rubel.

With this in mind, Ken Dean—a liberal activist and a member of Rubel's church, Northminster Baptist, which I still call the "Swinging Baptist Church," and a purported friend of Rubel's—convinced William T. Richardson to change his sworn testimony. Richardson was the acting director of the Mississippi Farmers Home Administration. Clarke Reed and I would not approve of him being the permanent director. It was alleged that an in-depth probe into Richardson's directorship had been completed and that Senator Eastland was squelching it.

Richardson had denied at least five different times under oath that he had signed the FHA Letter Commitment for $15 million and said that he did not know how his signature appeared on the letter. Dean arranged for Richardson to receive immunity from prosecution from any allegations if he changed his testimony and averred that Rubel Phillips had admitted to him that he had prevailed upon his secretary, Nelda, to trace Richardson's signature on the so-called commitment letter by holding it up against a window pane. (Nelda denied this allegation under oath.) Because of this reversal of testimony, Rubel was indicted along with the Sterlings, from whom the assistant U.S. district attorney prevented his extrication; consequently, Rubel was adjudicated guilty, ultimately causing him to serve time in the Federal Facilities at Eglin Air Force Base, Florida.

As a result of Firestone's devious machinations against Rubel, Dixie's application was subverted, forcing a compromise that split the ownership of WLBT four ways. Subsequently, Marty Firestone was heard to brag about how he had "done in" Rubel to sabotage Dixie's very strong decision from the FCC.

The settlement for WLBT was brought about for several reasons: 1) Phillips's situation had torpedoed the Dixie vessel and it was severely taking on water; 2) the interim operation of WLBT was lucrative for the United Church of Christ and they had a vested interest in not settling the matter; 3) Channel 3, Inc. was backed by a very wealthy Texan—Walter Hall—who would never agree to Dixie being awarded outright the license; 4) the legal fees were exorbitant, with Dixie's exceeding $500,000 and I absorbed almost half; and, 5) by 1979 there was an accumulation of a proverbial exhaustion of physical, mental, and financial resources.

The ensuing settlement dictated that the four groups, sans Lamar Broadcasting Company, would own WLBT with each group having 25 percent. Additionally, the overall ownership of the franchise would be 51 percent minority owned; thus TV-3 Inc. was organized to be the corporate owner.

Dixie was owned 40 percent by me, 40 percent by Dixie National Life Insurance Company, 6 percent by Phillips, 4 percent by its three African-American stockholders—Margaret Walker Alexander, Talmidge Portis, and Dr. Roland Powell (a veterinarian), and

10 percent by others, including Ambassador John Palmer. With only 25 percent ownership from the compromise, Dixie's TV-3 interest now was compromised to 8 percent for me, 8 percent for Dixie Life, 8 percent for our three from the black community, and 1 percent divided between Palmer and Zachary Taylor.

Part of the settlement was that the board of directors would be eight in number and consist of four white and four black members. The members were wealthy Texan Walter Hall, Al Flannes, Bob Neal (Dixie), and me, as the white representatives; and Dr. Albert Britton, Charles Young, Aaron Henry, and Reuben Anderson as the black representatives. Flannes was elected president and CEO; Henry, chairman; Anderson, secretary; and myself, treasurer.

All the staff of the United Church of Christ-run station were retained including Bill Dilday, one of the first black TV station managers in the country. It was difficult with such a diverse setup to run a facility worth at least $25 million with the large staff inherited from the United Church of Christ. Aaron Henry was chairman of the Mississippi National Association for the Advancement of Colored People; consequently, he conducted the board meetings as if they were NAACP meetings, and Dr. Britton, who imbibed too much before each meeting, caused the reading of the minutes of the previous meeting to be a lengthy ordeal. Also, Bill Dilday refused to pay attention to directives from the board and followed his own desires and inclinations in managing the station. All of these reasons caused my stomach to become nauseous prior to each board meeting.

Back in 1977 in the office of Forbes Blair, a Washington FCC attorney, I had had an experience with Aaron Henry that made it difficult to be comfortable with him at the board meetings. Representatives from the four WLBT applicants had met to discuss a compromise. Several hours of discussion ensued, with no real settlement attained and with me sitting at one end of the long table and Henry at the other end. When the meeting ended, Dr. Robert L. T. Smith Jr. (from the black community) approached me and said that I should speak to Aaron Henry because he thought the two of us could get along. Consequently, he took me to meet Henry and I prepared to shake Aaron's hand. As I neared Henry, Dr. Smith began to push the two of us toward a hug rather than shaking hands. My inner reluctance to hug Henry was not caused by his being black, but by his being a notorious homosexual; during my life I had never knowingly hugged a homosexual. I had testified before the FCC that I was not a racist, so in a split second within myself I thought, "Oh! What the hell!" and *whomp!* I hugged him good!

Consequently, at each ensuing board meeting Aaron hugged me upon entering the room. I eventually designed a way to flit through the door and take my seat while circumventing Henry. This situation added to my unease prior to board meetings.

After several years, with all this in mind, Flannes, others, and I decided to find a buyer for the station. The imposed requirements of the settlement agreement, together with the fifteen-year contest for WLBT and the attention WLBT received from the FCC, discouraged buyers; however, one emerged and offered $22.5 million, which was probably at least $5 million below true market value. Nevertheless, it was agreed to proceed because it was too onerous to operate the station under the imposed conditions.

Ultimately, Aaron Henry, Charles Young, and others teamed up with Buford Television, Inc., from Tyler, Texas, and they made an acceptable proposition to buy WLBT.

Interestingly, the representative from Buford was Frank Melton, an African-American with sound television management experience, who had sat in on board meetings prior to Buford's assuming control. The first act that Frank Melton performed upon taking charge of WLBT was to terminate Bill Dilday. Today I count Frank Melton a good personal friend. And on July 4, 2005, Frank Melton was inaugurated as the new mayor of Jackson, Mississippi.

CHAPTER 14

Carmichael's Debacle

In early November of 1975, I sat at my desk to pen a letter, the same desk where I'd enjoyed garrulous political conversations, the same desk where I fecundly fundraised for our promising growing party. Now, I sullenly stared at what seemed to be a sooty future. The paper was white, but I saw dark hopelessness.

The letter was necessary for two reasons: 1) my voice had been totally shot due to the strain of recent weeks of political activity, and I simply couldn't sustain another hard conversation at the moment, and, 2) this set of thoughts were permanent, without qualification, as fixed as the ink on the page.

The time had come to clear my conscience, shut and lock the door, about-face—if necessary, forever.

November 4, 1975

Governor Gil Carmichael
Governor's Mansion
Jackson, Mississippi

Dear Gil:

This letter is being composed prior to the election in order to set out some of my most deeply felt beliefs about this campaign. Additionally, my fears and trepidations concerning the direction of your leadership as Governor are also covered.

You are going to be elected but the specific issues will affect the election imperceptibly. You will be elected because you and Deanie are immeasurably more attractive, you are a businessman, you are more anti-establishment, he is a lousy person, the campaign is well-financed, and we are much better organized. Your compulsive orations did nothing but keep those of us raising money and organizing continuously apologizing for ridiculous positions. The ineptitude of your viewpoints on ERA, guns, the [State] Constitution and aid to N.Y.C., to name a few, have been incredulous.

Your campaign has been the most frustrating in which I've been involved. My monetary contributions ($12,800) together with my fundraising efforts (in excess of $250,000) were eagerly sought; but my input and advice were studiously ignored. My sixth generation Mississippi gut reactions have heretofore been good and my track record in personal recruitment and support (Cochran and Shanks) should have spoken for themselves. Knee jerk action based on polls is not foolproof for identifying issues and a miserable way to govern. Our steering committee steered nothing, but was constantly supposed to get the workers and raise the money. If you paid so little attention to us when you so desperately needed us, why should we expect to have any impact on your administration when we will no longer be such necessities?

You listened solely to DeVries and to David Brown (both liberals) and you had a proclivity to be on the ultra liberal side of almost all issues (a small morsel about penalties for crimes was thrown in). All the years, money, and money raising abilities that I have devoted to building a two-party system in Mississippi will be for naught if you follow in your Teddy Kennedy appeal to liberals and the northeastern media. We do not need a Linwood Holton in this state and I shudder to think that we may be heartsick for what we have wrought.

There is only one omniscient being. No human has the answer to every question. Your Messianic approach and your compulsive verbal diarrhea to expound on every subject caused this campaign abundant trouble. You must develop a little humility and admit that you do not know all the answers and that you will study certain things. The worst, however, is that even when you do not know what you are talking about you have a propensity to propound liberal solutions.

Another great fear is that those who have done the most over the years and during this campaign will be ignored. You have the most disconcerting ability to confuse your enemies with your friends. The structuring of your administration should be made up of those who helped whether Democrat, Independent, or Republican, but certainly not from the inimical power structure people or the opportunists who appeared at the campaign's end.

Gil, these musings are heartfelt and deeply seated. You know that all I want is good government; and I am absolutely convinced that the precepts of conservatism are the proper ones and that the future of this state and nation do not lie in the "do gooder" perfectibility of man's liberal direction.

Sincerely Yours,
W. D. Mounger (signed "Billy")

Gil Carmichael's 1975 run for governor against Cliff Finch exhausted me. I meant this letter to disassociate me from Carmichael should he win the governorship, and obviously I thought he would. I addressed the letter not only to Carmichael, but also showed it to a group of close friends and Republican insiders (Haley Barbour, Clarke Reed, et al)—there would be no mistaking: should Carmichael win, I was disavowing him.

I had helped Carmichael for years due to our party affiliation. When Wirt Yerger started the party in the late 1950s and early 1960s, he eschewed involvement from Carmichael and the Meridian Republicans. Clarke Reed and I, naturally, wanted to have a party that encompassed every part of the state, so we worked with Gil in organizing his district in east Mississippi. I really didn't think that he was as liberal as Wirt thought. I was wrong.

However Carmichael rated on the conservative-liberal spectrum, he had developed a desire to hold public office. I recall how seemingly from nowhere in 1967 Carmichael volunteered to run for lieutenant governor when Rubel Phillips ran as a Republican for governor. I thought at the time that the way he did it was rather peculiar. I guess it was demonstrative of the fact that he really had overwhelming ambitions for office; then 1972 came, when Carmichael ran for the U.S. Senate against Jim Eastland after defeating James Meredith for the Republican nomination. Carmichael had been hugely mistreated by the Nixon team and thus won the sympathy of many in Mississippi, including me. I even spoke up for Carmichael at the Agnew appearance in Mississippi and, moreover, shirked Clarke Reed's directive and let Carmichael have the microphone to announce Mississippi's vote at the 1972 Miami Republican National Convention. It was against my better judgment, and it was something that Gil should have immeasurably appreciated.

But appreciation is not part of Gil's character or internal being.

The snub by Nixon's team played to the benefit of Carmichael, who was able to garner tremendous sympathy from Mississippi media and voters. After a strong and improbable finish against Jim Eastland, Carmichael aimed for the governor's office. Gil interpreted the opposition he had faced as proof that he stood for what was right.

Gil just doesn't recognize reality as it is. He lives in a world designed by his imagination in his private dreamland. He decides the way a thing ought to be, and then he turns it around and decides that it is. That is why he could take such poor treatment from Nixon's staff, because he imagined, "All of this is not really happening; they are not really doing this to me; they should be supporting me and so really they are supporting me." It made him the perfect candidate to run in that particular race against Eastland in 1972. And, in the end, he did surprisingly well.

Another trait that I couldn't help initially but admire was that Carmichael didn't let up. Gil never quit running after the 1972 Eastland race, because he had to work especially hard with his party in the minority.

So when 1975 approached, Carmichael was a statewide personality and the prohibitive Republican favorite. He had everybody behind him because he didn't really step on any toes except Eastland's during that 1972 race. He certainly didn't step on any party toes, and people like myself felt an obligation to him.

In November of 1973, Ronald Reagan came to Jackson to speak. It was an important milestone, as Reagan had never visited Mississippi. His strong reception at the 1968 Miami Republican Convention led to gearing up for an historic 1976 run for the White House. Clarke Reed and I were very much publicly behind that idea;

Reagan and others on the national scene were relying on our influence.[1] I worked diligently and sold most of the tickets for the fundraiser. I decided that Carmichael should get the opportunity to introduce Reagan, a move that was strongly opposed by Clarke Reed and Wirt Yerger. I should have given the introduction to Wirt. But I was tired of Reed's protests. "Go jump in a damn lake!" I told Reed, "because you do not do anything to put these things on; I do."

Again, I stuck my neck on the line for Carmichael; again I ended up sorry. Carmichael accepted that opportunity and, instead of introducing Reagan, he made a campaign speech! Donors came to hear Reagan; instead, they heard too much of Carmichael. As 1975 approached, Carmichael's team was up and running. Gil's *modus operandi* in this election was to act as if he had a primary, not sit back and wait until the Democrats finished their primary before starting his campaign. We all joined in and concurred very strongly. Gil did everything he could to stay in the forefront.

His Democrat opponent soon became clear: Cliff Finch, who dressed like a "working man," wearing a hard hat and carrying a lunch pail. He drove bulldozers at campaign events. He appealed to the rural Mississippian.

The core of Republican state leadership met with Gil to discuss bringing a veteran campaign director on to his staff. Lyn Nofziger, a Reagan associate in California, said he was interested in running Carmichael's campaign; Clarke Reed, Tommy Giordano, Wilkins, and I felt that Nofziger ought to have the job since he knew how to run a truly conservative-based Republican campaign. Nofziger met with Carmichael and warned him that, in order to run the proper campaign, he would need "a great sum of money" committed up front. I don't know whether it was because we didn't have the money in advance or what, but Gil didn't really make any effort to hire a Nofziger type. Carmichael asked me to be his finance chairman, but I declined due to my heavy commitments to local races in Hinds County. Still, early in the campaign, I loaned Carmichael five-thousand dollars, a debt I later forgave.

Somehow, Carmichael hooked up with Duke University professor Walter DeVries to be on his steering committee. DeVries was an experienced pollster. Many Republican conservatives considered him an outsider liberal. The next thing we knew, Carmichael had hired DeVries. We were saddled with an advisor who didn't know anything about southern politics. I believe that Gil was wanting someone who agreed with all of those grandiose things that he had in mind, and not somebody who believed as I did that there are certain things that you must do to get elected and to do the right things for Mississippi. Gil had in mind all along that he had to be revolutionary, that he had to bring about all of these monstrous changes. You can only do so much changing; people don't like to change much. They like their changes in gradations, not in great leaps.

A pre-campaign meeting at the Holiday Inn Medical Center gathered all the key men and women who would work for Carmichael throughout the state's highways and byways during the upcoming campaign. Among other things, Carmichael brought up the fact that he had some TV spots that he was beginning to cut and that he was going to do something about a new state constitution. Everyone in that meeting hit the ceiling about him wanting to advocate a new constitution. There was no support there whatsoever. All the people at that meeting said, "Gil, it is just bad politics. Don't do it. The last governor who tried to do it was J. P. Coleman, and when Coleman tried to run again, he was just devastated."

Gil promised the group he absolutely would not pursue that. The next thing we knew, he started making statements about a new constitution. Gil was lucky to be running against Finch, because Finch didn't do anything with it since all Finch said the entire campaign was "I drive a bulldozer; I'm for the working man." Still, even Gil's closest supporters began to wonder: If he will ignore us and press for a new constitution, then what might he do next? All of us knew that you scare the voters badly talking about a new constitution—old folks versus young, liberal versus conservative, city versus rural, black versus white, ad inifinitum—it was a losing political position with all groups.

Carmichael never had enough money up front; eventually he hired a group of professional fundraisers. They did create some things and did cause some money to come in. But at the same time, they irritated the heck out of people. They were making everybody mad and we never really could work with them. The steering committee told Gil that those fundraisers had to go. Gil ultimately listened and dropped the group. He was, however, the first viable Republican gubernatorial candidate on a Mississippi ticket that was loaded with other Republicans running for all sorts of state, district, and local seats—and they all required money for their campaigns, too. It cost me! We Republicans were ramping up, but we lacked the myriad deep purses and good-old-boy system of our state Democrat rivals. We also lacked the number of competent campaign workers that the Democrats had; in Gil's case, he had locked up a good many of the better Republican workers, leaving slim pickings for the other Republican candidates.[2]

As the campaign crept on, Gil still operated without a finance chairman. The Republican National Committee assigned some help for a few months. Finally, I suggested to Gil the name of a close friend of mine for the finance chairman job—Victor Smith, an oilman who had shown great organizational skills when he headed a recent Billy Graham crusade in Jackson. Victor and Gil had some key conversations about Gil's personal faith, which was important to Smith. Smith also told Gil that, if Smith were to give and ask others to give, Gil had to agree to give commensurately. Gil convinced Smith that they saw eye to eye.

That sort of reenergized me to throttle up our state's fundraising engine. I decided to get a contest going between some key Republican constituents; it became so heated that some people would even go out and borrow ten- or fifteen-thousand dollars to give, figuring they would eventually raise it. I don't necessarily encourage outright competition, but I do encourage people to say, "By gosh, we can do it!" I would challenge a whole group to raise fifty- to a hundred-thousand dollars and said I would raise the same amount.

Victor and I raised money totaling about five-hundred-thousand dollars. The campaign had not been going long when Gil brought a bill into the campaign office, about the time when the money began coming in, to reimburse his businesses and all of his expenditures over there in Meridian for a substantial sum of money. Victor looked around and said, "What in the world is this for? I'm putting this money in, and Gil committed to leave his money in. Now that we've got money and need to spend it on all of these things, he wants all these reimbursements for telephone calls and traveling and stamps and all this other stuff. He is reneging on his pledge to me."

So Victor was understandably unhappy about that.

Instead of living up to his commitment to Victor, Gil got all of his money reimbursed to him, in addition to having eleven-thousand dollars of debt paid off! Not only did he not leave any money there, he came out eleven-thousand dollars to the good!

Over time, I became progressively disillusioned with Carmichael. It was a cumulative thing. There was Carmichael's surprise announcement to the key campaign people about his intent to seek a new state constitution. That was the first time I told Gil he was no messiah. You run a political race to get your philosophy through, but also to win. You don't run a political race to educate the people. Carmichael's brain trust was finding that our guidance was not any good. Victor and I loaned the campaign fifteen-thousand dollars to be paid if there was a surplus. There was sufficient money left, and Gil reneged. I was finally reimbursed after assiduous effort.

While I supported taking stances on key issues, Carmichael believed it necessary to take a stance on everything. Dreaming up the most controversial positions to take is foolish. We had some smart people telling Gil that, people such as Haley Barbour and Bill Wilkins.

As the campaign progressed, Carmichael finally secured someone to do his basic organization—Manion Milliken, a connection from the Goldwater days—but Milliken offered little help in guiding Carmichael and instead confined his efforts to organization. Nonetheless, money was arriving at a rate of about fifty-thousand dollars a week and Carmichael was looking like he had a strong chance to win against Finch. About this time, I organized a meeting of key Hinds County contributors at the Petroleum Club. I looked at the crowd and thought, "Boy, we're just going to get a lot of money out of this group."

The meeting unraveled before my eyes.

Gil arrived and disconcertingly announced that he had just taken a position on hand-gun registration. Boy! You talk about putting a blue funk on everything! I sat there and my gut just said, *"Oomph!"*

I started choking.

I said to myself, "Don't tell me he just said that!"

Mason Nooe spoke up: "You mean to tell me you've done that?"

I wouldn't have asked a soul in that room for a penny. I said, "Man, Gil just cut himself off." It's the most devastating statement that I've heard a politician make. Later I learned what had happened. DeVries was in favor of gun control and had taken a poll in which he asked a sampling of Mississippians a loaded question to this effect: "Would you be in favor of registering handguns just as you would register your automobile?" The poll came out about 60 percent in favor, and DeVries and Carmichael failed to run their decision by the steering committee.

Gil stirred up the National Rifle Association. He made all those people in the rural community, as well as some around Jackson, mad. Once you say "Gun," people in Mississippi do not think of a Saturday night special. They think, "You are interfering with my shotgun, my hunting rifle." And what Gil did was motivate the darnedest bunch of activists you ever saw. I'm as convinced as I am about the sun coming up tomorrow that that cost him about a hundred-thousand votes. I think that one statement cost him the race.

One indicator of the statement's damage was how the money flow dropped off, from about fifty-thousand dollars a week to about twenty-thousand a week. I lost any desire to raise money, and I quit. It took me about six weeks to get my viscera back into action. Gil's steering committee begged him to go back to the same message he had projected against Eastland—"blue sky" and "motherhood," etc. They told him, "You have taken all the positions that you need to take. Just let the people know you're a better quality guy than Finch."

But Carmichael was not finished. With about two weeks left in the race, he announced at a public forum that he was for federal aid to New York City, which left me stunned. Is there anything less astutely political to say in Mississippi? Nobody gave a compound darn about New York City. We Mississippians hate New York City. I've made this statement on TV: "What you do to New York City is take the world's largest band saw, saw it off and get all the tugs you can muster and tow it out to the abysmal depths of the Atlantic Trough and sink it." Now that's what you say politically in Mississippi.

I began to feel trapped. I had hooked Victor Smith into running Carmichael's finances. My own sister headed a number of North Jackson precincts. I had all my family and many friends working on the campaign. Every time I wanted to walk out on Carmichael, I would say, "Okay, but do I want Finch as governor?"

I lost my voice the weekend before the Tuesday election. I now believed that, whatever the outcome, I had to state clearly how I felt about Carmichael. I couldn't use the phone. I couldn't dictate. I was convinced that, despite Carmichael's bumbling, he was going to win. I was also convinced that I had played a major role in electing him. Yet, I also was convinced that Carmichael wouldn't listen to good advice by the most respected conservative Republicans in the state. The next four years might prove devastating. I could see Thad Cochran and Trent Lott losing their next race because this would reflect on them. People would say, "You guys are crazy." I was really fearful. To this day, I truly believe that, if Carmichael had been elected, we Mississippi Republicans would not enjoy the fantastic successes we do today.

So in November of 1975, I sat down to write a letter—one like I'd never written before, one that could have changed the rest of my life. I was going to totally break with Gil and have nothing to do with his administration and at least clear my conscience. I would let the world know, "Okay, he's governor, but I want nothing from him. I will have no connections with him."

I wrote the letter and showed it to several people, including Clarke Reed, Tommy Giordano, Bill Wilkins, and Haley Barbour.

On election Tuesday, Cliff Finch won. I did not have the heart to show Carmichael the letter at that point.

I am convinced that, as lousy as Finch was, the best thing that happened to us in the state GOP was for Gil almost to have been elected but lose. I think it ultimately worked out correctly. I have often told Cliff Finch supporters, "Thank you for saving me, the Republican Party, the State of Mississippi, the nation, and the world from Gil Carmichael!"

The Ingratitude of Doug Shanks

C armichael's campaign was one of many that I worked from my post as Hinds County GOP chairman in the seventies. In addition to an ability to raise money, I had the right to seek out and approve of potential candidates for local, state, and national offices. I now set my sites on filling city and county offices, in addition to state and national ones, using the strategies that I had learned in national and state elections.

The 1970s were big for us in statewide races and also in Hinds County and Jackson races. A number of local GOP candidates had run in 1967 and 1971, although none were elected, with the only viable candidate in 1971 being Dr. Tommy Davis, who ran for re-election as Hinds County coroner but was beaten by a used car salesman running as a Democrat. The race was notable for its absurdity, illustrating the vise grip that Democrats still seemed to hold in county and city elections.

The city of Jackson races followed in 1973 to fill the offices of mayor and the two city commissioners, and I felt we were ready to win one of the three races. The contested 1972 Hinds County Republican chairman's race helped stimulate Thad Cochran's Fourth Congressional District win in 1972. We had shown that we could turn out the vote for Cochran, and Nixon also carried Hinds County with 70 percent of the vote.

Racial voting lines were the most predictable patterns in the city; however, we seemed to be making headway in forming a serious Republican constituency within Hinds County's black citizenry—most notably with Charles Evers, the older brother of slain civil rights leader, Medgar Evers. President Gerald Ford had named Nelson Rockefeller as vice president of the U.S. in 1974; WLBT, a Jackson television station, assembled a group of people for a live roundtable discussion of the consequences of the appointment. I had been asked to be the token conservative among Aaron Henry, Charles Evers, Owen Cooper, Pat Derian, and others. Pat Derian married Hodding Carter Jr. and ultimately became a member of President Carter's State Department in charge of Latin American affairs. An unforgettable moment occurred during that live, televised discussion. To fully appreciate it, I need to hark back to 1971, when Ruby Stutts Liles, a black Republican, decided to run for the Mississippi Senate from Hinds County. Liles was from the Stutts family, which is a substantial oil royalty owner in the Tinsley Oil Field south of Yazoo City, and her father was a long-time "Black-and-Tan" Republican.

Ruby Stutts Liles was very insistent that I support her and introduce her at her campaign kickoff meeting. Her announcement meeting at Jackson's storied downtown Sun & Sand Motel was attended by about one-hundred people, mostly from the black community, and most conspicuously Charles Evers. This was the first time I met Charles; as a consequence, we became friends and today Charles is a full-fledged Republican.

When the WLBT roundtable discussion occurred in 1974, my turn came to speak, and I attempted to emphasize my cooperation with the black community by citing my support of Ruby Stutts Liles. I looked at Charles and said, "Aaron, we worked together with Ruby Stutts Liles and"—suddenly, Charles interrupted me, joking to the camera, "Billy, that's what's the matter with you white folks, you can't tell us n———s apart!"

I died laughing, although my effort at showing my connections to the black community had been totally obliterated. The program was being shown live, and I wonder to this day how the audience reacted to that impromptu dialog between Charles and me.

I combed the city in 1973 for mayoral and city commissioner candidates, approaching Derwood Boyles to run as a Republican; Boyles declined. Then, Mary Stikes, a previous Jack Breed supporter who was serving as my GOP assistant in Hinds County, mentioned a young man whom she knew in the city's public relations department—Doug Shanks. Stikes lived only a few houses down from him in South Jackson. I met Shanks and was impressed; Shanks was attractive and articulate. Stikes further offered to run Shanks's campaign, and I saw the green light to elect him, since Mrs. Stikes was the best organizer in the county.

Another man, Jim Williams, also impressed me. He entered Jackson's open commissioners' race, and that meant that we Republicans were fielding commissioner candidates for both seats.

Shanks rallied a lot of youth to work for him through the Jaycees. I sought to raise money for both candidates. I accumulated about fourteen- or fifteen-thousand dollars for Shanks, but only about five- or six-thousand dollars for Williams. I tried to be as impartial as I could, but it was obvious that there was more money out there for Shanks.

The city financial officer, Grover Allen, also considered switching and running as a Republican, but he wanted certainty of financial backing and I declined Allen's overtures. Allen was a gruff individual who seemed invulnerable. Tom Kelly was running for reelection as a city commissioner, and he appeared hard to beat. Later he became a Republican.

Midway through the campaign, Mayor Russell Davis, a Democrat who lacked any opposition, put out the word to several of his people asking, "Why don't you go out and help this young guy, Doug Shanks?" Davis knew Shanks, who had worked in the mayor's public relations office. Shanks finished a close second to Kelly and far outdistanced Allen and Williams.

Shanks hadn't been in office long, however, when I began to sense ingratitude in the young commissioner. His first thought was, "Why doesn't the Republican Party do more for me?" rather than saying, "I thank all of you Republicans who worked for me and delivered all of this unique help that I wouldn't have received if I had run as a Democrat." His mind was, "I'm city commissioner! I'm this great Doug Shanks and everybody is supposed to be doing things for me." This attitude is why he lost when he ran for mayor four years later. As is usual with many politicians, Shanks evinced no gratitude or appreciation; contrarily, he chose the confrontational route. He even said, "To hell with Mary Stikes." Ingratitude personified?

Shanks also didn't help himself any when, in late 1975, he took the position as state campaign chairman for then-President Gerald Ford. He did this despite the facts that Mississippians were largely for Ronald Reagan and that I urged him to decline the position because I was Reagan's state chairman. I had hoped to avoid a confrontation with my newly created city commissioner. In running Ford's Mississippi campaign, Shanks's true colors showed. That story is told in the next two chapters.

Part Three:

The GOP Storm

CHAPTER 16

The Republican Reed Begins to Bend

In 1975, Ronald Reagan visited Mississippi again. I foolishly had let Gil Carmichael introduce him in 1973 at the Mississippi Republican fundraiser; the next time, in 1975, I chose to make Reagan's introduction myself. I introduced him as, "Our Moses to lead us out of the political wilderness."

I could not have been more sincere. Goldwater had moved from the scene and Reagan had rocketed to the forefront in the minds of many conservative Republicans. Watergate had led to the fall of Richard Nixon; and Gerald Ford, Nixon's vice president, had taken office and was looking to win the 1976 popular election to gain his own full term of office in the White House.

The troubled 1975 Carmichael gubernatorial campaign had severely eviscerated me. Repeated disappointments with the Nixon administration had also left their mark. Clarke Reed knew this, and in November 1975 made the pitch that I become Reagan's Mississippi state GOP chairman for the 1976 presidential primary. "You will like it," Clarke crooned. "You can cleanse your soul after Carmichael. You can do something you truly believe in. If you will do it, you and I will work totally together, with you as the titular Reagan chairman. We will be working together but I won't take a public position so that I can be more influential in guiding to

Reagan the Southern Chairmen's Association (where Clarke was still in charge) and the national party."

I took the Reagan job, contemplating that I could now do something on a positive scale where I felt comfortable, and convinced that I was on the side of the vast majority of the Mississippi Republicans. Little could I—or anyone, for that matter—have foreseen what was ahead.

The ensuing 1976 struggle for the Republican presidential nomination—in Mississippi and nationally—became the stuff of fiction, epic in proportions, and emotionally crushing for many.

Here is my account of the events.

Jackson city commissioner Doug Shanks began toying in late 1975 with an invitation from President Gerald Ford's staff to be Ford's Mississippi chairman. The Ford team initially had looked at Carmichael for that position but I believe that Clarke became so jealous of Carmichael that he killed the idea.

Upon hearing that Shanks may become Ford's Mississippi GOP campaign chairman, I telephoned Reed. "Clarke," I said, "I'm Hinds County chairman because of you. I saved you. I have all these miserable headaches in this county. Now I'm the Reagan chairman. Certainly I don't want to be bothered in organizing the county, district, and state with Doug Shanks as city commissioner and Ford's Mississippi chairman."

Typical of Clarke and his spinelessness, he did nothing.

Normally, I would not care who was Ford chairman, but I did not want to worry about a confrontation with the first Republican city commissioner whom I had elected in Hinds County. Things were still in the process of healing from the 1972 Hinds County chairmanship rift; thus, I hoped to avoid future fissures.

After I learned that Ford had asked Shanks, I invited him for lunch at the Petroleum Club. "Doug," I said, "I'm going to give you some advice. Stay clear of the presidential nomination fight in the party. It is stupid for any person in a political office to get involved in an intraparty fight, certainly for the national party nomination for president. Steer clear of it. You're not going to see Thad Cochran involved in it."

Cochran had assured me that he planned to stay out of the Republican nominating process. I told Shanks: "It's stupid enough to be involved in a party controversy if you are on the vast majority's side; but if you get involved as Ford's top man in Mississippi, you will very much be on the minority."

Shanks seemed unfazed. I went one step further: "I want to ask you this as a personal favor. I do not want to have a confrontation in my homebase. I am asking you to decline as a personal favor and you know you would not have been elected without me."

We had about four conversations; notwithstanding, he took Ford's Mississippi chairmanship. His ambition eclipsed any appreciation he might have had for my previous help.

Reagan again came to Jackson in the spring of 1975, and I put on a hundred-dollar-a-plate function for the state party with 1,600 people attending. Reagan had not yet announced his candidacy nor made me his state chairman. Clarke Reed and I met Reagan and his wife, Nancy, at his plane at the Jackson International Airport. While riding from the airport to the Walthall Hotel, Clarke urged Reagan to run for president in 1976 and assured Reagan of his all-out support, and I committed my full support also. The morning after the fundraiser, Reagan and Nancy invited Clarke and me to breakfast in his Walthall Hotel suite, and Clarke repeated his unfettered support for a Reagan candidacy. These two outright expressions of support directly to Ronald Reagan are extremely significant; Clarke waffled and then totally collapsed in his support for Reagan during the next year and at the 1976 Kansas City Republican National Convention. Clarke's reneging on Reagan will be shown in detail in the next few chapters. The bottom line, however, is that I was in the car and in a hotel suite when Clarke told Ronald Reagan straight to his face that Reagan absolutely needed to run for president and that Reagan would absolutely have Clarke's complete support. It was unequivocal.

Some historical context on how the Ford-Reagan race developed may be helpful. Ford, a Michigan U.S. congressman and minority leader, ascended from vice president to president upon Richard Nixon's Watergate-induced resignation. Ford made several federal appointments during his brief time that were not conservative. I therefore hoped for a viable alternative to Ford in the 1976 Republican primary; consequently I was ready to support Ronald Reagan any way possible.[1]

Wirt Yerger had been concerned for a while that Clarke Reed was steering the state's party apparatus from a pragmatic position; conversely, Reed didn't want Yerger as Reagan's chairman. As the time approached to elect the 1976 Mississippi Republican delegation, I was like many who believed two things: 1) the Republican 1976 presidential nomination fight would be over early, with either Reagan or Ford knocking out the other not long after the New Hampshire primary; and, 2) there was, then, no reason not to elect a noncommitted delegation committed to unit rule as we had done for Miami in 1968 and 1972.

Meanwhile, Clarke Reed said often that he wasn't going to take a public position regarding whom he supported in the 1976 Republican race, but rather would allow the delegation to speak as a whole for itself when it arrived in Kansas City.[2]

Clarke was with me in Washington, D.C., when I formally accepted the request to be Reagan's Mississippi chairman. We visited in Reagan's campaign office with David Keene, Reagan's southern coordinator, and John Sears, Reagan's campaign chairman. Sears had been Nixon's campaign chairman in 1968 and he often joined Clarke and me during many Washington meetings. Clarke and I knew David Keene from his days on Spiro Agnew's staff. Reagan had selected David as his southern coordinator on Reed's recommendation. Every Reed action pointed to his supporting Reagan by assisting me in delivering the Mississippi delegation at the 1976 Kansas City convention.

It is important to understand that Clarke was our state GOP leader—our state party chairman—and that I had trusted and believed in him when he told me that we were working together to elect Ronald Reagan. Instead, Clarke proved to be working only to serve his own ego and to maintain his positions of influence.

Everything hinged on the thirty Mississippi delegates (and their thirty shadow alternates) understanding and complying with the unit rule voting system that Wirt had initiated in 1960. Clarke and I were ultimately responsible for insuring that this occurred. Unfortunately, Clarke's whole role, inclination, and almost total motivation was to be involved on the Washington scene and the

Southern Association of Republican State Chairmen. Clarke was not very effective within the state organization.

I, meanwhile, took my own party role terribly emotionally. That is why I could go out and raise the kind of money I did on behalf of candidates. On the other hand, it was devastating when candidates turned out to be less than desired, when candidates double-crossed me, or even when they lost a race. I became enmeshed and immersed in campaigns.

Clarke and I had been developing a pattern for years: I would do most of the work and he would take most of the credit.

For instance, I had organized a major statewide party fundraiser back in 1972; Harry Dent from Washington, D.C., was the speaker, and native Mississippian Mary Ann Mobley, an actress and former Miss America, attended. I sold virtually every hundred-dollar-per-plate ticket. Yet during the festivities, when it came time for the photos of the key event organizers and guests, Clarke stood with Dent and Mobley without pausing to wait for me to arrive in the room. I was furious with Clarke. I told him that he was selfish and egotistical.

It wasn't the fact that I didn't get my picture taken. It was really the principle of Clarke's taking total credit for something for which he deserved no credit. I walked out of the room and said, "To hell with Clarke Reed."

I wasn't the only one who came to this opinion of Clarke. Billy Powell, who entered into GOP state politics via working with me, experienced his own frustrations with Reed, as Powell eventually built Rankin County's GOP organization into a powerhouse in the 1980s. Powell recalls:

> I knew that Mounger was the finance chairperson of the party back then [in the 1970s]. I knew that he was doing all the work and Clarke was getting all of the credit. I could see that. But as far as being part of that particular time frame during the 1976 presidential race, I was not. But after the 1976 Reagan loss and then Reagan's rise to the presidency, Clarke resurfaced as a result of Kirk Fordice's election as governor of Mississippi in 1992. In the [1980s] Reagan era Mounger had gotten Clarke Reed cut out. . . . Mike Retzer [Clarke's protégé] was supporting Pete Johnson against Fordice. Clarke Reed also was

supporting Pete Johnson. . . . Greg Phillips, who was then the state
Fordice chairman, . . . got Clarke Reed to give Fordice five-hundred
dollars with the idea that it was not going to be reported. . . . Clarke
called back the next day to make darn sure that it was not going to
be reported. He was supporting Pete Johnson in the gubernatorial
Republican primary, but . . . he was playing both sides against the
middle.

We on Fordice's team won the [governor's race], there were about
seven or eight of us that were more or less on Fordice's finance team:
myself, Liles Williams, Jake Mills, Neal Clement, Tommy Wallace,
Bill Grêsham, and Greg Phillips. We had a meeting out at Liles's
office at Stuart C. Irby, Jr.'s business. And I can remember that there
was no particular person in charge of the checkbook at that stage of
the game. And Greg was the one who was handling it. Clarke was
there and he made the suggestion that he, in effect, handle the
checkbook. All of a sudden he was starting to show up, because now
we had won the primary. *Now* he's a strong Fordice supporter. . . .
Now Clarke shows up and he is a big Fordice supporter. . . . Well we
wound up winning the general election. After the election he had
the checkbook. We'd have the finance team meeting. . . . It's easy to
raise money once you become governor. Well, we had a meeting at
the governor's office. . . . We would report the contacts we each had
made and the money that we had raised for Fordice, and we would
pass it in. When everybody got through all their discussion, Clarke
would bring Fordice in to give us all a pep talk. [He] never mentioned
what anybody had raised.

It wasn't until we had gotten to that stage of the game that I
realized that what [Clarke] was doing was the same old thing that
[Billy] Mounger had talked about for years—[Clarke Reed] was riding
everybody's shoulders. He took credit for everything. He didn't necessarily take full credit, but he would not give a particular individual
credit to Fordice for having done anything.

. . . He didn't want Fordice to know that somebody else had raised
forty- or fifty-thousand dollars. He did not want them to have an
inroad. And at that stage of the game is when it really dawned on
me the type of selfish person that the guy is. He went up there to see
David Hicks up in Greenwood, who had raised quite a bit of money
for Fordice. So he [Reed] goes by and he picks up the checks from

David and says he is going to carry the money for him down to Fordice. [Clarke] never gave Hicks credit for that. . . . He just flat picked
it up, wouldn't give credit to the people who were actually out there
raising the funds.

Clarke's strong tendency is to take credit and garner glory, as Billy
Powell's story indicates.

The summer of 1976 saw the Mississippi GOP rising in national
prominence while Clarke began to wriggle as never before to hold
onto his own position of influence. He seemed withdrawn from
direct guidance. I received no input as the Ronald Reagan state
chairman from Reed. He chose to work more on the national level
from his post as head of the Southern Association of Republican
State Chairmen.

Doug Shanks, Gerald Ford's state campaign chairman, and I
were left to negotiate whom we would appoint as state party delegates to the 1976 convention. We actually communicated decently
about that. When all was said and done, I outmaneuvered Shanks
and procured ten pro-Reagan delegates to five pro-Ford delegates
out of the Fourth District. Getting a simple majority of Mississippi
delegates to support Reagan would ultimately win all our "unit" of
thirty votes, so I thought I was okay. I figured that Tommy Giordano had taken care of making sure Reagan had a majority in the
Third District, and that Charles Pickering and Victor Mavar had
done likewise in the Fifth District. The two northern districts—
the First and Second—were more liberal by my estimation, but I
counted on Clarke to insure Reagan's power base there.

The leadership for the state convention in 1976 seemed flimsy
and thin. Clarke told me he wanted to resign his post as state party
chairman; then he flip-flopped, saying he should keep the position
through the 1976 August Republican National Convention. He
maintained that his leadership at the national convention was important as chairman of the Southern Association of Republican
State Chairmen and as the "senior state party chairman in the
United States." Reed said he felt it was important to keep his position to continue the RNC rules committee fight that he had led in
1972 to ensure that delegation apportionment was not altered.[3]

Reed told me, "If I give that up, these other guys are so weak out there that they will play Ford's game," namely the state chairmen of Alabama, Louisiana, Georgia, and the likes. David Keene at Reagan headquarters thought Reed made sense on that count, as did I. In hindsight, however, what Clarke was really doing was engineering something to benefit himself, while he was selling it publicly in other ways. Charles Pickering's name had been strongly considered as the next state GOP chairman, but then Reed proposed that Pickering be "chairman-elect" at the national convention so that Reed could run the state delegation at the national convention. To assuage Pickering, Reed suggested without my knowledge that Pickering be "vice chairman" of the state delegation while Reed maintain authority through the national convention. The vice chairman position by long-established protocol belonged to the finance chairman of the party, and thus it had been mine at the Miami conventions of 1968 and 1972.

Haley Barbour alerted me to Reed's move. "He cannot do that!" I averred. I went to the state Republican offices in Jackson seeking Reed; I learned he was in Houston, Texas. I chewed Reed out over the phone in Haley's presence. "You have taken credit for my fund-raising efforts. You would have been ousted in 1972 without me. So how can you backstab me now?" I asked him, adding, "Because of what you just tried to do, I want to be chairman of the delegation. [In reality, my plan was to take the post and then cede it to Charles Pickering.] And everybody is going to know how rotten and sorry and ungrateful you are."

Clarke began backtracking, apologizing, actually crying on the phone. However, the next day, Charles Pickering called me saying that I deserved my protocol vice chairman's position in the delegation. It was obvious to me that Reed had conned Pickering since our conversation. I told Pickering: "You sucker! I had Clarke backed into a corner and you have just messed up the whole ball game."

Clarke had convinced Pickering that Clarke still should be chairman and that the party owed me so much that I should be vice chairman. I told Pickering that he should not have listened to Reed, and that I had planned all along to make him chairman; now, however, he would not have either position while Clarke preserved his position as chairman.

In the end, after all the infighting, Clarke and I kept our positions as chairman and vice chairman, respectively. But I wondered, "If Clarke will do such a disloyal thing for no good reason, what else will he do?"[4] Additionally, I elicited the pledge from Clarke that I would control the Mississippi microphone at the convention.

The vice chairman position was really titular, but it was my plum. The position of vice chairman of the delegation is weak like being the vice president of the United States, but there was principle involved. It might have been a wormy, mangy, desiccated plum, but it was mine!

Clarke's propensity to be totally egocentric demonstrated itself again when we attended the 1976 Mississippi Republican Convention. The newly elected national delegation met to elect the upcoming chairman and vice chairman for the national convention. The first nomination was for state chairman. The floor opened for nominations and someone said "Clarke Reed," and *"bam!"*—the gavel went down and nominations were closed. Reed was elected.

Then came time for vice chairman. Clarke should have had paramount on his mind to make absolutely sure that I was the vice chairman of the delegation. My vote could have been orchestrated just as Reed had orchestrated his own—quick and clean. Instead someone nominated Gil Carmichael; then another person, thinking that Charles Pickering might be getting slighted, nominated him; finally, I made Reed recognize Swan Yerger, who nominated me. Lillian Todd, the state's national committeewoman, was supposed to nominate me, but she was not in the room.

Pickering withdrew his name from nomination, saying the vice chairman's position traditionally went to the state party's finance chairman. Carmichael, however, kept his name in the running. Charles Pickering owed me nothing, yet did the right thing; but Gil just sat up there and persisted in running against me. "Now wait a minute," I said to myself, "this cannot be happening. This is not possible." I asked for a point of personal privilege. I told the delegation, "I know that this is not proper for someone to make a campaign speech for this position; but there are things that people in this room are unaware of. First of all, you know my position is the state finance chairman; but you may not know . . ." and I enumerated the favors I had done for Carmichael, starting with the time that I gave the microphone to Gil at the 1972 national convention. After each example that I listed, I'd say to myself, "Gil, get it through your skull, you can't run against me."

I was trying to give Gil a graceful chance to get out; but I'd make a point and Gil would just sit there. And I'd say, "I was the only one who made a speech for Gil in front of the crowd at the Old State Capitol in his race against Jim Eastland." He just sat there. Then I said, "You may not know it but, when Gil ran for senator in 1972, I was the single biggest contributor he had; even when I was raising money for Thad Cochran, I still raised more than 25 percent of his money." Nothing. . . . So I added, "I gave him the introduction of Reagan at the 1973 fundraiser."

I made each point like a guy zinging an arrow and—*whups!*—I would look at Gil and say to myself, "Gil, get out of this race. Don't just sit there."

"Last year," I continued, "when Gil ran for governor, I was the single largest contributor that Gil had." Then I mentioned the fact that I raised roughly a quarter-million dollars and that I was the only reason Victor Smith came in as Gil's finance chairman. I went through that litany and Gil Carmichael was like a sphinx. I was saying to myself, "I've given him every reason; all he needs to do is say, 'You are right. It's your position. I can't run against you.'"

Finally Gil did say, "You're right. I'll vote for Mounger," and he made a flourish of that. Then he wrote my name so that everybody could see. Gil lives in Never Never Land.

I beat him two-to-one. People tell me that I take politics too personally. Unfortunately, I do not know how to deal otherwise, because everyone is supposed to be appreciative. They are supposed to be trustworthy and they are supposed to be truthful. Some in the media said that the message from the event was not to cross me if I ever helped fund your campaign.[5]

My feelings actually were much deeper—Gil knew what he was doing and he knew the amount of help that I had given him, and it was inconceivable that one man would so thoroughly disrespect someone who had helped him so much.

Later, longtime liberal political columnist Bill Minor wrote that Gil almost beat me for delegation vice chairman; the vote was two-to-one—there is no "almost" about it. Minor said that Carmichael didn't know what was going on. That was not possible! Minor's Sunday, April 18 article had been entitled: "GOP Factional Quarrel Deepens."[6] I wrote a letter to the editor of *The Times-Picayune* of New Orleans; my letter, dated April 19, 1976 and the article, follow:

GOP Factional Quarrel Deepens
   By W. F. Minor

JACKSON, Miss.—Just below the surface, it was apparent at the Republican State Convention a week ago, is a deepening rift in the GOP ranks between the archly conservative leadership of chairman Clarke Reed and finance man Billy Mounger and the moderates of Gil Carmichael.

For years, the Republicans have projected an image that everything inside the party is apple pie harmony, in contrast with the divisiveness of the state's Democrats.

Mostly the Republicans who have disagreed slightly with the Reed-Mounger domination have been ostracized or relegated to positions of little influence over the past decade.

But Reed and Mounger never had to deal with a threat such as Carmichael poses to their continued leadership and also the philosophy of the Mississippi Republican Party.

While Reed and Mounger have held the machinery of the party close to their vests, the attractive, progressive Carmichael has gone out on the stump and given Mississippi Republicans a formidable candidate such as they have never dreamed of before.

Carmichael had to run his race for the U.S. Senate against Jim Eastland in 1972 with an ambivalent backup from his own state party leaders, since Richard Nixon was paying back some debt by supporting Eastland. But on the surface, Reed and Mounger were with Carmichael, even though avidly for Nixon.

It was evident to close observers of Mississippi politics that what Carmichael was saying in 1972 didn't correspond very closely with what Reed and Mounger had been saying in the past.

Carmichael ran his race, turned on a lot of young people who felt alienated by the Democratic mess, and won many converts to the Republican Party. That apparently was fine with Reed and Mounger who were unable to generate much enthusiasm until the attractive silver-haired Carmichael came along.

But the real dimensions of the philosophical gap which existed between Carmichael and the state party leaders became even more evident in the 1975 gubernatorial campaign.

Carmichael came on as a solid progressive, advocating a constitutional convention, registration of handguns, and making corporations and the petroleum industry pay more taxes.

Reed was quoted by one national publication which came down to cover the intriguing campaign of Carmichael that he (Reed) disagreed with most of the things that Carmichael was saying.

Mounger, who had made and inherited his money in oil and in banking, is even further to the right than Reed, so his differences with Carmichael's stands were believed even stronger.

Yet Mounger, the perennial money raiser of the Republican Party, and seeing a possible winner, put a good bit of his own money into the Carmichael race and raised more.

It would have been thought likely that Carmichael, just barely losing to Cliff Finch in November, could now lay claim to being the titular head of the Mississippi Republican Party.

Obviously, Reed and Mounger had thoughts to the contrary, particularly so when Carmichael announced last December he was going to support President Ford for the Republican nomination. Mounger became the state chairman for Ronald Reagan, and Reed, while maintaining public neutrality, leaned strongly to Reagan.

Both Reed and Mounger had made it known they planned to step out after a decade and let some other Republicans take their places. But they were not about to let Carmichael gain control.

Trouble was, Carmichael didn't mount any effort to gain control, just one seemingly innocuous effort was made to elect him vice chairman of the delegation to Kansas City.

That, however, hit the fuse of Mounger, who as finance chairman considered the vice chairmanship his province. Even after Carmichael announced that he was personally voting for Mounger, Carmichael nearly won the spot.

Afterwards, Mounger was implacable. He loaded his guns on Carmichael, charging that "Gil is a man of all-consuming ego with no vestige of humility." Mounger threatened to withhold his money-raising talents from Carmichael if the latter runs for the U.S. Senate in 1978.

I wrote this reply to Bill Minor's editor:

Mr. Ed Tunstall, Editor
The Times-Picayune
3800 Howard Avenue
New Orleans, Louisiana 70140

This letter is written in response to Mr. W. F. Minor's article (Sunday, April 18th) "GOP Factional Quarrel Deepens." I take umbrage with only one point in the article which is either an example of unmitigated ineptitude or a purposeful prevarication.

However, first, I would like to make a few general comments. Certainly, there is a minority in our Mississippi GOP which is considerably more liberal than Clarke Reed and myself; but this difference is good because it demonstrates a great deal of growth and expansion in our party and shows that we are not a monolithic entity with no room for differing opinions. The only votes in our State Convention which might demonstrate the conservative liberal strength in the Mississippi GOP were: the Alternate Participation-Unit Rule vote which was carried 161 to 62 (72%) and the Mounger vs. Carmichael vote which was two to one my way.

Second, I take great pride in calling myself a conservative and Mr. Minor compliments me when he says I am even more conservative than Clarke Reed. Of course, you must know that Mr. Minor is appraising the situation from the aspect of an ultraliberal. Once, in my presence, he expressed an opinion so radical that he had Hodding Carter, Jr. shaking his head in disbelief. Mr. Minor's opinion of my beliefs is proudly accepted by me; and, to put my opinion of him on record, *I believe that if Bill Minor moved one more millimeter to the left, he would topple over the inside of the Kremlin Wall.*

Now to the studiously misleading statement in the article. Mr. Minor said: "Even after Carmichael announced that he was personally voting for Mounger, Carmichael nearly won the spot." The vote was 31 for me and 17 for Carmichael with three of my avid supporters entering the room as the vote was counted. With their three votes, the margin would have been exactly two to one. How in any-one's reasonably fair-minded interpretation could the conclusion be drawn that Mr. Carmichael almost won? Obviously, that statement was made by either an incompetent reporter or one who consciously misstated the facts to serve his liberal proclivities.

Thank you for whatever response you care to give to this letter.

Very truly yours,
W. D. Mounger

WDM: pm
CC – Mr. W. F. Minor

A day later I supplied an April 20, 1976, addendum. The letter stated:

Mr. Minor refers to the Reed and Mounger ambivalent support of Carmichael and Nixon in 1972. Most assuredly, I backed both candidates. Even though I was Finance Chairman for the Committee to Re-Elect the President, my contribution to the Nixon campaign was only $1,000. In contrast, my individual contribution to the Carmichael senatorial campaign was $10,500 and I additionally raised in excess of 25% of all the money that Carmichael had to run that senatorial race. Yes, I will admit to ambivalence, but my support was considerably skewed to the Carmichael side. Therefore, the thrust of the Minor statement exuded his ultraliberal bias.

In another part of the article, Mr. Minor refers to me as "seeing a possible winner, put a good part of his money in the Carmichael race and raised more." Yes, I put $12,800 in the Carmichael race. Yes, I thought he had a chance to win. However, as I stated before, I put $10,500 in the 1972 Carmichael senatorial race and I knew he had no chance of winning. Mr. Minor's implication that my motivation was solely to back a winner is contrary to the facts; and once again, demonstrates his lack of desire or inability to dig out the facts for fear they might refute the preconceived conclusion that he propounds in his "so-called news article."

I told Gil later to his face, "Gil, you knew exactly what was going on and you did the unpardonable. You do not run against me after everything I've done for you. You showed what sort of person you were. You and I are totally finished now. You will have to accept that." Gil's actions led me to make one of the more well-known and accurate quotes I have ever issued to a paper. When the *Jackson Daily News* asked me about the standoff with Gil and about why Gil would challenge me, I said: "Gil is a man of all-consuming ego with no vestige of humility."

The *Jackson Daily News* ran the article with this headline: "GOP Split Developing?" The April 12, 1976, article by staff writer Tom Eppes in full read:

A millionaire who ranks high in the Mississippi Republican leadership says his confrontation Saturday with Gil Carmichael, 1975 GOP gubernatorial hopeful, may cost the candidate his financial backing in any future campaign.

That support meant at least $200,000 for Carmichael last year, says wealthy contributor and fundraiser William D. Mounger, a Jackson oilman and banker.

The rift between Mounger and Carmichael developed at the state party convention when the former candidate's name was entered opposite Mounger for vice chairman of the state delegation to the Republican convention.

The post traditionally goes to the state party finance chairman, who is Mounger. He won the post in secret balloting, but he was angered by Carmichael's challenge.

State Sen. Charles Pickering of Laurel also was nominated for the post, but he withdrew his name from the ballot.

Widely recognized for his political fundraising expertise, Mounger has figured in the campaigns of U.S. Reps. Thad Cochran and Trent Lott of Mississippi and of Jackson City Commissioner Doug Shanks.

He said he also contributed heavily to Carmichael's 1972 bid for the U.S. Senate seat held by James O. Eastland and to U.S. Sen. Barry Goldwater's bid for the presidency in 1964.

"At this point, I almost cannot see a set of circumstances when I would support Gil," Mounger told the *Jackson Daily News* Sunday.

"But I'm old enough to know never to shut the door; something could come up," he said.

Contacted by telephone in Denver, Colorado, where he is attending a conference on federal transportation matters, Carmichael said "it was an accident" that he was nominated.

"Before I saw what was happening, it was too late," he said. "I'm just sick in my heart, because Billy (Mounger) is a real champion. I regret it happening."

Said Mounger, "You don't upset something that was a basic, traditional right. I would say that I have a reason to be angry."

The finance chairman said he contributed $12,800 to Carmichael's 1975 campaign. That was the largest single contribution made, he said.

Mounger said he raised $200,000 from others for the Carmichael gubernatorial bid and said his influence was important in another $200,000 raised by the GOP candidate's finance chairman, Victor Smith.

When the amount of those contributions was related to the delegates, he said, the delegation elected him vice chairman by a two-to-one margin over Carmichael.

Mounger said he also was upset with the challenge because:

—Contrary to orders from the Committee to Re-elect the President (CRP), he made a speech in favor of Carmichael for U.S. Senate and against Sen. Eastland at a 1972 rally for former Vice President Spiro Agnew. He said CRP backed Eastland.

—He relinquished his right to announce the votes of the Mississippi delegation at the 1972 national convention so that Carmichael could appear on national television while his campaign was in progress.

"There are some things you don't violate, your word, integrity, loyalty to your friends, that's what's important to me," Mounger said.

"Gil is a man of all-consuming ego with no vestige of humility," he said.

Clarke Reed, state party chairman before stepping down Saturday, was also critical of Carmichael, but he said Mounger's decision to withdraw backing for any future campaign would not be the death knell.

"It's the question of overall gratitude, relationships," he said. "If you react that way to one person, how will you react to someone else; that's the whole question."

Said Reed, "It turned off a whole lot of people. It looks like Gil doesn't think anything about these things."

"He's now gone into another platitude [sic] or something. He's not in the real world," Reed said.

Reed and Mounger have been key leaders of the Mississippi Republican Party since 1966. That year Reed was elected state chairman and Mounger became finance chairman and chairman of the Hinds County party.

Mounger first became politically active in GOP affairs as an organizer for Goldwater in 1964 in Mississippi.

He said he made a name for himself as a fundraiser when he surprised the national party leaders with the promise that he would raise $150,000 from Hinds County for the presidential campaign.

"They bet me a steak dinner, and I raised $160,000," he said. "From then on I've been fundraising."

Mounger estimated he has raised over $3 million in Mississippi for various politicians in 12 years.

He said he raised two-thirds of Cochran's campaign money in his first bid for Congress and three-fourths of Commissioner Shanks' funds.

The Trent Lott campaign was only a sidelight in past years with $2,000 and $3,000 contributions, he said. But he said he plans to become more involved in that effort this year.

Lott and Cochran could not be contacted late Sunday.[7]

Reed and Carmichael both had at me, only later to apologize with a note of innocence in their voices. Those types of things set the stage before the 1976 state delegation appeared at the Republican National Convention in Kansas City. A poor moral tone was established leading up to the 1976 Republican national convention, and it went downhill from there.

Each state delegate was to remain "uncommitted" until the final vote at the Kansas City national convention in August of 1976. Only a few Mississippi delegates were to work for either Ford or

Reagan, among them Shanks and myself. Even Reed, the party chairman, had said he would remain mum.

Our 1976 delegation consisted of the following at-large delegates: Clarke Reed of Greenville; William D. Mounger of Jackson; Lillian Todd of Jackson; Gil Carmichael of Meridian; Dene Pace of Corinth; Odell Tucker of Greenwood; Swan Yerger of Jackson; Victor Mavar of Biloxi; Bill Patrick and Jerry Gilbreath of Laurel; Toxey Hall Smith of Wiggins; C.P. Ball of Starkville; and Dewey Lane of Pascagoula. District caucuses had further selected: Clyde Whitaker of Tupelo; Miki Cassidy of Quitman; Malcolm Mabry of Dublin; Roland Byrd of Louisville; Gloria Beale of Mound Bayou; Mike Retzer of Greenville; Ed Carruth of Carthage; Ann Tindal of Macon; Jack Lee of Union; Bill Dease of Jackson; Jan Rasch of Vicksburg; Gail Healy of Natchez; Charles Pickering of Laurel; Bobbie Thomas of Long Beach; and Tom Anderson of Pascagoula.[8]

Keeping all of our delegates quiet about whom they favored— Ford or Reagan—heading into the Kansas City convention was our strategy to help us deliver an uncommitted bloc of thirty votes at the convention that could swing the national party's nomination and amplify our state's influence, as it had at the Miami presidential conventions in 1968 and 1972. Our national committeewoman and Reagan's women's chairman on the delegation, Lillian Todd, who later reneged on me by voting against Ronald Reagan, told the *Jackson Daily News* on April 12, 1976, that keeping the unit rule was very important, stating she was "in favor of using our 1.3 percent of power at the convention."[9]

Our state convention in the summer of 1976 adopted a solid conservative platform. However, no presidential preference vote was taken of state convention attendees. Such a vote would have made it pellucidly clear to delegates how they should cast their votes at the national convention. We did, however, take a voice vote that strongly favored Reagan over Ford; it could not be called absolutely definitive, however, since it was not tallied. An actual count at the Mississippi GOP convention would have shown Reagan's original strength. I could have used it to help bring delegates into line later when things broke down in Kansas City. It would have established that the Mississippi delegation to the national convention was strongly for Reagan with the vote likely being three to one. I bollixed that situation by not insisting on an actual vote of state delegates to indicate outright their public support for Reagan.

The *Jackson Daily News* reported on April 12, 1976, that we as a delegation were on the record with our intent to keep the unit rule. "State Sen. Charles Pickering of Laurel said Sunday he felt the delegation would follow the decision of the state convention and go to the convention uncommitted. 'I think it's highly unlikely they would decide to support any candidate before the convention.'" The article further stated:

The convention also voted 161–62 to direct the delegation to vote as a bloc. The vote came despite arguments the unit rule is against party regulations and would deny delegates the right of individual choice.

"The national party will not enforce it (the unit rule)," Pickering said. "It was voted by the convention so it kind of imposes a gentleman's agreement on them (the delegates). If someone didn't want to abide by it they couldn't force them."

. . . Party leaders contended the unit rule debate was not a Ford-Reagan contest, but the candidates' state chairmen split on the issue.

Ford's campaign manager, Doug Shanks of Jackson, opposed the rule saying it was unenforceable. W. D. Mounger of Jackson, Reagan's manager, argued it could increase the state's political clout.

At no point in the convention were individual delegates asked their presidential preference.

Mississippi Republicans traditionally go to the convention uncommitted. Party leaders say delegate selection has been a reward for party service and is unrelated to a delegate's presidential candidate preference.

While a voice vote of the delegates seemed to favor Reagan, Reed said there is a long time before the national convention and votes could shift back and forth.[10]

That voice vote was important to me. I presumed that it made clear the state convention's strong leanings for Reagan. I also assumed that all our delegates understood and endorsed the obligations of a voluntary unit rule. This had been the state party's routine since 1960. I was surprised when Doug Shanks irritated us at the state convention by standing and speaking against the unit rule; that required me to stand and speak for it. The unit rule passed 161 to 62 at the state convention delegates, but the question of keeping the unit rule had publicly surfaced, and only just begun. Shanks, a newcomer to the party, started saying publicly that he was going to break the unit rule, and later Gil Carmichael did likewise. That indicated a lack of integrity, since they had just accepted the unit-rule conditions at the state convention.

This was only the beginning!

CHAPTER 17

Summer 1976: Mississippi Skirmishes Grow Hot

After the Mississippi delegation had settled down, I spent late May and early June in California with a special tennis instructor for my son, Bobby, who had been ranked fifth in the nation as a twelve-year-old. I returned with several weeks to work on the delegation, after which I spent three weeks running the USA Boys 16 National Clay Court Championships at River Hills Tennis Club in Jackson—a massive undertaking with 128 sixteen-year-old boys coming from all over the world. I had agreed to run this tournament for two years (1975 and 1976) to bring national sports acclaim to Jackson, and a teenaged John McEnroe won in 1975. These still are the only two national tennis championships ever held in the state of Mississippi.

I had told the Reagan people when I became chairman of the Mississippi Reagan campaign, "Now, look, there will be a period when I am going to be effectively comatose." That had been fine with Reed, David Keene, and the Reagan staff. While I was organizing and conducting the tennis tournament, Carmichael and Shanks were taking advantage of the unwatched Mississippi Reagan store. And at that time, President Ford, along with his wife, Betty, began making direct calls to members of the Mississippi delegation. If you had been a delegate in this Mississippi delegation attending a dinner party and the phone rang, you could almost have said, "That is probably the president of the United States or his wife calling," and it could easily have been true.

Ford even signed a note to me on his personal stationary, and I presume that he sent a similar note to all our state delegates. The note read:

April 30, 1976

Dear Billy,

Congratulations on your election as a delegate to the Republican National Convention from Mississippi. Although you are uncommitted at this time, I look forward to working with you in the challenging months ahead.

A GOP victory in November must be our common purpose, and I welcome any suggestions you may have which will help achieve that goal. Thank you for your continued support of the Republican cause.

Betty joins me in sending you our best wishes.

With warm regards,
(Personal signature of "Jerry Ford")

Mr. W. D. Mounger
Post Office Box 1200
Jackson, Mississippi 39205

Think about it: *A bunch of average Mississippians suddenly being courted by the president of the United States!* There had been no way to prepare for, or anticipate the efficacy of, those calls.

In a nonce, "uncommitted delegates" who were supposedly solid Reagan types were being promised great rewards to support the seated United States president.

Worse, however, were Clarke Reed's responses: the press were calling Clarke to investigate alleged rumors of shifts in the Mississippi delegation. We had not formally polled the delegation, and

Reed's negative statements were detrimental, throwing doubt on Reagan's support.

He implied that Ford's chances were rising. In turn, Harry Dent in President Ford's office released Reed's statements to key media; those statements, in turn, would be disseminated throughout the Northeast by Ford's public relations machine.

Dent hoped to use Reed's comments about Mississippi to preclude any serious pre-convention movement to Reagan. Indeed, Reed's comments effectively stalled any momentum to Reagan.

Clarke would call me on the telephone and say, "I think Reagan is weak. I just don't believe he's got the count. I think things are bleak." Behind Reed's words, I heard him equivocating that he had committed himself to Reagan and to me, but that now he feared that Ford could actually get the nomination, leaving him adrift.

I kept telling Reed, "Yes, Clarke, but the one thing we must keep in mind is, What do the people want, and what did we give our word to do?"

Reed would reply, "Oh, the people of Mississippi want Reagan. I don't care what happens, the one eventuality that cannot take place is for Mississippi to be perceived as the state that puts Reagan down—that sabotages Reagan."

Such an outcome had not even been conceivable for me up to this point.

In July during the tennis tournament, just three weeks before the Republican National Convention, could I—a West Pointer imbued with "duty, honor, country"—have believed that Mississippi Republicans would equivocate on Reagan?

Nevertheless, I could sense in Reed's phone calls and in his quotes to the press that something was amiss with Reed. When I was in Washington, D.C., on business in May, I visited David Keene at Reagan headquarters. "I can feel the point of Reed's dagger poised over the previous scar he left on my back," I informed Keene regarding Reed. This statement referred to his attempt to subvert my vice chairmanship of the delegation.

"Absolutely not!" Keene said. "There is no way Clarke Reed will abandon Reagan. I will never believe that Clarke Reed won't stay with us. His word is gold! He is absolutely an honorable man!"

"Well," I said, "Okay, if that's the way you feel, but Clarke Reed has darned well double-crossed me." Keene accompanied me to visit Reagan's campaign manager, John Sears, who iterated his belief that Clarke absolutely was a man of his word.

Keene and I did agree on one thing: No matter how much back-door campaigning Ford's people did prior to the national convention, there was no way that enough delegates could be swayed to turn the majority for Ford as long as Clarke Reed stayed firmly supportive of Reagan. "If Reed stays put," I told Keene, "There is no way the Mississippi delegation can go to Ford! No way!"

David Keene would later finger Clarke as the real problem behind the wishy-washy Mississippi 1976 delegation and as a contributing reason that Ronald Reagan picked Richard Schweiker as his vice presidential running mate. "Newsmen tended to focus on the angry reactions" by Reed and others to the Schweiker pick, stated Keene after the 1976 melee. "But as a matter of fact, if it hadn't been for the problems we had been having with Clarke Reed . . . *before the Schweiker decision*, (original emphasis) we might have taken an altogether different course."[1]

Keene continued: "Early in the campaign, Reed had personally indicated that he was with us, but refused to endorse Reagan publicly or deliver his delegation to us before the convention. I had urged him to do both in the spring while we were still ahead in most of the public delegate counts, but he told me then that, if he tried, a few Ford supporters on the delegation might get upset and break the unit rule. Therefore, if he were to try to bring out his delegates, he might only be able to deliver twenty-five or twenty-six and that, he assured us, would be viewed in the press as a victory for Ford, not Reagan. He was right, of course, since most people were assuming that we would receive all thirty of Mississippi's votes."

Keene further wrote about Reed in an article in *The Alternative*:

"Let me do it my way," he [Reed] said, "and I'll get you at least 28 and possibly all 30." . . . [Campaign manager John] Sears had only one question. He wanted to know if I thought Reed would in fact deliver for us later on. I remember hesitating for a few seconds, but I told him that I thought we could count on him. He had given us his word and I didn't think he'd break it.

My assurances were good enough for Sears. He told me to get back to Reed and tell him that we would be counting on him and that he could handle things his own way. I did just that, but added that we were both on the line. He because he had given his word and me because I had backed him up. He told me that he understood and that I had nothing to worry about.

Reed knew exactly what I was talking about when I said we were both on the line. He knew I would be taking some heat within the Reagan organization for backing him up—for trusting him. . . . Reed had made a personal commitment, and I was convinced that he would stick.

The reality was that Reed had told David Keene *and* me that we could count on him to stay with Ronald Reagan. And even more importantly, Clarke Reed had told Ronald Reagan the same thing. Reed had committed to the three key men that he would vote for Ronald Reagan and that he would help deliver the Mississippi delegation to Reagan.

Clarke Reed aside, I should have totally zeroed in on Reagan's nomination the whole time leading up to the August 1976 convention. But I was still confident that the delegation was in good shape. And, at that point, it was. All Clarke Reed had to do was be honorable; if he were, then the other delegates would not have deviated. However, Clarke's negative statements increasingly concerned me during the pre-convention weeks and days.

I told Clarke, "You are supposed to be for Reagan, but those statements you are making to the media sound like pro-Ford statements."

David Keene offers more in his *Alternative* article regarding that tumultuous summer:

The resources of the White House could prove unbeatable in such a contest and the President's people knew it. They began inviting delegates to the White House to see *their* (original emphasis) President, to talk to Cabinet officers about pet projects and to impress upon them the majesty of the *Office* (original emphasis) they were being asked to support. And they were beginning, by mid-July, to pull some of our own people as well as a number of the uncommitted. For the first time since March, we were on the defensive.

Clarke Reed realized about this time that if we didn't do something soon, we were going to lose—and the prospect of being on the losing side made him neither comfortable nor happy. We knew this and so did Clarke's old friend, Harry Dent, a former Nixon operative from South Carolina, now working virtually full time in the South for the President. Dent spent a good deal of time during this period badgering Reed about how it felt to be backing a loser. It didn't feel very good and Reed began to show it—publicly. He knew he couldn't just break his private commitment to us—at least, not without a good reason—but he began to move as far away from us as possible. He started telling reporters that our count was no good, that although he was leaning our way he fully expected Ford to win and, worse, that he wouldn't be at all surprised if his own delegation went for Ford.

This was devastating stuff. . . . One has to know Clarke Reed pretty well to understand him most of the time, but the message coming across didn't need much interpretation—Reagan was slipping badly in the South. . . .

As soon as he [Dent] finished one of his calls to Reed, Dent would call delegates in other Southern states with the corollary: Reed is about to jump so you'd better move first before it's all over and your vote doesn't matter.

The tactic hadn't worked by early July, but there were signs that our support was getting softer by the day. And the delegates we were talking to in other parts of the country began to use Clarke Reed and our weakness in the South as an excuse to stay away from us.[2]

Ford supporters including Gil Carmichael were calling delegates and falsely telling them that the majority of the delegation was for Ford. The Meridian politician was telling delegates that each of their votes was the key vote to deliver the delegation to Ford. Carmichael said, "I've been calling around and I have thirty delegates and alternates. All we need is one more vote." He interjected Clarke's statements, saying, "Clarke is saying that Reagan may not make it."

One other matter inordinately confused the Mississippi delegate count: alternate delegates were included as part of the Mississippi delegation since the unit rule was put into place. Alternates enjoyed the privileges of real delegates, except for convention floor seating. This helped our young Republican Party in Mississippi build and encourage new leadership. The unit rule had worked in the past, but when it sprung leaks in Kansas City, the whole notion became a disaster.

Alternate delegates were being courted as actual voters by Carmichael and Shanks as a tactic to disrupt and compromise the unit rule system. Alternate delegates, being one-half of a full vote, could thus nullify a full delegate vote. The matter was very confusing to delegates, much less everyone else.

Meanwhile, Carmichael and Dent worked the delegates assiduously. Instead of convincing "uncommitted" delegates to change their allegiance, Carmichael first pitched that they express interest in a face-to-face meeting with President Ford. The idea was that if enough real and alternate delegates seemed interested (at least thirty plus one of the total of sixty) then President Ford would come to Mississippi, which would stampede the delegation to Ford. In addition, Dent and Carmichael were using every conceivable stratagem and promise to entice delegates to Ford.

Word spread that enough delegates had interest to warrant a visit by the president prior to the national convention, Clarke called me: "Look, man, Gil Carmichael is out stampeding the delegation," he said. "You've got to get over and do something about it."

"Clarke," I replied, "I told you I could not perform the Reagan state chairman job during the National Tennis Championship. You can't ask me to do it. I made it clear to Reagan and you. I'll get on it the first chance I get, but I cannot do anything on it now."

I had been working around the clock for two weeks setting up the Boys 16 National Clay Court Championships. It was the Sunday before the first matches, with 128 players from throughout the world arriving to compete.

"Oh," Reed replied, "it's terrible. You've got me in a terrible position."

"Well, Clarke," I said, "aren't you with Reagan?"

"Yeah, yeah."

"Well," I said, "if you're Reagan then it's time for you to do something for Reagan, rather than play this devious game that you've played. Keep the delegation in line and stave off this coup and shortstop the lies and distortions that Carmichael and Shanks are spouting."

So Reed called a delegation meeting for the ensuing Sunday. Meanwhile, after a jam-packed Monday and Tuesday of all-day tennis matches, I maneuvered some time on Wednesday and started calling. I could not use the WATS line in my office, but I phoned every delegate I could reach using a River Hills Club telephone. I reminded them that the state of Mississippi was strongly supporting Reagan and that delegates had their original obligations. I told them, "Don't be rattled and don't be persuaded that the delegation is moving to Ford." Also, starting on Thursday night, Wirt and Swan Yerger and I worked the phones continuously.

The tennis tournament was over on Saturday, and the delegation met Sunday, three weeks prior to the August national convention. The Reagan and Ford camps sent representatives to speak—David Keene for Reagan, and Harry Dent and Dick Cheney for Ford. Privately, Reed called Carmichael to halt his misrepresentations. Only about twelve delegates and alternates (a total of six Mississippi votes)—far shy of the thirty plus one needed—indicated they were leaning toward Ford when the dust settled from that meeting. I later learned that Tommy Giordano had approached Charles Pickering after the Sunday meeting, saying that he felt Ford was going to win the delegation and proposing that the two sidle to Ford and receive credit for the delegation coup. Carmichael told the national press that he had forty commitments for Ford. Tom Pettit with NBC (who interviewed me a number of times) told the other members of the press to listen to me because Gil Carmichael was "a pathological liar"!

Unbeknown to me, before our Sunday meeting, another decision of momentous proportions was taking place. John Sears had toyed with the idea of Reagan announcing his vice presidential running mate prior to the national convention, an unorthodox tactic. It was an attempt to gain some traction in the slippery northeastern United States. So, on the following day, Monday, Ronald Reagan announced as his vice presidential selection left-leaning United States Senator Richard Schweiker of Pennsylvania, an anathema to Mississippi conservatives.

Keene had informed Reed but not me; in fact, Keene had never directly communicated with me as the Reagan state chairman. He had communicated with Reed instead. He definitely should have told me about Schweiker. Keene later told me that Reed hadn't "taken any offense" to Schweiker; Reed, on the other hand, said that he didn't have time to judge the choice upon initially hearing the news from Keene. Clarke would continue pointing to the Schweiker nomination as his proverbial "last straw" reason for jumping to Ford. Poppycock! Reed had not objected when Ford announced his choice of the liberal Rockefeller as his vice president.

On the Monday morning after Sunday's delegate meeting, I began feeling better about where the Mississippi delegation stood. I had not been informed about the Schweiker choice. Keene had asked on Sunday night how I might feel if Reagan chose his running mate early—prior to the convention, where the nominee traditionally announces his choice. I had responded that it would be fine; "fine," however, for me was predicated on Reagan's earlier assurances to Mississippians that he would pick a running mate compatible with our views. Then I received a call on Monday morning from the Reagan campaign that Reagan had chosen Schweiker, a liberal. I called Keene, who confirmed the choice, stating it was made to try to reach out to some northeastern delegates, mainly from New Jersey, Pennsylvania, and Ohio. "Well," I said, "I just believe that's going to be very harmful to us."

I hung up the phone and immediately thought—"Clarke Reed is gone."

I knew right then that the situation was difficult.

Thad Cochran called and said, "Schweiker is just the worst thing you ever saw." Some key conservative leaders around the country also sounded off. My phone never quit ringing. It was a terrible day. I ended up calling together some trusted Reagan delegate supporters. This group included Haley Barbour, Swan Yerger, Doug McCurley, Tommy Giordano, Charles Pickering, and Clarke Reed.

The press—national and local—found out that this group was gathered at my house. My large yard on Old Canton Road soon swarmed with media. They kept trying to get to me, but Jan kept putting them off. Finally, Keith Glatzer, a Channel 3 reporter, knocked and I answered. Glatzer said, "We know you are meeting in there." He asked permission for all the press to camp out on our driveway; I said they could. "I don't want to put you out in the street. After we finish, anyone who wishes will have something to say to you."

Inside, Pickering and Barbour advocated sitting tight and letting everything settle for a few days; Reed began saying that he didn't see how he could remain with Reagan since he had said in the press "a hundred times" that Reagan must pick a compatible running mate; Tommy Giordano, of Brandon, chimed in, saying something like, "I can't desert my people over there in Brandon. There's no other thing we can do except to stay with Reagan." I was encouraged by Giordano's seeming rock-solid statement. Tergiversatingly, Giordano was already working the other side and Gail Healy later told me that he had, days prior to the Sunday caucus, tried to convince her to support Ford. That night I overheard him waffling to someone on the phone and I told him to make no more calls.

I couldn't count the times that Reed had said that the most devastating thing that could happen to Mississippi was to be perceived as the state that undermined Ronald Reagan's candidacy. Notwithstanding, I had felt for some time that Reed had been groping for a reason to switch to Ford. That night didn't help my confidence; each man took time to call delegates and encourage them to stand firm. Reed's calls were namby-pamby, negative, conversations. I finally told Swan Yerger to keep Reed off the phone. As the meeting wound down, I felt strongly about two things: 1) Reed was gone to Ford's side, and 2) President Gerald Ford, who had been reticent to come down to Mississippi, would now be visiting the Magnolia State.

Barbour, Pickering, and I told Reed: "Clarke, okay, we are convinced now that Ford is coming here on Friday. We want you to say nothing about your apostasy—*not one thing*—until Friday. We want you to promise us and give this situation time to clarify itself."

Reed vowed, "All right. All right. I am a loyal party man. I follow the good of the party and I promise you." Reed lasted about twenty-four hours. It really was no surprise by that point. He had broken his word on other commitments, and once a man breaks his word, his integrity is obliterated.

The meeting at my house ended, and we met the press. There was CBS's Bernie Goldberg, among others. Reed told the press he didn't know what he was going to do but that he had always opposed a Reagan running mate who was incompatible with Reagan's philosophy; I told the press—"I don't like Schweiker, but I am still with Reagan."

The combination of the choice of Schweiker and then-President Ford's announced visit one week later was proving to be devastating. All this was roiling my stomach. Ronald Reagan called me at home on the Tuesday night after the Schweiker announcement. "Billy," he said, "how are things going in Mississippi?" I was honest: "Governor, you just gave me yesterday the worst dose of Ex-Lax I've ever had in my life. You not only purged everything that you were supposed to get, but you eviscerated me. You got all of my guts. I am a hollow shell. That's what you did."

"Oh, I'm sorry that you feel like that," Reagan replied. "Let me tell you about why we did what we did." Reagan explained that Paul Laxalt, his campaign manager, vouched for Schweiker, who was Laxalt's seatmate in Congress; William F. Buckley, Jr., the founder of *The National Review*, also thought it was a good idea. Reagan said, "I am still true to my commitment to you. I don't have any problem there. Yes, his voting record hasn't been that good, but he agrees that government can't solve all problems and that he has seen the light."

Reagan said that, even with the problems in the Mississippi delegation, he believed his chances required greater measures to accumulate enough other delegates to win the nomination. We both knew how the Ford administration was fending off Reagan's efforts to pick up key northeastern delegates. Whenever one thought about moving to Reagan, Ford's people could promise government contracts; in one case, the brother-in-law of a delegate received a big architecture contract for a hospital. The sitting president had the power of incumbency that made it devastating for Reagan. He then told me: "We are just getting killed."

My telephone was constantly ringing. The in-doubt Mississippi delegation became the *cause célèbre* to the national press. It was national news that Mississippi might be going for Ford and that Clarke Reed had abandoned Reagan. By noon on Tuesday, Reed was calling me. "Oh man," he said, "I just can't stay. You've got to let me out of that commitment. I just can't stay. That Schweiker thing is just too terrible."

"Clarke, no!" I replied. "I'm not going to let you off. You committed. You said you were a team player." I did not know that Reed had attended a state dinner at the White House honoring Queen Elizabeth of England. The Ford people had for a while been pressing Reed hard. Reed was now using the Schweiker issue as his justification to squirm from Reagan to Ford. Keene saw this as well, writing in *The Alternative*:

> Clarke Reed finally had the excuse he needed to move. I had told him of the Schweiker selection on Sunday, July 25, and he had seemed to take it fairly well. But by Monday evening his attitude had changed.
>
> He called me at least a half dozen times during the next few days and I called just as often. Harry Dent was also calling. So was the President of the United States. And the former Governor of California. And virtually every political reporter in America.
>
> Reed couldn't take the pressure.[3]

Harry Dent was pressuring Reed to switch to Ford, and soon. Dent told Reed that he would be a kingmaker; he would pull other big-name people like Joseph Coors of Coors Brewing over from Reagan to Ford. The chance to lead a break away to victory seemed to prove immensely enticing to Reed. The Ford people pushed for Reed to switch to Ford before his arrival in Mississippi on Friday. Reed finally committed to Dent, the President, and Dick Cheney to announce his switch on Wednesday. Haley Barbour kept the written statement off of the six o'clock news; it hit at ten o'clock Wednesday night. The following is David Keene's memory of that fatal time:

He called me at home at 11:30 on Tuesday evening to inform me that he was going to endorse Ford the next morning. I told him he couldn't do it because he had given his word and because we were going to win.

"The conservatives are sticking with us," I told him, "and if you desert Reagan now you will be deserting them. You'll be seen as a sell-out and you won't have enough influence left after this thing is over to speak for anyone."

Reed wasn't buying, so I made one more try. I told him that regardless of how he felt about Reagan or Ford or Dick Schweiker, he owed me something and I wanted it—24 hours. I was playing for the time we needed to further solidify our Southern and right flanks. . . .

The Mississippian agreed. We had another 24 hours. Or so I thought. Before noon on Wednesday, Reed was back on the phone asking me to let him break his promise of the night before.

I told him that he shouldn't run around making promises he couldn't keep. "I know that," he replied, "But I've made other promises to other people."

That said it all. I knew which of the promises he felt he would have to break. For the first time I let my anger show. I told him to do what he had to do, but to spare me the rhetorical justification. I also told him that I would remember the value of his word.

Reed switched that [Wednesday] evening, telling a mutual friend that he really hadn't broken his final promise because he waited until after sundown. Not 24 hours, but a day anyway.

By moving to Ford, Reed had for the second time thrown an almost insurmountable roadblock in the way. . . .

I told someone after the whole thing was over that a tight political campaign is a little like a war in that it reveals an awful lot about the character of the combatants.

And character *is* (original emphasis) important.[4]

The news of Clarke's switch rocked delegates in Mississippi and delegates in the Northeast who were already shaky. Bernie Goldberg of CBS showed up in my office Tuesday morning and interviewed me both for the morning and evening news. Goldberg told me, "You are like *As the World Turns*; you are on TV twice a day." NBC and ABC followed. I didn't have time to watch TV, but I topped the news nationally. Goldberg interviewed me twice a day Tuesday through Friday—morning and night, for both the morning and evening CBS national news.[5]

Keene, who before Schweiker had spent almost all his time on the phone with Reed but none with me, was now practically living on my line. Ford's impending trip on Friday was forcing Reagan's hand. I was reacting as quickly as I could, extracting a commitment from Pickering and Barbour not to take a nomination straw vote of the delegation because of Friday's Ford visit; I warned that, if they did, I would have Reagan and Schweiker come on the same Friday at the same time as the president's visit. The Reagan campaign had given me carte blanche authority to have Reagan visit Mississippi whenever I desired. The Ford group could visualize both campaign planes circling the airport, trying to land simultaneously! And I told the Ford campaign not to hotbox the delegation on Friday, and they agreed. Then I told Keene to bring Reagan and Schweiker to Jackson the following Tuesday. "Whatever you say, we'll do," Keene's Reagan people said.

What a day of maneuvering!

CHAPTER 18

The Day the President Came to Town

A Republican president was coming to town and I, who had nourished Republicanism in Mississippi from almost its infancy, was not invited to greet him. It made me for the first time in many a year feel like an outcast. The Friday that Gerald Ford arrived, I was not invited to meet him at the airport.

Ford did meet with the delegation, including me, at the Ramada Inn next to the Mississippi Coliseum. He answered questions on key policy issues such as the Panama Canal, and he shook hands personally with each delegate. The president knew who I was when I shook his hand. I told him, "Well, if you get the nomination I'll support you and be with you." Ford replied, "Well, I know you will. It doesn't concern me that you won't. I appreciate that."

The meeting left me and others feeling that, while Ford had not answered sufficiently key questions including national defense, the Russians, and the Rockefellers, he nonetheless was a decent, attractive, friendly person. Delegates were snowed under by the press upon leaving the meeting. It had the feeling of a mini-convention. As had been previously agreed, there was no straw poll or any other visible evidence to indicate that any major shift in the delegate vote had occurred, except for Carmichael boasting about Ford's visit and speculating that the Mississippi delegation now was forty-strong for Ford (unprovable and patently untrue).

Preventing a Friday straw poll vote of the delegation was a key victory for me. After the president's visit, the delegation might have been stampeded. Tom Pettit of NBC interviewed me after Ford's visit, and I said that the delegation was up for grabs; and another reporter stated that Carmichael said Ford had a solid forty-five of the sixty delegates and alternate votes. I learned that Tommy Giordano had been calling delegates, proposing that they switch to Ford with him soon; and that he was subtly competing for Ford's kudos with Reed to see who could pull the most people. Giordano was lying to me in spades; it was like Napoleon asking, "Where is Marshall Ney?" at Waterloo, if Ney had deserted to the enemy. Lillian Todd also told me that she couldn't take Schweiker; this was a disappointment because I had helped her gain employment at Deposit Guaranty, had persuaded the bank to let her serve as a traveling Republican committeewoman and to subsidize her, and had engineered her election as our committeewoman. I disgustedly told Lillian, "Just promise me you will keep your mouth shut and that you'll not publicly say you're for Ford." She agreed, hinting that she may even still support Reagan.[1]

People who I thought were iron-tight were slipping away. Our delegates received the same letter that I received from the president, on White House stationary, after Ford's visit with us. My letter read as follows:

August 5, 1976

Dear Mr. Mounger,

Mrs. Ford and I appreciate the warm hospitality and friendly welcome we received during our visit to Jackson on July 30. We know that a great many people contributed their time and effort in planning for this event, and we are grateful for all that you did personally on this occasion.

With our thanks and best wishes,
(Personal signature of "Gerald R. Ford")

The press was constantly in my Jackson office. Reagan's headquarters was persistently calling and I was inundated with mail. I did not have a moment's peace. Although "lieutenants" like Giordano were shifting, I found solace in the support of Victor Mavar from the coast, along with Charles Pickering and Swan Yerger, together with his nondelegate brother, Wirt. We made calls to delegates around the state, many of whom were being promised personal perks in their businesses or relatives' businesses by Ford's team. We could only counter with, "Reagan is the right person who is conservative and compatible with the people of Mississippi."

I was growing severely weary, a fatigue caused by weeks of sleepless nights, running the tennis tournament, and a frenzy of press. It was very debilitating and I was finding it hard to think clearly and to manage the immediacies of the dire decisions I needed to make; and Kansas City was still ahead.

Days passed hectically and I scheduled Reagan and Schweiker to meet the delegation on the Tuesday after Ford's Friday visit. When I went to meet Schweiker in the airport's commercial arrival area, the press surrounded me; however, Schweiker was diverted to the Delta Airlines freight terminal, leaving me joking and laughing with the press. I made my way there to meet with Schweiker and his wife, who were waiting in the freight terminal. Bert Case of WLBT, Jackson's NBC affiliate, approached me, cameras and lights blaring: "Billy, is there something significant about this? I guess this is an example of how y'all feel about Schweiker. Is it symbolic where you are meeting him?"

"Yes," I joked, "I guess it is symbolic that we're meeting him here at the Delta freight terminal, because there are certainly a lot of people, myself included, who consider him excess baggage!"

Inside the freight terminal, Charles Pickering and I met Schweiker and his wife, Carol, and I wasted no time. "Senator, before we talk about anything else, I want to tell you that you offer me a problem worse than normal."

I continued: "Your total voting record is not what we would desire at all. Additionally, I am the main person in Mississippi who is responsible for national oil-and-gas legislation. I have often visited

Washington to work on oil-and-gas problems, and you have voted 100 percent against everything that I have ever tried to accomplish for it. Your situation is especially exacerbated with me."

Schweiker started to say something such as, "Oh, well, I represent a consumer state and I have all of these consumers. . . ."

"Now, wait a minute!" I said. "I haven't time to get into a debate with you. Obviously you don't understand the picture at all. It is your vote, and those who vote like you, which has brought on a shortage of natural gas and other fuel, which has undermined the free enterprise system. And now let us change the subject, because we haven't enough time to debate it."[2] [I also told Schweiker that, someday, there would be an obvious energy shortage and then Schweiker would understand. The next winter Pennsylvania suffered badly from a shortage of natural gas.]

Reagan flew in from California a few minutes later. It was the first time that he and Schweiker made a joint appearance after Schweiker was chosen as his vice presidential nominee. I boarded Reagan's plane with Schweiker and we conferred about strategy, then drove to the Ramada Inn. The Mississippi delegation awaited us, and some of the Ford delegates prodded Reagan and Schweiker with questions provided by Ford's staff.

Schweiker handled himself surprisingly well, as did his wife. But he could not pull off a miracle, as hoped. I then arranged for Reagan and Schweiker to meet with key delegates one-on-one after the main session. Clarke Reed perforce had not been invited. He had cast his lot on Wednesday before the Ford meeting, proving his apostasy. All around the country, people such as Joe Coors and Roger Milliken had jumped vertically, as I had, and every single one of us had landed right back in our previous Reagan shoes, except for Reed, who was the only committed Reaganite who moved laterally.

Reagan and Schweiker's visit probably helped maintain the status quo, not unlike Ford's visit. Schweiker admitted that he had a bad voting record on key issues and that he was rethinking his political proclivities.

The media called Wednesday night for my reaction to news that Tommy Giordano and Tupelo mayor Clyde Whitaker, (who was promised an appointment to the Tennessee Valley Authority Commission) had defected to the Ford camp. That news undermined the effect of Reagan and Schweiker's Tuesday visit; nonetheless, no one except Carmichael was denying the vote of the delegation was not a close proposition.

CHAPTER 19

The 1976 Convention: Mid-Political Life Collapse at Kansas City

At least two things had proven true, given all the pre-convention squabble over Schweiker: 1) Reagan's naming of Schweiker as his vice presidential candidate stopped any major defection of northeastern delegates over to the Ford camp and had kept Reagan's ticket to Kansas City alive, but 2) Reagan's hope that Mississippi's hard-core support would win him the Magnolia State was undermined by the Schweiker incident.

Every Mississippi delegate except the two presidential chairmen—Shanks for Ford and myself for Reagan—were supposed to be uncommitted, keeping silent until the voting day at the national convention. There was to be no public talk, in theory, about how delegates were voting prior to the convention. Theory had been smashed, however, and the only delegates who seemed willing to stay mute on their votes were the Reagan backers—people of honor who remained faithful to the unit rule system and stayed quiet, as in years past. A new breed of delegate in Mississippi had emerged, however, willing to talk and to consider breaking unit rule. Clarke Reed had spoken so negatively to the press that he had helped Harry Dent and his Ford team unravel many well-intentioned people around the country; the press, like a laughing flock of crows, had flown to Mississippi to help capture those delegates lacking equilibrium. As the campaign neared time to travel to Kansas City, NBC's Tom Pettit asked me to suggest the name of an "uncommitted" Mississippi delegate whom he could interview and also conduct follow-up interviews through Kansas City. I recommended Gail Healy, and Pettit later profusely thanked me. She was an example to the nation of how the "uncommitted delegate" system was supposed to have worked. She was terribly mad at Clarke for breaking his word and for committing to Ford when he was the chairman of the delegation and had been instructed to maintain an uncommitted delegation until the final moment. On the final vote, she laudably voted Reagan!

Reagan had figured correctly that many in the Mississippi delegation wanted to stay with him and to help him; however, the problem was that the Mississippi delegates wanting the most to help Reagan were the most committed to the principle of staying passionately "uncommitted" until the national convention floor vote. That, of course, meant they couldn't, or wouldn't, publicly recruit delegates, unlike Carmichael and others who broke traditional protocol to do so. An uncommitted delegate cannot proselytize. How can you sell somebody else when you're not publicly identified and committed?

The Mississippi delegation arrived at our Independence, Missouri, Ramada Inn, immediately before the Sunday start of the convention. Those of us in leadership had gone a few days earlier. Crews from NBC, ABC, and CBS, greeted us, along with writers from the *New York Times*, *Washington Post*, and *Los Angeles Times*—all assigned to cover us throughout the convention. The press and the Ford team well out-numbered Reagan's, and our delegates were surrounded constantly by them, even on the national convention floor. Ford had in excess of one-hundred floor passes for his people to work the delegates. Reagan only had fourteen floor passes. Most of Ford's people proselytized the Mississippi delegation! And poor Reagan only had fourteen passes to work the entire convention floor.

The convention sentiment was for Reagan, but too many delegates had previously committed for sentiment to prevail. It was obvious that the platform was a conservative Reagan one, which

Charles Pickering had helped to write and which demonstrated that generally the delegates were inclined toward Reagan conservatism.

I had decided to cease any more calls to delegates by the Tuesday prior to the convention. I had tried every angle, fearing that any more calls might hurt, not help. I, therefore, had arrived at the pre-convention commotion on Wednesday, attending the Southern Chairmen's meeting, where I saw Clarke Reed. It was just like being around a stranger.

Ford's southern campaign organizer, Harry Dent, sneaked up behind me in the Muehlbach Hotel's entranceway and cracked, "Schweiker!"

"Kissinger!" I shot back.

We both laughed—knowing that as much as Schweiker had hurt Reagan, Kissinger was an albatross to Ford. I remained outside the room as the Southern Chairmen's meeting was held, knowing that I was no longer Reed's ally. I sat with CBS newsman Mike Wallace, chatting for about an hour; Wallace seemed very much personally for Reagan. Both Wallace and Robert Novak told me that the only Republican capable of winning the presidency was Reagan.

Meanwhile, the Reagan headquarters was in high gear. I went there, but decided I was most needed with the Mississippi delegation if there was to be any hope of winning key votes. "What is your delegation count?" asked David Keene, Reagan's southern campaign organizer.

"David, I've got twenty-eight for Reagan and I don't have many other possibilities. There are four or five I have a chance to get."

"What can we do?" Keene asked.

"Pray!" I said. That comment was overheard by the *Wall Street Journal*'s Al Hunt and ended up in a *Wall Street Journal* article.

Pat Boone led a host of Hollywood notables who met with the Mississippi delegation to speak for Reagan. Boone said that Reagan was a fine Christian and Boone made a religious-like plea for him. The Reagan headquarters, however, had its own plan for trying to win the nomination—it proposed a convention rule designated "16-C." They wanted state Reagan chairmen to persuade their delegates to vote for proposition 16-C. I thought, "How can I get a count on 16-C when I can't get a damn count on Reagan?"

The 16-C rule proposal that the Reagan camp espoused would have required the presidential candidates to name their vice presidential choices before the actual presidential nominee had been chosen at the convention. Reagan already had named his—Schweiker. The Reagan team strategy was to make Ford specify his vice presidential running mate with the idea that, if he did, this would keep Ford from appealing to other states' delegations whose favorite sons, such as Howard Baker of Tennessee, were being dangled as possible vice presidential running mates. In other words, it would have possibly loosened the log-jammed river of the presidential nomination contest. Perhaps then, Reagan's people could have persuaded some disaffected delegates from those states that were snubbed.

I thought, however, that all the talk regarding 16-C didn't apply to Mississippi. Whatever they were saying in the Reagan strategy sessions didn't apply in our unique position, or so I assumed. I did not, therefore, pay sufficient attention to it. Proposition 16-C, however, became the deciding vote on whether Reagan would have a chance to win the nomination.

I knew for sure that Reagan faced an uphill battle after the 16-C vote was taken. The Mississippi delegation voted 31-28 against 16-C. I lost one of my previously predicted Reagan delegates, Rev. Baker, and Charles Pickering failed to deliver his incoming party executive director, John Simms. Clarke voted with me only after there was no chance for 16-C to win; he was trying to assuage his undermining of the Reagan cause.

The defection of Rev. Baker on this vote epitomizes the vicious battle for Reagan delegates. A so-called minister from the Rankin County black community, his selection was engineered by Tommy Giordano, who was at the time the Reagan chairman for the Third Congressional District. Giordano's treacherous shift to Ford made it obvious that he would pressure the reverend to join him; and I desperately needed Baker's vote. I was on the board of directors of the Rankin County Bank at the time, and two of my co-directors—Irl Dean Rhodes and Long John McLaurin—were the most powerful Democrat politicos in the county, effectively controlling it. I asked their assistance (they were strongly pro-Reagan), and they delivered in spades by informing Baker that he had better not return to Rankin County if he did not support Reagan.

When Baker arrived in Independence on Sunday, he immediately informed me that "Mr. Irl Dean and Mr. Long John have told me what to do," and he said he would vote for Reagan. His vote made twenty-eight for Reagan. Ex-New Hampshire governor Meldrum Thompson, who was monitoring our delegation for Reagan, on Monday informed me that one of the delegates was being threatened with his life and viciously berated. Immediately, I knew that it was Rev. Baker. Giordano and John Rushing, a Jackson contractor—both burly—kept him incommunicado. The next time I saw Baker was during the delegation vote on 16-C when the standing vote was taken. Baker was lifted to his feet with Giordano and Rushing holding each of his arms. The count would have been 30–29 with Baker's vote, not a majority, which would have negated the unit rule. Then with only full delegates voting on 16-C, the convention floor vote would have been 16–14 in favor of 16-C. Reed would have reversed his vote, however, in order to keep the Ford margin safe at 31–28. To compound the issue, if Pickering had delivered Simms's vote, it would have been 30–29, again, not a majority. *C'est la Guerre!*

After the meeting I was approached by Tommy Giordano and Doug Shanks. "I don't have anything to talk to you about," I said.

"Well, we just need to talk," they said.

Victor Mavar and I, with misgivings, agreed to meet. Giordano and Shanks wanted to compromise the unit rule and allow the delegation to vote proportionately on the nomination. I felt that for Reagan to win, he had to carry all of Mississippi's votes. I told them that I needed all thirty by unit rule. They could have any number of votes and be equally happy, but I felt that we in the Reagan camp had to win them all—thirty or bust.

Frustration was building. At the meeting, I told Shanks: "You are a fool because regardless of who wins this fight, you have lost! There is no way you can come out ahead. You're on the wrong side of the majority. Even if Ford wins, you have alienated the vast majority of your voters in Hinds County, and if Ford loses you are in real trouble. If Reagan loses, I will just play more golf—my life will not be altered—but you have gained my enmity and you will pay a price for that." I also stated that Ford could not win the general election, even if nominated.

David Keene came to see me early Tuesday.

"What's your count on 16-C?" Keene asked.

"Hell, David, I don't know."

"You don't know? Well we've got to know!"

"Damn," I said, "how can I tell you? I can't tell you how this delegation is going to vote between Reagan and Ford. How in the hell am I going to tell you how it is going to vote on 16-C?" After this exchange, Victor Mavar, Swan Yerger, and I belatedly promoted 16-C to our delegates.

Keene was focusing on the Reagan 16-C strategy that would play out in a vote on Tuesday night. I had my sights set on Wednesday night and the delegate vote on the nomination. Meanwhile, another move had arisen in the Mississippi delegation—some were pushing on Tuesday after 16-C for the delegation to voluntarily vote on Wednesday to end unit rule and allow everyone to vote on a proportionate basis. I opposed it. Reagan needed all thirty. Others argued to allow both the delegates and alternates to vote—a total of sixty votes; then, if the vote was thirty-two, twenty-eight, the vote could be proportioned down to sixteen/fourteen, etc.

We in Mississippi were infighting terribly. I missed the Tuesday morning all-or-nothing strategy Reagan's staff had hatched on the 16-C proposal. Unfortunately, the vote became its own referendum—or straw poll—on Tuesday night of how each state delegation would vote on Ford/Reagan. But David Keene never told me, "Look, go all out to get the darn thirty votes tonight (Tuesday)! If you don't get the thirty votes, get whatever you can. Because if you lose it 30–0 tonight, tomorrow is down the drain."

I still did not really understand the true significance when the Mississippi delegation gathered under the unit rule for the delegates to determine Mississippi's vote on 16-C. This was on Tuesday afternoon, before the actual convention-wide vote of each state would be cast on Tuesday night. I told the delegation that, as far as I was concerned, "This is not a Reagan-Ford thing." In hindsight, I didn't make a sufficiently strong pitch for it. It's one of those *maybes* that you have to live with the rest of your life—if I had made one of my impassioned Baptist preacher-type speeches and had reminded Lillian Todd, Clarke Reed, and others of their extant due bills and had appealed to them not to be dishonorable—I don't know.

When the 16-C vote came, it was twenty-eight for 16-C, thirty-one against. Since unit rule was still in effect, all thirty delegate votes from Mississippi were to be cast against 16-C. Realistically, the actual idea of 16-C stinks and was a rotten issue. It had no idealistic content. Yet I should have still battled harder to win 16-C. Earlier, Haley Barbour had told me, "Look Mr. Mounger, they've got you in a bind. The thing isn't any good. You know it's really and truly not fair."

In retrospect, if we had voted our delegation for the 16-C, and had the message been disseminated to other states' delegates regarding Mississippi's support for 16-C, our vote could have been decisive. Even if Reagan had gotten a majority on the Mississippi delegation's 16-C vote, Carmichael, Shanks, Giordano, et al, would have broken the unit rule when it was time to cast our vote that night at the convention, and Reagan would have gotten somewhat less than thirty votes. With the dishonorable, it was "heads I win, tails you lose."

At the time, I did not understand that the 16-C issue had disemboweled Reagan's chances in the Mississippi delegation and in the convention. For all the anxiety I had endured, Clarke Reed was almost a zombie. He was a shell of a human being. Reed sat among the delegation on the convention floor just dormant, sighing. It was deflation, not elation.

Finally, Tuesday night arrived, when Mississippi would announce its tally from our afternoon unit rule vote on the convention floor. Before that floor vote on 16-C, Swan Yerger, Victor Mavar, and I met on the periphery of the convention floor to plot a strategy for somehow still salvaging the final Mississippi nomination vote for Reagan on the following night. We knew we needed five additional votes. Suddenly a CBS reporter approached us—"Clarke Reed has just shifted from Ford back to Reagan!"

We were stunned. We looked over and noticed what seemed to be a Mount Everest—a pile of reporters and bodies swamping Reed. I knew that if Reed had shifted, it would change things. So I pushed and prodded my way into the pile, calling out to Reed, "What's happening? What's happening?" He was uncommunicative.

Reed had been shown an Alabama newspaper that quoted Ford advisors stating that they had written off the South, which had prompted Reed to say to CBS that, if true, he was switching back to Reagan from Ford. The comment was like a match to gasoline. Press erupted everywhere. Ford's people started calling and trying to calm key delegates; Reagan's people dove into the melee, trying to make hay. Press, delegates, and others swamped me with quick questions for which I had no ready answers; I was still trying to communicate with Reed. He was sitting there among the media, in an absolute trance. Finally, Haley Barbour called for all the Mississippi delegates to have a meeting.

Ford's Mississippi representatives feared a new caucus vote and immediately bellowed, "Don't go! Don't go!" But Barbour was careful in his words—this was only a meeting to get to the bottom of Reed's statements, and I agreed. Delegates were scurrying into the hallways and could find no privacy from the media; finally, someone suggested going into the CBS trailer parked immediately outside the hallway.

It was embarrassing. A large number of delegates and alternates entered the CBS trailer where we met CBS reporter Mike Wallace, who refused to leave. "You can't throw me out, I'm not going to leave," Wallace was saying. Somehow, Victor Mavar contacted a key CBS official who told Wallace to let the Mississippi delegation have their privacy. Soon after, Reed entered the trailer, shadowed by Bill Wilkins, whom he had enticed back to help him. And Wilkins was buffering Reed to stay with Ford.

I felt a measure of relief. "Now we'll find out what the score is," I thought, turning to Reed and saying, "Clarke, okay now tell us—please tell us—what has happened and what is going on?"

The look Reed gave the delegation is etched in my mind. He just kind of gazed around and then left. He did not utter a word! We were stupefied. Here we've conducted this rigmarole with all of the national TV audience watching the Mississippi rabble going into the CBS trailer. And now, the leader of the delegation, the state chairman, said nothing—*nada!*

Our entourage was left groping for direction. In just minutes we were to take the national convention floor to cast our votes on 16-C. Some Reagan backers now were threatening to break the unit rule. One of them was Sam Alford, supervisor chairman in Pike County, who was mad about the actions of some Ford backers, particularly Shanks and Carmichael, who had never intended to honor unit rule. Alford felt that Reagan's people should be allowed to cast their unfettered votes for 16-C. I understood his sentiment. But undoubtedly, because of my West Point notion of absolute honor, I knew that we had to keep our commitment. Keene had acquiesced that it was my call.

The moment spread like a pall over many in the Mississippi delegation. Their vote would probably condemn Reagan's chance.

Clarke and I had walked onto the convention floor earlier that evening and I figured I might as well give it one last shot. "Clarke, you know that you told me that you would do anything I ever wanted you to do. Now is the time that I'm calling on you. I want your vote."

Reed replied, "I just can't do it. I just can't do it."

We reentered the convention floor from the CBS trailer with cameras rolling. All of us were somewhat dumbfounded. Clarke Reed had promised that I would control the microphone as a partial payback for his earlier attempt to sell out my vice chairmanship of the delegation. Consequently, I put the onus on Reed to cast Mississippi's abominable thirty votes against 16-C. The states moved in alphabetical order, announcing their vote tallies, and I reasoned that the best move for Mississippi would be to pass for two reasons: 1) if the vote total were to cinch against 16-C before Mississippi voted, it would perhaps ameliorate the impression among constituents at home that our delegation had sabotaged Reagan; and, 2) the pressure on those Reagan backers who still wanted to break unit rule would be alleviated.

When the spotlight and cameras focused on Mississippi, Clarke was feeling heat from two sides—Tommy Giordano and Doug Shanks were urging him to announce the vote, hoping to win points for Mississippi with Ford; I was vociferously pressuring Reed to pass.

"Mississippi passes," Reed said.

A massive groan filled the convention hall.

The nation had waited with bated breath for a decisive word from Mississippi's delegation, and we had passed. Florida cinched the failure of 16-C on the second time around, thereby killing Reagan's hopes of beating Ford. Clarke Reed finally announced the 30-0 Mississippi vote against the rule, and the convention hall again erupted. Mississippi officially was now indirectly on record for Ford. I most remember in that moment the eyes of Dick Obenshain, Virginia's state party chairman. Virginia, along with Mississippi, were considered avant-garde leaders in the new conservative push for smaller government; Virginia was Reagan country. Dick and Clarke had been good friends. Now, Obenshain tossed a thick sheaf of papers to the floor and stared at Reed with venom in his eyes. Obenshain was state chairman of Virginia and very attractive; he was later killed in an airplane crash while campaigning for governor of Virginia.

If there were ever abhorrence in a person's eyes, it was in Obenshain's.

I was almost devoid of feeling.[1]

John Hart interviewed me for NBC after those momentous proceedings, as did Mike Wallace for CBS; Sylvia Chase of ABC also wanted an interview, which I delegated to Swan Yerger. In both of these interviews, I stated that the delegation the next night would in all probability option for a proportional vote, which would be sixteen for Ford and fourteen for Reagan.

Charles Pickering approached me on Wednesday morning, concerned that, as incoming party chairman, he would return home to a state party in shambles. "Look, let's go ahead and work this thing out and do it proportionately, just let the votes fall out," Charles said. Reluctantly, I acquiesced, not wanting to shackle Pickering with such an onus back home. There was not any sense in trying to be Don Quixote about the unit rule issue. You get tired of being whopped on the head by the windmill blades. I wouldn't have minded forcing the apostates to cast a 30-0 vote against Ronald Reagan, against the sentiments of the vast majority of the party and of the people of Mississippi. I truly felt that Reed, Shanks, Carmichael, and their confederates had made their bed and they should lie in it. Get full credit or full discredit. The Mississippi voters probably would have dismembered them.

I again designated Clarke to cast our abhorrent Mississippi vote when Wednesday night arrived. This vote was the actual Ford-Reagan vote for the presidential nomination. The Mississippi vote, after the loss of 16-C, was not the crucial vote in determining who got the presidential nomination. We Mississippians cast our vote proportionally at Pickering's request, and it was 16–14 in favor of Ford. The final convention vote tally of every state gave Reagan one more vote and Ford seven more votes than the total tally on the 16-C vote. The total national tally on 16-C was 1180 for Ford to 1069 for Reagan. Now, the final national tally on the presidential nomination was 1187 for Ford to 1070 for Reagan.

After this anticlimactic Wednesday night presidential vote to nominate Ford, the biggest news around Kansas City was the grass-roots campaign promoting Reagan as Ford's vice presidential running mate. A vast wave of sentiment for Reagan rumbled through each state's convention delegates.

A draft-Reagan campaign was instigated that night by Paula Hawkins of Florida, that state's national committeewoman and later a U.S. senator. She worked all night, galvanizing a broad, majority spectrum of delegates to draft Reagan for the vice presidential post. Some believe that Reagan would have declined, but I believe that he would have accepted. All Ford had to say was, "I would like to let the convention decide," and Reagan would have been the vice presidential nominee.

I must state that there were two occasions during the convention when I almost reverted to my fisticuff days. The first was with Carmichael after he had *ad infinitum* pushed a Ford/Reagan ticket to entice Reaganites to support Ford before the convention, and to do so during it. Carmichael sorely vexed me, and I told Giordano and Victor Mavar, "I've had enough of Ford/Reagan. If Carmichael opens his mouth one more time, you will have to restrain me. I am ready to assault him. You had better keep him quiet!" Subsequently, Victor Mavar firmly related to Carmichael, "Gil, I want to tell you to shut up!"

The second occurred in the Mississippi area on the convention floor where Harry Dent was continuously lurking, shoring up

Clarke Reed and generally working the delegation. I forcefully told him, "You are not from Mississippi! So get away from here, or I am going to get physical." He could tell I was severely irritated, and thereafter kept his distance.

At an early Thursday morning caucus, the Mississippi delegation unanimously voted to support the draft-Reagan initiative. Pickering, Reed, and I went to Reagan's hotel to present the draft information to Reagan. While we were traveling to inform Reagan, Ford precipitously named his choice for vice president—Senator Robert Dole of Kansas—to thwart Reagan. When we arrived at Reagan's hotel, he was meeting with his staff and many people who had helped him. Ronald and Nancy Reagan were in a large hall, which we entered very disheartened. Clarke was greeted like the floating repulsive object bobbing in the punch bowl. I approached Reagan, and Clarke Reed was already there.

Everybody looked at him, saying, "What is that rotten *blankety, blankety, blank* traitor doing in here?" Clarke was shedding tears and just saying, "I'm sorry."

Reagan said, "Well, you might be sorry, but why *do you* always have to do it *to me*? Now that's twice!"

The magnitude of the moment sticks in my mind. It was an immeasurably devastating time to see Reagan almost be nominated and realize the detrimental role that Mississippi had played. I also was cognizant of my own shortcomings with regard to the selection of the delegates and other ineptitudes, which had contributed greatly to the fiasco. Our party field man, Joe Sims, drove our car and, when we left that meeting and reached the car, I uttered a scatological expletive and burst out in copious tears. Never have I been so lachrymose; Clarke and Pickering began bawling, also. You could almost float in that car. I've never been that upset. Part of it was the realization that everything was down the drain; it was all over. I realized that the ballgame was lost. It was just horrible. Horrible.

The only uplifting occurrence at the convention was on Thursday night when Ford and Dole were presented as the party nominees. Reagan was also invited to speak. Everyone went wild when he spoke in his incomparable way. The convention was in a frenzy—myself included—and it was obvious that the majority queasily finally realized that they had nominated the wrong man for president!

The remainder of the convention week was completely anticlimactic. I had slept very little for six weeks. My battles were done. The only thing I wanted to do was go home. I felt that there was a vacuum inside of me. I was eviscerated.

The media were interviewing all of the key Mississippi players, critiquing the week before a national viewing audience, as if it were a postmortem. This was happening before the supposedly most celebrated night of the convention when the running mates are presented to the convention. I spoke straight into the cameras at a press conference to apologize to the people of Mississippi for being a part of electing a delegation so contrary to the wishes of the state party and the people of Mississippi.

Never in my life have I been involved with more people who so egregiously violated their obligations to me, to the party, and to their pledges. This dishonor was the most devastating and ugly byproduct of the 1976 delegation selection process and it demonstrated once more the weaknesses of human beings.

All of the Mississippi delegates were not loathsome, however; some need to be praised just as others deserve to be abhorred. Among the abhorrent, enough has been said about Clarke Reed. But Tommy Giordano was very despicable because as the Reagan Third District chairman, he attended the Reagan-Schweiker meeting at my house long after he was deviously working for Ford. The most ungrateful was Lillian Todd, Republican National committeewoman at the time. When her husband, Dr. Norman Todd, a very admirable individual, passed away, I helped her become employed at Deposit Guaranty National Bank; and when the opportunity to contest for national committeewoman arose, I convinced John Maloney, president of the bank, to approve of her doing so; and then I was instrumental in engineering her election. Next, I prevailed on the bank to allow her time to fulfill her Republican duties and to be subsidized in those activities. Lillian was my Reagan women's chairman on the delegation, and she apostatized! However, she at least did not do so surreptitiously. Mike Retzer was not so rascally, since he was an absolute toady of Clarke's and would have supported Beelzebub if Clarke had done so.

Others were naïve and not sufficiently conversant with their obligations, and they followed the lead of so many apostatizing leaders; consequently, they were easily swayed by personal telephone calls from President Ford. Some, like Clyde Whittaker, mayor of Tupelo, changed because he thought he would be appointed to the Tennessee Valley Authority. When I bought forty copies of Jules Witcover's book, *Marathon*, that detailed the 1976 campaign, I inscribed the following in each book, which I sent to the twenty-seven other delegates who admirably stayed with Reagan: "To _____, an indispensable right hand in our deplorably perfidious delegation! With your help we almost beat those squirmy, slippery, slithery, slimy worms. If only three more had been people of honor and integrity, such as you, we could have reversed the tide of history." [2]

Now, let us discuss those stalwarts who withstood tremendous pressure and remained with Reagan. We've described Gail Healy, who was uncommitted, but when the crunch arrived, voted for Reagan, knowing he would lose. Danny Jaber of Natchez supported Reagan despite a deceitful promise to him that his friend Howard Baker would be Ford's vice presidential choice in exchange for his vote for Ford. An African-American alternate delegate from Gulfport—Jean Long—voted for Reagan on the final vote, again knowing she was on the losing side. Further very commendable things could be said about the other faithful Reagan supporters who never deviated from the principle of honor; sadly, many more uncomplimentary stories could be told about the devious and weak Ford "squirmy worms."

I finally arrived home after all the tumult culminating in the Ford-Dole ticket. I had taken only one sleeping pill in my whole life up to that point. I took one when I hit home. I also had a drink. I never drink in my house unless I have company—it is a phobia with me. That night I had a couple of stiff shots of something, together with that sleeping pill.

Jan and I went to bed. Early in the morning the phone rang—it was Clarke Reed. He called to take exception to something I had said in the press. He said he and his wife were mad at me. "If this were in the days of gentlemen," Reed said, "I'd have my pistol out at twenty paces." I replied: "Well, Clarke, I just always speak what

I think. I'm sorry if it upset you. I just said what I believe and it's the truth." I rolled over, turned out the lights, and bowed out of the 1976 Ford-Dole campaign against Jimmy Carter. I needed a break from politics.[3]

Duplicitous means "double-dealing." "Du" means two and "quadri" means four; therefore, at this time, I coined the adjective "quadriplicitous" to describe Reed.

CHAPTER 20

Giving the Shank to Shanks

Doug Shanks decided in 1977 to run for mayor of Jackson as a Republican. I, meanwhile, was involved with helping Nielson Cochran, brother of Thad, run for a city commissioner's seat. My public position was that I was vacationing in the mayor's race, that I was supporting Nielson Cochran. That same year I had passed the state finance chairmanship to my Laurel friend J. W. "Judy" King with little public fanfare. Gulf Coast newspaper columnist Wayne Weidie devoted a column about my contributions to the party. "The growth of Mississippi Republicanism in no small way is a tribute to Mounger, perhaps even more than Clarke Reed," Weidie wrote. "Laurel's 'Judy' King . . . may be a financial whiz, but he won't likely match Mounger, . . . a solid cornerstone of the growing GOP. He was the most important kind of cornerstone—financial."[1]

Shanks had alienated many people during his city commissioner days. He also took the position in 1976 as state chairman of Gerald Ford's campaign, opposing Reagan and inviting the fury of staunch Mississippi GOP conservatives. Political columnist Paul Pittman even went so far as to say that Shanks and Carmichael "alienated themselves from their fundraising genius, W. D. (Billy) Mounger, an intractable Reagan man, whose memory is elephantine and who felt bartered off."[2]

I found a place to channel my energy in Nielson Cochran, who seemed in touch with the common man. Not many people of consequence knew Nielson, the brother of Thad. I had to promote him with, "He is a chip off the old block of his brother, Thad," and, "Nielson is a good man. Give me some money for Nielson."

Nielson had heard me preach continuously about the unappreciativeness of Doug Shanks and he was very cognizant that I was raising his funds. I would talk a guy out of five-hundred dollars or whatever and would say, "Nielson, do you know why he gave that money?" He would respond, "Yes, I understand. He gave that money to *you*, he didn't give it to me." I said, "That's right."

There is more to some situations than meets the eye. A case in point is Dale Danks. Danks was Shanks's Democrat opposition for mayor in 1977. Danks decided to run for mayor and visited me. We had known each other for a while—our children had attended Jackson Prep together—and also Danks had originally run for office back in the 1960s as a Republican. Danks asked me to support him for mayor. I told him, "If you will run as a Republican, I will do all I can for you because you are a good candidate. But if you run as a Democrat, don't look for me to do much." He said, "Well, if you can't do that, what role are you going to play in Doug Shanks's campaign? Are you going to support Doug Shanks?"

I said, "Absolutely not. I will not back Doug Shanks. He will absolutely get no support from me. I will not do anything publicly and I will not say anything publicly anti-Doug Shanks, but if any of my friends ask me, they will know that I am not backing him and I will attempt to shut off his funds."

Dale did tell me, "If you will not support Shanks and will not work against me, I am going to run, because that solidifies the decision for me."

I said, "Dale, I will do for you what I can in my way, but don't look for me to say anything, nor am I going to give you a direct financial contribution, and I am not going to go out and raise money for you."

He said, "I understand that. But if you will do what you said for me, that is all I need."

In actuality, I cut off virtually all of the Republican finance support for Shanks.

Dale Danks handily defeated Doug Shanks.

I knew Doug Shanks wasn't going to win because so many of our very strong Republicans were not supporting him, and there is no way you can be elected as a Republican unless you get practically all of our Republican support. Dale Danks called me the day after the election to express his appreciation for the role that I had played in the campaign. I reiterated then to him, "Well, you know I didn't do anything publicly."

He said, "I know, but you did everything that you told me that you were going to do."

Jim Eastland later met with me to discuss old battles and the upcoming political landscape. Eastland was planning another run for office, and I told him I thought that he should run, since there was no Republican I considered a better man for the job at present. "Well, Senator, I imagine my role to be similar to what I did in the mayor's campaign in Jackson," I told Eastland. "There's no way to expect me to ever say anything publicly. If anybody asks me, I'll say, 'I'm taking a vacation in the campaign.' The senator told me then: 'Yes, it's exactly what I want you to do because, except for you, Dale Danks would not be mayor today."

I told the senator that I had never made such a claim. The senator replied: "Dale Danks gives you credit, therefore you take it."

Part Four:

Days of Fame (and Shame)

CHAPTER 21

Jumbled Alliances: The GOP Swarms Eastland

The election of Jimmy Carter to the presidency in 1976 ensured that the Mississippi political landscape would never be the same. Ronald Reagan would see to that. When Carter beat Gerald Ford—sweeping the South and carrying Mississippi—Republicans were thrust into serious soul searching.

I devoted my energies to specific races after I handed the reins of state finance over to a trusted associate, Julius "Judy" King from Laurel. By now I had my share of enemies within the state party apparatus, but I had stayed the course, says newspaper columnist Wayne Weidie. My name was good after 1976; Reed's was becoming suspect with some. "While Mounger wasn't exactly an unpublicized wallflower during his days as state GOP finance chairman, he was always in the background when compared with former state chairman Clarke Reed of Greenville. Reed basked in the limelight as much as any Republican state chairman in any state. . . . Mounger is an outspoken fighter for what he believes in and can't be controlled by anybody."[1] As Charles Pickering recalls me once telling him, "You have to take me—warts and all."[2]

Strange colors splotched Mississippi's political canvas in the mid-1970s: Cliff Finch's governorship coalesced an unlikely voter group of blacks and rural conservative whites. Jimmy Carter occupied the White House, spouting born-again Christian rhetoric while making left-leaning decisions that confounded Bible Belt-style Christians. Some may say that Carter is the epitome of a born-again Christian, but I believe the Bible had something else in mind. Finally, "Big Jim" Eastland was drawing his last puffs of power, but his shadow still hovered over Mississippi.

United States senators John C. Stennis and Jim Eastland had been human plows, moving Mississippians like dirt as they willed. Two great boulders, rockhard with their Senate seniority, Eastland and Stennis piled up political favors like treasure on which they sat, holding court. Subjugation to these old-school Democrat kings—with the power, influence, and prestige they channeled for Mississippi—still seemed preferable for many to choosing untested leadership. Yet if both men guarded their lair like dragons, they also were seen as political dinosaurs. The all-Democrat-run state system of the middle-twentieth century that had maintained a segregated South was now increasingly an anachronism. But Eastland's and Stennis's seniority in the Senate representing their impoverished state kept people feeding at their troughs.

Would the seventy-three-year-old Eastland run again in 1978, or would he give his seat up for good?

Who would eventually seize the new prize created by his vacated seat?

Several considered running for Eastland's seat, including Democrats Finch and William Winter, along with Republicans Charles Pickering and Thad Cochran. Besides attaining the governorship, winning a U.S. Senate seat would be the next step toward Republican Party dominance in Mississippi.

Amid the uncertainty, Tom Hederman (whose family still owned the *Clarion-Ledger* and the *Jackson Daily News*) heard me say that Eastland should run again and, as a consequence, Buddy Sheppard of Sheppard Building Supply approached me with a strange proposition—a personal meeting with Jim Eastland. Sheppard, who lived across Old Canton Road from me, asked if I would come to his annual Christmas party to meet with Eastland. "Who can say anything if I go to a neighborhood party?" I thought. When the night arrived, I walked across Old Canton Road for a visit.

I arrived early, and had a long meeting with the senator. I walked into a room and saw the bear of a man, his handkerchief sprouting from his pocket, and we shook hands. I spoke first: "I want to take this opportunity to apologize for having done anything for Gil Carmichael relative to you because it would have been a disaster if we would have elected him [in 1972 for the U.S. Senate] with the way he thinks."

"Well," the senator answered, "I appreciate you telling me that."

It became evident that Eastland was putting out feelers concerning one last run for the Senate. "The role that I'm going to play is to be quiet and not really to be involved," I told Eastland.

Ruleville's baron king stated, "Well, I appreciate that. I understand that you're the one who elected Dale Danks mayor of Jackson."

"Now wait a minute, Senator," I said. *"I'm* not claiming that. Certainly in my way I played a role in that because of what I did or didn't do—what I didn't do, mostly."

"Well," said Eastland, "you may not claim credit, but Dale Danks gives you credit for it and I give you credit for it. You elected Dale Danks mayor of Jackson."

Our conversation expanded. "There is one thing you are known for," I said to Eastland. "Whether people like you or not, nobody has ever accused you of lack of loyalty to the people who helped you. You don't go around and stab people in the back."

As Democrat toadies congregated in the house—chattering louder by the minute—we wrapped up our discussion. I exited to the stares of newly arrived state politicos. They could draw from my presence whatever they would, but the meeting added to my already strong urge to lay low in the coming political matches. In 1982 I even counseled Haley Barbour to think twice about running against John Stennis for Senate. "Haley," I said, "as much as I like you, and as close as we've been, if you get in there, fine. But I just want to tell you, and I don't want to mislead you to any extent, you're doing it without me. I am not going to do anything." Actually, I was not disposed to help him because of his role in the 1980 convention regarding the credentials fight that saved Clarke Reed.

Charles Pickering, on the other hand, eyed Eastland's seat with few reservations and a firm conviction that the time was now for the GOP and for him. Pickering, an Ole Miss law school graduate (first in his class), began a law practice in Jones County years earlier with the goal of a political career. After winning a county attorney's election, Pickering eventually was elected as a state senator. Now, in 1978, as state GOP chairman, he hoped to harvest a statewide and national political post.

I firmly felt that Charles had a lot of great things going for him, including being highly respected among both parties in the state legislature. His philosophy was conservative, plus his father was still a farmer, keeping him in touch with the average Mississippian.

Still, I told Pickering, "I don't see us really beating Eastland. If you get in there just count me out. I don't think you should run."

Nonetheless, rank-and-file Mississippians were, first and foremost, conservatives and Pickering—among other aspiring Republican politicians—longed to lead them in a fresh direction. These same voters scorned the 1976 Mississippi delegation's Ford vote but still-aspiring Republican leaders could see the political fruit hanging on the tree for an unabashed conservative. Two years into Carter's administration had sufficiently sickened Mississippi's majority toward Democrats in the coming 1978 races, causing Republican leaders to stop licking their 1976 wounds and plot a rebound. Whomever you ask today, be it Clarke Reed, Charles Pickering, or a host of others—including myself—we all agree that, in hindsight, Ford's losing to Carter was the best thing that could have happened to the Mississippi GOP and to Ronald Reagan.

Either by ouster or retirement, Eastland's departure meant not only a Senate vacancy, but also potentially a vacant U.S. Congressional seat, should Thad Cochran or Trent Lott run and win. I knew both were mulling a run. But I feared what might happen if Trent and Thad butted heads with each other in the same primary. Whoever survived such a divisive confrontation would probably cause the loss of both of the U.S. House seats and the survivor could not be elected to the Senate against Jim Eastland or anybody else. Many agree that Thad Cochran felt more compelled to go ahead and make his run for Senate or retire altogether from politics. Thankfully, that was not an alternative that really appealed to Trent.

Cochran privately had told Eastland's people that he would not challenge the powerful Democrat if he ran again, which created a rapport with Eastland's supporters. So when Eastland opted out and Thad ran, he inherited a substantial group of the Senator's people. Pickering in the meantime had gotten into the race regardless of whether Eastland ran for reelection or not. Eastland eventually announced that he would not run again.

I had talks with Pickering and Cochran, even though my whole personality is to leap wholeheartedly in one direction or the other; I felt I could not publicly choose between the two. I did not gain any goodwill from either one, and I particularly engendered ill feelings from Thad because he felt I should have openly supported him.

I was in a contretemps. I had recruited Cochran in 1972 and had been instrumental in his reelections in 1974 and 1976, but Pickering had voted for Reagan as a delegate in 1976 (although I felt Pickering gave me no assistance with other delegates) and Haley Barbour was Pickering's campaign chairman, having committed to Pickering before Cochran decided to run. (Barbour told Pickering that, though he felt closer to Cochran, he would stay on as Pickering's campaign chairman if Charles wanted him. Pickering kept him on board.)

A jumble of new alliances ensued that may have strained some relationships short-term, but proved in the long haul just how much stronger the GOP in Mississippi now was. I gave both Cochran and Pickering one-thousand dollars but made no public endorsement; privately, however, I told many people that Thad was the most electable candidate. Cochran won the primary with a hefty margin. Afterwards when I joined his key staff workers to celebrate the victory, Thad visibly showed his displeasure that I had not overtly supported him. Consequently, I was left off of Cochran's steering committee; nevertheless, I raised more money by far for him than anyone else during the campaign.

In the end, I had made amends with Cochran and attended most Cochran gatherings. Yet after Cochran's election, rumors soon flew that Cochran was not going to support the conservative side during the Senate Republican organizational meetings prior to the U.S. Senate Session of 1979. Consequently, I wrote Thad the following letter:

November 20, 1978

The Honorable Thad Cochran
212 Cannon Office Building
Washington, D.C. 20515

Dear Thad:

Your victory was an accomplishment that many of us have been struggling to consummate for twenty years. It was certainly a great personal triumph achieved with the help of a large number of dedicated people working individually and collectively.

Personally, I am immeasurably elated over your success. You, especially, know (I trust still remember) the role I played in your original recruitment and campaign which ultimately culminated in victory. You have not needed my talents as much since that time; but I did raise more than $150,000 for you this year, which I daresay is considerably more than any other individual can claim.

The Jon Hinson election also gives me immeasurable satisfaction. The parallels between your 1972 race and Jon's are eerie. With the exception of original recruitment, the similarities are astounding. Mike Allred recommended you to me in 1972—this year he prevailed upon me to back Jon in the primary, which ultimately was the key to his victory. Additionally, I raised in excess of $125,000 for Jon compared to the $80,000+ for you—representing more than two-thirds of the money for each campaign. In 1972, it was obvious that we were lacking in the necessary person to push fundraising from an organizational aspect. Considerably through my efforts, Jim Keenan shouldered the responsibility and performed magnificently. In an almost repetitive respect, I recruited Wirt Yerger this year who supplemented my efforts to solidify the campaign financially. Jon's campaign and election were quintessentially déjà vu.

Enough reminiscing! My main purpose in writing is to urge you to support Orrin Hatch for the Republican Senatorial Campaign Chairman instead of Heinz. In 1976 you indicated you did not care for Dick Schweiker and now I cannot see how you could possibly consider his fellow liberal Pennsylvanian, Heinz, for such a position. My grapevine—I hope an unreliable one—informs me that you are undecided between the two. The choice is so blatantly clear cut that

I am devastated that I even need to bring the subject to the fore. My gnawing fear in politics is to have been instrumental in electing a Southern Chuck Percy. Please! Do not begin your term as Senator with an evisceration of those who have meant the most to your success. The future of the Republican Party nationally, and particularly in the South, is with enlightened conservative leaders. Please! Do not send us such a debilitating signal as a vote for Heinz over Hatch.

You probably have already committed your support to Howard Baker as Minority Leader because he controls the Committee Assignments. Even though his reelection is terribly repugnant and unpalatable to most of us grass roots Republicans, I do not visualize the symbolism and effect of his reelection as I do that of Heinz over Hatch. Baker is a sufficiency of indigestibility without compounding the malady.

In 1968, I played a large role in the nomination and consequent election of Nixon—only to be rewarded with Watergate. For ten years Clarke Reed parasitically existed on my endeavors; and in 1972 (as you may recall) my control of Hinds County preserved his tenure as Chairman—only to enable him to be the quadriplicitous soul he is as to sabotage the Reagan nomination. Equivalent examples could be demonstrated for Doug Shanks and Gil Carmichael. With devastatingly disappointing experiences such as these, I have developed a degree of paranoia. Therefore, I plead! Not, *et tu Brute!*

Hinson's victory can only be judged as an additional complement [sic] to you for representing this district so well for six years. Both successes were overwhelming in their importance and in the satisfaction that they have given to those such as myself. Most certainly, they were *mirable dictu.*

Sincerely yours,
(Personal signature of "Billy")
W. D. Mounger

WDM:pm

CC—Mr. Al Smith
Mr. Grady Jolly
Mr. Julius Ridgeway
Mr. Jim Furrh

In late 1978 when the Senate Republican Caucus was held, Thad voted for Pennsylvania Senator H. J. Heinz III over Orrin Hatch for chairman of the Senatorial Campaign Committee; Heinz won 21–20. Oregon Senator Robert Packwood, a liberal, won 22–21 over conservative Idaho Senator Jim McClure for the position of chairman of the Senate Republican Conference; I preferred the opposite side of each of Cochran's votes, which decided the elections.

One of my pet peeves had always been the election of Republicans who then toed what is perceived to be the liberal line. I now worried that I had helped create another stealth liberal senator. I wrote another letter berating Thad for these votes, and I carbon-copied the letter to a large number of people, engendering an extended breech with Cochran. I have regretted very few of my political activities; however, today I wish I had never written this letter. It took several years for the two of us to become amicable again. Today, I consider Thad a very good friend, and we have great respect for each other.

CHAPTER 22

Jon Hinson

A boyish Jon Hinson came to see me early in 1978. We had known each other from the days when Hinson worked for Democrats Charlie Griffin and John Bell Williams, and then later when Hinson worked as the administrative assistant to Thad Cochran.

"Would you back me for Congress?" Hinson asked me.

I offered no commitment to him at that time. I was undecided, because to be honest with you, he had a baby-fat, soft kind of look about him. And I felt a little leery of him, his not being an athletic type and all; but I knew he liked to act rather than being an athlete. He was not married, with what that might indicate.

Soon after Hinson's visit with me, Charlie Griffin called on me. Charlie had been John Bell Williams's administrative assistant and had taken John Bell Williams's place as the Fourth District U.S. Congressman, and he had named Jon Hinson as his chief of staff. When Griffin decided not to seek reelection, he elicited Thad Cochran's promise to keep his staff in exchange for Griffin's quiet support. So when Thad took office, he kept Jon Hinson as his chief of staff.

Cochran later named Wiley Carter to the position and Hinson departed Cochran's office amicably. Also, since Hinson had an apartment on Capitol Hill near Cochran's House office building, Cochran recommended that Wiley live with Jon Hinson, proving that Thad Cochran did not know Jon Hinson's proclivities or he would never have recommended that Wiley live with him.

After Griffin retired from Congress, he became secretary of the Mississippi State Senate, and he was in that position when he told me that Jon Hinson would make a great congressman. We spent several hours together, talking about Hinson's father—the chairman of the board of supervisors in Walthall County—and his mother, a schoolteacher, and about Jon's abilities. If I would back Hinson, Griffin said he would help behind the scenes and could do the campaign more good by maintaining all his connections to the Democrats.

At that time, three others (one being Gray Jackson) had entered the Republican nomination race for the Fourth District seat. I knew, however, that there was a reasonable possibility of taking Jon Hinson and selling him because he had such good Washington experience with John Bell Williams, Charlie Griffin, and Thad Cochran—and I could see using that as a basis for a campaign. And with his father as a supervisor, he could count on much help from the old power structure supervisor types.

My energy was still depleted from the 1976 debacle. I hadn't planned on actively working for anyone in 1978. Then Mike Allred, who had first suggested Thad Cochran to me for a congressional run, called. "Billy," he asked, "what are you doing in the primary?"

"Well, right now I am sitting it out," I replied.

"Well," said Allred, "who do you think can win?"

"The only one of the four who could win is Jon Hinson, because of his experience."

"Then you better step out and make certain he gets the nomination. You mean to tell me," Allred continued, "that you've worked all this time for the Republican Party and you think one of them can win and continue our success and you are going to just sit there and do nothing? You can't do that." Duty, honor, country tugged again at me, and I mulled the matter, inquiring with key people about Hinson. I asked Thad Cochran whether Hinson would make a good congressman and if Thad would work with him. I also asked whether he knew any reason why I should not back him. Thad said, "No, Jon would make a good congressman. He knows how to operate in the Washington sphere and he would be an extremely good congressman if you elect him."

Then I talked to John Bell Williams. "Now John Bell, you were the first one who hired him," I said. "What do you think?"

"Jon is from a great family, super," John Bell said.

I had checked with the three people who knew him best: Charlie Griffin, Thad Cochran, and John Bell Williams, all of whom gave me the go-ahead. Moreover, Hinson had been elected president of an association of Mississippians in Washington, D.C., leading me to think: "These Washington people worked with him and they elected him, so he must be all right." In a few weeks, I had moved from the sidelines to lacing up my cleats for Hinson's team.[1]

TV producer Stuart Stevens—a native Jacksonian who would eventually win many national awards and whose father, Phineas Stevens, was the "Stevens" of the Butler, Snow, Cannada, Stevens & O'Mara Law Firm—was living in Washington at the time and he and Jon were friends. Stevens agreed to put together the advertising for the campaign. One ad had Jon Hinson in a grocery store, talking about prices and taxes, demonstrating the TV effectiveness of the amateur actor.[2]

With the primary over, Hinson faced the son of Senator John C. Stennis—John Hampton Stennis, who had great name association, but a poor presence. Charlie Griffin visited with me from time to time about campaign strategy. When discussing the campaign, Charlie would laugh and say, "You know, all those Democrats are not aware that I'm for Jon Hinson, and I can inject all sorts of barbs and Stennis naively takes my advice. My main advice to him is: 'John Hampton, you need to meet as many people as possible by going to every shopping center and to every county, and mingling with the people.' That is the worst thing he can do because if he talks to ten people he is going to turn six of them off."

A second win in the Fourth Congressional District was looking possible. I had beaten the bushes for money early but for the final financial push to election day, I sought more help. I informed Hinson that the time had come to call Wirt Yerger and ask my old Republican buddy to jump back into the trenches. I said, "Jon, you go to Wirt's office, and wait as long as you have to. Go in there and sit down with Wirt and stay in his office as long as necessary and repeat the same things to him that you have relayed to me. Both of you agree on most issues, as I do. You only have to sit there long enough for him to understand your conservative beliefs."

That night Wirt called me and asked in his characteristically gruff fashion: "Why haven't you done anything for Jon Hinson?"[3]

"That darn Wirt," I muttered to myself.

Yet Wirt agreed to help with fundraising and the next day I ran into Lillian Todd, who was still national committeewoman. She asked me how things were going. "Well," I said, "I'll tell you what; we just put it together. We are going to elect Jon Hinson, because I just helped maneuver Wirt Yerger to come on board and between the two of us we are going to be able to render a one-two punch to successfully raise the money."

On election day that November 1978, Hinson won. He rode the coattails of Thad Cochran's historical Senate win and he benefited from Eastland's retirement. For the first time ever, the Fourth District had a Republican U.S. congressman and senator.

Immediately, Hinson's voting record won conservatives' kudos. However, one question kept coming up at social gatherings. Was Jon ever going to get married?

He began telling people about a girlfriend in Washington. Wiley Carter told me that Hinson often brought a very attractive girl, Cynthia (who worked for Democrat Congressman Bo Ginn of Georgia), over to cook at their apartment. Then the two were married and a subliminal sigh of relief exuded from Yerger, me, and other key Hinson constituents. Cynthia was really a cute girl, and my friend Neal Clement chided me about remarking on her good looks. Wirt threw a party for the couple at his Jackson home. Everyone had their photo taken with the new couple and everything appeared great. To the present day, Wirt and I agree that Jon Hinson showed more appreciation and attention to his serious supporters than any other person we have supported. Jon constantly sought my advice.[4] And best of all, he married Cynthia!

The year was 1980. Ronald Reagan was seeking the presidency. I voluntarily relinquished my Mississippi Reagan chairmanship to Trent Lott, and meanwhile, I was made Reagan's mid-south finance chairman. Wirt Yerger was not interested in working an-

Right: My mother when she was reputed to be the most beautiful girl in Covington County.

Above: A 1944 *Clarion-Ledger* photograph during World War II of my mother and father, proudly holding pictures from right to left of me at West Point, my sister Marjorie, and her fiancé Ernest Nevels, an heroic P-38 pilot in the South Pacific War Theater.

Right: My father in a typical, legendary pose as president and CEO of Deposit Guaranty Bank and Trust Company, circa 1942.

Left: I am on crutches in 1931 as a five-year-old after being run over by a car on North State Street near Power Elementary School.

Below: My Power School sixth-grade class in 1937 included future esteemed beauties Jane Ross, Deanie Wallace, Doris Johns, and Polly Wells; it also included my close life-long friends Fox Garraway, Sam Sanders, and Leigh Watkins, together with three officers of our 1944 graduating class at Central High School—Ann Porter (secretary), Alma Van Hook (treasurer), and me (vice president); note that, somewhat predictive, I am pictured on the far right.

Left: The *Clarion-Ledger* featured several fathers with their children for a special 1942 Father's Day section. M father is flanked on his right by Marjorie, with Henry in h lap and Libby to his far left. am standing to the rear.

Above: A "power" photograph, from left to right: Nat Rogers (far left); my father (fourth from left); Herman Hines (fifth from left).

Right: A football photograph of me in 1942 when I made 3rd-Team All Big Eight and with my hair bleached by the sun after being the pier lifeguard all summer for the White House Hotel in Biloxi, Mississippi.

Below: The sole photo of my Chrysler Highlander convertible, given to me while at West Point by my father. The photo was taken at Mount Holyoke College in Connecticut, after I had wrecked the car.

NOT A PASS • FOR IDENTIFICATION ONLY

HEADQUARTERS
UNITED SSTATES CORPS OF CADETS
WESST POINT, NEW YORK

IDENTTIFICATION CARD

William D. Mounger
First Namme   Initial   Last Name

C4 5683   1948
Serial No.   Class

Date Issued
2 SEP 1947

William D. Mounger
Signature

USCC Form No. 31—15 July 1947

Left: My photo in the West Point yearbook, "The Howitzer," in dress whites prior to my 1948 graduation with my United State Miliary Academy crest and cadet identification card.

Middle: Feeding Billy in New Orleans after cleaning bugs from the drilling rig while working for Humble Oil and Refining Company in 1957.

Bottom: With Jan and Billy outside our Short Street apartment in New Orleans, while working for Humble in 1957.

Left: In 1966 with Nixon before he had announced for president and when he spoke to more than one-thousand people at th[e] fundraiser where I botche[d] the flag ceremony.

Right: During the 1968 GOP national convention in Miami Beach, I gave a lengthy interview with NBC's John Chancellor, minutes before the voting began for the presidential nomination.

Above: "Claudius Maximus" Kirk, governor of Florida, Clarke Reed, and myself at the 1967 Mississippi Republican Party fundraiser, which I emceed.

Above: I am shown moving about the floor at the 1972 Republican National Convention in Miami Beach, Florida, wearing a ridiculous red hat and adorned with much paraphernalia.

Above: The last trip that President Nixon took from Washington, D.C. before resigning as president in 1973. It was to the Naval Air Station in Meridian, Mississippi. With Air Force One in the background, those in the photograph from left to right are: myself, Gil Carmichael, Marjo Denson, President Nixon, Victor Mavar, Clarke Reed, and Virginia Waggoner.

Above: With then-Vice President Gerald Ford at the noon fundraiser that I emceed, which was six days before President Nixon resigned and Ford was elevated to the Presidency.

Above: In 1969, the first time I met Ronald Reagan in his office, while he was governor of California, he gave me goose bumps.

ove: Clarke Reed, me, Nancy and Ronald Reagan, at
rke's townhouse office in Greenville, Mississippi, in
1.

ddle: At the Democrat National Convention in 1972,
h delegation had reported that it was boycotting let-
e! (Labor Leader Ceasar Chavez was striking lettuce
ducers in California.) We originated this "Elephants
e Lettuce" stick-on that was the hottest item at the
2 GOP Convention. You can tell this elephant *really*
s lettuce.

ow: Jan and I with Ronald Reagan before he spoke
ur 1973 fundraiser, which I emceed.

Above: Congressman Trent Lott, Governor Ronald Reagan, Congressman Thad Cochran, and myself at the 197 fundraiser.

Below: In June of 1976 with Ronald Reagan, Jimmy Stewart, and "Festus" in a meeting with the delegates to the 1976 convention, when the delegation was solid Reagan. Afterwards, we flew to Biloxi for a fundraiser for Trent Lott's reelection, the only such event where Reagan appeared that year.

Right: Myself, Trent Lott, and Senator Paul Laxalt (Reagan's National Chairman) discussing our Mississippi role in the incoming Reagan Revolution the 1980 inauguration.

To Billy Mounger – With Best Wishes
Ronald Reagan

Above: The "Group" lunching with President Reagan in the Cabinet Room adjacent to the Oval Office. Left to right: Ed Rollins, White House Political Director; John Powell of Missouri; President Ronald Reagan; Diana Evans of Oregon; Ted Stivers of Georgia; Bob Rowland of Texas; the redoubtable Jimmy Lyon of Texas; and myself, with White House Chief of Staff Jim Baker fretting at the door.

Above: Bobby and Billy with Governor Ronald Reagan at the 1973 fundraiser in Jackson.

Below: Charles Pickering and I are attending the 1980 Republican National Convention in Detroit, Michigan, where I was wearing my Reagan Leadership white cap, prompting NBC's Tom Pettit to say to me that I "looked like Idi Amin in a white hat"!

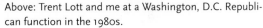

Above: Trent Lott and me at a Washington, D.C. Republican function in the 1980s.

Left: At the ensuing celebration of Trent Lott's 1988 swearing in ceremony for U.S. Senator, Trent told all those present that I, as his finance chairman, was the key to his success and then he reached into my pocket in search of more campaign funds.

Below: Circa 1968 at the Independent Petroleum Association of America meeting in Washington, D.C., prior to electing any Republican U.S. Representatives from Mississippi. I am shown with Congressman "Sonny" Montgomery, Emmett Vaughey, Congressman Tom Abernathy, and W. M. (Bill) Vaughey.

To Jan and Billy
Best Wishes

Above: With George W. Bush, when he came to Jackson to support Haley Barbour for governor in 2003.

Above: The National Review Board of the East-West Center in Honolulu, Hawaii, in 1972 with me seated first on the left.

ove: At home during the 1986
S.A. International Ballet Competi-
n with myself, Donna Godwin, Jan,
na Novak (a famous prima ballerina
m Poland), and Alexander Grant,
owned danseur from England.

ddle: Left to right, a Russian film-
ker; Natiali Kasatkina (director of
Moscow Classical Ballet); Gen-
di Afterko—all three were probably
B—with Jan and me.

ow: I am holding the 2000-year-
Roman coin I excavated at the
thsaida dig at the head of the Sea of
lilee in Israel in 1991. It prompted
to write the poem, "The Coin."

Above: Memorabilia from the January 27, 2005 Republican Elected Officials Association Roast of me. Attendance was over 600.

Above: On January 28, 2006, I roasted Lt. Governor Amy Tuck and teased her about her fear of flying by giving her a parachute. Photograph by Brian Broom

other campaign, so I convinced our mutual friend, Jim Furrh, to be Hinson's finance chairman for his reelection. Then, during Hinson's re-election campaign, reports issued that Jon had been caught in 1977 in a burning porno movie theater, the Cinema Follies, in Washington. "He was rescued from under a pile of bodies—one of only four men that survived."[5] Later we learned that "while a Cochran aide, he was arrested on a charge of committing an obscene act."[6]

Upon learning of the porno-movie theater, we who had helped Hinson to power had some serious talking to do. John Bell Williams, Charlie Griffin, Jim Furrh, Wirt Yerger, myself, and a few others gathered at Wirt Yerger's house on Northside Drive where we listened as Jon Hinson attempted an explanation. He told us he was trying to escape from the theater when he was overwhelmed by smoke, but made his way to a locked door. He lay by a crack under the door where some air was getting in, passed out, and almost died. Then Hinson described how the incident had caused him to seek out his Baptist minister and get right with God. Eventually, Charlie Griffin spoke.

"This is not a negative," Griffin said, "this is a plus! The guy was in a *porno* house and almost died. And, as a result, he was born again! Man this is a political plus. Here is a guy who was in a place he ought not to have been, he almost died, he survived, he really got religion."

We weighed the circumstances and decided to continue working with Jon and to relate the story as Griffin had laid it out. Furrh kept running Hinson's finance campaign; and I also kept raising money.

The campaign regained steam. Meanwhile, I left town for one of my regular Independent Petroleum Association meetings, this one in Aspen, Colorado. When I returned on a Friday night, I flipped on the 10 P.M. news and heard the report about park police in Washington, D.C., arresting Jon Hinson with a red bandanna draped down his front like a codpiece, walking near the Iwo Jima Memorial by the Potomac River. The *Clarion-Ledger* blared the facts the next day. The Iwo Jima Memorial was a regular gathering place for gay men, who would drape red bandanas from their front waistline if they were seeking a sex partner. The paper stated that Jon Hinson had been among those arrested.

I analyzed, "The porno theater, we can live with—but not a homosexual situation." At that time we still believed the porno place had been a heterosexual theater. We did not know it was a homosexual porno joint.

I decided that confrontation with Hinson now was necessary. I told Hinson's staff, "We are going to see Jon at his downtown Jackson office for a Monday morning meeting." I called Jim Furrh and said, "Jim, you are going to go up there to see Jon Hinson with me."

I remember Jim saying, "Oh, I can't go. I'm going to Europe."

I said, "When are you going to Europe?"

"On Tuesday."

"Your fanny is not going to Europe on Monday," I insisted. "Jim, you are the finance chairman. You are going up there with me."

Wirt Yerger was unavailable, so I prevailed on Swan Yerger and we three went to Hinson's office, where we first encountered Hinson's wife, Cynthia.

"We've got to go in and see Jon," I told her.

"Well," Cynthia replied, "I'm going to go with you."

"No, Cynthia, you must stay out," I said. "You can't go in there with us."

We three entered his office. With something as important as this meeting's subject, I have always believed in mincing no words. I looked my United States congressman, Jon Hinson, right in the eye, and said, "All right, Jon, are you a homosexual?"

He gave us a soliloquy, enumerating multiple reasons why he was not a homosexual, and propounded the fact that he preferred females, not males. Hinson lengthily detailed all the erroneous things that people were saying. And he said he did not know why he happened to be at the monument, but that with the pressure of the campaign on him, he just ended up there.

We asked him how Cynthia was responding to the situation and he replied that she was taking it fine and that he was constantly conferring with his minister.

We left asking ourselves, "What do we do?" This situation was awful. Jon was strangely swearing that he was not a homosexual; but it accentuates the fact that, if you are a closet homosexual, you live the life of a lie and become a consummate liar; but also, sadly, it makes for a good politician. Many politicians will tell you what he is going to do when he does not care whether he does it or not. If he has convinced you, he has accomplished his goal.

None of us really knew the next step to take or how to proceed.

Wirt Yerger and Ralph Lord went to see Dr. Don Patterson, our minister at First Presbyterian, and asked his opinion. Patterson told them, "Well, he is telling you that he is not a homosexual. His minister is saying he is not a homosexual. He is married and his wife is saying he is not. Who are you then to judge and say that he is? Then you are being judgmental and you are not in a position to judge him."

I went into neutral and the *Clarion-Ledger* was running articles regularly. After a period of neutrality, I finally decided, "I do not know what else we can do except to continue and not disown him."

In August, Hinson issued a long statement in which he admitted to having been both in the porn theater and the Iwo Jima Memorial; he said he had rediscovered his religious faith and planned to continue to serve as congressman if reelected.[7] Admittedly, I did not enthusiastically campaign after that, but Jon kept campaigning. Towards the end of the campaign, a *New York Times* reporter came down to research the campaign.

"I've got to visit with you," he told me over the phone.

We had lunch. The reporter told me, "I've been surveying around here, and Mississippi is such a religious state that it's hard for me to see that the voters will accept anybody who may be a homosexual; however, in my research, I'm beginning to believe that Jon Hinson is going to win this race."

The reporter added, "I don't understand this."

I said, "Let me tell you this. Some people say they had rather have a conservative queer than a macho all-man liberal." Again, my tendency for colorful language spawned a quote that ended up running in several large papers around the nation. The *New York Times* ran an article entitled "Mississippian Gains Despite Sex Issue" on Wednesday, October 4, 1980, quoting me on Hinson's conservatism.

JACKSON, Miss., Oct. 4—When Representative Jon Hinson chose on an August morning to disclose his past involvement in homosexually related incidents, even his most ardent conservative supporters began to mourn his political suicide.

By now, a month to go until Election Day, the first-term Republican is not *persona non grata* in his hometown, district or state, as might have been expected just a few years ago. To the contrary, even his opponents acknowledge that not only is he a contender; he is also leading in the race.

"You'd think that a man who had acknowledged frequenting a homosexual theater would have been run out of Mississippi," said W. D. (Billy) Mounger, a wealthy independent oil producer who proudly claims residence in the philosophical right wing of Mr. Hinson's campaign financing for both his elections. "But he's got a great voting record. He's been with us conservatives on every issue right down the line."

"There are folks that think we would rather have a queer conservative than a macho, all-man liberal, and they may be right," he added, "but he says he is not and was not a homosexual and never performed a homosexual act, and I believe him. If I didn't believe him, I couldn't support him."[8]

When the election occurred it was a three-way race between Democrat Britt Singletary, a thirty-year-old lawyer; Leslie McLemore, a black independent and professor of political science at Jackson State University; and Hinson, who was elected with a minority of the vote. Singletary told the *New York Times* that Hinson "played it masterfully," referring to his admission of being gay. "He's as fine a political actor as you've ever seen, and I think many, many people believed him when he said he was not gay. When you add to that his religious conversion and his marriage to a pretty young lady, they believed him more. Of course, there's nothing Mississippians like more than forgiveness, but there are a lot of Christian conservatives out there who are going through a lot of mental gymnastics in order to justify their support of something that would otherwise be anathema to them."[9]

Hinson headed back to the nation's capital as Mississippi's Fourth District Congressman. When Reagan was inaugurated in 1980, Hinson let me use his special parking pass at the Cannon Building and he loaned me his personal car and driver on occasions.

After the election, in November or December, I was visiting across Hinson's desk in his Washington office when the famous columnist Bob Novak called for me. We had been friends since the 1968 convention. And I said, "Bob, how did you know I was here?" He replied, "Well, I called Jackson and your secretary told me where you would probably be and I called."

"Well," I said, "what is it that you need?"

"I need for you to help me obtain a job next summer for a young man in Mississippi." Novak is a University of Maryland graduate and Maryland had recruited a Mississippi basketball player.

I hung up. Hinson asked, "Who was that?"

"That was Bob Novak."

"What did he want?"

"He has a basketball recruit out of Jackson, and he wants me to get him a summer job."

Jon was sitting right there across his desk and he immediately said, "I will put him on my staff." Within seconds I called Novak. "Bob, I already have your player a job."

"You found him a job!" he said, astonished.

"Yes," I said, "Congressman Jon Hinson is going to put him on his staff this summer in Mississippi."

In January 1981, Novak hosted a lavish party during the Reagan inaugural festivities for Washington VIPs at his home in Maryland. Jan and I drove there with Hinson and his wife, Cynthia. In February 1981, I was back in Washington on business when I rode the Capitol tram with Hinson's wife, Cynthia, to meet Jon for lunch in the House dining room. Afterwards, Cynthia took the opportunity to give me some news: "Jon and I are trying very hard to have a baby."

"Cynthia," I replied, "there couldn't be anything better that y'all could do with all Jon's problems. If you had a baby that would go further towards allaying these negatives than anything else you could do. That would be wonderful."

That was the last time I ever saw Cynthia or Jon. Soon afterwards, in February 1981, Jon Hinson was caught in the men's room on the sixth floor of the House Cannon Office Building. The Capitol police conducted a sting and Jon was caught in a homosexual act, and was arrested on a morals charge.

Hinson's administrative assistant called to inform me about the arrest and soon TV stations called to interview me. Bert Case called and asked if I would do a live interview on the WLBT news and that night on TV I stated that Hinson must resign.

Several other key local Republicans called for Hinson's immediate resignation.[10] Along with Wirt Yerger, Jim Furrh, Ralph Lord, and Mike Allred, on February 6, 1981, I sent Hinson a very plain message. It read:

MAILGRAM
Western Union

You have deceived and disgraced not only yourself but those of us who put our confidence and reputation on the line for you. You lied to us and all the constituents of the fourth congressional district. We feel you have no choice but to resign immediately from Congress.

Ralph Lord, Jim Furrh, Billy Mounger, Wirt Yerger

With the television lights blaring and the statewide broadcast rolling, I told Case that I'd tried to give Hinson every benefit of the doubt. Now, however, Jon Hinson had no course but to resign. That was the only service he could do for the district. The next morning, again with TV cameras rolling, I walked to my office in the Deposit Guaranty building and looked at my door, which was adorned with bumper stickers and political paraphernalia.[11] I reached up and ripped the Jon Hinson sticker off the door. Period.

Jon Hinson all along had said he was not a homosexual. But now I believed Hinson had to do his duty and resign. Hinson entered a hospital. His wife was sticking with him; his minister was remaining with him. Eventually, under constant pressure, he resigned, though constitutionally he did not have to. He could have stayed as a United States congressman, with more than a year and a half left on his term.

I never talked again to Hinson, who eventually became an activist for the homosexual lifestyle. His wife, Cynthia, divorced him.

According to an Associated Press July 25, 1995, article, Jon "later publicly acknowledged his homosexuality and became active in the gay-rights movement. He helped organize the lobbying group "Virginians for Justice" and fought against the ban on gays in the military. He also was a founding member of the Fairfax Lesbian and Gay Citizens Association in Fairfax County, Va. A native of Tylertown, Miss., he never returned to his home state, but lived quietly in the Washington, D.C. area, first in Alexandria, Va., and then Silver Springs."[12]

Jon Hinson died in July 1995 of AIDS.[13]*

*See note 13 for an explication of an historic caucus and election that we held to succeed Jon Hinson.

CHAPTER 23

Political Years
of Joy in the 1980s

"This is Billy Mounger. We're out of the office right now. If you're a
conservative Republican I *know* your phone call will be returned. If
you're a moderate or liberal of any stripe, *we'll see*. If you're a liberal
Democrat, you probably don't have much of a chance!"
—Phone Machine Message since 1989, W. D. Mounger's Office

My famous phone message actually was recorded in 1989,
when my son Billy and I shared an office from 1982 to 1989;
he bought the answering machine in early 1989. Billy told
me to leave a message and the statement above is the first outpouring that emerged. The expression summarized my feelings and
my approach to political life, and it still does today. But in the
1980s, how much more so! Wherever we Republicans in Mississippi turned, it seemed that victory greeted us. Going on almost
two decades now, callers to my Jackson office—without discrimi-
nation—have been greeted by the above.[1]

In the 1980s, our party not only had "arrived" in Mississippi, but
had inundated the political scene like a tidal wave. Ironically, the
events of the 1976 convention—and the way average Mississippians perceived it—had foreshadowed this eventuality. The people
back home were incensed at the Mississippi delegation when it
came back from the 1976 convention. Our rank and file, the door-

knockers, the little old ladies in tennis shoes, the precinct captains, the executive committee members in the counties, the people who give the ten dollars—those people were overwhelmingly Reagan.

No other time in my political years was like the 1980s, when the fruit of so many past battles finally yielded a bumper crop of near epic proportions. The 1964 Goldwater race was exhilarating in the sense of awakening my mind to politics; the 1968 Nixon race—my first to serve as state finance chairman and state delegation vice chairman to the national convention—was special; and following that, with the election of Ronald Reagan in 1980, all those previous years' efforts came to fruition.

Ronald Reagan was an entirely different type than Nixon. Nixon was very appreciative of what Clarke and I had done, but Nixon also was such a cold character with whom you could not feel close. With Reagan, every time I was around him I would put my arm around his back and felt as if he were a good friend. I expounded on his amazing charisma when I wrote a tribute that ran in the *Clarion-Ledger* just after Reagan's death on June 5, 2004.[2]

When we elected Reagan in 1980, I was very close to him, having gone through that '76 fight. It was tremendous. It really made me feel overwhelmingly good, particularly after going through the most traumatic experience of my whole life, which was the delegation fight of '76. As for Clarke Reed, he became *persona non grata* during the Reagan years, as national political reporter Al Hunt recalls: "Mr. Reed, once one of the most influential conservative Southern Republicans, never recovered [from the 1976 Reagan debacle]. After Mr. Reagan was elected four years later Mr. Reed sought a spot on the non-controversial foreign intelligence board; he didn't get it."[3]

The Reagan people remembered my efforts from 1976 and as 1980 approached I received credit for many things, some that I didn't exactly do. I tended to take credit if it were good. Everybody in the Reagan group knew who I was. One apocryphal story was that Ford had asked me to the White House along with Clarke Reed when Queen Elizabeth was there and that I had refused!

A 1981 front-page *Clarion-Ledger* article boldly stated that I could "contact friends, and those friends can contact other friends, and campaign funds would grow exponentially. In an interview last week, a candid Mounger estimated that he could get as many as 300 friends to donate to the [Liles] Williams' campaign, and Mounger, who was finance chairman for the state Republican Party for 12 years but is currently at odds with the state party's leadership, isn't even officially connected with the campaign or its state party fundraising drive."[4] Still, I wrote David Keene on July 10, 1981, expressing my disgust at the low-level tactics the Democrats used to defeat Williams. In one advertisement that ran on black radio stations on campaign day, the following inflammatory rhetoric was used to galvanize an unprecedented African-American vote:

> Martin Luther King and Medgar Evers gave their lives so that you could have the right to vote. Now Ronald Reagan and Liles Williams are trying to take your vote away. In fact, you could lose that right by 6 o'clock today if you don't vote. Today you must go and vote for Wayne Dowdy. Wayne Dowdy has the courage to publicly say that Wayne Dowdy would vote for extending the 1965 Voting Rights Act.

Everybody in the White House knew what position I had taken on behalf of Reagan and how firm I had held my ground. Once I ran into Newt Gingrich, then a fledgling politician: "Oh man, you did so great," Gingrich told me regarding the 1976 convention. "I'm one of your fans."

In truth, I was still the blocking guard, the West Point cadet, the Air Force A-bomb commander. Any name that I had made for myself was based on my advocacy for others. "Fundraising is a passion with Mounger and he enjoys keeping a running score as the money trickles through him to a candidate," the same article said about me. I told the *Clarion-Ledger*, "It's like a football score."[5]

The article added: "Mounger thinks about politics all the time, even scouting potential contributors at funerals." Meanwhile, my Democrat opposition in Mississippi was beginning actually to use me as a fund-raising tool, or an attempt at one. In a June 22, 1981, letter from Danny E. Cupit that was written on the letterhead of the Democrat Party of the state of Mississippi, Cupit urged Democrats to resist the election of the Republican congressional candidate, Liles Williams, in the Fourth Congressional District, adding, "In the next two weeks we must work together against the Republican Fat Cats who will use every influence of the White House against us. We cannot afford another Billy Mounger-Wirt Yerger puppet in Washington." The new battle lines were now clear in our state. The aforementioned letter was forwarded to me by my old friend and mentor, W. M. Vaughey, with a handwritten note from Vaughey saying, "I don't know whether you should be complimented or insulted!"

The truth was, when the Reagan political strategists chose officers who would help carry Ronald Reagan's standard in the state and, ultimately, to the White House, my work in earlier years was rewarded with the position of Mid-South Reagan finance chairman. Trent Lott, then the relatively new Minority Whip of the U.S. House of Representatives, took the job as Mississippi Reagan chairman—handpicked by myself. I told Charlie Black (the executive director of the national Republican Party) that either I would take the position, which I was in line for, or it must be given to Lott. I said to Charlie, "You work on Trent, I'll also work on Trent. If Trent will come in and do it then you don't have to worry about hurting my feelings or pushing me out of the way." So we convinced Trent to be chairman, which was even more efficacious because he was now Republican Whip in the United States House of Representatives.

In a personal interview, Lott recalls how he and I agreed to work as a team in 1980.

> Billy was never the one that wanted to have the title or get the credit. He was willing to do jobs that nobody else would do. Therefore he got stuck with them—the titles *and* the responsibility—but his goal and my goal in 1980 was to win. And Billy knew . . . from my organizing the Fifth District and how we've turned that into a Republican district . . . that I would put together an organization and he and I would work together and trust each other and I'd be the chairman and we'd have an advisory committee, and finance committee, and we'd raise the money. So I knew that in 1980 the goal was 50,000 Republican votes in that district. You had to have that many basically to hold your own [statewide] because we were going

to lose the rest of the state by 10 or 20,000. So at any rate, Billy agreed for me to be the chairman and we got it organized. And I mean we did it right. We had a finance chairman; we had an advisory committee; we had an executive director; we were organized; we had headquarters; we had offices. And sure enough, we carried my old district by a little over 50,000 and we carried the state by 10,000 for Reagan; against, by the way, Jimmy Carter, a Southern Democrat incumbent president, "born-again." And we took him out. Billy and I will always remember that very fondly.[6]

Even though I had resigned as party finance chairman in 1977, I remained its national convention delegation vice chairman because of my close relationship to Reagan. I asked oilman Neal Clement to be Reagan's state finance chairman. But I essentially raised nearly all of the money.

I just have a passion for fundraising. "I will honestly call people more than ten times for a donation," I told the *Clarion-Ledger*. "It's human nature to love money more dearly than anything else and some can't understand that even old King Tut couldn't take it with him. One reason I like to raise money—I'll be honest with you— you can find out more about the innate character of people when you're asking them to give you money [than] you can by doing almost anything else. Over the years, I have people in this town categorized—some of the biggest money people that y'all write about in the paper, man they don't give anything."[7]

After four years of Jimmy Carter, the favored nominee of the Mississippi Republican delegation selection process for the 1980 convention was a foregone conclusion—Ronald Reagan. However, whom the delegates would be and how the delegation would be picked still provoked infighting among state factions. Delta Republicans tried to institute some strange approaches for proportioning delegate selection. One of my greatest frustrations and one of my worst mistakes was not attending the 1980 state convention in order to confront those men whom I now distrusted and who, in my mind, were trying to rig the system.

Wirt Yerger, along with Reagan campaign organizer Kenny Kling, urged me not to attend the state gathering because of friction with Jack Breed, who wanted to be national committeeman

and whom I had defeated for the Hinds County party chairmanship. I had subverted his desire to vote the Hinds County delegation (the largest in the state) using the unit rule for him.

I erroneously let them convince me to do something totally
against my will. They stated that I would harm the Reagan campaign by attending the state convention. I should have adamantly
resisted, but they were persuasive. I let Wirt and Kenny Kling prevail. It turned out to be a horrible mistake. The delegates were
involved in a big credentials fight at the state convention. Haley
Barbour was sergeant at arms on the other side working to preserve
Clarke Reed's faction. Ultimately, Trent Lott, not having my buffering presence there and with no experience in a state convention,
caved at an inopportune time enabling Clarke Reed and Mike Retzer to stack the deck improperly using their Delta counties, which
helped them to control the delegate count.

Prior to and during the precinct and county conventions, I commissioned attorney T. Cal Wells to analyze the legality of the votes
in Washington County, the home county of Reed and Retzer, as
well as in LeFlore County (Greenwood), which kowtowed to Reed
and Retzer.[8] Wells's overwhelming conclusion was that Reed and
Retzer broke the law. States Wells: "It is obvious that after viewing
the system and the vote totals that an illegal system was used."

In Washington County, Reed and Retzer disallowed a legitimate
precinct, then substituted their own people; they also allowed Retzer to vote improperly in the wrong district and at the same time
contrarily disallowed one of our votes. With these shenanigans, Retzer won the Washington County chairmanship of the party delegation 21–20. In LeFlore County the disproportionately and unfairly
distributed precinct delegates stacked one precinct very much in
their favor; otherwise they would have lost LeFlore County.[9]

If I had participated in the convention, I believe I would have
steeled Trent Lott to fight successfully, which would have undone
Reed and Retzer. Haley Barbour was playing his own game since
he, Reed, and Retzer were for John Connally before he was defeated
in the primaries.

As a result, Mike Retzer kept his post as state party chairman.
However, he did not serve at the 1980 Republican National Convention as the chairman of the Mississippi delegation—Trent did

and I was vice chairman. Retzer, however, turned around and helped push the vote through for Clarke Reed to remain the state's Republican committeeman. Clarke Reed had been in an airplane accident while flying around caucusing and promoting himself. At the state convention as people waited to vote for the state's national committeeman, he had himself shuffled in on a hospital bed, trundling down the aisle. Clarke won. In the end, Clarke's ego was served again.

Trent folded on this battle. All of us who had held the line four years earlier for Reagan should have held the line in choosing the state party officials for the 1980 national convention. They booted us out in 1976 when they got control. So we shouldn't have given in. Trent gave in.

I had to vent my concerns about what I felt was a bungled, rigged 1980 state convention. I did so in the following letter to U.S. Senator Paul Laxalt of Nevada:

Senator Paul Laxalt
326 Russell Senate Building
Washington, D. C. 20515

Dear Paul:

You, undoubtedly, recall the inextricably miserable position the tergiversator Clarke Reed and others put me in as Chairman of the Reagan Campaign in Mississippi in 1976. You know how supposedly irretrievably committed Reed was to Reagan, to me, to David Keene, and others—yet he consummated the ultimate apostasy.

Well, here we are again with Clarke Reed surviving as National Committeeman and his sycophant, Mike Retzer, as State Chairman. Retzer was also elected as one of the five at large delegates and he has yet to say that he is for Ronald Reagan.

The scenario that unfolded at the State Convention was almost surrealistic. Our Reagan Organization was, at best, inept and, at the worst, a cabal to procure and swap paramours. What occurred at the State Convention was an inexcusable imbroglio.

As I stated, our organization was incomparably ineffective—I had almost no input relative to its formation and virtually no influence on its performance. Our candidates for State Chairman and National Committeeman were not willing to openly campaign until after the County Conventions on April 26th. Consequently, myself and Wirt Yerger were set up as bogey-men-straw-men and we were maligned all over the State. Also, the facilities and employees of the Mississippi Republican Party (which we all pay for) were used for a full time campaign organization to re-elect Reed and Retzer.

Despite the incompetence of our so-called organization, the incomprehensible existence of a complimentary Reagan Campaign telegram to Reed, the reluctant and belated candidates, the power of incumbency, and the opposition of the Mississippi Republican Party machinery, we could still have won the State Convention.

Reed and Retzer were elected as delegates in their home county solely due to chicanery (our own Duval County). The enclosed information from our attorney, T. Calvin Wells, clearly demonstrates their impropriety. Retzer, in particular, participated in disqualification of two of our delegates when he, himself, was in the same category; i.e. not registered thirty days prior to the election. The $7^1/_2$ votes from his county should have been disqualified at the Convention. Additionally, the most inequitable apportionment imaginable was contrived for LeFlore County to benefit the Reed-Retzer (anti-Reagan) forces and is so patently egregiously unfair there is no way they could have survived proper scrutiny.

Alas! Just when we had won a procedural vote 100 to 95 to hear the credential challenges in alphabetical order by county (a procedure that would have increased our margin to 17 when hearing the LeFlore challenge), unfathomably and inexplicably, Trent Lott, our State Reagan Chairman and floor leader, capitulated by accepting the stacked-deck credential's committee report in its entirety. Our cause was thus totally undermined; and upon seating the four contested delegations, a Retzer majority (17-13—the 17 composed of mostly Bush with some Connally) Executive Committee was elected. With the momentum then on their side, they wheeled Clarke Reed in on a portable hospital bed (he walked around plenty before that), and he carried the National Committee seat by a twelve vote margin. In further debasement to our cause, Retzer was elected as a delegate and to this day, is not pledged to Reagan. The injustice of it all!

Enclosed is a three page summary on the challenges that should have been sustained by the State Convention. Several of us are desirous of pursuing these challenges at the National Convention. Of course, if we won, all business of the State Convention would be invalid including seating five delegates (Cochran, Lott, Hinson, Pickering, and Retzer) who are pledged to abide by the vote in our June 3rd Preferential Primary which will be Reagan all the way. We understand this is an immeasurably difficult request, however, for us to proceed, it is necessarily imperative that we have the unqualified support of Ronald Reagan and the Reagan Campaign.

Paul, please peruse the enclosed information and let me know whether you will bring it to Ron's attention and whether we will have his and the campaign's total support in this endeavor.

Further, I beseech you to proceed with this request; but, at least, give me the assurance that neither the Reagan Campaign nor a Reagan Administration will deal with the "quadriplicitous" duo of Reed and Retzer.

Please give these matters your immediate consideration and render me an answer as expeditiously as possible.

Sincerely yours,
Signature (Billy)
W. D. Mounger

WDM:pm

For me, such issues weren't small things—the key issue was always about doing the right thing.

The 1980 convention was in Detroit, and I went up two or three days early. Trent Lott was head of the national platform committee, so he controlled the national Republican agenda for Reagan's campaign, and Charles Pickering also served on the platform committee.

Trent did extremely well and he did not put up with a lot of static from the liberals. He put through the right kind of anti-abortion stance and covered other issues, as well, but he had naively allowed Retzer to control the seating on the convention floor

rather than the Reagan forces. Too many good things were happening to make noise about that; still, state political columnists including Bill Minor were writing that we in the Mississippi GOP
were "Babies in Bath-water" who were splitting into a moderate
faction led by Cochran, Reed, and Retzer and a conservative faction
led by Lott, myself, and people like Wirt Yerger.[10]

More than Clarke Reed had been sidelined in the 1980 Reagan-
fest. Also nowhere to be seen in 1980 was Gil Carmichael. (He
would resurface when George Bush ran for president in 1988, and
would become U.S. Assistant Secretary of Transportation). Also
gone, now, was the unit rule. It had served its purpose early in the
young Mississippi Republican Party's life, but 1976 had shown its
weaknesses. The 1980 state party delegation scuttled it.

Lott wore a red golf cap in his capacity; I wore a white one,
which designated me as the Mississippi Reagan coordinator. Network journalists once again sought me out for interviews. My notoriety from four years prior caused many to desire to interview
me. Tom Pettit, who had interviewed me numerous times in 1980,
once again asked me for an interview. When it came time for the
cameras to roll, I had my white cap on. I was proud of my Reagan-
leader white golf cap.

Pettit, however, felt otherwise. "Billy," he cracked, "if I were
you I would take that cap off. You look like Idi Amin in white
face."[11]

"Tom, if I look like that then it sure is coming off."

It was nice to have a good laugh with an old journalist buddy—
the pressure of 1976 only a whisper in the distance of time.

Tom Brokaw also approached me for an interview. Even though
I was not chairman of the delegation, the TV people still wanted
to interview me instead of Trent. I felt a bit embarrassed. Brokaw
asked about the growing number of black Republicans, particularly
about the recent redistricting of an unusually shaped Second District comprised of the Mississippi Delta on down through Jefferson
County to Natchez, which created the state's most densely popu-
lated African-American district.

In the first congressional election after redistricting, we Republicans retained the Second District seat, electing Webb Franklin
over African-American Robert Clark. Much had been written

about the whole matter, with many liberals saucing their articles with fuzzy accusations of racism. I, on the other hand, suggested in a *Philadelphia (Pa.) Daily News* column (November 13, 1984) by Adrian Lee that Mississippi blacks simply showed "apathy." I said that Jesse Jackson had "campaigned more times that I can count" in the district and still, a black Democrat couldn't win, adding the issue wasn't "color but fairness." I accused liberal activists of not wanting fairness, but rather "guaranteed success," and suggested that they had, in turn, sent all the white Democrat vote in the Second District into the Republican Party. I said in the article, "It was as if all the whites voted for Franklin, and the blacks who could have made a difference didn't bother to vote at all."[12]

Some national journalists probably considered such statements by me—a white, upper-class Mississippian—as a show of racism. Those who knew me—including black Republican Charles Evers—knew better. Rather, it was simply me being candid and honest, ignoring silly taboos and speaking my mind.

Unlike four years earlier, the 1980 convention was one where journalists had to dig for a story. The only kind of stew that year was over the vice presidential selection. Though some talked of the prospect of Jack Kemp—a politician on a first-name basis with me—Reagan clearly wanted George Bush. I had long ago made my feelings about Bush known.

If Reagan wanted him, it was futile to oppose his selection. Bush never appealed to me because I always thought he was too moderate and his eventual presidency failed because of the very reasons that I was always reluctant to support him.[13]

When in 1992 George H. W. Bush was seeking renomination as president of the United States, he traveled to Mississippi on the campaign trail. I will let my good friend Jim Furrh recall the rest of this story: "I was asked to meet President Bush at the airport upon his arrival in Jackson. I was happy to do so. When Bush arrived at the airport, I greeted him and we got into a limousine to ride to his speaking engagement, where a great number of solid longtime Republicans were waiting. But one person who was not there was Billy. Billy did not support George Bush and had even accepted the responsibility of being Phil Gramm's Mississippi campaign chairman. President Bush obviously knew this, and he turned to me and asked: 'Jim, why isn't Billy Mounger supporting me?' I simply replied, 'Well, he just doesn't think you are conservative enough.'"

That was the truth, and I believe that history proved me to be right. Of course, George W. Bush is altogether another story. He has been a solid conservative whom I am proud to support. But Jim and I laugh to this day when he recalls how George the First was befuddled by my absence at his campaign gathering.

Making George H. W. Bush his vice president was one of the worst things Ronald Reagan did because out of that we were saddled with Jim Baker as chief of staff, a non-Reaganite. Baker consequently brought many George Bush people into the Reagan administration, diluting the Reagan Revolution. As a consequence, Bush was positioned to engineer his own nomination to succeed Reagan. Thus, Reagan's successor was not philosophically attuned to truly continue his revolution.

I helped squelch a mini-revolution in the 1980 delegation when several delegates wanted Jack Kemp instead of Bush. In the end, I persuaded them not to oppose Reagan's choice which would only have embarrassed the Mississippi delegation. Still, the Republican Party, both nationally and within the state of Mississippi, left the Detroit Convention more unified and energized than it had been in years.

Reagan was now a friend of Mississippi's and was personally close to Trent Lott and myself. Reagan proved this when he decided to attend the 1980 Neshoba County Fair. No other event in Mississippi so symbolized political passion within the state, and for Reagan, the Republican presidential candidate, to attend was unprecedented.

Trent Lott had helped secure the deal, which would further solidify the love relationship between Mississippians and Reagan. Trent called me and he said, "I've got it approved to have Reagan come down to the Neshoba County Fair."

"Trent," I said, "I'm the number one Reagan guy in the state and I can't be there."

I had an imperative Independent Petroleum Association of America meeting in Colorado. Undoubtedly disappointment was evident in my voice as I realized that I would miss this historic and potentially intimate time of politicking with Reagan. It just killed me.

Still, I was thrilled at history in the making. It was a great moment and it was a brilliant move politically. It solidified Reagan with those types who attend the fair.

When the 1980 election was over, Reagan not only had won the White House, but Republicans had won the U.S. Senate. Suddenly Trent Lott was launched into greater prominence. A year after Reagan's election, Trent was elected House Minority Whip. I now was very close to the president of the United States and the U.S. House Minority Whip, as well as Thad Cochran.

Mississippians at the 1980 inaugural festivities were ready to celebrate. Mississippi—once again—had stomped other states in percentage-of-quota fundraising, second only to Kentucky, a state much more affluent and with a much-too-low quota. Master Mississippi strategist Bill Wilkins was no longer there to arrange grand seating and gala events for state leaders attending inaugural functions, but Mississippi's implicit clout sufficed. I maneuvered a great box for our Mississippi inaugural ball in the United States Museum of Natural History. It was the next-best box in the house, immediately adjacent to the George H. W. Bush family. Four couples joined Jan and me in the box: Stuart C. and Bitsy Irby, Jim and Mary Lee Furrh, and Victor and Gayle Mavar.

During that ball I met a young George W. Bush for the first time. Everyone at the ball was elegant. Reagan arrived at the Museum of Natural History with Nancy on his arm and then gave his typical inspiring speech. I was eyeball to eyeball with history, as Reagan spoke right next to my box.

Reagan's first term did not disappoint. Reagan cut taxes and reduced government. And when Mississippi's own newspaper— which had only recently ended family ownership when the Hederman family sold to the national Gannett newspaper chain— recommended tax increases, I cracked my knuckles, cleared my proverbial throat, and wrote a letter to the editor entitled, "Champion Taxing Yourself First." It read:

> The audacious arrogancy of your March 9 editorial headline, "No Backbone," is putrescent with hypocrisy. The extreme rigidity of

your backbone is unsurpassed in recommending tax increases on others; however, the backbone of a jellyfish is admirably firm in comparison to yours pertaining to paying your fair share of taxes.

You, your Howard Bakerite moderate Republican executive editor, and your Gannett (Rochester, N.Y.) puppeteers with their $120 million purchase of the Hederman newspaper empire have arrogated unto yourselves the task of intimidating the provincial bucolics residing in Mississippi into accepting oppressive tax burdens to accomplish your desired social engineering purposes.

The proverbial "pot" is pristine white compared to your "tax kettle." Why don't you recommend a sales tax on newspapers? You pay none now! What about a sales tax on newsprint? You pay none now!

Naturally, you are for sales tax increases—zero times an increase is still zero taxes to you. Undoubtedly, you also have structured your $120 million purchase to avoid paying any corporate income taxes whatsoever. Again zero!

You advocate increasing the oil and gas severance tax by 50 percent (6 percent to 9 percent)—a tax off the top before considering any costs, when business is severely depressed (down 60 percent), and with natural gas and crude oil prices plummeting.

You carp about MP&L with its monopoly and its commission-controlled rates. What about your newspaper monopoly, your uncontrolled rates, your ever-increasing profits, your avoidance of taxes, your expanding, not decreasing, business?

You relegate excellent senators, such as Ellis Bodron, to the "Hall of Shame." You categorize most taxpayers who voted against your pet bond issue as bigoted racists. Yes, and you say that legislators who don't genuflect to you are devoid of backbone.

You certainly don't come to the taxing table with merely unclean hands. Your uncleanliness is better described in scatological terms. Consequently, before you again advocate raising any taxes on anyone or anything, you owe it to the taxpayers you have demeaned to champion taxing yourself first!

Bring back the Hedermans![14]

> W. D. Mounger
> Jackson

To be fair, I was not inclined even to hold my punches with the president of the United States—even my friend, Ronald Reagan. When in 1981 Reagan had supported an extension of the original Voting Rights Act of 1965, which focused unfairly on seven southern states including Mississippi, I voiced to Reagan many Mississippians' concerns.

A certain section of the Voting Rights Act required seven southern states (Alabama, Georgia, Louisiana, Mississippi, South Carolina, Texas, and Virginia) to obtain the U.S. Department of Justice's explicit approval for any change—even minor ones—in their voting codes. It made no such requirement of other states. Southerners were irate from its initial passage during Lyndon Johnson's presidency. Southern Republicans felt the Voting Rights Act should apply the same standards to all fifty states.

Reagan planned not only to extend the original act for ten more years, but to ignore pleas by southern Republicans that the act at least require all states to submit to the same level of scrutiny. Mississippi Senator Thad Cochran urged Reagan to be careful, saying: "Voting is important in every precinct in every state, not just in the old South. The time is past when the South should be treated differently."

I wrote my own missive to the president. The letter follows:

July 27, 1981

Dear Ron:

Please! Ron! Not you too? Do not destroy our faith in you by supporting the inequitable, invidious, and iniquitous Voting Rights Extension with its egregiously sectionalistic pre-clearance provision intact.

Whose counsel are you receiving? Harry Dent's? That's like Solzhenitsyn being advised by Brezhnev. Dent's machinations serve only his egocentric purposes and not yours. I've experienced his Machiavellian manipulations in the White House and as your Mississippi Chairman in 1976. Beware!

You've listened to Charles Evers. He may have delivered his own vote to you in 1980 and that is all. You have met with Aaron Henry, our antagonistic enemy. Why haven't you counseled with me, Trent Lott, or Bill Alexander (Alexander's letter is enclosed with a pertinent article)? We have fought your battles. We are your loyal supporters. Do not draw and quarter us.

We vociferously apologize for not winning the Fourth District. The wrong message has been sent to Washington and apparently to you too. We lost by 912 votes because 25,000 additional black votes were corralled in two weeks. These votes were delivered by scare tactics and organization. The fear syndrome was used in the Voter Rights Act, but welfare checks and Government largesse were the *sine qua nons*. Mostly, the N.E.A., AFL-CIO, and the NAACP put their national organizers in the field to turn out the votes. (Refer to the enclosed Political Report.) You lost precinct 27 (1195 to 22) when the Act was not an issue. We lost precincts 27–31 (3180 to 34) and you lost them (4628 to 90). Black votes are only for sale through Government handouts. If you go for that, we have little in common.

We can regain this seat; but not if you undermine our ability to show the grossly racist campaign run by our opponent. We can and will motivate our voters and succeed the next time, if you do not eviscerate us by supporting the Voter Rights Act.

Ron! You know this legislation is unfair. No one should be considered guilty until proven innocent. However, if you contortedly believe that this Act is innately good, then you are disserving your fellow Californians and others by not allowing them to be the recipients of its blessings.

Ron, I beg, I beseech, and implore you to do what is right and not further impose this insidious legislation on a small section of the country. You would not have carried a single Southern State if the voters had thought you were weak on this issue. Be alert to *agent provocateurs!*

Sincerely yours,
William D. Mounger

I believe Reagan appreciated me shooting it to him straight. I have no reason to think otherwise.

It was about this time that I also began to write not only prose but poetry. And at times, my subject matter was none other than the sad liberals whom we conservatives were now soundly thrashing in Mississippi. Never having attempted to write poetry or rhyme, it was as much a surprise to me as to everyone else when I suddenly did so. The first outpouring spontaneously welled up out of me in London, England, all (except for the title) on the night of June 3, 1982. To set the stage for this spontaneity, one needs to know why we were in England and what significant event occurred before we departed.

In explication, the January to March 1982 session of the Mississippi Legislature took up a proposed severance tax increase on oil-and-gas production from 6 percent to 9 percent. This tax increase was instigated by then-Governor William Winter to pay for his education reform bill, which was ridiculous for it would have ruined the business, and one industry should never shoulder the total tax burden for a cause which benefits the state as a whole. Governor Winter, disingenuously, stated that the increase was only three percent when any rudimentary math student would know it was a 50 percent increase. This specious and unfair tax increase was thwarted, predominately due to the efforts of Charles Williams, who was then president of the Mississippi-Alabama Mid-Continent Oil and Gas Association, along with some help from its chairman, Jim Furrh, and others.

After winning this hard-fought battle with the governor, a number of Mid-Continent members decided to take a trip to England, Scotland, and Ireland led by Charles Williams. On the last night we were in London, June 3rd, we went to the St. Catherine's Dock to eat, drink, and be entertained. Our restaurant had an Elizabethan ambiance with a Henry VIII character, ladies in waiting, courtiers, serving winches, court jesters and other assorted costumed characters. We sat on huge benches around a long thick slab of a table and we were served roast pig, beef, lamb (mutton?), Johnny cakes and other examples of period food. Additionally, we were coaxed to drink copious quantities of red and white wine, beer, ale, mead, and whatever other alcoholic drinks one desired. During the dinner, our leader, Charles Williams, was adorned with a cloak and a crown as if he were a kingly or Ducal personage. Having imbibed an inordinate quantity of all of the aforementioned beverages, my mind evinced a degree of perspicuity which resulted in (at least I thought) a streak of brilliance resulting in my proposing a toast. Which was: "Here's to our Hero, Sir Charles of Williams, for his great victory over that dastardly villain, Sir William of Winter!"

After sitting down and continuing to imbibe a variety of drinks, I concluded that my toast had a profundity to it which began to elicit rhyming verses welling up within me which had an Elizabethan format involving battles and jousting like knights of old. My mind kept conjuring verses on the bus returning to the Hilton at Hyde Park and then continued after arriving at my room. At that time, I began to put the verses on small pieces of paper and continued thusly until about 4 a.m. on the 4th of June. After a short sleep, I collated what I had written onto sheets of hotel stationery amounting to ten four-line stanzas.

Later on the 4th, we departed for Edinburgh, Scotland, and I read my poem to a couple of people on the plane, who stated that a title was needed for my outpouring. Somehow, in a flash, it came to me that, if I changed the last word in the effusion from "defender" to "conqueror," I could keep an English, if not Elizabethan, motif and I could then title my verbiage, "Williams the Conqueror."

Anticlimactically, I read my final product to all assembled at lunch in a restaurant north of Edinburgh. Then, upon returning to Jackson, I had it printed in Old English-style script in pseudo-scroll fashion. Each member of the trip was sent a copy and Charley Williams and myself had ours framed, which he keeps in his office and I keep on my dressing room wall. The poem follows:

Williams the Conqueror

Here is a proud story for all us to hear,
It certainly contains what all hold so dear,
It's that tale of our hero, Sir Charles of Williams,
Versus that great villain, Sir William of Winter.

The contest took place on the banks of the Severance,
And Sir Charles gave Sir William no amount of reverence.

The battle unfolded on the famous Tax-on-oil;
And reached a decidedly magnificent turmoil.

Sir Charles of Williams was caparisoned,
With things most good and a truthful bond.
He had—Moons and boons, Furrhs and myrrhs,
Hughes and News and right and might!

Sir William of Winter was most cleverly festooned,
With things most bad and raucous tuned.
He had—goons and loons, curs and slurs,
Loos and phews, and shite and trite!

Then, that most desirous day did appear.
Both contestants, regalized, did draw near.
Our knight did charge with lance held firmly,
But, Sir William of Winter's felt most squirmly.

After the clash most highly resounded,
Sir William of Winter was the most confounded.
The clangor and tumult were much calamitous,
But fighting and winning were well worth-the-fuss.

And, after the crescendo of war had subsided,
Sir Charles had emerged with what we abided.
Sir William of Winter appeared most unhappy,
And in furtherance we wish him to be most clappy!

In accord with the outcome, each must feel,
It was assuredly for all the truly ideal.
All should praise our champion deterrent,
Our true and good, Charles, our Knight Errant!

Of all such things I've seen most recent,
The deeds of Sir Charles are the most decent.
With a huzza and a jubilation,
We all rejoice in Sir Winter's humiliation.

Now hear you thus that we all concur,
That Sir William of Winter is an awful cur.
However, our champion, we do most prefer,
Sir Charles of Williams the Conqueror!

William Mounger
Ye bard and Poet Laureate (?)

Eventually came the 1984 reelection campaign for Ronald Reagan. His staff in Dallas, Texas, in 1984 tapped me as the Reagan-Bush coordinator for all the southern delegations on the Republican National Convention floor. If we had had a problem on the floor relative to the Reagan campaign or platform, then it would have been my job to try to coordinate the forces among all the southern delegations. Nothing major came up to effectively use my power, but I proudly wore my red cap symbolizing my position.

Due to the focus of the convention—which offered less suspense and more hype on Reagan's first term and promise of a second term—floor machinations were minimal. Trench warfare was nil. I was less in demand among the TV anchors. There were, however, other new experiences.

I attended one unforgettable gathering (where I spilled a cream-puff down the cleavage of a very buxom Jewess) hosted by the Jewish-American/Israeli Political Action Committee with my friend, Jimmy Lyon. Jimmy was especially important to the Reagan campaign because, after Reagan had lost New Hampshire in 1980 and was desperately in need of a cash infusion, he faced a win-or-fold scenario in North Carolina, and Lyon loaned $350,000 to Reagan's 1976 campaign, thereby winning North Carolina.

At the convention the party held a thousand-dollar-per-person fundraiser, and Jimmy purchased a $10,000 table, including me as his guest. Charlton Heston was among Lyon's other guests. One of the young ladies working for Reagan knew I would be there and asked me to obtain Mr. Heston's autograph. She told me, "Oh you're going to sit with Charlton Heston; he is my biggest hero; please get his autograph."

And I said, "Well I don't usually get autographs, but for you I will get one."

During that gala, I found Heston to be very kind and approachable. For her sake, I said to him, "I don't normally do this, but this is for a female Reagan worker"—and I gave him her name and stated that she worked with me on the Reagan campaign and that she would love to have his autograph. And he said, "I'll do you one better!" And he reached into his pocket and pulled out a picture of himself; it was just the size to fit in a coat pocket, and he wrote on it—"To Cheryl with my love."

I ran into her after it was over, and I said, "Look, I've got to tell you, I'm sorry, but I couldn't get you what you wanted."

Very dejectedly, she said, "Oh well, I know you tried. But thank you anyway."

And then I added, "I couldn't get you what you wanted. I got you something better!" I produced that picture; talk about elation! Since Heston had been so willing, I asked him also to autograph a photo for Jan. He wrote one to her and Jan could not care less!

Heston didn't act like he was a big shot or an arrogant movie star. He was just a natural guy. Later on with Jan, I saw him again at a private party that Jimmy Lyon hosted in his suite atop a hotel. A number of people were there, including Anita Bryant, whom Jimmy was dating, and Jan and I rode with them to the convention in Lyon's limousine.

In the 1984 Reagan-Bush election, we all knew our roles. Still, the money had to be raised and Trent Lott arranged to have Reagan appear one day on the Gulf Coast during the fund-raising push for the campaign. Meanwhile, I already had a major fundraiser planned at my house for that same evening in Jackson for the reelection of Second District Congressman Webb Franklin.

It seems that every time a major happening occurred, I was always in Aspen, Colorado, but I was coming home on Friday before the Monday that Reagan was to speak on the Coast. Upon arriving in Jackson on Friday night, I was asked to put on a fundraiser using the presidential visit on the Coast for the Mississippi Election '84 campaign, of which I was chairman. I stated that I did not know how I could accomplish that task with only Saturday, Sunday, and part of Monday left to raise the money, and that I had to be in Jackson Monday night for the Franklin fundraiser.

Saturday morning I went to work with the assistance of a dynamic young man, Dan Davis, who was finance director of the Mississippi Republican Party. It was ironic that Reagan would visit the state and once again I would have to miss him. But then I was able to get Dudley Hughes, who owned a jet, and his wife Robbie, to go to the Coast. Dudley gave me $10,000 and I raised about $105,000 in two-and-a-half days after Reagan announced he would be coming. I hustled other people and filled up the plane. Billy Walker Jr. gave $10,000, and was so impressed that he gave an additional $10,000 after he returned home.

I have been consistent in flushing "four-flushers" from my fundraisers. If you let them in, they will shove aside those who pay and will occupy the time of whoever is the important personage. Consequently, I made the Reagan campaign promise that only those designated as paying could attend the fundraiser. Everyone who attended, as I promised, did have a personal visit with the president, had an individual picture made with him, and participated in a general discussion with him on any subject. Beforehand, Haley Barbour sidled up, but I told him, "Give me five-thousand dollars or you don't get in." Ebbie Spivey, then the state GOP chairperson, swished her skirt, but got the same treatment. The Reagan staffers were really guffawing at the tight ship that I ran.

After all the donors saw Reagan, Dudley Hughes and our party boarded his plane and returned to Jackson, where I barely made the seven o'clock function at my own house. The guest speaker at my home that night was Senator Connie Mack of Florida, whose grandfather was Connie Mack McGillicudy, the longtime original owner of the Philadelphia (Pa.) Athletics Baseball Team.

After I had orchestrated Reagan's private five-thousand-dollar-a-person meeting on the Coast, he delivered his public speech. In his opening remarks he mentioned that "my friend Billy Mounger [is] having a fundraiser up in Jackson," explaining why I had to leave to host another event that same night, an allusion that did not escape the arch-liberal columnist of Mississippi, Bill Minor, who wrote in the October 7, 1984, issue of the *Clarion-Ledger* of "the Mississippi Republican Party, the infant not long ago that has grown overnight into adulthood," adding: "One night back in 1975, Billy Mounger, the longtime state GOP bankroller, introduced

Reagan as a modern 'Moses who will lead us.' Evidently Reagan has not forgotten Mounger, whom he described as 'my friend, Billy Mounger,' in his remarks here [in Gulfport], the only person mentioned so. Word that Mounger had become the state party's most controversial figure had apparently not reached the presidential ears." Minor was alluding to the charges that some of us had levied during the gubernatorial election of Bill Allain. (The Allain issue is detailed in Chapter 24.)

Or *Camarilla* in the case of Ronald Reagan, loyalty, not controversy, was the measure of friendship. I was privileged to enjoy many enriching times with Reagan in a gathering of key influential Reaganites that we called "the group."

This group, in particular, was special to me. My Reagan counterpart from Atlanta, Georgia, Ted Stivers, was a member; so was John Powell, the renowned Republican kingmaker from Rolla, Missouri, who was responsible for starting the political careers of John Ashcroft and many others. Others in the group included Bob Rowland from Austin, Texas; Diane Evans from Salem, Oregon; Marcy Lear from Roseville, Minnesota; Frank Whetstone from Cut Bank, Montana; and most formidable of all, Jimmy Lyon from Houston, Texas.

Ted Stivers pulled us all together. In aggregate, we became one of the most effective advisory bodies to Ronald Reagan.

We convened from time to time for White House meetings with Reagan and White House staffers, but we mostly congregated in Lyon's private suite in the Madison Hotel with Jimmy's limousine permanently waiting outside to whisk us to the White House or wherever else we needed to go. Many cabinet-level officials came to the suite to brief us about whatever we desired or needed to know.

Once the group, in a lunch meeting with President Reagan in the White House cabinet room, mentioned that the most loyal Reagan supporters were too often left out of the selection process for high administration positions. I admonished chief of staff Jim Baker, "You do not really know the true Reagan backers, especially those who have been Reaganites the longest. You may not intend to overlook them, but you appoint those whom you know the best and they are Bush people."

Consequently we then proposed that the president add a fourth person to his White House triumvirate of Jim Baker, Ed Meese, and Mike Deaver to represent Reaganites. Senator Paul Laxalt, Reagan's presidential campaign chairman, thought our idea preposterous, until Ted Stivers convinced Bill Wilson, the ambassador to the Vatican and member of Reagan's original kitchen cabinet, to accept the position. When we informed Laxalt, he stated, "I thought you were crazy, but this is a ten-strike."

Unfortunately, Baker and Deaver constantly occupied the president's ear and thereby dissuaded him from creating such an office. Obviously, Baker and Deaver (not Meese) feared diminution of their influence. Even though we were foiled, we were somewhat assuaged when Bob Tuttle—whose father, Holmes Tuttle, was an original member of the Reagan kitchen cabinet—was appointed assistant to the president for personnel, which increased our influence over presidential appointments.

Another Bill Wilson episode occurred during the 1984 inauguration when he informed Ted Stivers that my name had arisen at a meeting of the Reagan kitchen cabinet alleging my support of Reagan's new tax bill, which I adamantly opposed. I called Wilson and ascertained its veracity; and as a consequence, I exchanged a series of letters with the president (Reagan had given me a secret code to put on the outside of my letters that insured passage directly to him) explaining my true position. I had discerned that the real culprit was a Democrat oilman from Texas whom Don Regan, Reagan's then-chief of staff, misrepresented as me; but before our correspondence was completed, the president unfortunately became a little testy with me. Nonetheless, the tax bill was passed, and was not as detrimental to the oil-and-gas industry as I had feared and, in retrospect, was politically excellent for the president.

The group also often participated in conference calls to discuss prospective Reagan appointments, and during one such meeting Reagan staffers mentioned that an opening needed to be filled on the United States Military Academy's Board of Visitors. During the Nixon administration I had served on the presidentially-appointed National Review Board of the East-West Center in Hawaii, which had afforded Jan and me many pleasant trips to the islands and the Orient and had allowed us to make many new acquaintances.

Now, however, when Reagan's staff informed our group that an opening existed for a 1984–86 term on the Board of Visitors of my alma mater, West Point, someone remarked, "The Board of Visitors of West Point. . . . Anybody have any ideas about that?"

And I said, "Yeah, I have an idea."

"What's that?"

And I said, "Me."

And they said, "Great."

So I essentially appointed myself to the Board of Visitors. And for insurance purposes I obtained Trent Lott's support for the appointment, as well as the White House's.

Trent Lott says that he was happy to aid me in this single request: "The only thing [Billy] ever wanted me to do was help in getting him on the West Point Board of Visitors. And I was more than glad to accommodate."

In 1985 I dropped by the White House and told Bob Tuttle, who had received his position because of the "group": "You guys don't need to look for a replacement for me. I have the replacement for me."

He said, "Who is that?"

And I said, "Me."

So I reappointed myself, something that is not normal; however, Reagan had set a precedent by reappointing a friend of mine who had been the GOP chairman of Florida to the Air Force Academy Board of Visitors. After being reappointed for the term of 1987 through 1989, I was elected as chairman of the Board of Visitors in 1988, and again in 1989.

The West Point Board of Visitors originated in 1817. It originally was composed of academics from other institutions who conferred with the superintendents of West Point about curriculum and other matters. After the Civil War, it was still comprised of people from outside of the academy, but with a new set of goals. Today, the board is made up of four United States senators, five United States representatives, and six presidential appointees. The president appoints two people each year to serve three-year terms. And the board must report directly to the president each year.

The Board of Visitors has *carte blanche* powers to delve into anything pertaining to the academy and must send a final report directly to the president each year. It is the duty of the board to inquire into the morals, discipline, curriculum, instruction, physical, fiscal, academics, and any and all matters relating to the academy that the board decides to consider.

Some of the topics of studies during my tenure on the board have included: "Admissions and Attrition"; "Cadet Basic Training and Discipline"; "Faculty Composition"; "Curriculum"; "Governance of the USMA"; "Cadet Pay"; "The Cadet Honor Code and System"; "Long Range Planning"; "Cost Price Worth of West Point"; "Cadet Appreciation of the Constitution"; "Women's Issues at West Point"; "Fourth Class System and Disciplinary System"; "West Point Admissions Criteria"; "Active Duty Service Obligation"; plus numerous other topics.

At least two of the studies that occurred during my service merit further discussion. The first, "Active Duty Service Obligation," has to do with the required time a graduate must serve in the military after graduation; at that time the requirement was five years. Over the years, this requirement had provoked much debate and the board concluded and recommended that upon graduation a graduate should serve a minimum of four years in the regular military and four years in the reserves. The second, "Women's Issues at West Point," produced by an attractive female lawyer from California named Marta Caldera, caused the most consternation with the board because of the gravamen of the report. Its main complaint was that West Point accentuated the combat arms too much and that women were excluded from the combat arms. I was astounded! Preparing for combat is what West Point is about and should emphasize. Women were shoe-horned into an all-male academy after 175 years, and they complained about West Point's main mission. What did they expect?

In my years of service on the Board of Visitors and in other West Point affiliations, my love of the Point has grown. I didn't really appreciate West Point when I was there as a cadet but when Jan and I attended my tenth class reunion, it dawned on me what a privilege it has been to be a West Point graduate. My life has been immeasurably affected by my West Point experience and I have attended class reunions every five years starting with my tenth, with the last being my fifty-fifth. Also, we have enjoyed many mini-reunions, the last being the spring of 2005 in New Orleans. Among my classmates are thirty-one generals, including four four-star generals, two three-star general superintendents of West Point and one of the Air Force Academy, plus six more three-star generals and numerous other leaders including former Secretary of State Alexander Haig and former National Security Advisor Brent Scowcroft—both my classmates for two years.

In 1984, when I walked around Trophy Point on my first tour as a member of the Board of Visitors, I reflected on my father's desire for me to be a cadet, my own skewed reasons for attending, the hardships I had endured, and my service with so many great men. "Who would have thought," I said to myself as I strolled the grounds, "that when I arrived at the academy, that forty years later I would be here as a VIP with everybody at West Point holding nothing sacrosanct from me?"

In 1989, the second year that I was chairman of the Board of Visitors, the superintendent, Lt. Gen. Dave Palmer, chose a young lady, Karen Baker, as First Captain among her peers. She was absolutely in the top ten of the cadets there, and she was really sharp. She became West Point's initial female First Captain.

I was with her when she was named First Captain, and then, the next day, she led a fourteen-mile march in full pack. The whole route traversed West Point property, which covers 18,000 acres. At the end of Karen Baker's historic march, the Plebe Class and First Class "Beast" leaders marched through the West Point gates and passed in review with me standing on the stand in front of Quarters 100, the superintendent's home.

I had always dreamed of having a parade in my honor. Well, I had that parade—it may have been only 30 percent of the Corps of Cadets—but at least I got a 30 percent parade.[15] And it was military history, too, as Karen Baker was the first female First Captain.

I am happy to have assisted West Point in the halls of the United States Congress as well. In Trent Lott's first year in the Senate, after he took his oath in January 1989, an issue arose in the Senate concerning all the academies. In June of that year, Lt. Gen. Dave Palmer, superintendent of the United States Military Academy, called me (I was still chairman of the Board of Visitors of the academy) and desperately asked for my help.

The Department of Defense appropriation bill for 1989–1990 had been put before the Senate for approval, and the bill included a provision that graduates of all United States academies (Army, Air Force, Navy) be required to serve not five, *but eight*, years in the military in addition to four years at the pertinent academy for a total of twelve years.

Lt. Gen. Palmer had received no warning of this new provision, nor had any other academy, the Secretaries of the Army, Navy and Air Force—not even the Secretary of Defense. All the affected parties were capitulating regarding the service requirement except for Palmer, who was convinced that academy recruitment efforts would be devastated if sixteen- or seventeen-year-olds were made to commit the next twelve years of their young lives. Lt. Gen. Palmer did not believe the academies could recruit enough preferred entrants to survive.

I told Palmer, "I will do what I can through Senator Trent Lott, who is a member of the Senate Armed Services Committee and who will do anything to help me provided it is proper, legal, and the right thing to do." But I added, "Senator Lott is a freshman senator who is supposed to be seen, not heard; however, I will contact him."

When I relayed the story to Trent, he was genuinely concerned; he actually believed the required service should be even less (four years rather than five); he said he would see what he could do. Additionally, Palmer had uncovered that the culprit who had inserted the proviso was Senator John Glenn of Ohio, an ex-Marine and astronaut who obviously had run afoul of Annapolis graduates in the Marine Corps and now was exacting his retribution.

Trent visited with Senator John Warner of Virginia, the immediate past chairman of the Senate Armed Services Committee, who told Trent to talk to Senator Glenn. When Trent contacted Glenn, Glenn lectured him that he could care less what a freshman senator such as Lott wanted and the provision would remain. The arrogant rebuff from Senator Glenn, together with the positive encouragement of Senator Warner, motivated Trent to advocate an amendment to reduce the requirement from eight years to six years; and that the change be held in abeyance until sufficient hearings had taken place. When the vote was taken on his amendment on the Senate floor, Lott defeated Glenn, 55–45 amid a Democrat-controlled Senate.

I like to say that I gave Lott the issue that demonstrated his leadership potential and propelled his climb towards Majority Leader; in addition, it made me a hero at West Point. The other academies averred that they wished they had a "Billy Mounger" on their Board of Visitors. As a postscript, the Congress held hearings, studied the situation, and voted to leave the service requirement at five years.

One more piece of history remained to be made in the late 1980s: I had helped elect the state's first Republican senator; I would help elect the state's second—insuring that for the first time in the history of Mississippi the state would have two Republicans serving as its senators. I just discussed how Trent Lott entered the Senate with a bang by besting seasoned Ohio Senator John Glenn. Briefly, here is how I helped Lott win his Senate seat.

While Thad Cochran's climb from congressman in 1972 to senator in 1978 pleased me greatly, Trent Lott's climb from congressman in 1972 to senator in 1988 also made me proud. More and more, I had grown closer to Lott, whose conservative philosophical leanings were more compatible to me. I was Trent's finance chairman for that race and the finance director was the very capable young man, Dan Davis; together, we made a tremendously effective team.

Lott ran against Democrat Wayne Dowdy, a former McComb mayor who had become U.S. Fourth District Congressman and had strong financial backing. When Lott asked me to be his finance chairman, I conditioned it on Davis being the paid finance director; I had developed a strong respect for Davis while we worked together on Reagan's 1984 reelection campaign. With Trent's connections, being House Republican Whip and all his national connections, he produced a lot of PAC money from Washington. What Danny and I accomplished was to raise more than $3.5 million dollars for Trent to win that campaign.

It was tremendously satisfying. We finally elected someone whom I still believed in after the trauma of 1976, which to this day remains the worst experience of my life. Then in 1980, working together, Trent and I carried the state for Reagan; and finally, we won the U.S. Senate for Trent in 1988.

Trent recalls our election effort: "He [Billy] knows I'm an instinctive conservative. I think Billy trusts my philosophy of government. He knows my background. He knows what I believe in. He knows my voting record has been very steady with a high 90s conservative rating. Therefore, we trust each other philosophically. And then he knows I like to win and I play to win and so does he."[16]

In Lott's 1988 campaign for the United States Senate, a few of us put our foot down strongly at least once; it was when Trent was beginning to seek the help of a highly touted campaign advisor— Dick Morris—who eventually became embroiled in Mississippi governor Bill Allain's campaign and, more significantly, was a longtime campaign advisor to President Bill Clinton. Lott recalls:

In 1988 I was running for the Senate and Billy was my state finance chairman; and my campaign manager was Tommy Anderson, who used to be my chief of staff and had been ambassador to Barbados; and the chairman of my steering committee was General Mickey Walker. I had a steering committee, and Billy was on there by virtue of being my finance chairman. . . . It was a great group. . . . We had gotten out early with good television and the polls showed me well ahead. . . . We were looking at another series of three television spots. . . . The consultant was Dick Morris. And the media guy was Bob Goodman of Baltimore. So I had good television, good consulting. . . . Anyway, when I saw these three new spots that Dick Morris had talked me into, I said, "I don't know, I don't feel comfortable with those. I'd like for my steering committee to look at these spots." I had not asked them to look at any others. So Dick Morris flew down from New York to Jackson to show the spots to my steering committee. He set the scene, how we prepared those particular spots, the polling data and all, so they would look at the spots and let me know what they thought. Well, they looked at the spots and then they picked Billy—not Mickey, but Billy!—to call me. And Billy basically said, "We don't like the spot and who is this guy with alligator shoes from New York down here telling us what we ought to be doing?" And I laughed and I told him in effect, "Well those spots will never see the light of day and the guy with the alligator shoes will never come back to Mississippi."[17]

In summary, as the 1980s played out, I truly was enjoying the knowledge that my real conservative friends were ascending to places of state and national prominence, that my guys were now in leadership, that people I had been associated with over numbers of years and my Reagan friends from all around the country now held the reins of government. There was Thad Cochran, whom I had recruited in 1972 for the U.S. House, and who won election to the U.S. Senate in 1978; Trent Lott, my longtime philosophical partner, was elected to the U.S. House in 1972 and the Senate in 1988. Ronald Reagan now lived in the White House. For a time, three U.S. congressmen also were Republicans, not to mention the eventual election of Kirk Fordice as the first Republican governor since Reconstruction. As of 2006, we have Haley Barbour as governor, Amy Tuck as lieutenant governor, Tate Reeves as treasurer, and Phil Bryant as auditor; two of four congressmen (due to reapportionment) and both senators are Republican. (See Chapter 25 for how we convinced Amy Tuck to switch parties.)

All the years of hard work had paid off!

Once, when I was much younger in about 1967, Trustmark National Bank (then First National Bank) CEO Bob Herrin had challenged my decision to work for the growth of a new Republican Party in the state. One day he stated, "Billy, what are you doing all this Republican stuff for? You can't make money or get any power through Republicans. You can't get anybody elected. How you make money and how you obtain benefits is to be a Democrat and you'll be rewarded."

I replied, "Well Bob, I'm not in it for reward. I'm in it for trying to do what I think is the right thing. I believe we need a two-party system and I think Democrats are bad for America."

Today I would like to look Bob Herrin in the eye and hear what he now has to say; but I would like to say to him, "You may have made millions of dollars, but look what my efforts have accomplished." However, he is deceased.

In January 1989, I received a letter, which was a wonderful way to close out the 1980s and earlier years that I had spent laboring for conservative Republicanism alongside Ronald Reagan. The letter was on stationary labeled "The White House, Washington" and dated January 13, 1989. It read:

Dear Billy:

As I prepare to return to California, I wanted to take a moment to tell you how much I've appreciated your support and help all these years. In 1980, you and I, with the help of the American people, started a prairie fire that has burned with ever-greater intensity, sparking one of the greatest political movements our Nation has ever known.

With the election of my trusted friend George Bush, you and I can rest assured that the revolution we've created and the great victories we've won during these past eight years will not be undone. Rather, they will provide the solid foundation for his administration to build upon.

Yes, we've done wondrous things together. We've cut taxes, revitalized our Nation's defenses, spurred the economy into the greatest peacetime expansion in history, and restored confidence in our Nation and the principles it embodies. America is back and standing tall again! Nothing we've done on my watch makes me happier than to see the renewed pride in our country and optimism for its future.

While I'm looking forward to spending more time around the ranch, I know that there are battles yet to be fought and—you know me—I'll be out there speaking my mind as I always have.

For now, just let me say that your tireless contributions to my many campaigns for office have provided Nancy and me with fonder memories than you will ever know. It was your unwavering support, enthusiasm, and commitment to our cause that sustained us through many a long and difficult hour.

God bless you, and God bless America.

Sincerely,
Ronald Reagan (personal signature)

CHAPTER 24

Bill Allain

Charles Pickering has long been a true Republican and community leader. While Pickering was doing well in Jones County, in 1979 he decided to run for the state post of attorney general of Mississippi, and I supported him. His opponent was the son of a Natchez river boater—Bill Allain. Pickering's political and legal career would flow into the twenty-first century, while Allain's would rocket in the 1980s and plummet then, as well.

Before detailing the difficult—and, yes, lurid—story of the battle to uncover the truth of Allain's sexual liaisons with male prostitutes, the background of Pickering's race against Allain will be instructive.

At an early finance meeting for Pickering at Jackson's Walthall Hotel, I made one of my typical spiels for raising money, telling the attendees, "If all of you will collectively raise fifty-thousand dollars, I will personally raise more than that." Newspaperman Paul Pittman erroneously claimed that I had promised to donate the money to the Pickering campaign to match anyone else who raised that sum. His article, printed below, elicited the following response from me.[1]

Seething beneath the surface of the neatly-groomed and increasingly successful Mississippi Republican Party is a power struggle, spawned by the now famous clash of Ford-Reagan forces in 1976 and fueled by the vanity of personalities and conflicting ideologies.

What is at stake is the long-honored hegemony on a tightly knit coterie of charter members of the modern Republican Party in the state—men like Jackson insurance man Wirt Yerger and oilman Billy Mounger, the party's consummate fundraiser and unabashed gadfly of the Republican right.

To put it mildly, Mounger was outraged when Gil Carmichael, the party's standard bearer in two recent statewide campaigns, supported Pres. Gerald Ford over Ronald Reagan in the 1976 GOP battle for the party's presidential nomination.

That rift has continued, and despite protestations to the contrary by party functionaries, it continues. If anything, it has deepened.

What is really at stake this year is whether the newcomers to the state party—men like Carmichael and Sen. Thad Cochran—will be able to wrest meaningful control of the party from Mounger and his associates.

Not only has it been Carmichael who has continued to be a burr under Mounger's political saddle blanket. Now it is Senator Cochran, as the logical temporal head of the state GOP, who is flirting with political heresy.

Cochran was credited, when he ran for Congress in 1972, with saying that he had never voted Republican until he voted for himself in the House of Representatives race that year.

Now, in spite of earlier reassurances from Mounger to the Republican right that Cochran would be okay on the issues, the freshman senator from Mississippi has set a moderate course in Washington, far from the positions that Mounger had promised.

Cochran, for instance, is supporting John Connally of Texas for the Republican nomination next year. Moreover, he backed President Carter's position on the Taiwan issue and supported the politically moderate Sen. Bob Packwood (R-Oregon) and Republican Sen. John Heinz of Pennsylvania for key GOP leadership positions in the Senate.

This and more was the subject of a 45-minute harangue Mounger delivered to a May 14 meeting in Jackson of the finance committee for state Sen. Charles Pickering.

Pickering, a candidate for attorney general this year, spoke briefly to the small group as did Haley Barbour, the shrewd Republican operative who is backing both Reagan and Pickering. But it was

Mounger who dominated the meeting unloading his invective on Gil Carmichael, a candidate for governor this year, and on Cochran, whose political turn is not to his liking.

That Pickering is but a foil in the internecine party warfare is incidental to Mounger's, perhaps fading, role as party kingmaker. But Mounger challenged the group to get busy on fundraising, vowing the he would raise or donate $50,000 to the cause.

The unfortunate beneficiary of the inner-party fight is without a doubt Toxey Hall Smith of Wiggins. Smith, an attorney in Wiggins and former FBI man, is also seeking the Republican nomination for attorney general this year.

But, with Mounger backing Pickering, it is probable that Smith has had difficulty in raising the funds to mount an adequate media campaign and the effort needed to make a successful statewide race.

Earlier on, Pickering had considered running for lieutenant governor. But, with the game plan forecasting bigger and better things for the Laurel native in the years ahead, the decision was made for him to seek the attorney general's slot. This would give him an independence from Carmichael should the Meridian car dealer be elected governor this year. And, it would bypass the historical dead-end blight on lieutenant governors who have sought higher office.

Whatever the outcome, this struggle is one to watch. Its resolution could very well determine whether the state GOP goes statewide on a permanent basis, or whether it will still have to grapple with the provincial charter members and kingmakers in the capitol city.

My June 7, 1979 response to Pittman follows:

Mr. Paul Pittman, Editor
The Tylertown Times
Tylertown, Mississippi

Dear Paul,
Our mutual friend, Jim Furrh, has furnished me with your Outlook article of May 24th. This article is replete with misstatements and misrepresentations which could have been easily rectified by a telephone call to me. A reporter of your experience and (deserved?) repu-

tation should at least check his story with the person primarily involved.

To disabuse you, my schism with Carmichael was not caused by, nor originated with, his support of Gerald Ford in 1976. Approximately 75% of my disillusionment with him was due to his inability to follow the advice of his Gubernatorial Steering Committee culminating in defeat. About 10% of my disenchantment was brought on by his extreme reluctance to repay a campaign loan to me (separate from my substantial contributions) after ending the campaign with a substantial surplus. About 14.9% of my irreconcilable difference was due to his opposing me, after being given every opportunity to withdraw, for my protocol position as vice chairman of the delegation to the 1976 GOP Convention. Subsequently—but not material to this critique—I won the post about 2 to 1. Now, in totaling my Carmichael irritation percentages, you will find that I was 99.9% separated from him prior to his support of Ford. Admittedly, that last .1% sealed the door with Elmer's Glue. These facts have been clear to anyone who has come within earshot of me (which you have made no effort to do) because my manner (your description "unabashed gadfly") is to let all and sundry know where I stand.

Now, as to my differences with Thad. Most certainly, I have made them clear to Thad and all who will listen, and will continue to do so whenever I differ with his stands on issues. Especially, will I do so when I am attuned to the desires of the average Mississippian and particularly the wishes of those who supported Thad. His Heinz vs. Hatch, Packwood vs. McClure, Taiwan, and Education votes all fall into this category. After all, I have at least earned the right to criticize.

Your insinuation that I was infuriated by Thad's committing to Connally is blatantly untrue. At no time did Thad ever lead me to believe that he would support Reagan; and his commitment to Connally was a pleasant surprise for I feared he would be for Howard Baker. Obviously, I am strongly for Reagan for many reasons; but, if he should fail and Connally succeed, I would have no problem in supporting Connally over any Democrat possibility. Baker would almost be impossible for me to digest.

Your statement that Thad had never voted Republican prior to his race in 1972 is also without foundation. He served as Treasurer of Democrats for Nixon in 1968, therefore, he must have voted for

Nixon then. Also, you misspoke when you stated that Haley Barbour was supporting Reagan. He is for John Connally and is working on the Connally payroll which a cub reporter should have known.

Your statement that I subjected the meeting to a "45 minute harangue" is fiction of the most dubious type. The meeting, including lunch, lasted an hour and was mainly about finances. Even you give me some credit as to my fundraising abilities; i.e. "consummate fundraiser." At a finance meeting is it not logical that I have the floor for a few minutes? My comments were limited to around 15 minutes, almost all were concerning campaign finances with a number of satirical and sardonic asides relating to the human desire to not part with money together with remarks about the lack of appreciation of candidates for assistance given during campaigns. Yes! As is my wont, those remarks included Thad and Gil.

You also accuse me of being a "kingmaker"—a mantle I have no desire to wear. The facts will probably bear out that I have been very instrumental in the elections of Thad Cochran, Jon Hinson, and others; but my motivation was the furtherance of good conservative government. However, your choice of the word "king" is apropos because too many candidates, after being elected, think they are endowed with "divine right."

In addition, your description of Charles Pickering as "a foil in the internecine party warfare" is totally without substance. Pickering is an immaculately honest, Christian, decent, well qualified person, with an excellent record in all his endeavors and in no way is anybody's foil. Judy King is Pickering's co-finance chairman and he supported Ford, served with Mike Retzer as the party's finance chairman (as my successor), and is still backing Carmichael. How you could say Pickering is a foil or is a candidate of a faction is another of your jaunts into space. Additionally, Toxey Smith is a fine man and my support of Pickering reflects no animus towards him individually or his capabilities. Certainly, no internecine conflict can be accredited to this situation as Toxey was a strong supporter of Reagan at the '76 Convention.

Your sensationalizing of my fundraising commitment to the Pickering campaign was also a gross misrepresentation. I did not state categorically that I would "raise or donate $50,000 to the cause." As has been my *modus operandi* in every campaign, I have challenged the other fundraisers by interjecting a figure for myself much in excess of what anyone else is expected to fulfill. Accordingly, I set a goal for myself of $50,000 for the Pickering campaign with the explanation to those present that I expected to raise that figure as a minimum and would probably do twice as much. Also, that commitment included both primary and general elections giving me six months to raise it.

Furthermore, in order to prove my sincerity, I stated that I would guarantee at least that amount, but that I did not expect to put any more of my money in the campaign and that I was taking no appreciable risk in making that statement. You make it appear that I was acting the "Big Shot" by saying I would contribute $50,000. Of course, if you reported fact instead of fiction, it would require a modicum of effort and would not be as entertaining as your conjurations.

In summation, there was a Pickering finance meeting and I did make a presentation before it. You have expanded these facts with flights of fantasy to supply your readers with a column. Surely, after so many years, your competence and veracity as a reporter are superior to this apocryphal verbiage.

Sincerely Yours,
W. D. Mounger

WDM:pm

Pittman profusely apologized to me for writing such an erroneous column and promised that he would run my refutation letter statewide, but he never did.

Pickering won his primary with a goodly amount of funding to spare. Then he faced Bill Allain, who at that time was relatively unknown. But Allain had served as an assistant district attorney in the case involving James Meredith, who was the first black to enter the University of Mississippi.

We were running a good race with Pickering, and I believed we were going to elect our first Republican in a statewide race. Then toward the end of the campaign, a conversation took place about trying to obtain black votes; heretofore, we had not been successful in obtaining many black votes. The Republican National Committee dispatched two black workers to help the Pickering campaign appeal to black voters with about ten days remaining before the election.

I did not know how to get black vote and I still do not know how to do so. Unbeknown to the steering committee, the two workers brought a substantial amount of money—perhaps $100,000—from the national party.

Thad Cochran's longtime friend, Grady Jolly, who later was appointed a United States appellate judge, had fought many good battles with me and was also helping with Pickering's campaign. Cochran had defeated Pickering in the 1978 senatorial primary, and afterward, Pickering did yeoman's work for Thad; therefore Grady was demonstrating his appreciation.

Grady suggested to Pickering that his campaign try to find out whether Bill Allain had ever been associated with the state's Citizens' Council. He apparently said, "Maybe some black votes can be enticed if it is shown that he belonged to the Citizens' Council."

If I had known, I would have said, "That is taboo, because almost every prominent white person at that time was a Citizens' Council member, and if I had been an adult living in Mississippi in the 1949 or 1950 era I would have probably been a member also. Perhaps my father was. I do not know."

The two young men did more than take Grady Jolly's suggestion. They came out with a radio spot.

Of all the things that I have seen in a campaign, that was the most disastrous. It had no pluses; everything was minus. When the campaign ran those spots on black radio saying that Allain was a member of the Citizens' Council and blacks should support Pickering rather than Allain, then in reality the spots were saying that Allain was really—as far as the race goes—more conservative than Pickering. What that did then was cause the particularly George Wallace-type Democrats who were having a difficult time voting Republican—the Eastland types—to reorient toward Allain.

The logic may have seemed convoluted to anyone but a Deep South conservative at that time. In an interview with the authors, Pickering said he had no idea that this whole campaign had been hatched and wouldn't have endorsed it at all.

With only two days left until the vote, Pickering announced that he did not approve the spots, but the campaign executive committee effectively had no time to disown them. Pickering was then forced to spend the last two days of the campaign apologizing and chasing ephemeral votes rather than emphasizing his strong credentials.

The final vote in the 1987 attorney general race in Mississippi was 315,831 for Allain to 294,560 for Pickering. I believe that Charles Pickering may have lost more than 100,000 votes due to those stupid spots. In response to this great blunder, I wrote to myself the following white paper:

Götterdämmerung, 1979; or,
How to Snatch Defeat From the Jaws of Victory

Charles Pickering was winning his campaign for Attorney General until some of his staff blundered to the ultimate degree by blatantly appealing for votes on black oriented radio stations with untrue and inflammatory statements. Mistakes have occurred in campaigns before; but none to compare with the disastrous one committed by this campaign.

Invariably, the greatest errors Mississippi Republican candidates commit are those concerning appeals for liberal or black votes. Assuredly, we should attempt to get all the votes we can; but we should never directly appeal for votes in a way which is contrary to our basic conservative philosophy and out of line with our natural constituency. And, we must never lose sight of what composes that constituency—Republicans, Independents, and George Wallace Democrats—all of which are predominantly conservative. In order to win, we must never alienate these groups.

Just such an alienation resulted in the incomparably stupid action of certain Pickering staff members. Every aspect, both negative and positive, of the ill-conceived radio spots enured to the benefit of the opponent. Superimposed upon this unfathomable blunder was the traditional burden of running as a minority party candidate compounded by the trouncing experienced by the top of the ticket. Any mistake was thereby multiplied many-fold.

The only possible favorable result was the addition of a debatable number of black votes. Pickering already was the beneficiary of more than normal black votes because the black community to some extent was already informed about Allain. For example, the pre-marked sample ballots handed out in Hinds County left the Attorney General choice blank. And, whatever the gains, they could easily have been more than offset by Allain's denial that he was ever a member of the Citizens' Council.

In general, the spots brought about the destruction of the "nice-cool guy" image that Charles has rightfully attained in the public's eyes. The charges smacked of gutter politics and were unsubstantiated. They seemed like desperation tactics when in reality, Pickering was winning thereby destroying the winning psychology. Lastly, they caused Pickering to give the impression that he was an incompetent manager even if it were believed that he didn't approve them. The negative effect was fortified when Pickering appeared on TV with an unsatisfactory and frenetic explanation of the event. Ironically, the TV appearances were scheduled in advance to enhance his "good guy" image by showing his extremely attractive family.

Maddeningly, this situation would not have arisen if the National Committee had not assigned their black consultant Wright to help out with the National money. Local campaign funds would never have been used in such a way. Consequently, this campaign was not sufficiently alert because this was outside help and money.

The spots redounded to Allain's benefit. They set forth aspects about Allain that he could not say himself. They stated he had worked against the Civil Rights Movement and that he belonged to the Citizens' Council. Both these points were persuasive in shifting great numbers of George Wallace type votes from Pickering to Allain. Exacerbating the situation was the interpretation that if Charles were demeaning Allain for his Citizens' Council membership, then Charles, himself, must be more liberal than was perceived.

Additionally, the intellectual types did not like the spots because they reeked of "mudslinging" and tied Pickering with the top of the ticket and its similar tactics. Also, to them, making charges that were unsubstantiated demonstrated unethical behavior.

Unfortunately, Pickering did not know about the particular offensive spot; but he received the blame even though the decision was made by people unauthorized and incompetent to make such a decision.

In conclusion, there are two basic lessons to learn from this unmitigated fiasco. The first is that we, as Republicans, must always represent the conservative side of the spectrum and we should be immaculately careful not to alienate our natural constituency of conservative Republicans, Independents, and Democrats. The second is that regardless of the technical and experience qualifications of campaign experts, control of a campaign must always be exercised by those people who are congruent with the mores of the people.

There were times like these—off and on—during the 1980s when our Republican cause in Mississippi seemed to have bogged down into a mid-life stalemate. For instance, Democrat Wayne Dowdy was able to win the Fourth District congressional seat two times in a row, confounding us Republicans. Meanwhile, Haley Barbour had run against John C. Stennis in 1982 and lost. Barbour then departed for Washington, D.C., where he would eventually become chairman of the Republican National Committee and a top lobbyist. (I did not actually support Haley for the Senate because of Haley's antics at the 1980 state convention; but when Barbour lost the race, I stepped in with a two-thousand-dollar contribution.) And, as mentioned before, Gil Carmichael had run for governor as a Republican and lost twice—to Cliff Finch in 1975 and William Winter in 1979. He also was effectively sidelined after Ronald Reagan won the White House in 1980.

The white-haired Allain served his one term as attorney general, then in 1983 turned his sights on the governor's office for the term running 1984–1988. William Winter, a liberal's liberal, was ending his tenure as governor. The residue of the Cliff Finch years in the late 1970s was still thinly spread throughout the state.[2] Jon Hinson had resigned in disgrace, creating an open Fourth District seat.

It was hard for many of us in the GOP to conceive that a Democrat might again win the Mississippi governor's race at the very time when Republican President Ronald Reagan was ruling the White House. We in the state GOP wanted very much to take that governor's office. So many of us key Republicans kept trying to find a new gubernatorial candidate.

We turned a second time to Greenville planter Leon Bramlett, who had run a solid Republican primary race against Gil Carmichael back in 1979. We all loved and admired Leon Bramlett, a graduate of the United States Naval Academy and an All-American football player there.

Former Governor John Bell Williams first suggested Leon to me in 1978, and I informed Wirt Yerger, who followed up with Leon. A former Democrat state party chairman, Leon was good-looking and a dedicated Christian. Regretfully, Leon did not file until the last minute in 1979, because his daughter was in a coma after an accident. Wirt Yerger, Neal Clement, Victor Smith, and I immediately dashed to Bramlett's side in 1979, pulling together a campaign infrastructure almost overnight. Carmichael barely defeated Bramlett after personally borrowing a hundred-thousand dollars and dumping it into the last week of the campaign. Carmichael's victory had proved Pyrrhic because many, including myself, would not support him and his silly positions.

In repetition of what he had done in 1979, Leon again did not make up his mind in 1983 to run until the last minute. As the Democrat first primary was finishing, we picked up rumors from Democrat Evelyn Gandy's campaign that Allain was a homosexual. When a second Democrat primary ensued pitting Gandy against Allain, the rumors permeated the air. But the Gandy campaign didn't do anything openly. I had met Allain earlier that year through my good friend, David New, an oil-well driller from Natchez, who asked me to attend a meeting with Allain. That was my second meeting with campaign strategist, Dick Morris, who became very famous later working for Bill Clinton, but who also worked for Republicans including Trent Lott.

I had no intention of backing Allain, and Bramlett's late entry in the 1983 race gave me a viable Republican candidate. The rumors were now rampant about Allain, and Leon Bramlett's campaign lacked luster. Leon was a bright and qualified man, yet he did not have a fire in his belly. He was a reluctant candidate both against Allain and earlier in 1979 against Carmichael.[3]

With the Bramlett campaign bogged down, I commiserated with fellow oilman Neal Clement from time to time, and Neal lamented that the state might be electing a gay governor, who, if true about his frequenting prostitutes, was breaking the very laws he was sworn to uphold as our state's attorney general.

We would not support someone proven to have broken intentionally other laws. Should we turn our heads as a state just because the laws potentially broken might have involved embarrassing sexual conduct?

Even today many seem to miss this larger point due to the sexual nature of the potentially criminal acts: prostitution and sodomy, not to mention potentially tampering with evidence or influencing witnesses.

U.S. Rep. Jon Hinson was arrested for similar, albeit actually lesser, criminal acts involving sex. Our state's largest paper reported that. Were we all to leave our state's attorney general, running for governor, unchecked?

After several conversations, Victor Smith, Neal, and I ate lunch at the old Petroleum Club where we discussed these rumors. Neal kept saying, "We don't want a person like that as governor. It would be terrible."

We three decided that someone ought to do something about it, and *voilà*. I don't know which one instigated the original thought, but we collectively looked at each other and said, "Well, we are the ones who must discover whether these rumors are true or not. Who else will do it if we do not?"

Our first action was to find the divorce papers between Allain and his former spouse. We contacted Scott Hemleben, an attorney and backer of Evelyn Gandy, who was also one of Neal Clement's attorneys. We were in Neal's and Howard Stover's office when Scott Hemleben came over and said, "I thought you guys were absolutely crazy, but after reading this divorce filing, I believe you are on the right track."

The divorce papers alluded to Allain frequently being gone at odd hours and failing to perform his "husbandly" duties as a spouse. We all looked at that and said, "What that says is that he isn't sleeping with her." From that time on Hemleben was an active, silent participant.

We proceeded to vet all the rumors. We needed a legal expert working more overtly for us so I suggested Bill Spell, a former Mississippi journalist and a lawyer. Spell had worked for the Mid-

Continent Oil and Gas Association, for Senator John C. Stennis as public relations director, and also for Liles Williams's campaigns. He was mainly a Democrat, with Eastland, Stennis and others, but I knew he was an independent thinker who had the fortitude of his convictions.

I called Spell and said, "I don't know whether there is anything to these rumors, but we need someone who has knowledge in this area to give us legal advice and to be involved—someone who has guts."

Spell was intrigued.

He began to research police records. We would hear about something that happened in Washington or in San Antonio or wherever, and we kept following other leads. When you are conducting a political campaign, you hear many rumors; however, we were frustrated because there were no police records anywhere.

We would hear that Allain had been seen and picked up by the police, and about other unsavory things happening in the local area; but there was nothing recorded on a police blotter. The police just did not want to get involved with the Mississippi attorney general. They would leave him out of their reports, compounding our investigative problems. Our efforts were bogging down.

About then, Scott Hemleben, single at that time, told us that a girlfriend of his had a homosexual brother and that she would sometimes accompany him to homosexual bars. Scott said his girlfriend had heard that Allain was attracted to black transvestite prostitutes. And that the normal, if you could say "normal," homosexual community did not like his preference for those weirdos. They did not like prostitutes, and they did not like blacks being with whites. They had no respect for him.

That is when Bill Spell, Neal, Victor, and I contacted Bob Pendleton of Pendleton Detectives. Pendleton's people interviewed patrons of homosexual bars who stated that they were aware of Allain's activities; they even gave the names of the black transvestites involved. Pendleton then located these designated individuals.

One of the gay prostitutes went by the alias "Devia Ross." Ross and others said that they had been involved with Allain and that they had been to his apartment. Allain's apartment was on North

Jefferson Street, and as a test, Pendleton asked "Devia Ross" if he knew where the apartment was. Pendleton then took Ross and others on separate car rides and attempted to get them lost. When Pendleton would head in the wrong direction, they would correct him, saying "No, you're going the wrong way. We know where he lives." And then they would lead him directly to Allain's apartment and would describe the inside of the apartment—sofas, pictures, etc.

They told Pendleton that they would park outside with Allain, and he would go in and determine if the coast was clear. Then they would enter his apartment. All our discoveries kept corroborating the story.

Next, Pendleton found a plumber who had gone to Allain's to work and uncovered many stacks of horribly erotic homosexual literature. What heterosexual guy is going to have anything around with homosexual literature in it? No normal person does that.

Our group, with Pendleton and Spell's overt help, deposed these characters, and the story progressively got worse. In addition, policemen began telling us, "We have picked Allain up any number of times in a certain area." One policeman actually had identified Allain talking to one of the prostitutes we were interviewing.

We were convinced that we had confirmed his unnatural activities, but except for the prostitutes, no one had ever witnessed Allain in *flagrante delicto*.

We tried another angle. We knew that when police picked up a person with a communicable disease, they asked the person to detail their sex partners for health purposes. That record is kept at the state health department and a contact in the department told Spell that Allain's name was mentioned by more than one of these very same prostitutes. That was on public record. We knew it was there.

Then a contact within the state department of health informed Bill Spell that the records had disappeared. At a press conference Spell let it be known that we knew that those records had disappeared and he warned just what the penal sentence for such theft would be. Miraculously, the records showed back up again; however, we never got our hands on them. But we knew they were there and that we could get them with a subpoena, which I believe is one of the many reasons Allain never sued us.

During this time Leon Bramlett did not know any of this. Spell, Neal, Victor, and I were conducting this investigation as individuals. Bill Spell never received a penny for the untold attorney hours he put in, but many people inferred, "Bill Spell made a lot of money off of this." *Au contraire!* He did not make anything, though it cost him some clients, and his son publicly came out against us. However, it did cost Neal, Victor, and me in excess of $150,000.

This period was the only time in my life that I have felt threatened; and, consequently, we provided guards for both Bill Spell and Victor Smith's houses. We were being tailed in our cars from time to time, and we received telephone threats and other intimidations.

We did not begin our investigation until after the Democrat primaries were over, and it required a lot of time accumulating the evidence. Therefore, we did not piece together the story until the latter part of the general gubernatorial election campaign.

Bill Spell's idea was to gather the information and proffer it to the *Clarion-Ledger* because Charles Overby, the editor there at the time, was Spell's friend. Spell had recommended Overby for his first job after college, as a staffer for Senator John C. Stennis.

I told Spell, "I don't trust the *Clarion Liar* to do anything." Still we figured we were giving them this great scoop, and they would proceed properly with it. We had compiled a seventy-one-page investigation with many depositions and presented it in bound form from Pendleton. The opening page of the investigative document reads:

Statement of William E. Spell
October 25, 1983
Jackson, Mississippi

An investigation has developed clear and convincing evidence that establishes beyond a reasonable doubt that Attorney General Bill Allain, over a period of years, frequently has engaged in homosexual acts with male prostitutes.

Some of the homosexual acts that the evidence shows Mr. Allain engaged in are described by Mississippi statute as "detestable and abominable" and are punishable by a sentence of ten years in prison.

The evidence includes the following:

> Sworn statements of persons who state they engaged in homosexual acts with Mr. Allain.
>
> Polygraph or lie detector tests of those persons that indicated the persons who stated they participated in homosexual acts with Mr. Allain were truthful.
>
> Statements of police officers and former police officers that they observed Mr. Allain in a pattern of conduct consistent with solicitation of male prostitutes and inconsistent with conduct not reasonable for any other purpose.
>
> Statements of persons who say they have seen in Mr. Allain's apartment pornographic items and activities consistent with homosexual activity.

The investigative tasks were performed by Pendleton Detectives of Mississippi and the Investigation is still in progress.

Everything was detailed fully and backed by sworn affidavits.

The *Clarion-Ledger* stagnated, even though Spell had assured the newspaper that we had given all three of the prostitutes lie detector tests and all three had passed. *The Clarion Liar* asked if they could see the male prostitutes.

Meanwhile, we decided to sequester the three prostitutes. We figured that we could not leave them walking the street to be subjected to whatever might befall them. So we moved them around—Shreveport, Monroe, Baton Rouge, various places.

Spell made the male prostitutes available to the *Clarion-Ledger*, which assigned reporter Wanda Cantrell to check on all these things. Bill Spell recalls how the *Clarion-Ledger* sat on the story; Says Spell: "Then began the greatest display of gutlessness I've ever seen in my life. . . . This was something amazing."[4]

Charles Overby had asked, "How can I make sure that these things occurred? How can I make sure they're telling the truth?" His experts advised the paper to give these transvestites lie detector tests and that if they each took separate tests—and all three passed—you could be sure they were truthful. Thus, the paper administered a separate test to each one, and each passed, meaning that each passed two tests, since they each had already passed the one we gave them. That is a total of six tests given and six tests passed. Even after all that corroboration, the paper would not accept the story.

Overby told one major out-of-state newspaper that did print details that he thought his role as a reporter wasn't to cover whether a man running as the Democrat candidate for governor of Mississippi frequented transvestites—a criminal act. The *Miami Herald* noted: "Spell and Pendleton compiled a report, bound in blue and, in a small box printed on the front like a Surgeon's General's warning: "Notice. The enclosed contains sexually explicit material concerning Attorney General Bill Allain. If such material is objectionable to you for moral, religious or personal reasons, please do not read the contents."

The article continued: "Inside were depositions and lie detector confirmations from three black transvestites: David Holliday (known as Devia Ross), Donald (Donna) Johnson and Grady Arrington (Nicole Toy). The Mill Street trio offered very graphic descriptions of sexual encounters with Allain. And there were statements from a pair of maintenance men who claimed they saw stacks of "queer magazines" by the water heater in Allain's apartment.

"On Oct. 14, Spell took his blue book to the media. Jackson's largest newspaper, the *Clarion-Ledger*, brought in the three drag queens and hired its own polygraph expert. They passed, said executive editor Charles Overby. "But I didn't think the newspaper's role was to expose sex habits."

"The *Clarion-Ledger* and other newspapers and television stations held the story."[5]

It was just too gory and there wasn't a picture of Allain in the act, so the *Clarion-Ledger* would not print it. Their reporter, Wanda Cantrell, whom I met, trolled the gay bars that Allain was reported to frequent, and after she researched the situation, she became convinced that our claims were true.

But again, Overby thwarted her; the paper emasculated her story so much that it was ineffective. Her immediate boss at the paper, Lew Cernel, supported her, and reportedly, there was a shouting match at the *Clarion-Ledger* about properly publishing her reportage.

The *Clarion-Ledger* definitely abdicated its faith with the people of Mississippi when it sat on verified facts about the moral and legal failures of Bill Allain. Senator Trent Lott still feels that the paper was derelict in its duty, and he hardly reads the *"Liar"* today. Trent Lott: "It was extremely irresponsible for the *Clarion-Ledger* not to reveal what they knew was the truth. I guarantee you they would reveal it if it had been a Republican. If it would have been me, they would have ripped my head off. There is no question that the *Clarion-Ledger* is an extremely liberal Democrat organization like most Gannett newspapers. The only decent Gannett newspaper is their flagship, *USA Today*. But they are prejudiced; they always have been and they always will be, and the *Clarion-Ledger* in my opinion is one of the two most negative factors in this state. They hold us back. They perpetuate racial distrust."[6]

Eventually, when the campaign was over, I wrote a letter to the *Clarion-Ledger* spelling out my incredulity that the paper had not reported pertinent information that concerned such key public figures—especially during a gubernatorial election. Along with my letter to the Gannett paper, I included a newspaper clipping from the *Miami Herald* reporting scores of details about the Bill Allain allegations that never saw the light of day in Mississippi's largest paper. The full, very thorough *Miami Herald* article is contained in this chapter's endnotes.[7] I alluded to the November 6, 1983 *Miami Herald* article, "Homosexuality Allegations Rock Mississippi Race," in the following letter decrying the *Clarion-Ledger*'s selective news coverage. My letter to the editor was headlined, "Truth about Allain Said Suppressed," and ran in the *Clarion-Ledger* on November 27, 1983. Its text follows:

> If (?) you deserve a Pulitzer for your efforts concerning the Education Reform Act, you unquestionably deserve a "Putridlitzer" for your suppression of the truth about Bill Allain's cavorting with black-female-impersonator-prostitutes.
>
> You, the arrogant executive editor, told numerous people that you believed the allegations to be true, and your investigative reporters ferreted out much information which buttressed the charges pre-

sented by Bill Spell. But you, in your elitist arrogance, decided the people had no right to know the truth.

If you suppress the truth when it doesn't benefit your ultraliberal proclivities, then what else might you do in support of your elitist predispositions? Your investigative reporters must feel as unclean as Allain's male prostitute friends after you "spiked" their stories. Your lack of reportorial candor deserves a spike to be placed in only one locus!

There was an article printed in the Sunday, Nov. 6 issue of the *Miami Herald*. In 24 hours, it uncovered more about the truth than you revealed from Oct. 13 to the end of the campaign.

Mississippi has been last in the nation for a number of years; but now we are the laughing stock of the nation! You could have prevented this embarrassment to the state if you had fulfilled the duty of a free press and pursued the truth!

If the *Miami Herald* could print interviews with transvestites and other inhabitants of the "trolling" area, why didn't you print your reporters' information? They interviewed several transvestites we could not contact, other individuals in the area, several policemen, maintenance men who had repaired Allain's apartment, and many other people. Obviously, their discoveries were not revealed because they corroborated our claims. If your reporters had uncovered refutations, you would have headlined them in red! Why not the truth?

However, you aren't the only culprit! Almost the entire Mississippi press corps participated in an intentional dissemination of disinformation. You and your cohorts in the Mississippi press arbitrarily decided that: (1) A candidate's sexual perversions should not be discussed in the theater of politics; (2) A person's moral, ethical, philosophical, and religious individuality should not be aired; (3) The late exposing of the charges somehow made them wrong; and (4) Most importantly, the voters might not support your choice for governor if they knew the truth.

Pulitzer! Maybe? Putridlitzer! Incontestably!

W. D. Mounger
Jackson

When the state's major paper ignored our information, Bill Spell, Neal Clement, Victor Smith, and I decided it was too important to just drop. So we decided to carry the burden of making the information public ourselves. We hired Bobby Peets, now deceased, who was in advertising, and he developed newspaper ads and TV spots featuring Bill Spell. We were not able to get any media to take our ads or productions; two exceptions were a station in West Point-Columbus and one in Greenwood that ran our half-hour TV production. But the stations had to run pro-Allain programs as well. We spent a lot of money producing our TV spots and advertising, but the media boycotted it.

Next, we held a meeting with prominent businessmen to present our evidence. At the meeting, some believed the information and others did not. Some said, "You have all this material but there are people who are never going to believe it unless you have a photo."

After that frustrating first meeting with the business community, we tried to persuade the Bramlett campaign to adopt our findings, but Leon Bramlett would not do so. If he had, the media would have had no option but to cover the issue fully, since it would be part of his campaign. Without the Bramlett campaign's imprimatur, the media said, "You are not a campaign. We are not going to run your material."

When we met with Leon Bramlett and his staff and showed them the material for the first time, Bramlett, who had no knowledge of what our research had shown, was appalled by what we presented. Leon listened to the entire presentation and said, "Oh, I just can't do anything with that. Besides I'll be sued."

Bramlett's daughter was still comatose in the hospital, and this tugged at him emotionally while on the campaign trail. We stated, "If anyone is going to be sued, we will be. First of all, all of us have substantial worth, so we are delectable targets. But they are not going to sue us because the truth is an absolute defense against libel. You should not be concerned. You are the candidate and you are not the one who might be sued."

But the fact was that the story was nauseous—the characters were horrible and the transvestites had been seen on TV. If I may use one of my facetious phrases, if they had just been "clean-cut homosexuals," it might not have seemed so obnoxious to the people. However, many people would not acknowledge that our community of Jackson had practicing homosexuals, much less black prostitute transvestites. And this guy was in the lead for governor, making unacceptable the repulsive story.

After we had met with Bramlett, we conferred and agreed, "We have made all this effort and we have uncovered all this information and no one will run our newspaper ads or TV spots. And now Bramlett has rebuffed us, too. If he is not concerned enough to prevent such a person from being governor of Mississippi, why should we spend any more time on this effort?"

So each of us said, "To hell with it. That's the end of it."

But the next morning, everyone of us simultaneously concluded that we could not terminate the effort. We talked on the telephone and agreed that we had to stay the course, with only two to three weeks remaining before the election.

We held our first really large press conference at the Jackson airport, and it really hit the fan. Bill Spell recalls talking with the *Clarion-Ledger*'s Charles Overby before Spell laid out our findings at the press conference:

> I called him [Overby] and I said, "Hey, I want to ask you a question. I'm about to have a press conference. I just want to know one thing. If I go out and have a press conference, am I going to pick up the paper in the morning and see that you have whacked my legs right out from under me by saying that your newspaper's research shows contrary to what I'm saying in my press conference?" And he said words to the effect, "Well, what are you going to say in your press conference?" And I said, "I'm going to say that Allain . . . is a practicing homosexual and has had homosexual activities with these transvestites and so forth and just generally that." And his response to me was, "Well, we're not going to cut your legs out from under you." That pretty much told me that Wanda Cantrell's efforts had confirmed what we had developed.[8]

Allain burrowed underground for about thirty-six hours after our press conference. He knew the truth of our accusations. If we had been lying, he would have immediately lambasted us; conversely, he went underground. He obviously thought, "The gig is up. They've got me."

We traversed the state, expounding our information. We went to Columbus, then to DeSoto County, next to Clarksdale and Tupelo, and then down to the Coast and Hattiesburg. I especially remember the Coast meeting where Victor gathered many religious leaders, among whom were two particular ministers, one Episcopalian and the other one Lutheran, and they both said, "Why is it any of your business what he does? What difference does it make?" Victor explained that we felt people ought to know for whom they were voting, and besides, the Lord condemns homosexuality. Victor read a pertinent part of the Bible and the two so-called ministers said, "Oh, you can't pay any attention to what's in the Bible."

It was terribly frustrating.

When nobody would pick up our information, Allain's advisors—Dick Morris and others—were telling him, "You can weather this storm because they can't get their story out. The media will not present their side."

After about thirty-six hours, Allain emerged and denied our accusations. He said, "Oh, I would never do anything like that. And I'm going to file a lawsuit against all of them." We knew he was not going to file a lawsuit against us.

Then we suggested, "What about taking a lie detector test?" Owen Cooper from Yazoo City, who was an active Baptist and Democrat and a very conscientious, decent person, gave me one of my greatest compliments; he said, "If Billy Mounger is involved in this, and if Billy Mounger says it's true, it's true."

We next challenged Allain to a public lie detector session with Owen Cooper supervising; the plan was for all of us to publicly take lie detector tests together with Allain, using a totally independent lie detector operator—not his, nor ours. I agreed to take one, even though I had never before taken a lie detector test. Notwithstanding, it was finally decided for only Bill Spell to take one, but Allain refused to show up. Spell passed the test with flying colors under the supervision of Owen Cooper. Owen was the only prominent Democrat who agreed with us about Allain. To my knowledge, that was the only time Owen Cooper ever deviated from the Democrat Party line, and he was the only one.

After Spell took the lie detector and passed it, Allain finally took an in-house, secret test, which he purportedly passed. We knew it was a controlled lie detector test conducted by a well-paid operator from New Orleans. We understood that Allain was secreted several hours south of Jackson and that the operator was paid around forty-thousand dollars for the bogus test. Allain's campaign just announced, "Well, he passed."

On the night of July 16, 2004, Scott Hemleben was watching *The O'Reilly Factor* as a discussion was ensuing about California Congressman Gary Condit and the young lady he had an affair with who was murdered. Dick Morris reacted in his inimitable fashion in response to O'Reilly saying, in effect, "Look, what I don't understand is why the guy won't take a lie detector test." Morris then stated, verbatim: "I had a client who shall go nameless, who was elected either governor or senator and whose name is not Bill Clinton who was accused of some horrendous sexual misconduct; and he offered to take a lie detector test—a private lie detector test. And we spirited him down to a city where he worked for four days to pass that lie detector test. And, finally, with the aid of drugs, hypnosis, and God knows what, he finally passed. And then the issue became, would he take it by the police? And I walked him around the parking lot and asked, 'Is there any reason why you wouldn't take it?' And he said, 'Yes there is.'"[9]

Then Bill O'Reilly said, "Yeah, 'I'm guilty.' That's why he wouldn't take it." Meanwhile, Morris nodded his head.

There was no way in the world Dick Morris was talking about anyone other than Bill Allain.

While we had the prostitutes under our care, I think it was when they were in Monroe, Louisiana, they told the Pendleton guard accompanying them, "We would like to spend some of our money which is building up for our benefit." We were giving them a per diem in lieu of income for "tricks" they would be turning.

Our guard asked, "Well, what do you want?"

"We want a Singer sewing machine and a lot of yard goods."

Our guard took them to buy material to make dresses and a new Singer sewing machine. They studiously sewed away making dresses. After the campaign, they participated in the annual gay ball in Jackson, which I did not know even existed! They won prizes for their dresses, and one of them won the grand prize for a dress made from those yard goods and the Singer sewing machine!

Some time after Bill Allain had been elected governor, a stringer from Memphis for Geraldo Rivera for the 20/20 television show on ABC, whom Bill Spell happened to know, informed Spell that Geraldo wanted to come down to uncover the truth. I told Spell, "Bill, I don't know if he really wants to come down here to find out the truth. I'm afraid he is just going to sensationalize it." Bill said, "No, the person who's arranging it wants to come down here to set out the true story."

Bill stated that we didn't have anything to hide. We agreed we would make everything available to him, and that is essentially what happened. Geraldo's advance people came down first, and we gave them everything—all the material we had used. And there was a large amount of information we had not been able to air publicly.

Unfortunately, upon arrival in Mississippi Geraldo had already concluded that we were louses who had demeaned Allain for political purposes. He took our information, used it on his program, and acted as if he had originated it.

Geraldo featured one of the transvestites on TV and browbeat him before ever putting him on camera. The assistant editor of the *Clarion-Ledger*, Lew Cernel, who was over Wanda Cantrell almost came to blows with Geraldo, whom he saw mistreating the transvestite into changing his testimony. He became vehemently incensed because Geraldo wasn't really reporting; he was forcing the transvestite to recant. Geraldo did not care about the truth but only wanted to depict his own, wild story.

Later, Geraldo interviewed Spell, Victor, and me. Geraldo questioned me for approximately forty-five minutes and was getting nowhere since I was telling the truth. Suddenly, in the middle of the interview, he stopped and said, "Tell me, you really don't like homosexuals, do you?" I said, "Well, it's not that I hate homosexuals or that I dislike homosexuals, but I will say that if anybody is around me whom I believe to be a homosexual, it sort of makes my flesh crawl." And then we went on with the interview. When I exited the interview room, Victor and Spell asked, "How did you do?" I said, "Well, I'll tell you what he's going to run. He's going to run a statement I made in the middle—he didn't care about any facts because I refuted everything that he threw at me because all I told him was the truth."

It took several months before the Geraldo show ran; by then it was 1984 and Reagan was running for reelection. I had been the mid-south regional finance chairman for Reagan in 1980. But in 1984 I was the Mississippi finance chairman for Reagan. It so happened that I was in Washington the first part of the week when the Geraldo program was to run on ABC two nights later. Whenever I was in Washington, I visited with Nevada Senator Paul Laxalt, who was also the campaign chairman for Reagan. Later, in 1992, I was even the "Laxalt for President" chairman in Mississippi because I did not want to be for Bob Dole.[10] After I visited Paul, I also met with Ed Rollins, Reagan's campaign manager, and Lee Atwater, the assistant campaign manager. I told each one, "I am going to be on 20/20 Thursday and I want all of you to view it. If I have done anything which would embarrass the Reagan campaign, I will resign as finance chairman, if you wish. I have finished raising the money for the campaign, therefore it would be of little consequence." They each viewed the program and called me that night to say, "Billy, they [homosexuals] make our flesh crawl too." They all agreed with me. They laughed and said that it didn't disturb them at all.

Bill Spell states that the funniest remark during the investigation was when it was reliably reported that Allain had been caught naked with only his shoes on. Upon initially hearing that report, Spell remarked to me: "Why would he do that?" And I answered, "He obviously is not scared of getting AIDS, but must be deathly afraid of athlete's foot!"

In the years immediately following the 1983 Allain-Bramlett campaign, I have been asked several times to speak about it. What follows is a reporter's account of a speech I gave at Ole Miss in 1985.[11]

The 1983 gubernatorial race and the homosexual allegations involved were discussed by Republican W. D. (Billy) Mounger as he spoke to Alexander P. Lamis's Mississippi Politics class Thursday.

"A thing or two happened that was out of the ordinary. In fact, you might term it as bizarre," Mounger said in reference to the homosexual allegations against Bill Allain.

Mounger, who supported Leon Bramlett, was one of three businessmen who financed an investigation looking into rumors that Allain had associated with homosexuals.

Mounger said after the second primary election, rumors were everywhere. He and two others decided to try and find out if they were true.

The investigation eventually led to interviewing transvestites that claimed to know Allain. Mounger said he never met any of the transvestites because he was afraid he might laugh. He did say he peeked around the corner once to get a look.

The group sent results of their investigation to newspapers throughout Mississippi; but only a few chose to publish it. The *Clarion-Ledger* declined.

"I think the press failed Mississippi more in that instance than any other," Mounger said.

Though the group tried to get Bramlett to bring out the allegations, "He wouldn't touch it," Mounger said. "Leon led kinda a cloistered life in Clarksdale. I don't think Leon realized that sort of stuff went on."

The uproar resulting from the verbal charges was one of the main issues in the last two weeks of the election. Allain, who threatened to file a libel suit, never did.

Mounger feels that it was Allain's threat of a lawsuit that helped him win the election. "That's the reason he won, people believed he was going after who accused him."

"If that had happened to me," Mounger said, "I'd say three people better get their fannies across the state line. Strap on those lie detector tests, all over me."

The only lawsuit that could come up now is the group filing against the television news show 20/20, Mounger said. He said when the reporter interviewed him, "I knew I wasn't telling him what he wanted to hear."

About halfway through the interview the reporter asked Mounger if he disliked homosexuals. Mounger replied, "If somebody gets around me who's homosexual, it makes my flesh crawl."

Mounger said he knew the show was going to use that one statement and try to make him look bad. He said it didn't work though,
because all his friends thought it was funny.

Before the charges were aired, Allain had been in a predictable
lead, as had nearly every Democrat nominee for governor in Mississippi before him—about 60 percent to 25 percent, with a margin
of error thrown in. After the news broke, Bramlett came up to
about 35 percent, while Allain dropped, resulting in a virtual tie.

But in the end, the people in Mississippi did not want to believe
anything that horrible, especially since we had no public outlet to
tell the true story, and particularly with Allain denying it and saying he was going to sue us. We actually offered at one point to pay
for Allain to sue us. He refused, because he was never going to sue
us and never did!

With only a few days left in the campaign, Bramlett finally partially took up the issue, but it was far too late. He volunteered to
take a lie detector test if Allain would, saying that if Allain passed,
he would drop out of the race. But he delayed too long, and it was
simply a peripheral approach to saying that Leon believed us.

It was close to election day and it was obvious that Bramlett was
not going to win. As election day approached, a bunch of us old
Republicans were gathered with Leon. Wirt Yerger told him,
"Leon, you are the football player. Let me tell you what happened:
These guys (Clement, Mounger, Smith, and Spell) took over for
you. They took the ball down to the two-yard line. They handed
the ball to you with first down and two to go and you stumbled,
fumbled, bumbled it back to where you were on your own forty
again. That's what happened."

Leon is the kind of person who doesn't react too much to anything. I couldn't say that he took offense to that. To be honest with
you, the whole endeavor cost us fifty-thousand dollars a piece, and
that was in addition to the money we gave to the Bramlett campaign. That was separate. I did not regret it and have never regretted it.

After Allain was elected governor, I attended a function at the
Jackson Country Club hosted by Toby Trowbridge, an Oldsmobile
dealership owner. When I entered the door to the room I saw Toby,

and standing right next to him was Bill Allain. I was abruptly facing Allain and he said, "Hello Billy," and all I could say was "Hello
Governor," and I shook his hand.

Ultimately, Bill Allain was not too bad a governor, because he
made no waves. I did become irritated with William Winter, who
is a member of my investment club. There are thirty-two members
in the investment club—thirty-one Republicans and William, the
only Democrat. William had appeared on TV and said how bad we
were and how bad it was of us to make that kind of charge. But if
we had been despicable with the charges, then why did William
Winter always go out of his way to speak with me at functions,
indicating that he knew the story was correct?

In a letter I wrote to the *Clarion-Ledger* four years after the 1983
race, I made it clear that what we did was tell the truth—the very
thing we trust the members of the Fourth Estate to do. The letter
follows:

January 8, 1987

Letters to the Editor
Attention: Mr. David G. Hampton
The Clarion-Ledger
Jackson Daily News
P. O. Box 40
Jackson, Mississippi 39205

Dear David:

There you go again with your typically *Clarion-Ledger*-tenden-
tious article titled, "Will Allain and Newman be back in 1988?"
written by your staff writer, Dan Davis, on Sunday, January 4, 1987.

Your egregious tendentiousness is confirmed by this partial
quote, ". . . the likelihood of another *smear* campaign like the one
that rocked his [Allain's] 1983 candidacy." By what right do you describe what took place as a smear? Smear means to malign; defame;
slander; calumniate. All those words define something untrue. How
do you arrogate unto yourself the wisdom to brand the charges un-

true? Obviously, you have not deigned to communicate with your own reporters who know the truth.

In 1983, Allain appeared on TV across this State and swore to the voters that the charges were unfounded and that he would positively sue those involved for libel (also refer to the *Clarion-Ledger* dated October 27, 1983, "Allain prepares to sue; Bramlett calls for polygraph test"). If the charges were *smears*, he should have filed the largest damage suit for libel in Mississippi history. Why did you and your paper fail to prod the Governor into fulfilling his sworn commitment? Why did you and your paper avoid publicizing that Allain allowed the statute of limitations to expire in the fall of 1984 thereby precluding him from suing? If the charges were untrue, a suit would have saved this state from the embarrassing onus of having a Governor with such degrading charges outstanding. Obviously, he did not sue because the truth is an absolute defense for libel!

You also quoted Allain thusly: "I don't know what else they could do to me. I don't think they could do anything worse." How true! In our wildest fantasies we could not have dreamed such demeaning revelations. Truth again is proven to be stranger than fiction! Any innocent, red-blooded, heterosexual male would spend his last penny and expend his last breath to remove such abhorrent disparagements from his record. Allain did nothing!

Furthermore, your paper commendably eulogized Owen Cooper; however, you studiously avoided mentioning that he completely accepted the truth of our charges. His religious convictions pertaining to perversion overrode his political propensities which is much more than our immediate (whom you sickeningly and ingratiatingly adulate) ex-Governor can say. Additionally, Mr. Cooper stated to me that: "To any thinking person, Allain's failure to file the suit for libel should forever dispel any doubt about the truth of your charges."

If any smearing has been done, your paper has smeared those of us who revealed the truth. You have inexcusably miserably failed to serve your readers and Mississippi voters by *your* obvious conspiracy to conceal the *truth*.

Sincerely yours,
W. D. Mounger

The black community also could see straight through this issue from the very beginning. The most liberal newspaper in Mississippi, the *Jackson Advocate*—an alternative black newspaper—actually wrote a pretty devastating piece about Allain. I will close this chapter with that article, which presents even more information beyond what Bill, Neal, Victor, and I gathered. In the end, the Allain issue was about morality. It was about sexual deviancy and addiction. It was about breaking the laws of Mississippi against pornography and prostitution. Even more so, however, it was about a sitting attorney general repeatedly breaking the laws that he was sworn to enforce. It was about electing such a man as the chief representative of our state, the governor. And it was about deceiving people and covering up the truth—even at the cost of allegedly asking state employees to purge files or alter police reports. Sadly, without a truly responsible press, this information was never presented as it could and should have been. Again, the following article by Jackson's alternative black paper, however, pulled no punches.[12]

JACKSON—My dear departed grandmother used to have a saying when something was related to her that didn't quite pass the truth test. "That don't quite set right with me," she'd say.

A recent experience brought that old adage very vividly home.

Three weeks ago, we were standing at the lunch counter of a diner, waiting patiently for our order, when we were approached by a man who mistakenly thought I was the sister of one James "Pee Wee" May. The mistaken customer immediately recounted a scenario of the "injustice done to Pee Wee."

Having a little time and a lot of curiosity, we listened and asked questions.

The tale related to us sounded much like a tale from "Alfred Hitchcock Presents." The man told us of plots and counter-plots, a diabolical sequence of events that began with the alleged pre-election scandal involving ex-Gov. Bill Allain. We were given names, places and dates—a mountain of information which staggered our imaginations.

The talkative man was certain Pee Wee's arrest was part of the counter-cover-up move to protect then-Gov. Allain. "They framed him," the man said, "And after all he had done for them."

"What had he done for them?" we asked. The answer to that question led us into houses of prostitution and into the underground world of homosexuality.

VIEWPOINT

After checking and rechecking the facts surrounding the arrest of May; after interviewing many sources, it soon became apparent there was much more to this story than had ever made the papers.

James "Pee Wee" May was arrested on Dec. 10, 1985. He was charged with sale of cocaine, possession with intent to deliver cocaine, possession with intent to deliver . . . and receiving stolen goods.

There were charges and more charges. The method of arrest was as "fishy" as three-day-old cat. Things just didn't add up.

According to sources, the story behind the story of the arrest of May is one of sexual misconduct, bribery, extortion and threats of violence.

This tale of intrigue revolves around the pre-election sex scandal involving ex-Gov. Bill Allain.

In 1983, sources say, Allain, a democratic candidate for governor of Mississippi, was embroiled in a sex scandal involving four homosexuals.

The allegations were investigated and documented by Atty. Bill Spell and the Pendleton Detectives of Miss., Inc. According to the admitted homosexuals, they had "engaged in sexual activity with Allain."

Sources revealed that Allain, usually represented by his attorney, Crimes Pittman, had investigated several avenues for "squelching these allegations."

"A lot of money changed hands, but the stories persisted," they say. "Allain was desperate, he knew these statements made by the homosexuals could spell disaster for his political ambitions. He had to do something, and he had to do it fast."

Enter James May.

Sources say Pittman approached May and appealed to him to intercede on Allain's behalf with the homosexuals.

Consequently, May contacted and arranged to meet with the four homosexuals. According to one of the homosexuals, who requested his name be withheld, May used bribery, threats and violence to protract a promise that they would recant their stories. After promising to do so, the homosexuals were promised money and "good jobs" for their efforts.

Exit James May.

After they had fulfilled their end of the bargain, the four homosexuals received none of what was promised them. Feeling they had been "crossed," the homosexuals once again tried to tell the story of their involvement with Allain. But, having gone on television and recanted their stories, their credibility was shot. They had been effectively neutralized.

This maneuvering served to silence the homosexuals, but what about James May? There was a more expedient way of silencing May, according to sources.

When the homosexuals attempted to push their allegations, May was arrested, or as sources say, "framed to get him off the streets."

When contacted, May refused to confirm or deny the story. He gave a half-smile, a grunt and an emphatic "no comment."

James "Pee Wee" may not be willing to talk, but there are many more people involved who are more than willing to come forward.

AUTHOR'S NOTE: Former governor, Bill Allain, was reached March 22, 2006 on the phone at his home, after numerous previous attempts. Governor Allain said he had no comment regarding requests to add his observations to this chapter. He said he did not think anyone would read this book. He added: "That story has been in the newspaper. It's twenty years ago. It's over as far as I'm concerned. I don't want to fool with it no more. It is something in the past that I don't care to talk about. I don't think anybody else is interested, to tell you the truth."

CHAPTER 25

Two Decades of Electoral Success: Fordice, Parker, Tuck, and Barbour

I was never of fan of George H. W. Bush, and always endeavored mightily to avoid being on his first team. By 1990 I became thoroughly disgusted and wrote a letter pertaining to his vacuous reneging of his "read my lips, no new taxes" pledge. I wish I were as prescient as the following letter appears to make me; nevertheless, the facts are that the Republican Party was devastated soon thereafter in the November 1990 races around the country, and Bush badly lost his bid for reelection in 1992. George H. W. Bush's inveterate problem was that he never understood how he became president. In fact, he was elected on Ronald Reagan's coattails, Peggy Noonan's speech writing, and Lee Atwater's machinations. But Bush undoubtedly believed he was elected because he had graduated from Phillips-Andover Academy and Yale University and because his father was Senator Prescott Bush of Connecticut. He once demonstrated this elitism when, while campaigning, he said, "I stepped in deep do-do." Who in America says "do-do" but a Yalie?

My letter follows:

November 2, 1990

President George Bush
The White House
Washington, D.C. 20515

Dear Mr. President:

As you know, my Republican credentials are long term and impeccable. But, for the enlightenment of your toadies whose *cordon sanitaire* this letter must breach, the following very succinct resume is included:

Delegate to Republican National Conventions 1968, 72, 76, 80, and 84
Vice Chairman Mississippi Delegations 68-80
Southern Floor leader Reagan-Bush 84
Nixon Finance Chairman 1968 & 1972
Mid-South Finance Chairman Reagan-Bush 1980
Mississippi Finance Chairman Reagan-Bush 1984
Recruited and Finance Chairman Thad Cochran
Finance Chairman Trent Lott for Senate 1988

Hopefully these credentials will circumvent whichever sycophant is designated to answer this letter. With circumvention assumed, here are my views.

Dispirited, disillusioned, disappointed, and disgusted—these words describe my reactions to the misguided apostasy of your "Read my lips" pledge. Did you not understand the depth of the people's concern with taxes? Did you not understand or care about undermining the Republican Party?

My deep seated fear is that you do not even understand the reasons for your election. The two most prominent being, an absolute no new taxes pledge; and Willie Horton (the social issues agglomerated). Do you have no feeling for the average American's revulsion to the excessive tax load? Did your Connecticut, Phillips-Andover, and Yale backgrounds isolate and insulate you from the social issues concerns of the average American? Nevertheless, you are to be commended for vetoing the infamous quota bill; but you substantially undermined your deserved credit by your severe equivocation.

Mr. President, I initially began working diligently for Republican candidates during the Goldwater campaign and consequently we have elected many, including both Mississippi Senators. Now you are devastating all that we have accomplished by your capitulation to the tax-tax-spend-spend Democrats.

To begin to make amends, you must terminate those pusillanimous prostitutes of pragmatism, John Sununu and Richard Darman. They have disserved you, the nation, and the Republican Party. Even if you don't understand how you were elected, at least your coterie should. Without such a drastic move, I fear you have squandered almost 30 years of effort, reducing the Republican and conservative causes to shambles. Next Tuesday, I fear, our Republican candidates will be routed.

In the hope that this missive somehow penetrates your *sanctum sanctorum*, I have enclosed three items which have probably been withheld from your view. All of these are very indicative of the harm you have wrought by playing the Democrat's game. First is an article from the *Wall Street Journal* titled "John Q. Republican Answers Back"; second is an article from the *Orlando Sentinel* titled "Is Bush Man in the Empty Suit?" and third is a cartoon depicting the insuperable contretemps caused by the violation of your solemn (inviolable!) pledge. How can your word ever be trusted again! A Minister of God cannot disown the Lord! Your position is comparable when you disavow your sacred covenant with the electorate!

Most of us loyal Republicans are:

Dejectedly, disquieted, and disemboweled,
Signature (Billy)

Now we arrive at the 1991 election of Kirk Fordice as governor of Mississippi, an election for which I can take virtually no direct credit. My admired friend, Billy Powell, the "Czar of Rankin County" (a cognomen I awarded him!), was the essential person who won the primary and the general election for Kirk.

I was not for Kirk because I supported Pete Johnson in the primary; Pete was elected state auditor as a Democrat and mid-term switched to Republican, but he was burdened by a $160,000 debt, which I co-endorsed because he changed parties. With my monetary obligation, I could not support Fordice; also, over the years, I had had many confrontations with Kirk, who was endowed with a combative spirit.

When the general election commenced in 1991, I began having heart problems, starting with two angioplasties, culminating in successful open-heart surgery by friend and renowned surgeon Dr. Henry Tyler; in December I was also tended by my friend and unsurpassed cardiologist, Dr. Jimmy Hays.

However, for Fordice's reelection in 1995, I was a major factor, raising a substantial portion of his funds. Trudy Nickles, his finance director, came to me with the idea of raising $500,000 all in one day for Kirk. She had been naysayed by everyone she contacted, until she talked to me. I agreed that it was a doable idea and said that I would take care of a $10,000-per-couple function at the Governor's Mansion with ex-president George H. W. Bush as our guest. (You can not raise money at the Governor's Mansion but you can raise it before you get there.) However, before absolutely shouldering this task, some commitments were necessary. Beforehand, Fordice came to my house for a wedding function, and I told him that I needed a pledge that no one could come to the mansion function unless they had previously given the $10,000. (If you let one four-flusher in, how do you exclude others? And if you do, they inevitably will elbow out the legitimate people and occupy most of the guest of honor's time—this is a fetish with me.) Kirk agreed but I needed more specificity. I said, "That especially means Clarke Reed." Reed had a notorious reputation for attending affairs without paying. Fordice laughed and said, "Man are you tough. But you have my promise." With these agreements, I raised more than $300,000 in $10,000 pledges, and Trudy raised more than $200,000 from a $1,000-per-person function and from a greater-attended $250 per person affair, raising more than $500,000 in one day. Fordice, the first Republican governor since the Reconstruction period, was a great governor and the only governor in history who has ever served two successive terms.

After my two angioplasties and the campaign, I was playing tennis with my regular Monday partners—Ralph Hines, Gus Primos, and Wirt Yerger—when my chest began severely hurting. Gus and I won the set, and I walked off the court announcing that I could not continue because I was going to have open-heart surgery. Later, I had two stents put in and prior to each procedure I repeated that tennis scenario.

Dr. Henry Tyler operated on me on December 22, 1991. A day later I was in intensive care and still hooked up to all the life supporting and monitoring equipment, when Jan stood behind me, out of sight, and said, "I have someone to see you. It is Jim Furrh and he has given you a pint of his blood." (I had needed five pints.) I exclaimed, "Oh my Lord, I hope that doesn't make me a Bush-ite!" Jim, an old Texan, was a longtime backer of the first George Bush, whom I disdained as a moderate. Jim Furrh now recalls that incident: "I knew once I heard Billy joking about Bush that he was going to be just fine!"

Jim and I have been the closest of friends for more than four decades. We have enjoyed many trips abroad together with our wives.[1] And we have worked together in a number of political battles, including early efforts to elect Richard Nixon and our admittedly problematic efforts to support Jon Hinson. But we always have politely parted company when it came to Jim's public support for the first George Bush.

My friends Trent Lott and Billy Powell, and I are credited with Lt. Governor Amy Tuck's conversion from Democrat to Republican and reelecting her as Mississippi's Republican lieutenant governor. Trent said during an interview in the fall of 2004: "I sat down with Amy Tuck, our current lieutenant governor, three years ago to convince her to run as a Republican. And she said, 'Well how do I go about it?' And I said, 'Well, step one is I'd like to recommend that you contact a certain number of people and here they are and Billy Mounger was one of them.' I said, 'You need to go and sit down and talk to Billy and ask his advice and ask for his support and if you do, and he will [give you his support], he'll make a hell of a difference. And she did and he did."[2]

Quite honestly, I had been very impressed with Amy from the beginning. My admired friend, Billy Powell, however, who in the 1980s became the real force behind the GOP party in Rankin

County, had for a long time been cultivating a friendship with Amy and her brother, Al. Billy was chairman of the state Republican Party at the time and switched more Democrats to Republican than anybody else has ever done. Billy has a rapport with them since he grew up in rural Texas; truthfully, he's just a great guy and I really think a lot of him. Billy Powell recalls:

> If I really ever had a particular question, I would always go talk with Mounger. We had been friends for a long time through attending IPAA events together. And he over a period of time helped to bring me into Republican Party circles in Mississippi. He and I worked together on campaigns. . . . For instance, I got him to support Charlie Ross for senator. . . . I got him very much involved in the Amy Tuck switch. . . . I worked on Amy for eight years. When I was the party chairperson, Chris Webster was my executive director. Amy was going to run for secretary of state. I had her up to my office to see about switching. And she wanted to switch, she was conservative. . . . She didn't switch, with the idea that she couldn't come out of the Republican primary. Her brother, Al, was a strong person, really behind her, pushing her to run. Then she lost to Eric Clark. And I called Al and I took him out to lunch. When Amy won against Bill Hawks as lieutenant governor, of course I supported Bill. I went over to congratulate her. . . . She was very much appreciative. And I kept in contact with Amy. And she became more and more conservative, you may say. She was getting more and more out of favor with the Democrats. I went to Al. He and I talked. "You know, Amy has problems because she is getting too conservative. We really need for her to consider switching." Finally I talked to him one day and I said, "Well, let's you and I have lunch with the current state GOP chairperson, Jim Herring. I trust him. He'll help you. The previous chairperson, I would not have suggested it because he wouldn't have helped you. I don't particularly care for Mike Retzer, . . . He and Clarke Reed are close buddies. And Mounger and I are close buddies. And they don't like us probably for the same reasons we don't like them. But at any rate, I carried Al out to lunch with Jim. Al felt good about Jim. Eventually I said, "Jim, do me a favor. Have Trent call Amy." He did. Not long afterwards, I get a call from Amy, "Mr. Billy," she always calls me "Mr. Billy," "what do I do?" I said, "What

do you mean, 'What do you do?'?" "Trent wants to come by and see me." I said, "Amy, look him straight in the eye and ask him, 'What are you going to do to help me in the primary?'" And I said, "If he will not agree to help in the primaries, you don't need to change parties. We can't afford to get you beat in the primaries." And she did, and he agreed to support her. . . . She had guts. Mike Moore and Ronnie Musgrove and everybody tried to put the bead on her when Al Gore came down, for her to come to that event. She said, "I'm not going to do it." . . . And she was already on the tort reform type deal. She had done a couple of things that had gotten the Democrats mad at her. . . . Right before Thanksgiving I gave her a list of people. I sat down with her and said, "Now here's a list of people that you need to call and make them feel like they had a part in this thing." And on the top of the list was Billy Mounger. I said, "Go by and sit down and visit with him."

Trent, especially Billy Powell, and myself and our very effective state Republican chairman, Jim Herring, convinced Amy to switch. As was my wont, I felt an especial obligation to show a very warm welcome to elected Democrats who had the fortitude to follow their true convictions. Therefore, Billy Powell and I adopted Amy and worked assiduously for her—Billy more from an organizational standpoint and I from the financial side; and consequently Amy Tuck was elected lieutenant governor as the second Republican since Reconstruction, following Eddie Briggs who served from 1992 to 1996. Amy states that Billy Powell and I elected her lieutenant governor, but we do not make that claim, for she is the best campaigner of all the many candidates I have been associated with. However, if she wants to give credit—as Senator Eastland advised me—I'll take it!

Mike Parker, who owned a funeral home in Brookhaven, ran and won the election for Fourth District Congressman as a Democrat in 1988. He spent his own money and ran particularly effective TV spots because he has the ability to sell himself well, possessing a great voice. Mike defeated Republican Tom Collins, a seven-year Vietnam War prisoner. Mississippi admires heroic military people, which made Collins a good candidate on paper; nevertheless, Collins was not a good campaigner, and Parker went on to win the race.

While Mike was Fourth District United States Congressman, his assistant, Steve Guyton, originated the idea of having an academy day and inviting kids who were thinking about attending a national military academy. Guyton suggested my name to Mike Parker.[3] Consequently Parker asked me to speak to his first academy day. By this time I recognized that Parker was voting conservatively, and obviously he was not nearly as liberal as the other Democrats, creating a natural rapport. Parker probably had three hundred people at the War Memorial building in Jackson, including many young people and representatives from all of the academies. I rattled off my spiel and enjoyed forcefully favoring West Point in my speech. Mike Parker was greatly amused by my effusively touting West Point over the other academies. As a consequence, we became good friends.

I became a regular speaker each year for his academy days, growing ever closer to Mike. When in Washington, I would visit him even though he was a Democrat congressman, and I began to mention that he ought to switch parties.

We Republicans had high hopes of switching enough Democrats to Republican so that we could control the United States House and Senate. Billy Powell also became friendly with Mike Parker, trying to convert him, and Trent was working on him in Washington. Billy convinced Rusty Fortenberry, immediate past Mississippi Public Safety Commissioner, to switch parties when he was the district attorney for Covington, Jasper, Simpson, and Smith counties. Rusty's change helped set the stage for Mike Parker to switch, since he and Mike were good friends. Before he switched, Mike was instrumental in convincing three or four other Democrat U.S. congressmen to switch to Republican; and after converting all he could, he then switched.

In 1997, Trent, Billy Powell and I discussed needing a candidate for governor, and we agreed Mike Parker was the man. As a Democrat, Mike had received a lot of black support, and he had hired a number of black leaders on his staff, and even after he turned Republican in 1996, Mike was able to win reelection, maintaining a fair amount of black vote.

In Washington in early 1998, I opined, "I would really love to have a Republican governor succeed Fordice." So I met with Parker in his office, and he asked me to accompany him as he worked and visited with his fellow congressmen. I blurted, "Mike, you ought to run for governor. If you will, I will do what I swore that I would never do again—I will be your finance chairman."

Later I told Trent about my commitment, and sometime later, Parker publicized that he was not going to run for reelection to Congress. Parker lived in a nice house surrounded by several hundred acres southeast of Brookhaven where he desired to spend more time, and he was tired of Washington. These two factors convinced him to return to Mississippi, and finally, in October or November of 1998, he telephoned me stating that he would run for governor.

His campaign account contained about $350,000, and I decided immediately to raise $150,000 to get things moving. I called my good Republican contacts, such as Victor Mavar on the Coast, and asked for $10,000, thereby raising the $150,000 by early December. I was ultimately able to raise more than $3.5 million for the campaign with the invaluable assistance of our talented finance director, Kevin Kellum.

I envisioned a steering committee giving advice, but not controlling the campaign. Mike, however, took the early money to his media advisor and produced a brilliant TV spot making fun of hunting with his son, and whether they had shot anything. It was a father-and-son relationship situation, with guns and hunting— much appealing to Mississippians. It was the best opening spot that I have ever seen a candidate offer, causing people to perk up and talk about Mike.

In the long run it backfired, because from then on, all Mike wanted to produce was what I call "cutesy-wutesy" TV spots. Thereafter, everything he did had to have a tricky gimmick to it. Throughout the campaign, he never explained his philosophy or why he should be governor, or even who was Mike Parker. None of us key supporters were informed about what he was going to run on TV until we viewed it in our own homes.

Our steering committee only met once and, therefore, was ineffective. Mike did not want to be bothered. The voters kept saying, however, "When is he going to give us some substance?"

Mike Parker held a constant five- or six-point lead in the polling data, making him so confident that he would not campaign as he should; he would not go to a shopping mall and shake hands or attend any political gathering.

Leslie Lampton, a substantial Mike Parker backer from the beginning, once entered a barber shop after Mike had gotten his shoes shined, and the barber stated that Parker never spoke to a soul in his shop. Barbers are very politically influential with their customers. Leslie telephoned me, saying, "Billy, we have a candidate who cannot win because he is too indifferent to even speak to someone in a barber shop." Leslie also said that anyone wearing a big diamond ring could not win.

Mike also neglected campaigning in key voting areas, such as DeSoto County south of Memphis, a very populous Republican county. During the entire campaign he only went there twice and both times only meeting with a small group of people, perhaps twenty, to raise funds. They gave him money, but he made no effort to publicly promote his campaign. He followed the same routine in Tupelo in Lee County, another very good Republican county. He visited Tupelo twice, but never accomplished anything politically. He only raised money, which he used to air his cute TV spots.

In retrospect, Mike had essentially won his congressional campaign by spending his own money to run TV ads. He did not go out and hustle votes, even after he was a congressman, and he devastatingly continued that losing tactic during the gubernatorial race.

If he had made a modest amount of effort, he would have won. In the end, he essentially did nothing the last couple of weeks. While Musgrove was diligently campaigning, Mike was playing golf at the Deposit Guaranty tournament, and at the end of the campaign, the only TV he aired featured a female named "Musgrove" shelling peas, saying, "My name might be Musgrove, but I am voting for Mike Parker." It was cute, but what a miserable culminating TV spot. If he had just told the people, "I am Mike Parker and I am running for governor because . . ." instead of a comedy skit, he probably would have won. In finality, he lost by approximately eight-thousand votes from across the state.

There was not much you could say the night of the general election when he lost the governor's race. All of us were devastated. We kept watching that very close count, and Mike never would give in. The vote was so tight that it had to be decided by the Mississippi House of Representatives, where under Democrat control, Musgrove was judged victorious.

I heard that Mike blustered, "The Republican Party did not do enough for me." Well, essentially I represent the Republican Party, and I supervised raising $3.5 million from all our good Republicans. That was an absurdity—he had only himself to blame.

The following callous indifference demonstrates his lack of appreciation. I was diagnosed with prostate cancer (Level 6) in July of that year but I felt obligated to fulfill my duty as his finance chairman until after the end of his campaign. Jan had attempted to persuade me to immediately have an operation, but I insisted on finishing the campaign. After the losing campaign in November, I underwent a prostectomy by the highly competent Dr. Joe Ross, and by then my cancer was a Level 7 on an asymptotic scale, much worse than the previously diagnosed 6. Mike Parker never inquired about my condition and to this day has never expressed thanks to me for delaying my operation or for any of my efforts for him.

We now are at the election of Haley Barbour for governor in November 2003. Haley's prominence had initially been propelled as a twenty-two-year-old law student when we in the Mississippi Republican Party had named him as the 1970 Mississippi Census chairman. This was an awesome job supervising more than 3,500 people. When Bill Wilkins departed as executive director of the Mississippi Republican Party in 1974, we named Haley as his successor. He was later elected as our Republican national committeeman, and ultimately he engineered his own election to the chairmanship of the Republican National Committee. In that position he demonstrated more effectiveness than any other Republican national chairman in my lifetime. Helping him in these endeavors was his very adroit co-chairman, Evelyn McPhail, also of Mississippi. After leaving the chairmanship, Haley organized the lobbying firm of Rogers, Griffith, and Barbour, which evolved into one of the most successful in Washington, D.C.

After succeeding immeasurably monetarily and prestigiously in

Washington, D.C., Haley decided to forgo his tremendous income to serve his state by running for governor. He did not need me to be his finance chairman (he was an early *summa cum laude* graduate of the Mounger Finance Academy); consequently, I substantially offered my fund-raising abilities to Amy Tuck for lieutenant governor but gave the most generous monetary contributions of my life to Haley, who was elected the sixty-third governor of Mississippi.

Billy Powell and I coordinated the campaign for Amy Tuck after she switched parties. Amy was a tremendous campaigner and her term as lieutenant governor has been an invaluable benefit to Mississippi and the Republican Party.

The team of Haley Barbour and Amy Tuck has produced many benefits to the state, including tort reform, fair redistricting for the Third Congressional District, needed bond issues, and many other pluses for the state. Without the assistance of Amy and Travis Little, president pro tempore of the Senate, Haley's programs would have been in dire straits.

At the time of this writing, Haley Barbour and Amy Tuck are demonstrating tremendous effectiveness in dealing with the incomparable natural disaster of Hurricane Katrina. It would have been disastrous if "Old Squeaky" Ronnie Musgrove were still governor. It gives me much pleasure to see the entire country recognizing Mississippi's effectiveness in dealing with the hurricane disaster—particularly in contrast to the ineptitudes of the leaders in Louisiana.

CHAPTER 26

Saving the USA International Ballet Competition

B ack in 1975, well before I had evidenced any public connection to ballet, there were two ballet companies in Jackson: Ballet Mississippi and the Jackson Ballet Guild, which was formed to develop a professional ballet company and school to benefit Mississippi. The Jackson Ballet organizers were informed about a New Yorker, Thalia Mara, who owned the National Academy of Ballet, whose studio lease was terminating, necessitating that she reevaluate her future.

Thalia was invited to Jackson to confer with a number of people, including Walter Lydick Jr., Claudia Hogg, and Martha Underwood; that group urged her to come to Jackson and head the Jackson Ballet Guild. After settling here, however, she realized that she had previously met with the sum total of all Jacksonians who really cared one whit about ballet. Concomitant with that, she recognized that these Mississippians loved athletics, football, basketball, golf tournaments, and tennis tournaments, a realization that caused her to surmise: "These southerners like anything competitive; perhaps they would like an international ballet competition." This aggressive and talented lady had developed incomparable international and national ballet contacts, on which she began to capitalize.

At that time only two places in the world produced international ballet competitions. Varna, Bulgaria, had held the first in 1964 with Mikhail Baryshnikov winning in 1966 and then joining Leningrad's Kirov Ballet. Moscow, the capital of Soviet Russia, envied its satellite country of Bulgaria with its very successful international ballet competition, and thus decided that it must have its own competition. So Moscow, Russia, and Varna, Bulgaria—both behind the iron curtain—became the two locations for international ballet competitions; and, naturally, they stacked the deck with Russian judges at both places and as a consequence non-Communists faired poorly. They were not really that "cricket" or international, even though they were titled "International Ballet Competitions."

Thalia concluded that an international ballet competition ought to be held in the West; and she was aggressive enough to dream, "Why not in Jackson, Mississippi?"[1] Thus, she used her incomparable contacts to get the International Dance Committee of the International Theatre Institute of UNESCO to sanction an international competition for Jackson in 1979. Robert Joffrey, artistic director of the Joffrey Ballet and jury chairman of Jackson's first three competitions together with Estelle Sommers of Capezio Ballet Makers, became involved, injecting much prestige into the event. Governor Cliff Finch and his wife, Zelma, were both very bucolic, but Zelma convinced her husband to get the legislature to appropriate $300,000 for the resulting competition. In that competition, our native Jacksonian, Kathy Thibodeaux, was the senior silver medalist. Kathy later capitalized on her deserved recognition by founding "Ballet Magnificat!," a Christian ballet company that has justly earned national acclaim.

In 1982, U.S. Senator Thad Cochran was able to prevail upon the United States Congress to pass a resolution signed by President Ronald Reagan designating Jackson, Mississippi, as the official site of the USA International Ballet Competition. Thus, in 1982, Jackson held its first USA IBC. However, my involvement preceded this 1982 event when my wife, Jan, in 1979 hosted the English judge, Pamela May, a famous English ballerina, and I reluctantly attended three or four performances. Then, in 1982, Jan and I with Donna and George Godwin co-hosted Alexander Grant, a famous English *danseur* and ballet *raconteur* who was chosen as the Canadian juror, and thereafter, Donna's fervor motivated me to enthusiastically attend six or eight performances.

My first ballet experience had been in 1945 when a ballet company from New York City performed at West Point. I liked the music and I liked the dancing, but knew nothing about ballet. More foretelling, however, when I was stationed in San Antonio, Texas, in 1948 learning to be a USAF pilot, the movie *The Red Shoes* played featuring Moira Shearer, a famed British prima ballerina. I attended the movie theater together with West Point friends and was intrigued by it so much that I furtively sneaked back to see it again. I obviously did not want any of my friends to know that I was returning to see "a ballet dancing movie" a second time.

Virtually all my friends tease me about my involvement with ballet, because I am not built like a ballet dancer and no one would normally associate me with ballet. I stated in a speech on the opening night of the 2002 USA IBC that people cannot comprehend why I am into ballet; they mostly think it is very odd, since my forte has been football and my stature is short and thick. I specifically said, "When you are built like a fireplug, if you stand still at a street corner, you have to beware of dogs!" Naturally, Jan was severely chagrined; but the audience was greatly amused.

The 1982 event surpassed 1979; but the defection of the Romanian judge, and world-famous ballerina, Magdalena Popa, to the West during the event caused international repercussions.[2] Further and ominously, the first indications of financial problems with the IBC were emerging.

During the 1982 competition the Russians dispatched a famous prima ballerina, Sophia Golovkina, and others to investigate us, accompanied by several KGB operatives, all of whom came to determine whether our competition was viable. We treated them well, and I befriended all the Russians, which made the event more interesting for me and, as a result of their reconnaissance, the Russians committed to participate in the 1986 USA IBC. The Jackson competition had successfully run the gamut.

After 1982, I determined that the Jackson IBC was retrogressing financially; Finch and Mabus were out of office, and Bill Allain was now governor. Thus, I felt partly responsible for the decision by Governor Bill Allain that harmed the IBC. The legislature had approved giving the IBC $375,000 in 1984, but Bill Allain vetoed it, and I am convinced that one of his reasons was that many of the male *danseurs* had a bent towards homosexuality. At this point I am attempting to read Bill Allain's mind that his perception was that if he helped the International Ballet Competition, people would say, "Yeah, he's doing it because so many are his type."

My associate, Sue Lobrano, has worked for the USA IBC since September of 1980 and has been since 1986 the executive director. She is the most knowledgeable person in the world concerning international ballet competitions and recalls how I became more involved about this time:

I was amazed at Mr. Mounger's love of ballet, because he's definitely a man's man. The fact that he thought this was good for the city was instrumental in him really getting involved in it.

The IBC had no money period in 1984. We had received a $375,000 appropriation from the legislature, but then Bill Allain vetoed it. So that left us with nothing, and we were just two years away from the 1986 competition.

Dale Danks was mayor at that time. He was very supportive of the IBC. He called a series of meetings of some of Jackson's most influential business people and said, "Look, we are losing it and we need to come together and save it." Mr. Mounger was a part of that, and he stepped forward. That was my first real association with him. He worked along with some other people to save the Ballet in Jackson in 1986.

He became a member of our board of directors right after 1986. He began working toward the 1990 competition. He and Warren Ludlam Jr. joined forces to head the fund-raising campaign. They basically did it on their own. And that continues to this day with Mr. Mounger—he just does all the fundraising on his own.

This office does not fundraise. We write grants and that sort of thing. He has such amazing contacts that he can literally raise two-million dollars just over the phone.

We have been enormously grateful. His capacity to lead has been very strong. He's been very agreeable and glad to help us. He wants the IBC to succeed; he also wants to help us make sure how the money is spent. I am very proud of the fact that we have been very good stewards of the public money.

We were established in 1978 and our first IBC was in 1979. Since 1990 we haven't had a deficit, and that coincides with when Mr. Mounger stepped on board. He raises it and I watch it. He likes to tell people that I count paper clips.

Back in 1984, I told Dale Danks, the then-mayor of Jackson, that the USA IBC was a tremendous asset for the city of Jackson and that I was fearful that the competition was not successfully raising funds and that he should insure that it did not fail. As I have stated, Governor Allain vetoed the state appropriation, and additionally an abortive pursuit of a nebulous TV contract was being sought. Perhaps this was partially due to the fact that the 1982 competition was featured in a ninety-minute ABC-PBS film, *To Dance for Gold*, which aired around the world and has been reputed to be the most watched ballet film of its type.

Previously, there may have been a businessman's support group formed, however, I had no knowledge of, or connection with it; nevertheless, about six weeks before the 1986 competition, Danks together with Warren Hood Sr. called me to say that if I did not step forward and rescue it, the Jackson USA International Ballet Competition would be kaput! Consequently, I hustled and raised $350,000 from myself and several others, thereby saving the competition. At that time, I had no official involvement with the IBC board and consequently no influence on any of the decisions made for the 1986 competition. Nonetheless, the competition attained renowned international acclaim because the Soviet Union entered their three best young dancers (surveiled by appropriate KGB guards). Not unexpectedly, these three triumphed with Nina Anan-iashvilli and Andris Liepa winning Jackson's first ten-thousand-dollar "Grand Prix City of Jackson Award of Excellence"; additionally Vadim Pisarev won the men's senior gold medal. Nina remains a prima ballerina with the American Ballet Theater in New York and the Bolshoi in Moscow; and Andris is a premier *danseur* with the Bolshoi. From that time, with ballet *cognoscenti*, the USA IBC has been recognized as the premier international ballet competition in the world.

After 1986, my friend Warren Ludlam became the IBC chairman, and he asked that I join the IBC board and be its finance chairman, and I agreed, with certain provisos. One being that a complete staff must be working the prior four years leading to the next competition (not agglomerating one a year or so beforehand as had been done for the first three), and that I had to control all fundraising, especially including the perquisites for the major donors. After saving the 1986 competition, and contributing twenty-five thousand dollars myself, Jan and I were perfunctorily allocated two mediocre tickets with no tickets being issued to any of those from whom I had obtained the additional $325,000. It was obvious that no others than the Ludlams who had done anything financially to help save the IBC occupied any of the preferred seats; in other words, it was satiated with four-flushers!

One of my axioms in fundraising is that major contributors must be recognized in a unique way providing it is not too costly. Therefore, I determined that I would set aside the best 360 seats in the house—allocating two seats for each five-thousand dollars contributed; i.e. fifty-thousand dollars would procure twenty seats. I bulldozed the four-flushers and, with some assistance from Warren Ludlam, filled all 360 seats at two-thousand-five-hundred dollars per seat. That competition cost $1.9 million, all of which was funded. And a $150,000 deficit from the previous competitions was absorbed, which resulted in $200,000 remaining in the bank to prepare for the 1994 IBC. Naturally, thereafter, all complaints were squelched, and for all further competitions I have asked six-thousand dollars for each pair of preferred seats.

After 1989, Jan and I joined Sue Lobrano, the Ludlams, the Crystals, Larry Johnson (with Bell South), the Stovers, and others from Jackson to attend the Moscow International Ballet Competition. I thoroughly enjoyed that trip, especially seeing the historic sites.[3] Lobrano: "I don't know if Billy ever picked up on this or not, but there was a small group of us who tried to stay near him when touring historic sites, because he always knew more than our guides."[4]

We all enjoyed seeing the Bolshoi Theatre, where we met a famous Russian ballet artist—Valery Kosorukov—who in 1990 came to Jackson; we then toured the internals of the Bolshoi Theatre, which was an extra treat. And I am proud to say that I own several Kosorukov paintings and drawings. During a press conference during that trip while promoting our upcoming 1990 competition, Valeria Uralskaya, a renown national Soviet ballet writer, stated: "The Jackson competition is not only the jewel of international ballet competitions. It is the diamond!"

Representing the ballet, I've been to Helsinki twice and to Moscow once; and after our 1990 competition, Jana Kurova, a ballerina from Czechoslovakia and our USA IBC senior silver medalist in 1982, was producing the World Stars Gala in Prague, Czechoslovakia, following the Helsinki competition. I was aware that she had invited Jose Careño of Cuba, our 1990 Grand Prix winner, so I surmised, "I can travel to Prague as chairman of the USA International Ballet Competition to see the gala featuring Jose Careño, enabling me to boast, 'I am really proud that Jackson, Mississippi, produced the number one performer.'"

When Sue, Jan, and I attended, Kurova had recruited twenty dancers from all over the world, twelve of whom had danced in Jackson. We three Jacksonians were in Prague, Czechoslovakia, attending the World Stars Gala, comprising twenty of the best young dancers in the world, and not only the number one dancer, but eleven others, had danced in little ole Jackson, Mississippi. We were justifiably proud!

In 2000, Jan and I were in London traveling with Flo and Howard Stover when we attended the English National Ballet, which performed *Sleeping Beauty* in the Royal Albert Hall. The primary reason the choice was made to go to the English National Ballet was because I conjectured that a competitor from a Jackson competition might be performing. Immediately, upon receiving the program, we noticed that the stars were Toomas Edur and Age Oks (now anglicized to Agnes Oaks), both from Estonia, who had won our award for Best Pair in 1990.

Interestingly, the two dancers almost missed competing in Jackson in 1990 because they were short of money and even had to be supplied with sufficient dance equipment to be able to compete. During the competition, they announced that, upon returning to Estonia, they were going to be married; consequently, Sudie's, a prominent Jackson women's clothing store, presented them with a beautiful wedding dress. I guarantee that that wedding dress was finer than any other in Estonia.

Upon first seeing the program, I exclaimed—"Toomas Edur and Agnes Oaks—they danced for us!"

I then showed my USA International Ballet Competition Chairman of the Board calling cards to each and all, announcing "Look, they danced for me. How can I get in touch with them?" Finally, I found the stairs leading to the performers' dressing rooms, and I asked, "May I come back down and see them?"

The guard said, "Well, maybe I can get them on the phone."

He rang Agnes just minutes before the opening curtain, and I told her that I was there with others from Jackson. She said, "Yes, yes, please come back after the performance is over."

After the performance, we visited with Toomas and Agnes, a little bitty thing, and my first question was, "Agnes, what did you do with your wedding dress?" She answered, "Oh, I have it at home in a box." She also joked, "When my sister was married, she tried to wear it but she was too large." She added, "As soon as we finish these performances for the English National Ballet, we are returning to Estonia for our tenth wedding anniversary and I am going to wear my dress again."

After the 1990 competition, I became chairman of the board of the USA IBC and continued to raise essentially all of the required funds for the competition, and I am very proud to say that under my chairmanship, we have successfully produced the 1994, 1998, and 2002 USA IBCs—all of which are still recognized as the best in the world—and in June we will produce the 2006 USA IBC. Also in addition to the upcoming 2006 competition costing $3 million, I am proud to say that we have set up a well-funded foundation to help ensure the continued existence of the USA IBC in Jackson far into the future and that the USA IBC will remain by far the best-financed arts organization in Mississippi.

I became involved with saving the IBC in Jackson for several reasons: being a Mississippian, I was tired of everybody constantly denigrating Mississippi with comments like: "The people are rednecks down there"; "They don't know what they are doing"; "You are racists." The Jackson USA International Ballet Competition, being number one in the world, goes a long way towards refuting those stereotypes.

Bruce Marks, artistic director emeritus of the Boston Ballet and chairman of our Jackson jury since 1988, has said more than once, "This is the best ballet competition in the world." He also often has said, "I don't know that you people in Jackson, Mississippi, really know what a superior competition this is."

For the IBC, my fund-raising modus operandi has been to begin raising money for the next competition during the current one, and fortunately I have been able to ask for commitments to be paid on the donor's schedule, since we have sufficient operating funds and are not insistent if someone prefers to wait until the last minute to contribute. Over the years, I have raised more than $6.25 million for the USA IBC, and our pledgers have reneged on only $36,000, which calculates to less than .06 of one percent. *Mirable dictu!*

Today, the IBC enjoys tremendous respect around the world, and it is not uncommon for any of us to be traveling in this country or elsewhere and to encounter someone of cultural or governmental importance who, upon hearing the words "Jackson, Mississippi," will say, "Oh, that is where the USA International Ballet Competition is held." Actually, many refer to us as "The Jackson Competition." The IBC is undoubtedly something that many Mississippians don't fully appreciate; but it has contributed more than any other thing towards enhancing the image of our state around the nation and the world.

I've often told people that they have probably dreamed of being connected with the best on the block, neighborhood, city, county, state, or nation. Well, how about being involved with something that is the best in the whole world?

Another thing that we can point to with pride as Mississippians and Jacksonians is our great tradition of historical and cultural exhibits that we have been able to sponsor in Jackson since the early 1990s. I have been happy to be a part of these from the inception of the idea.

CHAPTER 27

Exhibiting for Mississippi

After Kirk Fordice was elected governor in 1991, his wife, Pat Fordice, became involved with a group of young Russian singers from St. Petersburg who performed in Jackson. After their performance, Pat asked if there were anything our state could do for them, and they stated that their city was in dire need of medical supplies; this was after "Perestroika," and the Russian medical system was in such disarray that they were even reusing needles.

Pat contacted William L. "Buck" Stevens, head of the Mississippi Pharmacists Association, who formed "Mississippians Reaching Out" to amass medical supplies. The organization included two Russian doctors at the University of Mississippi Medical Center, Dr. Yuri Zubkov, whom I later came to know well, and Dr. George Beneshvilli.

Upon Pat's instigation, the committee shipped between $25 and $35 million worth of medical supplies into St. Petersburg, Russia, including a $2.5 million G.E. magnetic resonating machine (MRI). Up until then there was only one MRI in Russia, located in Moscow.

After this demonstration of generosity, Mayor Subchok of St. Petersburg (incidentally, Vladimir Putin—the current Russian president—was his deputy mayor) said, "Jackson, Mississippi, is my sister city and for all that you have done, there ought to be something that we can do that would be mutually beneficial." (As a side, five of us, including Pat Fordice and myself, were also knighted, "Knights Hospitaller of St. John of Jerusalem," under the auspices of the Russian Orthodox Church and the czarist Romanov heirs.[1] One night, Pat invited the knights to dine with the governor and her, and for that occasion I wrote a poem—Grand Dame Pat and her Knights.[2]

Pat and her group invited Subchok to Jackson, but when he could not come, he sent Sergei Vlasov, who was the curator of the three Russian national museums in St. Petersburg. My good friend, Billy Powell, the person most responsible for electing Governor Kirk Fordice, told Pat and the group, "Well, if you are going to do anything concerning international affairs or art, you need Billy Mounger involved." So Jan and I were invited to dinner at the Governor's Mansion with Vlasov, where the idea emerged of organizing a cultural exhibit in Jackson of historical and artistic items from St. Petersburg's museums.

I was the only one present who was conversant with raising money for cultural events and especially for international events. Vlasov was motivated to discuss an art exhibition in Jackson since St. Petersburg's museums contained thousands of art objects never-before-seen outside Russia, and, as a consequence, we arranged a trip to St. Petersburg to explore that possibility.

I had been to St. Petersburg when we went to Russia for the Moscow IBC in 1989, but this was a special treat to meet the mayor of St. Petersburg and Putin. After our meetings, Vlasov took Pat Fordice, Billy Powell, myself, and the rest of our delegation into the inner sanctums of the museums holding a tremendous amount of gorgeous art, much of it paintings by unfamiliar Russian artists, along with icons. We recognized that the art might be great, but if the artists were unfamiliar to our anticipated visitors then an exhibition would not succeed. It also became obvious that we would have to pay them about $250,000 to pack and ship the art to Mississippi.

Dr. Yuri Zubkov had arranged for us to be housed in one of the nicer hotels in St. Petersburg, The Astoria, which he had paid for in rubles at about thirty dollars a day. Upon arriving, we had given him dollars and he paid our bill.[3] We dined as a group and Yuri always brought along his briefcase. We would order Georgian cognac for our group of about fifteen, and when we finished each bottle of cognac, he would pull a new bottle out of his briefcase and put the empty bottle in it; that way we paid much less for our cognac.

One night, we went to Yuri's apartment, which was very nice by Russian standards, and afterwards we attended the ballet. While we were walking to the ballet, I asked him, "Aren't you worried about the KGB?" I was prompted to ask because he had been paying our bills everywhere, saving us money.

"No I am not worried at all," he said. I could not help but be skeptical.

The next day some of the group, including Billy Powell and Pat Fordice, went to the Russian black market. Dr. Bob Smith, a medical doctor in our group, traveled outside Moscow with Dr. Yuri Zubkov, also a doctor, to render medical assistance. I also skipped the black market because I was more interested in Russian history and wanted to see the Yussupov Palace where Rasputin—the "svengali" of Alexandra, the last czarina of Russia—was assassinated.

But the rest of our group cared little about Rasputin. They shopped at the black market where they bought a variety of things. Unbeknown to me, Billy Powell had purchased a soldier's overcoat and a KGB hat. That night all of us congregated in Pat Fordice's room in the hotel and, suddenly, there was a *bam, bam, bam*, on the door.

Everyone was startled and said, "What's that?"

The outside demand was, "Open up, open up!"

It was a man in a KGB uniform. Billy Powell had donned that KGB cap and that overcoat, acting like he was the KGB. Bob and I were the only two patsies. The others thought that was really hilarious, and it was.

A year later, Yuri Zubkov was killed—murdered right outside his apartment. Someone had bashed him in the head with a metal bar. It was never proven that it was KGB, but he had made decisions on a medical school board that had raised the KGB's ire. Some think his murder was committed by those jealous that Yuri's power had been enhanced because he was instrumental in procuring so many medical supplies from America.

When we returned to Jackson, we organized the Mississippi Commission for International Cultural Exchange, with Buck Stevens as its chairman and me as honorary chairman and a member of the five-member board. We continued corresponding with the St. Petersburg officials, but it came to no fruition. Finally, we became aware of Jack Kyle, a native of Booger Den, Mississippi, who had been involved in all the Memphis exhibitions and had some unique ideas for an exhibition. Remarkably, Kyle proved to be a person of extraordinary persuasiveness who could convince foreigners to part with priceless artifacts, which they had never dreamed of letting any other country display.

Jack came aboard and the Metro-Jackson Convention and Visitors Bureau committed funding. Consequently, another group including Kyle made a second trip to St. Petersburg, which I declined, a regrettable error. My biggest regrets have always been those things that I did not do and one of those was not returning to St. Petersburg.

Jack Kyle was sated with ideas and went to St. Petersburg to explore a plan. His unusual plan had originated with the National Gallery of Art in Washington, D.C., headed by J. Carter Brown, who conjured the idea of replicating a room from a St. Petersburg palace in its entirety with all of its pertinent artifacts. Jack decided, "If we have an exhibition, why stop at one room? Let's replicate four rooms from four different palaces." He approached the Winter Palace, which was not interested, but Catherine's Palace, Peterhof, Gatchina, and Pavlovsk—all palaces—agreed to our proposition, thereby generating our first exhibit, the 1996 "Palaces of St. Petersburg: Russian Imperial Style."

We approached many businesses, with BellSouth our biggest sponsor for funding, and naturally we called on the banks for help. Next, we convinced the legislature to come through with $2 million and the convention bureau with $1 million.

"Palaces" cost about $11 million to produce, and the city provided us with the old county administration building, where we created spectacular miracles. During the time span of all the Jackson exhibitions, we would spend more than $5 million on that building, a fact that ultimately contributed to our long-term financial problems. We contracted with the artisans from Russia who after World War II had rebuilt those Russian palaces, which had been destroyed by the Germans in the siege of Leningrad (St. Petersburg). The floors in those replicated rooms contained sixteen kinds of inlaid wood created by the Russian artisans at a cost of $100,000 each. When it came time to ship all the artifacts, we were short $2 million to pay our local contractor, who threatened to sue us. We knew if we were sued it would be an international disaster and an ugly black mark on Mississippi.

In January 1996, we appealed to Bud Robinson, Chairman of the Board of the Deposit Guaranty National Bank, who helped engineer a $2-million line of credit from Deposit Guaranty, Trustmark, and Bancorp South; had the banks not loaned us the money, we faced a catastrophic fate.

We drew 554,000 people to the St. Petersburg exhibit, which was the most attended event in the United States in 1996. It was utterly fantastic. No one could have dreamed of anything being that successful. Those 554,000 people additionally bought gobs of merchandise from the gift shop, which turned a large profit. The St. Petersburg exhibit was so outstandingly good that it received untold recognition around the country.

After the St. Petersburg exhibition, Jack Kyle conceived a French exhibit about Versailles, and we produced that one in only two years. I was able to visit the Palace of Versailles a total of three times. Our commitment to the Palace of Versailles was $1 million to refurbish two rooms: the king's bedroom and right next to it, the king's dog room, where his dogs had been immediately available.[4] Versailles contained a dearth of artifacts, so as the *piece de resistance* Kyle suggested replicating an equestrian Bernini-sculpted statue of Louis XIV, king of France. The French experts protested, "That is ridiculous." In reality, however, they had already copied the original statue, which is stowed from view in the stables of the Palace of Versailles. It had been across a large lawn and a lake when, in the seventies, some radical students rioted, broke off parts of the statue, and doused it with red paint. The directors of the Palace of Versailles commissioned the restoration expert, Michel Bourbon from the Louvre, to replicate the statue out of a mixture of epoxy and powdered Carrera white marble. If you visit the Palace of Versailles today, you see that replica.

We commissioned Michel Bourbon for $300,000 to create another copy; consequently, today there are three replicas of that statue—the first sits next to the Versailles Lake; a lead copy is in Louvre's main courtyard near the I. M. Pei Pyramid; and our copy is in Jackson, Mississippi. Supposedly, there will never be another copy made.

The "Splendors of Versailles" exhibition was designated the "1998 Top Event in the U.S." by the American Bus Association.

That exhibition cost about $10.5 million and was open over a five-month period. We had projected that 450,000 people would attend, down from 554,000 for "Palaces." Based on the success of the Russian exhibit, the legislature approved $2 million and the same three banking institutions extended a $2-million line of credit. But, unfortunately, as the exhibit progressed, it became obvious that we were not going to attain our attendance estimates; of necessity, the banks had to intercede to control expenses. Ultimately, only 275,000 attended, necessitating that the banks collectively absorb a $1.8-million loss. Thereafter, they had zero interest in helping any future exhibit, even though Versailles again had received a tremendous amount of national acclaim. To recoup some of our costs, we considered selling the Louis XIV equestrian statue, but the statue by law and contract with the French had to remain in Jackson.

Undeterred, Jack Kyle began looking towards Spain for a third exhibit, and we traveled to Spain to examine several palaces with their artifacts and to plumb their history. In 2001 we produced an exhibit titled "The Majesty of Spain: Royal Collections from the Museo del Prado and Patrimonio Nacional," whose head was the Duke of San Carlos.[5] It also received the designation as the "2001 Top Event in the U.S." by the American Bus Association. As usual, we contributed $1 million to Spain—$500,000 each to the Museo De Prado and the Patrimonio Nacional. The Patriminio used the funds to refurbish a fifty-five-foot golden encrusted gondola and a magnificent royal carriage, and we replicated the porcelain room from the Palacio Real Aranjuez at a cost of $700,000 and a stucco room from a casita at the Palacio de El Pardo. We juxtaposed Goya cartoons with the tapestries copied therefrom, together with much other incomparable art. Their Majesties King Juan Carlos I and Queen Sofia actually visited the exhibition in Jackson. I stood next to her and she exclaimed: "These artworks are beautifully displayed and I have never seen most of them."

The Spanish exhibition drew only 320,000 visitors and accumulated a deficit of a little less than $200,000. The guarantors—E. B. Bud Robinson, Kane Ditto, Ambassador John Palmer, Leland Speed Jr., Charles and Stuart M. Irby, Dudley Hughes, and myself—digested that loss, with minor gastric troubles; however, before we committed to produce "Majesty," we had approached Harvey Johnson, Jackson's mayor, and stated, "We cannot do another exhibition unless you agree to provide security," which he committed to do. After we had signed all the contracts, he reneged. If our esteemed Hinds County sheriff, Malcolm McMillin, had not saved us by providing our security, our debt would have been terribly indigestible.

I was, to say the least, ambivalent when the idea of an exhibit from Dresden, Germany, arose for 2004, because we had run two deficits in a row and no one knew anything about Dresden, nor that Germany could possibly have a sufficiency of interesting artifacts to attract people. We were taboo to the banks. Our guarantors, myself included, were decidedly leery, and the legislature and convention bureau were considerably iffy concerning a fourth exhibit. Regardless of these facts, we approached the legislature and received a commitment for $1 million a year for three years; the convention bureau followed with $1 million, and finally the guarantors signed a note for $950,000. "The Glory of Baroque Dresden" cost about $10 million and its projected attendance was 320,000, the same as for Spain. We traveled to Dresden, which contains more well-preserved beautiful porcelains, paintings, and other artifacts than any other small city in the world. We again committed $1 million to the state of Saxony, Germany, and $200,000 to refurbish a Vermeer painting, *The Procurer*, one of only thirty-five Vermeers in the world. The exhibition in attractiveness, quality, and abundance of artifacts—including a 42-caret green diamond—was on a par with "Palaces of St. Petersburg," but, alas, our attendance was only 133,000—devastating!

Again, that great public servant Sheriff Malcolm McMillin stepped into the breech and, in addition to providing security, performed our janitorial services. All total, we were about $1.5 million in abeyance and, at the time of this book's printing, are still whittling at the remaining balance owed to Saxony to prevent an international incident. Meanwhile, the guarantors—the same as for "Majesty" with the exception of Dudley Hughes—are unhappily masticating that indigestible note.

These four exhibitions drew more than 1.3 million viewers and created tremendous goodwill, economic benefit, and priceless publicity for Jackson and Mississippi. Notwithstanding these facts, those of us who brought these exhibitions to the community say, "There ain't no mo' in the kitchen."[6]

CHAPTER 28

A Life: Enjoying Family and Friends

W hat I have become would not have occurred without the genes and the heritage from my ancestors and from my parents. My first Mounger ancestor was John Monger, who arrived in the Isle of Wight County, Virginia, circa 1660. He probably came as an indentured person; nevertheless, in a short time he became an owner of substantial acreage in Virginia. Two generations later my branch of the family added the "u" to our name, resulting in my "Mounger" branch. I am kin to Moungers, Mongers, and Mungers, and even other variations of the spelling. Many in the Munger branch from Birmingham, Alabama; Midland, Texas; and other locations became very wealthy, thus my father would say, "When the Moungers get the dough they drop the 'o'."

Ultimately, my fourth great-grandfather, Judge Henry Mounger, moved to North Georgia, and his son Edwin (my third great-grandfather) married Francis (Fanny) Clark, the daughter of a very famous Revolutionary War militia general, Elijah Clark, also from North Georgia. Clark, my fourth great-grandfather, was so renowned that an elucidation must be made of him.

Mrs. Louise Frederich Hays, archivist for the state of Georgia, in 1946 wrote a biography of Elijah titled: *Hero of the Hornet's Nest.* The Hornet's Nest was an area around Augusta, Georgia, north along the Georgia/South Carolina border and well into South Carolina. If only a small portion of this book is true, Elijah was one of the most interesting characters in this country's nascent development.

He was a backwoods settler with little formal education, who fought and killed many Indians. When the Revolutionary War began, he fought in many battles suffering eight to ten wounds. He won the Battle of Kettle Creek, Georgia, by conducting a fortuitous flank attack causing the British to retreat to Augusta and never to return to the "Hornet's Nest." He is also credited with ousting the British from Augusta and being instrumental in winning several other battles in South Carolina.

After the war, he occupied a huge amount of Indian land in West Georgia and organized his own independent country, "Clark's Republic." This helped precipitate an early Supreme Court decision confirming the federal government's sole power to make treaties with the Indian nations.

Consequently, President George Washington ordered the U.S. Army to oust Elijah from his republic; thereafter, he was tried before three justices of the peace, one of whom was, fortuitously for him, Henry Mounger, and not unexpectedly he was adjudicated as not guilty. Later, he was commissioned as a lieutenant general in the Revolutionary French Army, and he invaded Florida; however, before he had traversed to St. Augustine, the countries of Spain and France signed a peace treaty. "Atavism" means "resemblance to a remote ancestor." Since I have a propensity to charge into the fray, whether fist-fighting, footballing, confronting Democrats and perverts, or battling other perceived injustices, could it be because I am atavistic? As a matter of fact, my original title for this book was: "Atavist or Iconoclast"!

Edwin Mounger, a son of Henry, was the first treasurer of the state of Georgia and was on the first board of trustees of the University of Georgia. He had several sons, including Henry, my great-great-grandfather and Elijah Clark Mounger, who entered West Point but flunked out in 1822.[1] One hundred and twenty-six years later, I redeemed our Mounger reputation by being the only Mounger who has ever graduated from West Point. Henry became a lawyer, moved to Alabama, and next settled in the town of Paulding in Jasper County, Mississippi, circa 1830. He became a very prominent landowner, lawyer, judge, and ordained Methodist minister, and was a delegate to the Democrat National Convention in 1848 in Baltimore, Maryland. Additionally, on his deathbed, he was appointed United States Minister to Spain. He died in 1852. Henry had several sons. They were: the Rev. Edwin Hartfield Mounger, a prominent Methodist minister; Uriah Millsaps Mounger, who joined the Jasper Grays in 1861 and was killed in the Battle of Seven Pines, Virginia on May 31, 1861;[2] Elijah Clarke Mounger, who also joined the Jasper Grays and was killed in the Battle of Corinth on October 30, 1862; and my great-grandfather, William Harris Mounger. With the capture of William, my branch of the family—the Henry Mounger branch—was almost down to one. William Harris fought in several battles in the Civil War and was wounded and captured during the Battle of Chickamauga, Tennessee, and then was interred in Camp Douglas, a notorious Yankee prisoner-of-war camp near Chicago where he almost perished. Postwar, he became sheriff (Republican) and supervisor of Jasper County. He fathered several children, among whom was my grandfather, Milton Uriah Mounger.

We have discussed my grandfather, M. U. Mounger, a very dour and cold individual who was very protective of his honor. Once a bank he owned with a partner went bankrupt and even though legally he was not required to pay its debt, for the rest of his life he deprived his family in eradicating that total debt. He also served Covington County as county attorney, and as representative and senator in the Mississippi Legislature.

Once a Mr. McRae besmirched his name regarding a legal issue and also threatened his life; consequently, my grandmother, Alma McKenzie, who died before I was born, sewed a secret pistol pocket inside my grandfather's coat. When he and McRae faced each other, my grandfather shot him five or six times, but not fatally, bespeaking little for his marksmanship. Remarkably, no charges were filed against him.

My father also had two brothers. Dwyn, who became a very successful Presbyterian minister, graduating from Millsaps and entering the ministry; and Carleton, who also graduated from Millsaps College, entered the workforce during the heights of the Depression and thereafter attained little success. My father also had one sister, Marion, who is only twelve years older than I, thus I have never called her "aunt." She taught school until age sixty-five, then served as a Presbyterian missionary to Christ College in Taipei, Taiwan, until past the age of eighty. In the middle 1980s, I traveled to Taiwan as a guest of the Taiwanese government, where Marion utterly amazed me at her spryness. Today, she lives, still fervently espousing her Christianity, in a retirement center in Jackson.

Over the years, I have benefited greatly from my association with my brother, Henry, despite a large discrepancy in age.

Belatedly it is time to discuss my wife of more than fifty years, a beautiful lady and a great helpmeet. Jan Gore was a Depression baby, born November 13, 1932, in St. Louis, Missouri, at a time when her father was working in southern Illinois. Shortly thereafter her family moved to Montgomery, Alabama, where she attended school from elementary through the eleventh grade. They then moved to New Orleans, where she spent her senior year and enrolled as a town girl at Sophie Newcomb College, the female adjunct of Tulane University. In 1953 her father became treasurer of Knox Glass Company in Flowood, Mississippi, just outside of Jackson. She graduated from Newcomb in 1954, and I luckily met her at a Cotillion Debutante function that year.

Instantly recognizing her attractiveness, I asked her out. (This was during the last phase of my hell raising with Parham Bridges, and immediately before attending the University of Oklahoma.) We dated during Thanksgiving and Christmas of 1954, going on a Petroleum Club trip to the 1955 Sugar Bowl, where Ole Miss lost to Navy 21–0; we steadily dated throughout the summer of 1955, while I worked in Jackson for Union Producing Company. We were engaged during Thanksgiving of 1955 and were married on January 21, 1956, in the First Presbyterian Church of Jackson, Mississippi, with my Uncle Dwyn performing the ceremonies. We honeymooned in the Natiónal Hotel in Havana, Cuba (pre-Castro), and then we moved to Norman, Oklahoma. We had the G.I. Bill for $160 a month, a Standard Oil of Indiana fellowship at $150 a month plus books and tuition, and a new Pontiac from the dealership I partially owned. We lived in a great two-bedroom apartment with a living room, which cost us fifty-five dollars a month. We were in "high cotton."

On December 28, 1956, our son Billy was born. We named him after my father, William Malcolm Mounger II—the name I personally had desired; but my father had wanted to avoid a "junior," a failure because most people thought I was a "Jr." anyway. On January 26, 1960, Jan gave birth to our second and last child, whom we named after her father, Robert Gore Mounger.

I am deservedly proud of my two sons.

Billy was always an excellent student who was endowed with incessant scientific curiosity. In adolescence, he was not a natural athlete, but developed into an all-star baseball player and took up football without my urging. He played on the first-team junior high football in the eighth grade for Jackson Prep and made first-team senior high as a tenth grader on Prep's championship team. With four games to play his junior year, he almost ruined his left knee. My good friend, Dr. Jimmy Manning, operated on him and stated that Billy probably could not play football again. He did not know Billy! He worked more diligently to rehabilitate his knee than most any other person would have. Consequently, he was able to start every game on Prep's championship team his senior year, earning all conference and the Paul LaCoste coach's award. Additionally, during his confinement and dedication to rehabilitation, he became a very devout Christian. Truthfully, his Christianity was the predominate reason that I finally became a Christian, but more about that later.

Billy graduated near the top of his class, and the faculty at Jackson Prep designated him the winner of the Danforth Award for his all-around academics, athleticism, leadership, and character. Oh, how proud I was at that time!

Billy then entered Vanderbilt University, applying himself assiduously to his studies and other activities. He ultimately graduated *magna cum laude* in political science. His faculty advisor, Leiper Freeman, told Jan and me, "You will never have cause to worry about Billy because he always operates with 110 percent effort and productivity." No more perspicacious words have been spoken.

Billy maintained his dedication to Christian principles and chose his roommates accordingly. After graduation, I believed that he would become involved with Youth for Christ, Fellowship of Christian Athletes, or some other Christian organization. First, however, he frugally traveled Europe and the Mid-East for three months with a one-month diversion in Israel traveling and studying biblical history and visiting Kibbutzim. Upon returning to the United States, he worked as a landman for my friends Buddy Lloyd and Bob Thomsen (Lloyd and Thomsen), thereby, learning the rudiments of the oil-and-gas business. Next he enrolled at the Reformed Theological Seminary (RTS), which is one of the top-ten seminaries in America and is headquartered in Jackson, having been founded by members of my own church, First Presbyterian of Jackson, with large branches in Orlando, Florida, and Charlotte, North Carolina. Billy earned a master's degree in Christian studies while attending RTS. Afterwards, I explained to Billy that the business community was in desperate need of Christian leaders, which would enable him to accomplish two goals: living as a Christian witness while becoming a productive businessman. Consequently, he came to work for Delta Royalty Company Inc. with me, and later branched out on his own with Will Yandell to form MYEX Energy, which discovered several oil-and-gas fields.

Meanwhile, Dick Wilson, working with Vanguard Cellular of North Carolina, organized a cellular application for Jackson under the Federal Communications Commission. Because the limited partnership/FCC lawyer was Joe Hennesee, who had become my friend while serving as my lawyer during the WLBT application era, I signed for thirteen units out of thirty-nine in the limited partnership, giving one each to my sons Billy and Bobby; thereafter, I served as the general partner. Later, Billy's companies assembled groups that won licenses in subsequent lotteries.

When the FCC changed its procedure from a comparative hearing to a lottery process, we were given dispensation to make multiple applications. And if one of us were chosen, the FCC allowed a "settlement group" structure wherein the ultimate owner would be a larger partnership.

Fortunately, Billy's name was drawn in the FCC lottery as the winner of the Jackson, Mississippi, cellular license. Even though Billy's license was contributed to a "larger entity," Billy insisted on participating in every facet of the process—legal, technical, financial, and bureaucratic—thereby acquiring a virtual master's degree in cellular communications.

Billy recognized the potential value of cellular licenses and inquired as to ways to participate in applications for other licenses. He assembled nine applicant groups. Three of the nine won lotteries and retained majority control interests, and all groups won numerous minority interests in cellular licenses. Collectively the groups made more than fifteen-million dollars on a total investment of one-hundred-and-eighty-thousand dollars.

Later, Billy's companies assembled groups that won licenses in subsequent lotteries. Many other spin-off groups from Mississippi were successful, skewing a favorable disproportionate portion of winners in the national lottery for Mississippi.

Billy extended his operations by buying and selling minority interests, building, owning, and operating systems with Bobby also participating in these goings on.

Ultimately, he led a company that bid on new wireless frequencies (known as Personal Communication Services, or PCS) and combined these with frequencies won by AT&T. As chairman and/or CEO, he led this company, named Tritel, into AT&T Wireless in a multi-billion dollar merger. Needless to say, Billy has been fabulously successful. Billy and Bobby were also founding partners of Mercury Communications. Billy's precious wife, Cissye, has been a great blessing to me, as have their beautiful daughters, Callie and Catherine, and their son, William.

My son Bobby, as well, has led an eventful and productive life. At age seven he evidenced great baseball ability and at eight, with Sam Sanders as his eight-year-old partner, won the twelve-year-old Mississippi Tennis Doubles Championship. Thereafter, as a nine-, ten-, eleven-, and twelve-year-old, he was the twelve-year-old Mississippi champion. When he was ten years old, I took him to many tournaments, including the Southern Closed and Southern Open, and no ten-year-old ever defeated him. At twelve years old, he won every tournament he played except for the semifinals of the National Hard Court Championship in Abilene, Texas, and the semifinals of the National Championships in Charlotte, North Carolina. He was ranked number five in the nation (he should have been number four, since he had defeated number four), and also was ranked number one in the South. At fourteen years of age, he was still very good, ranking fifteenth nationally and second in the South. Bobby played tennis successfully through the 16s, ranking 16th in the South; he helped Jackson Prep win six state championships, playing on the high-school team from his 7th to 12th grade years.

Bobby, in his ninth-grade year at Jackson Prep, was named the Danforth winner by the faculty—the same year as Billy. Both sons winning the Danforth Award in the same year. I was bursting with pride!

Bobby attended Ole Miss and graduated from Belhaven College with a bachelor's of science in business administration. He worked very successfully in commercial real estate for Maurice Joseph and then associated with Billy in the cellular business. Bobby helped found Mercury Communications, which proved to be one of the predecessors of Tritel. Mercury owned or managed 15 cellular markets. In Tritel, Bobby was the manager of M-3 and Mercury PCS Investors, two of the original investment partnerships that started Tritel. When Tritel began operating wireless systems, Bobby managed its real estate affairs. Bobby and I now have offices together managing numerous business investments and we enjoy seeing each other regularly.

When Bobby attended Ole Miss he joined the Phi Delta Theta fraternity, where he made many enduring friends; these carried over to Jackson with the addition of many more. He is again involved in tennis, currently on the Board of River Hills Tennis Club.

Bobby is one of the most caring individuals I've ever known, and when myself or any others need help, he is always there. Everyone likes him and he has been the most attentive parent imaginable to his children, Robert and Anne Rivers. His wonderful wife, Rivers, has been a great joy in our family. As has Billy with his son, William, Bobby has spent an enormous amount of time coaching and fathering his son, Robert. In other words, he is an extremely well-liked person and a great family man.

CHAPTER 29

My Faith

rowing up, I received almost no guidance in religion. My father was Methodist and my mother, Baptist, and neither, to my recollection, ever attended a regular church service. Nevertheless, as a young child, I sometimes attended First Presbyterian Church's Sunday school, and later, my Aunt Marion escorted my older sister and me to Fondren Presbyterian, where I was baptized at nine; thereafter, I spasmodically attended First Presbyterian.

Aunt Marion, my father's sister, was attending Belhaven College and spent a great deal of time with me and my siblings. She was very religious and saw that we went to church at Fondren Presbyterian. Marion was only twelve years older than I, consequently, I have never called her "aunt." She became a school teacher and, upon retirement, became a missionary for the Presbyterian Church in America at Christ College in Taipei, Taiwan. While she was there in the mid-1980s, I traveled to Taiwan as a guest of the Taiwanese government. Marion showed the college to me and I was very impressed when my little aunt missionary wended her way along a circuitous route down a steep escarpment in the dark to escort me to a taxi; then she climbed that steep slope in the dark to return home. She is now retired, living in a senior's facility, and still maintains her total dedication to the Lord. What an inspiration to me!

Such a paucity of religious foundation ill prepared me to enter West Point, where there was compulsory chapel for all cadets. If you were not stipulated Catholic or Jewish, you were required to attend Protestant chapel. Every Sunday required marching up a mountain to an awesome gothic-style church, where the choir, accompanied by the second largest organ in the Western Hemisphere, sang praises to an institution (West Point) in the form of the "Alma Mater" and the "Corps," each of which did have a very spiritual content. After three years of compulsory chapel, my religiosity showed no improvement whatsoever. During chapel my "First Class" (senior) year, Herb Barineau, Chuck Wurster, and I sneaked off through a hidden door and climbed a winding staircase up to a narrow corridor paralleling the nave, where we removed dress coats and, in our T-shirts, read, slept, played cards, and, best of all, sneaked peaks of the superintendent, Major Gen. Maxwell Taylor, and the Corps of Cadets, who were properly attending chapel below. Upon completion of services we rejoined the rest of the cadets as if we had been in proper attendance.

After we graduated, I became fearful that the Lord was going to exact just retribution when Herb Barineaux crashed in a P-51 in December of 1949. He was the first in my class to die. Furthermore, in 1951 during the Korean War, Wurster crashed in an F-80 with a load of bombs and was almost killed. From then on, I deathly feared my time was next; however, instead of misfortune, the Lord has blessed me in every way.

Nonetheless, my religious indifference persisted, even after Jan and I were married in First Presbyterian in 1956. I still avoided church on Sunday by continuing to commune with Mother Nature on the golf course. Even after Billy and Bobby were born, I golfed while Jan took them to Sunday school and church. My disposition finally was altered around 1970, when Victor Smith was born again and headed one of the most successful Billy Graham crusades in the South. His devotion to Christianity caused me to reassess my *weltanschauung*. In 1973, when my son Billy was diligently pursuing his rehabilitation from knee surgery, he became a very devout Christian. With Jan's persistence, Victor's conversion, and Billy becoming a devoted Christian, the message finally penetrated my "case-hardened" skull and I recognized God's great design in sending his only Son to sacrifice his life for all of us.

Now I must state that several times each day I thank the Lord

for all he has bestowed on me, which has been tremendously boun-
tiful. For I realize that his guiding hand has been on my shoulder
my entire life. And whatever choices I have made, he has always
been at the helm. Words are not available to sufficiently express
my gratitude to Jan, Victor, and most of all, to my son Billy, for
leading me to see the light!

GALLIMAUFRY

Several businesses and other involvements have heretofore been sufficiently described, especially my early oil-and-gas activities, which now fortunately, in my eightieth year, are rivaling those early successes. Also, I need to elucidate my association with the Deposit Guaranty Bank, which includes thirty-five years on the bank's advisory board and board of directors and on the board of the Deposit Guaranty Corporation, the executive committee, the loan committee, and chairman of the audit committee. Additionally, I am a major stockholder of the bank, with about 80 percent of my stock purchased by me.

Other business activities have been as a board member and major stockholder of the Rankin County Bank and executive board member and major stockholder of Delta Industries, which owns Ready Mix Concrete Plants from Memphis to Mobile. In addition, Allen Torrence, Manny Crystal, and I previously owned the cable television system in Rankin County. Real estate has been one of my brightest successes with my partner, Larry L. Johnson of Landmark Homes. In our initial involvement, Larry needed my financial help; but now he has evolved into one of the most successful builders and real estate developers in this area. Of the various business partners I have had, Larry has handled our joint affairs the most fairly and successfully of any of my partners.

Outside of business, I have been vice president of the Southern Tennis Association, and I ranked southern junior tennis players for many years and coincidentally devised a ranking system superior to that which had been heretofore used. Additionally, I supervised many tennis tournaments including Mississippi State Championships, Southern Closed and Open Championships, and as previously stated, the only two national championships ever held in Mississippi.

Not much coverage has been given to my oil-and-gas organizational involvements, other than my being chairman of the Mississippi-Alabama division of the Mid-Continent Oil and Gas Association in 1968 and 1969; but I dedicated untold hours and trips to benefit the Independent Petroleum Association of America, serving many terms as vice president and member of the executive committee, and as chairman of the membership and finance committees. After many years of devotion to the IPAA, I abruptly removed myself from contesting for the presidency when I was undoubtedly in the lead. Perhaps I should have agreed to serve, but Reagan was no longer president and my oil-and-gas production had dwindled so low that I was embarrassed to be classified as an oil-and-gas producer.

I am also justly proud of being the *sine qua non* in helping János Radványi initially fund the Center for International Security and Strategic Studies at Mississippi State University. Radványi had defected to the USA while serving as ambassador from communist Hungary and is the highest ranking communist official ever to defect. After I met János in the 1980s at Charles Pickering's farm, he asked my help in funding his proposed center, and I orchestrated his visits to selected individuals who, along with myself, initially financed the center. János is an absolute jewel for Mississippi State University and the state of Mississippi, as a person who knew Nikita Khrushev and has incomparable international contacts. He has brought renowned programs and guests to this state.

Leota Hayes—whom I had President Reagan appoint to the Kennedy Center Board—chaired the now-defunct Mississippi Art Association in 1978. She asked me to be its finance chairman. At that time the Philadelphia (Pa.) Museum of Art made available for $28,000 the Robert Henrí painting, *Young Woman in Yellow Satin*, exclusively for purchase by another American museum. Leota and I promptly called on our generous friend, Lyle Cashion Jr.—an oil-and-gas producer—who agreed to fund the painting and additionally donated the grand piano that is still in the Mississippi Museum of Art. That Henrí painting is probably worth between $500,000 and

$1 million today and is the most valuable painting in the Mississippi Museum of Art.

In 1986, when I traveled to Taiwan with David Keene as a guest of the Taiwanese government, we visited that country's "grand canyon" area on the island's eastern side, where the government exhibited stone animal carvings. My fellow travelers knew of my incomparable collection of elephant carvings, and they promptly discovered a 350-pound elephant—about two feet in height and three feet long—carved from a metamorphic stone. They began pressuring me to buy it, and I said, "Jan will say, 'Put it in your office!' and I don't have enough room there, but the price is very attractive." A few minutes later, we were informed that, as governmental guests, everything was available to us at half price. Unable to resist such a bargain, I made the purchase, and consequently it was shipped by sea to Los Angeles and transported through the Panama Canal to New Orleans. Jan and I then hauled the 350-pounder to the house, where we had it uncrated. She immediately said, "Put it in your office!" My prediction was accurate *to the letter!* After two weeks, she said she had a name for it. I had intended to name it Sidney Chu for my Taiwanese escort, but I mulled, "If she names it, she will let me keep it in the house." She said, "I want to name him 'Tai,' because you purchased him in Taiwan." I answered in the affirmative, and Tai remains to this day a proud permanent resident our den.

Of all my overseas trips, the most comprehensively beneficial and educational was an eleven-day journey to Israel led by Dr. Luder Whitlock, president of Reformed Theological Seminary, Dr. John Currid, Old Testament scholar and biblical archeologist, Dr. Reggie Kidd, New Testament scholar, and Bob Bailey, now assistant to chancellor/chief operations officer of RTS.

Wherever we traveled, we were imbued with the archeological, Old Testament, New Testament, and all other significantly pertinent aspects of, the sites. One day we participated in an archeological dig at Bethsaida, where I uncovered a two-thousand-year-old Roman coin (it remains as part of Bethsaida's historical record); and in my usual effusive character, I celebrated in my inimitable way. That night the muse prevailed upon me to write the following poem that I recited to all on our bus the next morning.

The Coin (1997)

Our group has come to Galilee,
The land of Our Lord we've come to see.
Luder, Bob, Reggie, and John Currid,
They lead us on just like El Cid.
We've desired to be where Jesus tread,
That One who gives our daily bread.
We've seen where He fed the multitudes
And where He preached the Beatitudes.
It's easy to feel His definite presence,
Even to vision in iridescence.
Then yesterday was archeological,
In search of what's historical.
The site was Bethsaida a famous tel,
Each hoped that after good fortune befell.
We all climbed up enthused to dig,
And each was issued sufficient rig.
Before we started, Jim toppled a wall,
Unfortunately, he took a very bad fall.
He fell in a pit with a great slam,
And then we named him the battering ram.
I also, while carrying a thirty pound stone,
Stumbled and fell but broke no bone.
Each worked at his designated task,
Hoping in the end in glory to bask.
While the others decided a tea break to take,
Only one assiduously pursed the stake.
Diligently wielding that very last trowel,
He spotted something with great avowel.
A coin! A coin! He shouted with glee!
He held it aloft for all to see!
And I'm most proud that he was me!
It then was checked for historicity,
And then for true authenticity.
This coin was made in a Roman land,
Our Saviour could have held it in His hand.

Yes! Finding that coin was a great thrill,
But the only true one, is doing His will!

March 10, 1997, W. D. Mounger, Tiberius, Israel.

Two years after China was opened to visitors, our Mid-Continent Oil and Gas group in 1981 traveled there, as well as to Hong Kong. Even though our accommodations were primitive, our travel efforts were well rewarded. Among the memories and collected artifacts, I returned home with several of the then-new Rubik's Cubes, which I was inherently predisposed to master single-handedly.

After months and untold hours of manipulating the cube and plotting my results graphically, I finally defeated the cube! Afterwards, I repeated the solution four or five more times through diligence and perseverance, but without truly comprehending how I had solved the puzzle. Thereafter, I purchased a Rubik's Cube Solution book in order to understand my previous manipulations and, today, I realign all the colors in about three minutes.

In 1966, Mary and Emmett Vaughey (Emmett was the energy czar in Washington, D.C. during the Korean War) asked Jan and me plus Joyce and Fred LaRue to cruise on his yacht, a converted PT-Boat, from Fort Walton Beach, Florida, across the Gulf of Mexico and around the tip of Florida to Miami Beach. The captain of the vessel was an excitable Italian and his wife was the cook, and the first mate was an incoherent Bahamian.

The first night while cruising approximately one-hundred miles off the Florida coast, and after enjoying a sumptuous feast preceded by many Martinis and accompanied with copious quantities of wine, and, thereafter while playing a lively game of Scrabble, the captain burst into the cabin in a frenetic panic, stating that the boat was taking on water; the bilge pumps were not working and we were sinking.

Totally uncoordinated, we plunged into saving ourselves in a "Chaplinesque" slapstick way. The Bahamian, Emmett, and I attempted to lower the life boat in a veritable comedy of errors. The boat wobbled and tilted and almost fell overboard several times. When we finally lowered it to chest height, I saw that it included a large outboard motor and I lifted it as if a feather out of the life-boat. A superhuman task!

As this comédie Bouffe was taking place, Jan was continuously grasping my arm and Mary Vaughey had donned a rain suit and grabbed her immensely valuable bag of jewelry. Upon reaching the deck Mary distributed lifejackets, issuing Joyce LaRue—a very small person—one large enough to float a 350-pound man, and Emmett, even though he was somewhat scrawny, one suitable only for a tot!

As these totally inept actions were taking place, Fred LaRue nonchalantly had changed his clothes, obtained several towels, and thus proceeded to caulk them around a propeller shaft where the packing had failed, and from where the water was pouring into the engine room.

Concomitant with our farcical activities, the captain had radioed a "mayday" SOS signal and the Coast Guard was on its way with a gasoline powered portable bilge pump.

LaRue finally succeeded in stemming the influx of seawater and simultaneously our incompetent captain belatedly discovered that he had never flipped the proper switch to activate the bilge pumps and they were then functioning properly.

As this time the Coast Guard plane arrived and parachuted the portable bilge pump to us, which we obviously did not really need. We then diverted our destination to Fort Myers, Florida, and plodded our way through very stormy seas powered by only one engine.

After arriving at Fort Myers, the LaRues returned to Jackson and we remaining four drove the Tamiami Trail to Miami Beach, our ultimate destination, where we spent several enjoyable days, which proved to be very beneficial to me when I went to Miami Beach for the 1968 Republican National Convention.

During my life I have been blessed with many honors, but I was tremendously honored on the night of January 21, 2005, by being "roasted" by the Republican Elected Officials Association. Among the roasters were: Senator Trent Lott, Governor Haley Barbour, Lt. Governor Amy Tuck, U.S. Representative Chip Pickering, Peggy Mize, Pat Fordice, Jim Herring, Leland Speed, Representative Rita Martinson, Bert Case, Ashby Foote Jr., and Jim Furrh Jr. The night overwhelmed me and, to top it off, Charles Irby awarded me the first Stuart C. Irby Jr. award for philanthropy. This honor was especially humbling because Stuart was the epitome of philanthropists and I have strived inadequately to approach his example of generosity. Only one additional honor of all the awards I have received equals this one: it was the Mid-Continent Oil and Gas Association Bill and Emmett Vaughey Wildcat Award at the 50th Anniversary of the organization. This touched me deeply because of my respect and admiration for Bill Vaughey.

Many people have helped immeasurably towards my being able to be involved in so many varied activities. The two most beneficial have been my forty-seven-plus-year CPA, Homer Watkins Jr., and my forty-five-year unsurpassable assistant, Peggy Mize.

Homer has assisted me through all the complicated financial maneuverings of my business affairs, and without his advice, personal attention, and caring, my business activities would have been immeasurably curtailed. However, the best favor he ever did for me was to recommend that the bank and I hire Peggy Mize as my assistant in 1962.

Peggy has been ineffable as my right hand. It is almost impossible to contemplate what my life would have been without her incomparable assistance. The following three poems that I wrote about Peggy in 1987, 1997, and 2002 describe our association better than anything that could be written today.

The Irreplaceable (1987)

Inauspicious though it may have seemed,
But truly more than could be deemed,
The day that Peggy became my aide,
And all this time there's been no fade.

When she commenced, I was not there,
She must have thought I did not care?
For I was coasting with Bridges Parham,
Skirting most dangerously with degrees of harm.

Now, that day is ages past.
Twenty-five years—don't be aghast!
We've done many things in all these years,
And some could easily engender fears.

When it all started, we served the bank,
With many good customers but some most rank!
Along the line, much politics,
Not much appreciated and many bricks.

Low offices to high to Presidents,
Some good, some medium, some awful scents.
And Peggy helped regardless of whom,
Even when she knew the direction was doom.

The TV interviewers were most persistent.
She handled them well even though resistant.
Reporters galore sought me out,
And she protected me without a doubt.

Involvement in TV, cellular, and cable,
So many different things it seems like fable.
Uncommon, banks, Ready-Mix, and catfish,
Sometimes I'm sure against her wish.

Tennis, ballet, IPAA, and Mid-Continent,
With Rankin County a frustrating descent.
Through all this turmoil she's always been there,
And whoever's unfair had better beware.

Interpreting a lexicographer,
Could never phase her nor deter.
Convoluted letters with animadversion,
Were handled well with no desertion.

We've even been involved with one most queer,
Jon Hinson's the one—which brings a tear.
But worst of all is Bill Allain,
Who's perversion elicits a horrid refrain.

Now even with Billy coming on board,
There was never a hitch and nothing untoward.
With Cissye, Will, and Jennifer too,
She easily adjusted with little ado.

For Bobby and Jan, she goes the last mile,
With never a grumble and always a smile.
And all my friends, even from afar,
Avowedly say, "She must be a star!"

Through all of this she has been most straight,
For it's God, Church, family with no abate.
Yes I've been lucky that she works for me,
Her efficiency is there for the world to see.

Irreplaceable she's been for twenty-five years,
Without her my fortune would be in arrears.
Many a person she speaks to as love,
Because she's at peace with Him above.

September 15, 1987 W. D. Mounger

Still Irreplaceable (1997)

Another ten years have transpired,
Thank the Lord, Peggy has not retired.
When the time arrives, that she must go,
That's when I say, "There ain't no mo!"

Endured we did, Bush's presidency,
And seen Trent to his, ascendency.
Ninety and ninety-four were the IBC,
Ninety-eight also, with us the key.

We've partnered with Larry in real estate,
Due to bad fortune in oil of late.
Compounding it all is E.B. Inc.,
Causing us sometimes, to be out of synch.

She weathered a very sad tragedy
When the Lord took her dear Tall*ey.*
She handled it well, almost unperturbed,
'Cause Faith made her, very well gird.

We've suffered with this amoral Clin*ton,*
Who's made our lives, a lot less fun.
For upcoming "Splendors" and for "Palaces,"
She deserves to stretch her galluses.

For Vanessa she fought the IRS,
Trent and Homer brought them through distress.
To Houston, Danny, and grandchildren,
On trips of joy with many a grin.

Peggy's past the age of retirement,
But zips around with much fervent.
Yes, she's still the one irreplaceable to me,
As long as she'll stay, our work will still be!

September 20, 1997 W. D. Mounger

Still Irreplaceable II (2002)

We have lasted five years more,
Even not knowing what was in store.
We persisted in doing tasks galore,
But working with Peggy was no bore.

We continued in politics with one a larker,
Due to overconfidence in Mike Parker.
Bush, Trent, Thad and Chip Pickering,
Altogether with no amount of bickering.

This five we've had no involvement with gays,
And put on two USA Ballets.
We produced "Splendors" and "Majesty of Spain,"
And now with "Dresden" we're at it again.

Our business has expanded to offshore oil,
And real estate with Larry brought to a boil.
Cellular has been mostly Sun-Com,
With Billy and Bobby almost a bomb.

We dare not stop, too much on our plate.
After forty years there's still no abate.
But she always takes care of family and church,
She will never leave duty in the lurch!

September 20, 1997, W. D. Mounger, In appreciation of forty years of
    service as my Irreplaceable assistant.

After a prolonged excruciating bout with cancer, Peggy passed
away on June 2, 2006, and shortly thereafter I created the Peggy
Mize Foundation to benefit dancers in the International Ballet
Competition; forthwith I also composed the following quatrain:

Peggy suffered much awaiting her fate,
But the Lord in His wisdom set the date,
With open arms, He has welcomed her in,
Because He knew she was truly Christian.

EL FINI!

If you have slogged this far, I want to close with a poem I wrote the night of March 8, 1996, while flying over the darkened Amazon jungles on my way to Rio de Janeiro, Brazil.

I could not sleep for reminiscing of all that I was thankful for and all that the Lord had allocated to me in his plan for my life. Consequently, I wrote this poem on a semi-plastic table cover and read it to my fellow travelers the next morning. It was shortly before my seventieth birthday; therefore, I titled it "My Seventieth Year." I added to it later by inserting a line about my newest grandchild, Anne Rivers. With that exception, it is exactly today what I had penned that night.

I have conveyed directions for my funeral, requesting that this poem be read.

Essentially, all of my blessings are contained in this poem.

So here goes the poem, and I hope its message will be comprehended!

My Eightieth Year

It is now my eightieth year!
Praise the Lord! With a mind still most clear,
And also for the years with Jan so dear,
For Billy and Bobby so cavalier,
For Cissye and Rivers of the upper tier,
For Callie and Catherine none beautier,
For Anne Rivers no hint of veer,
And William and Robert, they have no peer!

But ther've been times, parlous and sheer,
Engendering in them their share of fear,
Lachrymose at times yielding a tear.
However, I'm happy I'm not a queer,
That Peggy has kept me from stripping a gear,
For abundance like the high frontier,
For awards and honors prior to my bier,
For Republican politics as grenadier,
For West Point and protection to be free'r,
For many friends to share a beer,
For the USA with loyalties most clear,
And most of all, through the Bible as seer,
Our LORD AND SAVIOR for this worldly sphere!
Oh yes, THANK GOD! for this eightieth year!

Adapted from
"This Seventieth Year"
Written on March 8, 1996
To be read each Christmas Day beginning in 1998

Paterfamilias W. D. Mounger

My Fund-raising Philosophy

Over the years I have conducted many fund-raising forums for the Republican Party and for the NCPAC (National Conservative Political Action Committee) at such places as Dallas, Texas, Birmingham, Alabama, Puerto Rico, and several times in Washington, D.C. In these forums I have lectured future U.S. senators and representatives, governors, and many other elected officials, as well as Republican Party candidates, finance chairmen, finance directors, and other fundraisers in general. The gist of my lectures was the following.

When conducting fund-raising meetings, particularly for political purposes, I have two opening ice breakers. The first is (to paraphrase the Bible): "In the beginning was the word and the word was money!" In actuality, this beginning would be operable for most any charity for without money, an organization cannot function. The second introductory is: "There are nine requirements for a successful political campaign. One—there must be an electable candidate; Two—there must be sufficient money; Three—there must be a platform with proper and saleable principles to propound; Fourth—money; Five—there must be sufficient management over an effective organization to conduct the campaign; Six—there must be money; and Seven, Eight and Nine are money, money, and money!" Again, instead of political specifics, the particulars pertaining to any charitable fund-raising campaign can be substituted into the nine requirements.

The next move to accomplish the fund-raising campaign is to set the goal. The goal needs to be as high as possible and explicated so that everyone can comprehend the necessity of the amount to be raised.

Next, a chairman must be designated and a fund-raising committee formed which is preferably composed of five to fifteen people. (Too large a committee cannot be managed.) Each member must fervently believe in the cause and the attainability of the goal. He must be inherently generous and his generosity must be demonstrated by his immediately giving an amount, relatively speaking, on a par with whatever he will be asking others to give. And, he must be willing and able to devote the time and the effort to make the project succeed. The finance chairman must particularly exemplify all the aforementioned attributes and must be constantly alert to "four-flushers" for they can terribly hobble the best laid plans for they will take names, promising to make calls, but do nothing, thus inordinately occupy the chairman's time.

With the committee formed, a list of prospects must be compiled and desirably listed on cards containing whatever applicable information is available. The names should be prioritized with the previous donors first; second, those who have a history of generosity; third, those who have a reason to contribute; fourth, those who can afford to give, but need the right prodding or incentive; and fifth, those who can afford to give, but love their money so much they are reluctant to part with it. This latter group is what I term my "dreg list," which is invariably satiated with doctors. The chairman should examine the list and choose those with whom he would be the most efficacious. Then, each member of the committee should choose from eight to twenty prospects with a general discussion of who would be most effective with each individual prospect.

With the goal set, the chairman designated, and the committee formed with prospects assigned, how do you raise the money? There is only one secret to raising money, "YOU ASK FOR IT." Most people want to write a letter, send a card, or have a publicity announcement and wait for the funds to roll in. It doesn't happen that way! It takes personal contact, preferably in the flesh, not on the telephone. When you look a person in the eye on behalf of an excellent cause which you are generously supporting and are expending your time and effort to support, it is much harder for your prospect to turn you down.

If you have a history of generosity and are substantially contributing to the cause, it very much influences possible donors and with such a background, you are much less likely to accept all the excuses for not giving. If you are a cheapskate, you know all the dodges because you have used them yourself and psychologically you cannot be insistent with the person. Ergo, no skinflints on the committee!

When each person works his list, call on the best prospects first. Number one is yourself, which clears the way to ask others. And the success that you have with the best prospects enthuses and encourages you to be more persuasive with your lesser prospects.

Always ask for at least two times what you believe the possible donor will give! If you leave the amount open, it is human nature to give as little as possible; and if the amount asked is considerably more than the subject intended, quite often, that person will give more than he intended even up to what he was asked and sometimes even more.

Don't think that a rich person will necessarily be a good fundraiser or even an excellent prospect. If he has inherited his wealth, he will most likely be very stingy, because he will normally only see the outgo and will fear he cannot replace the money. If he is a parvenu and has made his own fortune, he is much more likely to be generous! He will replace his gift by selling another life insurance policy, drilling another oil well, selling another house or lot, selling another car, or continuing to do whatever he has successfully done to attain his economic success. Yes, the *nouveau riche* are by far the most giving!

A fundraiser needs to use whatever persuasive angle he can contrive to get his possible contributor to give. That angle may be friendship, personal, familial, business related, school ties, philosophical, belief in the cause, an obligation, pure generosity, response to effort and fervor, or any other influential point that can be conjured.

Do not let your prospect dodge you. Make repeated calls, ten or more times if needed, until you can finally get an answer. Some people will avoid you but when finally cornered will say yes. Always, do all you can to get an answer because in finality certain people cannot say no if finally penned down.

If a person states that he must confer with his spouse, it is either an avoidance or the spouse truly controls and seldom will you succeed; however, still follow up and make the person render a final answer.

There are few efforts in life where you have an absolute score as to the success of your endeavors. Fundraising is a notable exception; when you succeed with a prospect it is like scoring a goal or touchdown and as each amount is raised, it adds to the total and you absolutely know how well you have done. Also, you truly get to know people when you ask them to part with their money, for most people think they can take their wealth with them and consequently have not discovered the immeasurable pleasure of giving. Therefore each success causes an elation and rush because the fundraiser knows what an accomplishment it is to get someone to part with his beloved money.

Many people cannot raise money because they love wealth so much that they cannot imagine others being generous with theirs. Also, if you ask others for money, then you are going to be asked to donate to their causes, which makes fundraising a very costly activity; however, our American way of life would not function if there were not fundraisers who obtain money from people and businesses to insure that the charitable, political, and religious underpinnings of this great country will properly function.

The defining of a successful fundraiser is whether he can continuously call on the same person or business and succeed. If he can obtain money after ten or more different campaigns, he is successful. To be in that position, he has had to be truthful without exception and whatever was promised the donor must be done, whether it was a party, meeting a celebrity, published recognition with differing categories, pins, tickets, ties, or other paraphernalia. Many organizations relegate the givers to limbo once they have given, which is a horrible mistake and failure is the consequence.

One last forewarning! If you have a meeting or party with an important person as the special guest, do not let anyone into the room who has not paid the required amount to attend. Again, no four-flushers! If you let one in, others will bellow to also attend and in addition, the freeloader will invariably inordinately occupy the time of the special guests and will shove aside all those who properly paid. Make no exceptions to this rule!

An Addendum of Letters and Notes

Western Union Telegram

The Honorable Richard Nixon
The White House Wash DC

In Miami, I vice-chairmaned the Miss. Delegation and instrumentally guided its twenty votes to you. In 1968, Miss. led the states in fundraising as a percentage of quota predominately because of my efforts. When you retreated from your Houston commitment on the oil depletion allowance, I stayed with you. Your reneging on your Atlanta and Miami commitments regarding schools was unpalatable; but I continued my support. And I stood by you when your strongly biased oil import committee recommended an ill-considered tariff on oil imports. Your IRS ruling to Gestapo-like police private schools was intolerable, politically idiotic, and totally inexplicable; but I still remained a supporter. Now, your disembowelment of the oil industry may have exceeded the limits of my tolerability. How does an 8% increase in crude oil prices in 13 years constitute inflation? Your chief economic advisor stated in Dallas last month that the oil and gas industry needed incentives not disincentives. Are you incommunicative with him? The oil industry has probably been the most pro-Republican and pro-Nixon of all industries and as a reward has fared worse under you than any other administration. Virtually every other industry has contributed significantly more towards inflation than oil; so, why single it out? Have you sold out totally to the Ripon Society; or are Kennedy, Muskie, and Proxmire running this government? Is it not reasonable to expect Republican policies from a Republican administration? Are we heretofore loyal supporters expendable in your quest for a new constituency? My disillusionment and evisceration are overwhelming.

William D. Mounger Republican Finance Chairman of Miss.

Western Union Telegram

Harry Dent Special Counsel to the President
The White House Wash DC
Jackson Miss
President Richard M Nixon
The White House Wash DC

As finance chairman of the Mississippi Republican Party, I am convinced that I speak for the vast majority of Mississippi Republicans and most other Mississippians in insisting that you immediately grant executive clemency to Lt. Calley. The people of this country, who have steadfastly supported your Vietnam policies, especially the people of the South, are severely demoralized and disillusioned by this conviction. This administration made an egregious mistake in allowing Calley to be tried and now that error must be rectified by granting clemency. We patriotic Americans who believe in fighting for our country cannot condone the condemnation of a loyal American who thought he was properly following orders and protecting his men. If this callous attitude towards an American soldier is allowed to stand, it is difficult to see how this administration can hope to remain in office after this present term. For the defense of America, the justification of the dead and wounded in Vietnam, the past, present and future members of the Armed Services, the parents of those who have served or may serve their country, the survival of the Republican Party, and possibly even the survival of the Republic, I plead with and beseech you to grant executive clemency to Lt. Calley immediately.

W. D. Mounger, State Republic Finance Chairman of Mississippi

---

May 22, 1981

Mr. T. M. Hederman, Jr., Editor
Mr. Dennis Camire, Staff Writer
The Clarion-Ledger
Jackson, Mississippi

Dear Messrs. Hederman and Camire:

In your less than apt article concerning the Justice Department in this morning's *Clarion-Ledger*, you refer to Senator Cochran as the "sole" Republican Senator from Mississippi. Your inept attempt to use a pejorative adjective to serve your polemical purposes of demeaning Senator Cochran and the Republican Party was despicable.

You could equally as well refer to Senator Stennis as our "sole" Democrat Senator; therefore, the word "sole" in this case is a surpassing inanity. Prior to Cochran's election, you could have stated that the Democrats had only two Senators from Mississippi. Perhaps your deprecation is due to ignorance and you do not know that the Constitution provides for only two U. S. Senators from each state.

You would be well advised to stick to the facts in your stories and not let your biases exude from your stories through inclusion of inappropriate adjectives.

Sincerely yours,
W. D. Mounger

WDM:pm

CC—Senator Thad Cochran

March 16, 1983

Mr. David E. Hardin, Editorial Director
The Clarion-Ledger
Jackson, Mississippi

Dear Mr. Hardin:

The audacious arrogancy of your Editorial headlined "No Backbone" (March 9, 1983, *Clarion-Ledger*) is putrescent with hypocrisy. The extreme rigidity of your backbone is unsurpassed in recommending tax increases on others; however, the backbone of a jellyfish is admirably firm in comparison to yours pertaining to paying your fair share of taxes.

You, your Howard Bakerite moderate Republican Executive Editor, and your Gannett (Rochester, New York) puppeteers with their $120,000,000 purchase of the Hederman newspaper empire have arrogated unto yourselves the task of intimidating the provincial bucolics residing in Mississippi into accepting oppressive tax burdens to accomplish your desired social engineering purposes.

The proverbial "pot" is pristine white compared to your "tax kettle." Why don't you recommend a tax on newspapers? You pay none now! What about a sales tax on newsprint? You pay none now! Naturally, you are for sales tax increases—zero times an increase is still zero taxes to you. Undoubtedly, you also have structured your $120,000,000 purchase to avoid paying any corporate income taxes whatsoever. Again zero!

You advocate increasing the oil and gas severance tax by 50 percent (6 percent to 9 percent)—a tax off the top before considering any costs, when business is severely depressed (down sixty percent), and with natural gas and crude oil prices plummeting. You carp about MP&L with their monopoly and their commission controlled rates, but ignoring your ever increasing profits, your avoidance of taxes, your expanding not decreasing business?

You relegate excellent Senators, such as Ellis Bodron, to the "Hall of Shame." You categorize most taxpayers who voted against your pet bond issue as bigoted racists. Yes, and you say that legislators who don't genuflect to you are devoid of backbone.

You certainly don't come to the taxing table with merely unclean hands. Your uncleanliness is better described in scatological terms. Consequently, before you again advocate raising any taxes on anyone or anything, you owe it to the taxpayers you have demeaned, to champion taxing yourself first! Bring back the Hedermans!

Sincerely yours,
W. D. Mounger

January 21, 1983

Mrs. Lloyd Spivey, Chairman
Mississippi Republican Party
357 East North Street
Canton, Mississippi 39046

Dear Ebbie:

It was utterly dismaying to read in Bill Minor's column in last Sunday's *Clarion Ledger* that the Mississippi Republican Party Executive Committee was contemplating incestuous proliferation by adding five members—all from the black community.

Any reasonable attempt to increase black participation in the Republican Party is commendable. All of us have been devastatingly frustrated by the small amount of black support for the party. However, we claim to espouse the cause of individual freedom and opportunity within our incentive system which rewards the deserving person and this proposal diametrically refutes this maxim.

Such a move would be violative of the principles of fairness. Such policies are egregiously abhorrent and have been thoroughly disproven and discredited with no demonstrated instance of efficacy. We have been steadfastly and adamantly opposed to quotas and affirmative actions and this idea is considerably worse than any quota.

This proposed expansion reeks of "Uncle Tomism" and would be demeaning and degrading to those participating from the black community. It would deservedly be vulnerable to public scorn and ridicule. And, it smacks of transparent toadyism that would be so odiously obvious that you would deserve unremitting derision.

Republican black votes will be attained when members of the black community realize that our ideas of government are more conducive to their well being, and not before. If we violate the precepts upon which our party was founded in a ridiculously vain attempt to procure the black votes, we will have surrendered our right to exist as the alternative party (devoid of George Wallace's dimes worth of difference). We should then retire from the political arena and retrogress to the old One Party System.

Yes! We do need black support. Yes! It is frustratingly irksome that very little black support has been realized. However, paranoia does not justify violating right principles. Just as a person who will not steal to satisfy his desires, a political party may not heinously subvert its foundations to satisfy an insatiable craving for more support. You are beseeched and implored to remain faithful to those who elected you and the principles upon which our party was founded.

Sincerely yours,
Signature
W. D. Mounger

January 28, 1983

Mr. William D. Mounger
Post Office Box 1200
Jackson, Mississippi 39205

Dear Billy:

I got out my dictionary and read your letter to Ebbie Spivey with interest. For a nice person who means well, you sure play hell. "Incestuous"? "Egregiously abhorrent"? "Public scorn and ridicule"? Really now.

To begin with, Thad Cochran proposed this egregious, abhorrent and ridiculous idea and the Committee *voted for it*. Not Ebbie. I for one agree that we cannot surrender principle to pander to blacks, or anyone else. But—is it all that unsound to have the Republican Party move the short distance from having a Black Republican Council to having the Party resolve, as far as its membership acting through its democratic processes will allow, to elect one black per district? I am unalterably opposed to "subvert(ing) (my) foundations to satisfy an insatiable craving for more support," but I do not equate putting 5 blacks on the State Committee with that ignominious end. We need, as you agree, black support. Let's find 5 blacks who already agree that Republican ideas are conducive to their well being and put them to voting on how our program and principles can best reach the rest.

Let's also lower the tone of our rhetoric.

With very best personal regards,
Yours very truly,
Signature
Michael S. Allred

January 31, 1983

Mr. Michael S. Allred
Satterfield & Allred
P. O. Drawer 1120
Jackson, Mississippi 39205

Dear Mike:

No apologies are forthcoming concerning the tone, rhetoric, or polemics in my letter to Ebbie; nor would it be changed one whit if recomposed.

Someone had indicated to me that this proposal was instigated by Thad Cochran which in my nonsycophantic posture does not make it sacrosanct. If Thad believes this type proposition to be efficacious, then he should add a black staff member for each Congressional District.

You and I have diverged considerably since we believed each to be a fellow "Roundhead," but in my lexicon you are now a "Pointyhead." Your condoning of chicanery and other shenanigans in the 1980 State Convention to abet your "Riponesque" cohorts in controlling the State Party, severely tested our friendship. And, now, it appears we are even more antipodal.

Your name has been appended to my compilation of those whom I have considerably helped, but have proven to be so overwhelmingly disappointing: i.e. Reed, Carmichael, Shanks, Cochran, T., Cochran, N., Todd, Giordano, et al, and now Allred.

Alas! I must state the Party is inexorably treading a path which has little comparability to that which I have dedicated so much of my time, effort, and money.

With undeterred pertinacity,
W. D. Mounger

WDM:pm

April 1, 1983

Dear Billy,

Just a note to send you the enclosed, to show you the trash they're publishing about you here in North Mississippi.

However, knowing your feelings about Bill Minor, I suspect that a) you've already seen it; and b) you don't give a damn!

Hope we can see you all soon. We haven't been near Jackson in ages; can't think why, other than keeping our collective nose to the grindstone.

We will go to Atlanta mid-May, however, for Syd's graduation at Emory. Ironically, even tho' he will get a Master of Divinity degree, he still has another 6–9 months doctoral courses to take! Is there no END!

We think of you all often, and recall the great time we all had with you here in Corinth on the occasion of the Biggers wedding.

Give our love to Jan and the boys.

Thine,
John (Signature)
John E. Bell

April 11, 1983

Mr. John E. Bell
WCMA
P. O. Box 471
Corinth, Mississippi 38834

Dear Johnny:

Thank you for Bill Minor's article. No, I had not seen it. Yes, I don't really give a damn about whatever he might say. It is ironic, though, that he is accepted as a good newspaper man when he has no desire to tell the truth—only to sensationalize on behalf of his ultra liberal proclivities. (See enclosed letter to *Times Picayune*.)

There would be nothing to gain by my sending a refutation or explanation to any of the newspapers that printed it. My answers would only allow him an extra opportunity to distort the truth for his own ulterior purposes. However, I will express to you what I could propound to the appropriate editors.

Some of what he said pertains to the truth: 1) I did write a letter to Ebbie Spivey (copy enclosed); 2) He correctly quoted me, but out of context; 3) The committee did add five members including three blacks; 4) And finally, I believe that Cochran did suggest that adding five blacks would be efficacious.

All other expressions in the article were either outright prevarications or spurious suppositions: 1) My letter engendered a great amount of opposition and all concerned highly regretted its conception; 2) The proviso that the additions be all black was eliminated; 3) The vote was 14–10—no great defeat to me. Also, four of my allies were absent and one was conned into voting pro. At best, they would have had a tie! Consequently, their "expansion" was purely Pyrrhic.

Actually, my letter was much more successful than I envisioned. They had the votes to quietly ramrod it through and I spoiled that act. I entered the fray solely because the situation demanded action and I felt compelled to step into the breech.

Additionally, his alleging that the party has done better financially without me is extremely misleading: 1) The party has been greatly helped by Cochran since '78 and Reagan since '80; 2) Without me there would have been no Cochran and I did raise over 25 percent ($300,000) of his Senatorial money; 3) I raised 90 percent of Nielson Cochran's money and elected him City Commissioner; 4) I raised 75 percent of Hinson's money in '78 and 50 percent in '80; 5) In '80 I was Regional Finance Chairman for Reagan and the Campaign '80 Chairman for Mississippi which raised all the Reagan and party money for the State and in addition, the party rat holed a large amount for the future.

Minor's scurrilous article was designed to undermine my reputation thereby enhancing the moderates and in consequence serving Minor's liberal ends.

Thanks again for the article, and Jan and I also enjoyed seeing you in Corinth and hope to see you in Jackson sometime soon.

Sincerely yours,
W. D. Mounger

AUTHOR'S NOTE: The following article about Mounger and Spivey's disagreements, etc., was written by Mississippi political columnist Bill Minor and appeared in the Daily Corinthian *on Thursday, March 31, 1983:*

"'Moungerisms' Snap at State GOP Heels"

Good old Billy Mounger, . . . He's back snapping at the heels of the present state GOP leadership which he considers hopelessly liberal.

This has produced a recent spate of Moungerisms, those deathless bits of prose that sound like they came out of the lexicon of Spiro Agnew, occasioned by the Jackson oilman's displeasure with the State Republican executive committee for expanding its membership to add some blacks.

Such a move, Mounger recently wrote to State GOP chairman Ebbie Spivey and members of the committee, would be "Egregiously abhorrent," and smacked of "transparent toadyism that would be so odiously obvious that you would deserve unremitting derision."

But against Mounger's wishes, the GOP executive committee the other day proceeded to fill three of five added seats with blacks, giving black Republicans their first representation as full executive committee members.

The young black professionals who have been active in the Mississippi Black Republican Council weren't altogether pleased with the selections nor the process of having five whites from each congressional district make the selections, but overall the move seems to be viewed as opening another door to black participation in the GOP.

As reported here previously, the impetus for expanding the committee to add black members had come from Sen. Thad Cochran, who is carefully seeking to build a broader black voter base for his re-election campaign next year.

Incidentally, this column learned that a Lance Tarrants poll done for the National Republican Party several weeks back showed Cochran had only a 25 percent name identification among blacks in Mississippi, indicating he still has much work to do in that area.

The episode involving the Mounger letter has underlying meaning in where the Republican Party is now headed in this state, showing the former bankroller of GOP candidates no longer has the clout he used to have in party affairs.

Mounger was thought to be indispensable to the state party as the perennial finance chairman for both presidential campaigns and individual Republican candidates for state office.

A public outburst in 1976 by Mounger aimed at Gil Carmichael, the two times GOP gubernatorial standard-bearer, revealed Mounger considered he bought total personal loyalty of any candidate for whom he raised money.

When Cochran made his successful race for the U.S. Senate in 1978, he purposely put distance between himself and Mounger, relying on others for his primary fundraising.

Gradually, the party leadership eased Mounger out of the picture as the chief finance man, replacing him with Julius Ridgway, a friendly, low-keyed type who also had independent wealth from oil and gas. Ridgway has proved to be a more effective fundraiser than Mounger, according to GOP insiders, and doesn't make anyone mad.

Mounger, however, evidently still has visions of regaining his place as the chief elephant rider in Mississippi and tossing out the forces allied with Cochran, and former state GOP chairmen, Clarke Reed and Mike Retzer.

But the heavy-handed move Mounger engineered with the aid of Rep. Trent Lott after the 1980 presidential election to throw out Reed and Retzer ended in a disaster, and helped to further draw the lines within the party between the Cochran and Lott camps.

Interestingly, freshman Republican Rep. Webb Franklin seems to have allied himself with the Cochran faction within the State GOP although he is walking a tightrope so as not to alienate his House colleague, Lott.

Cochran, meanwhile, is busily trying to keep the party unified, while at the same time pulling over as many Democrats as he can to support him in 1984, and possibly head off any major Democratic opponent.

A few more letters from Billy Mounger, however, could change all that.

House of Representatives
Washington, D. C. 20515

Jack Kemp
Thirty-First District
New York
Nov. 8, 1984

Mr. & Mrs. W. D. Mounger
P. O. Box 1200
Jackson, MS 39201

Dear Billy & Jan,

Just a rather belated note to say how much I enjoyed my visit to Jackson last month.

It was a delightful evening, and I appreciate so much your warm welcome and the wonderful hospitality.

Hope you'll enjoy this copy of my new book, and please let me know if I can ever be of help.

Best regards,
Signature (Jack)

"Mounger Cheered by Talk with Bush"
By Rowland Evans and Robert Novak
Excerpt, *Clarion-Ledger*, April 10, 1985

WASHINGTON—Independent oil producers ("wildcatters") may be switching from Rep. Jack Kemp to George Bush as their candidate for president in 1988 in view of the vice president's more sympathetic attitude on tax reform.

Oilman Billy Mounger of Jackson, Miss., a force in Mississippi Republican politics, is a longtime Kemp booster not happy with oil provisions in the congressman's tax reform bill.

Mounger chatted recently at the White House with the vice president, a former Texas oil driller himself, and was cheered by his concern for the industry's tax treatment.

In visiting administration offices in Washington, the staff of the Independent Petroleum Producers found the most sympathetic ears on Bush's staff. A Kemp supporter cautioned that sympathy is easy for the vice president's men because they have nothing to do with the tax reform fight. Nevertheless, the wildcatters were impressed.

WILLIAM D. MOUNGER, Oil Producer
(Letterhead)

April 22, 1985

Mr. David Hardin
The Clarion-Ledger
P. O. Box 40
Jackson, Mississippi 39205

Dear Mr. Hardin:

Thank you for the opportunity to critique the article dated April 16, 1985, headlined, "Mounger May Leave Kemp's Camp." Most assuredly, this headline was descriptive of the conversation I had with Steve Riley.

Factually, the major discrepancy concerned the "depletion allowance" for independent producers, but that inaccuracy was corrected the next morning. Additionally, the statement that Jack Kemp favors altering the manner in which dry holes are charged off was also incorrect. Tax matters are inherently very complicated, but they are even more arcane when pertaining to oil and gas. Especially confusing are the various proposals emanating from Kemp-Kasten, Bradley-Gephardt, the "Treasury Proposals," and several other versions. Keeping them separated is very difficult.

Desiring not to appear punctilious, I did find some fault with the leitmotif of the article which was that my re-evaluation was due in toto to my own economic well being. There are several more persuasive factors which have caused me to be less of a Kemp supporter and other reasons why I feel more amenable to George Bush. Furthermore, my irritation with the negative oil and gas proposals are engendered mostly because of their deleterious effect on this country's economic well being and national defense capability. In addition, the oil industry has been so predominately supportive of all that President Reagan has espoused that it would be emotionally devastating to me, personally, for any proposal from this Administration to tend to destroy this vital industry.

This response is, undoubtedly, much more detailed than you anticipated, but the opportunity to assiduously analyze an article in your paper could not be resisted.

Sincerely yours,
Signature
W. D. Mounger

WDM:pm

"Mounger May Leave Kemp's Camp—Proposed Tax Reforms May Sway His Support in '88 Race"
By Steve Riley
Clarion-Ledger, April 16, 1985, State-Metro Section B

The politics of tax reform may push Republican oilman Billy Mounger of Jackson into an unlikely corner for the 1988 presidential campaign.

Mounger, 59, a prominent GOP financier, long has been a supporter of New York Rep. Jack Kemp, considered a certain candidate for the Republican nomination. But Kemp's widely discussed tax reform plan would hit Mounger and other independent oil producers in the pocketbook—and it could send them scurrying to the camp of Vice President George Bush.

A switch to Bush would be unusual for Mounger, who favored Kemp for vice president in 1980 and never has been a supporter of Bush, suspected by conservative Republicans as being too moderate for their tastes.

But Mounger, who discussed tax reform with Bush in a meeting in late March, said Monday he is undecided whether to support Bush or Kemp.

"If I am tilting anywhere, I am tilting toward George Bush," Mounger said. "But there's a long way to go and a lot of things can happen."

Mounger said Bush, a former Texas oilman, "does understand our problems."

Mounger's dissatisfaction with Kemp stems from Kemp's tax reform plan, which would hurt oil producers by reducing the oil depletion allowance and by limiting write-offs for dry holes.

Currently, producers can deduct 27.5 percent of their income from their tax returns. That allowance is provided, Mounger said, because when oil is taken from a well, the resource is gone forever. "It's like dismantling a building and selling it brick by brick."

Kemp's plan would reduce the depletion allowance to 15 percent and force producers to pay a minimum tax on that amount. It also would allow producers to deduct the costs of drilling a well that is dry only if they terminate their lease on that land.

In Mississippi in 1983, an average of 10 to 1 wells were dry holes. Drilling a well costs an average of $1 million, Mounger said.

Mounger said the changes would discourage independent producers, and—in the long run—increase the country's dependence on foreign oil. "People will be standing in the damned lines all over again," he said.

With the proposed changes, "I wouldn't put another penny into the oil and gas business," Mounger said. "Nobody wants to drill oil and gas wells under those conditions."

Mounger, President Reagan's Mississippi finance chairman in 1984 and his regional finance chief in 1980, met with Bush at the White House on March 26. He also talked to Treasury Secretary James Baker and Reagan about his objections to Kemp's tax plan.

"I did get in a lick or two with the president," Mounger said, adding that Reagan still was uncertain about what parts of the plan he would support.

The feisty Mounger has been a controversial figure in state politics. In 1983, he and fellow Republicans Neal Clement and Victor Smith financed a private investigation that reported that Gov. Bill Allain had engaged in homosexual activity.

In 1976, as state GOP finance chairman, he led a fight at the Republican National Convention for the Mississippi delegation to support Reagan against President Gerald Ford. That led to a bitter split between Mounger and GOP National Committeeman Clarke Reed of Greenville and separated him further from Republican moderates.

While he worked for Reagan during the 1980 campaign, Mounger said he "was 100 percent Reagan, which would make me 100 percent against Bush."

"But I never have been absolutely negative Bush," he said. "I've never disliked George Bush as a person."

In an informal poll at the 1984 Republican Convention, state delegates narrowly favored Bush over Kemp for the 1988 Republican nomination. Many who favored Bush said Kemp would be an attractive running mate.

Mounger said one factor about Bush still bothers him. "Almost everybody I don't like in the Republican Party is for George Bush," he said. "That makes me uncomfortable to a degree."

———————

January 20, 1989

Letter to the Editor
The Clarion-Ledger
Jackson Daily News
P. O. Box 40
Jackson, Mississippi 39205

Dear Sir:

How ironic of you to print on January 18, 1989, the article "News Dissemination Perverted" by Charley Reese; especially, since, yours is probably the most blatantly guilty paper extant of perverted news dissemination. This article is so contrary to and incompatible with most of your reporters' practices that its inclusion on the page opposite the names of your culpable hierarchy should have caused an atomic explosion.

Mr. Reese stated, "What people object to is the perversion of the news into political commentaries." Among other instances, virtually all your articles on the Lott-Dowdy Campaign were political commentaries. Your egregious bias oozed from almost every word written during that campaign. In particular, your reporter, Jeff Copeskey, should have been on "Howdy Doody" Dowdy's payroll. Do you only hire reporters, be they carpetbaggers or scalawags, who agree to propagate the elitist dictates of your Gannett empire bosses? Do they compel them to properly enlighten us dimwitted provincials in Mississippi? Is the *Clarion-Ledger* the Gannett cudgel to bludgeon us recalcitrants into submissive obedience to your elitism?

You were extremely self-serving in allowing Copeskey to justify his perverted campaign coverage by stating in an article that the Dowdy campaign was more accessible. You mean news coverage is determined by accessibility? What about digging for facts? What about the truth? What about fairness? Ah yes! Accessibility is the key if it serves your version of what us ill-informed rabble of an electorate should know.

Mr. Reese's penultimate conclusion was "A journalist is an unelected representative of a constituency of people, but unfortunately, they cannot vote him out when he fails or neglects his duty to them." We cannot vote Mr. Copeskey out, but you can! However, he is undoubtedly kowtowing to your editorial board, who dutifully performs obeisances to your Gannett bosses.

What have so many of us done to deserve the oppressive yoke of your publication's bias. Oh! How we yearn for the good old days of the Hedermans!

Sincerely yours,
Signature
W. D. Mounger

WDM:pm

Wednesday, 1/18/89

"News Dissemination Perverted—'News Judgment' Is Being Used as an Excuse for Distortion or Censorship"
By Charley Reese
Orlando Sentinel, January 18, 1989

David Broder, *Washington Post* columnist, raised a point and some ire with an observation that it wasn't a good idea for journalists to criss-cross back and forth between journalism and government.

As usual, however, Broder missed the main point.

It is a problem but it is not men like Bill Safire and Pat Buchanan, who worked in Republican White Houses and campaigns, who are the problem. Nor is it men like Jody Powell and Hodding Carter, who worked in Democratic campaigns and administrations.

These men are all opinion peddlers, out in the open, commenting on political affairs as political people. No one expects them to be disinterested observers nor do they pretend to be. They are all men of well-known allegiances and opinions and make no effort to hide them.

It is not editorials and commentaries, be they liberal or conservative, which are the problem confronting journalism. Columns and editorials are arguments and the fun of them is the argument. If anything, most of them are too bland.

What people object to is the perversion of the news into political commentaries. It is this betrayal of journalism and this attempted deception of the reader or viewer which has lowered the public's opinion of journalism to one of its lowest points in many years.

A reader, as a consumer of news, has the right to expect that the news he purchases consists of accurate, balanced reports of events and people. When he doesn't get that, he has a just complaint.

Many editors and reporters think they are getting away with something by hiding behind the excuse of news judgment, but people have become too sophisticated to fall for that anymore.

They know that when one side of an issue is consistently presented and the opposing viewpoints consistently ignored that what they have is not journalism but political propaganda.

It matters not whether a newspaper or television operation is a publicist for the political right or a publicist for the political left. Consumers of news have the right to demand fair reporting across the political spectrum. They have the right to demand that the mistakes of public officials the editors like are reported exactly the same way as mistakes of public officials the editors don't like.

They have a right to be upset when a newspaper reports in great detail a peace demonstration but ignores a public seminar on the strategic defense initiative. They have a right to be upset when a journalist resorts to that hackneyed old trick of quoting an eloquent and elegant spokesman for the point of view he likes and seeks out an inarticulate lunatic to represent the other side. Is there any journalist over the age of 30 who still thinks the public isn't on to this trick?

I am of the firm belief that self-government will not work if the press fails of its responsibility, either as a result of dishonesty or incompetence. The basic premise of self-government is that the people can make the right choices if they are given the facts. That is the reason behind the First Amendment—not to protect the right of a dancer to show her genitalia, not to give the owners of the press a public license to distort therefore the result is the same whether the government denies them the facts or the press denies them the facts. Every journalist knows his rights; not every one knows his responsibility, how important he or she is, to the functioning and survival of democracy.

A journalist is an unelected representative of a constituency of people, but unfortunately, they cannot vote him out when he fails or neglects his duty to them.

In the long run, however, the journalist suffers the same fate as the people. Too bad some are too dumb to realize that.

William D. Mounger
(Letterhead)

July 20, 1993

Mr. Carlton D. Adams, Commentator
WAPT
Channel 16 Road
Jackson, Mississippi 39209

Dear Cal:

Sometime ago, when the U.S. House of Representatives barely voted for Clinton's so-called Deficit Reduction Bill, your reporter Cynthia Bowers flagrantly misused the adverb "only!" Her statement was that "only two of Mississippi's Congressmen voted against Clinton's bill."

Cal, the word "only" should not have been used at all; but, if it were to be used, she should have stated that "only" three of our Congressmen voted for Clinton's bill. Two out of five is forty percent of our Democrat representatives and if forty percent of all Democrats had voted that way, Clinton would have suffered a devastating defeat. If even one out of five had voted against it, he would have lost by a wide margin. Consequently, how could anyone innocently diametrically distort the significance of the two negative votes by inserting the word "only."

Two conclusions can be drawn, neither complimentary. One that it was used for tendentious purposes to obfuscate for philosophical proclivities. Or, two, Cynthia does not understand what the placement of words in a sentence structure can connote.

The improper usage of words by TV reporters to influence the listeners is always galling, but the egregious misuse of the word "only" in this instance has reverberated within me until I felt compelled to write this letter.

Cal, please impress upon your staff that they are reporters of news not promoters of a liberal agenda!

Sincerely yours,
Signature (Billy)
W. D. Mounger

WDM:pm

"Readers' Views"
"Continue to Oppose Clinton Invasion/Occupation of Haiti"

Your tendentious distortion and beration of the opposition to President Bill Clinton's absurd Haiti policies in your Sept. 21 editorial titled "Haiti: Clinton's Emissaries a Telling Trio" is appallingly contorted. You are so enmeshed in the smog of your ultra-liberal bias that you cannot discern the glaringly obvious. There is no compelling reason to invade/occupy Haiti! Actually, there is no truly legitimate reason whatsoever to be there.

Everyone in this country should be vociferous in opposing this stupid and vapid policy. Mark Helprin in the *Wall Street Journal* stated, "Mr. President, in trumpeting this gnatfest at a hundred times the volume of the Normandy Invasion, you have invited challenges from all who would take comfort at the spectacle of the U.S. in full fluster over an object so diminutive as to be a source of wonder."

Why shouldn't Republicans or all true Americans continue to oppose such an ill considered policy? What true national interest do we have in Haiti? Why should any soldier, or parent of a soldier, want to invade/occupy a trash-pit country just to satisfy the domestic concerns of a failing presidency, especially when the commander-in-chief lied to avoid the armed services, demonstrated against his country on foreign soil, and traveled to Russia under the auspices of the KGB and stayed in a KGB hotel in Moscow? Your draft-dodging hero wouldn't serve; but he has no reluctance in using American armed forces for his political pay-offs.

Even though we should not be in Haiti, you are right that we must support our troops. They did not create this fiasco and are only doing their duty. You, however, are extremely wrong in that we should all adamantly continue to oppose such manifest inadequacies of policy.

Your admired president would not have had to send his emissaries if he did not have such a dissembling and equivocating history! With his previous record of waffling, why should anyone believe him?

W. D. Mounger
Jackson

October 21, 1994

Letters to the Editor
The Clarion Ledger
P. O. Box 40
Jackson, MS 39205-0040

Dear Sir:

Mirable Dictu! (Marvelous to tell!) In your editorial, "Church Welfare: Governor Makes a Valuable Reminder," you have actually agreed with Governor Fordice! Your editorial was especially commendable since your philosophical alter ego the ACLU slams this same proposal for breaching its skewed interpretation of the separation of church and state.

You were on target with your comment: "If the church was doing the job it is called to do, perhaps welfare would be obsolete." Historically the church and family predominately took care of those in need, and consequently, our almost total dependence on government sustenance has undermined our ethos. You were especially cogent with your statement, "But there are greater dynamics at play here than perfect plans in an imperfect world." Yes, give this plan a try! It just might succeed where the inefficient intrusive social engineering of government has failed.

It was pleasingly refreshing for you to be positive about a Mississippi proposal, especially one coming from your "bete noire" Kirk Fordice. Please! Don't let this be a deviant aberrancy, find more to be positive about in our great state!

Sincerely yours,
Signature
W. D. Mounger

William D. Mounger
(Letterhead)

September 26, 1994

Letters to the Editor
The Clarion Ledger
P. O. Box 40
Jackson, MS 39205-0040

Dear Sir:

Your editorial, "Lawyer Ads/What Makes Lawyers Any Different?" is self serving to the ultimate degree. You champion lawyer advertisements when you, with your arrogant monopoly, would be the greatest local financial beneficiary. If a business, organization, or politician, especially Republican, pushed something so blatantly monetarily beneficial to them, you would have blasted them all over your paper! Lay off editorializing when you have so much to gain!

Additionally, you also are promoting your ultra liberal pro-Clinton agenda by advocating the advertising cause of the trial lawyers who are the greatest supporters of Clinton. And that lawyer group is terribly escalating the cost of all businesses in this country, particularly the cost of the health industry!

Quit hiding behind a legitimate good such as the First Amendment to further your profitable and leftish political agendas!

Sincerely yours,
Signature
W. D. Mounger

WDM:pm

"Fordice's Words Distorted on 'Draft-Dodger' Clinton"
Letter to the Editor, *Clarion-Ledger*, drafted October 18, 1994

There you go again! You misled your readers by distorting what Gov. Kirk Fordice said about President Clinton in your Oct. 13 editorial entitled "Leadership: Criticize the Person, Not the Office."

Gov. Fordice did not ". . . cast aspersions on his (the president's) ability to issue orders for our military now." Lamar Alexander, former governor of Tennessee, asked whether President Bush would have been better than President Clinton to rally the troops for possible combat. And Fordice responded correctly that since Clinton was a draft dodger (the record shows he lied to avoid the draft) and George Bush was a war hero, that the military and others would assuredly be more comfortable under Bush's command.

You disingenuously imply that Bill Clinton was the same as all other draft evaders. Not so! He lied while most of the others took advantage of legitimate means to avoid service.

Also, Fordice stated that Clinton demonstrated against his country on foreign soil while young Americans were dutifully serving and yielding their lives in combat. Clinton undeniably did demonstrate several times in England and across the socialist Baltic States and entered Russia when the KGB controlled the visas, and he stayed in a KGB-controlled hotel in Moscow.

You do not like these facts, but they are true. To mention them about Clinton does not demean the presidency, but does definitely demean the deserved-to-be-demeaned Bill Clinton.

Fuss about some other of your liberal fetishes, but please quit distorting actualities in order to hurt the governor and to help your unpopular president in his desperate time of need!

W. D. Mounger
Jackson

William D. Mounger
(Letterhead)

October 19, 1994

Letters to the Editor
The Clarion Ledger
P. O. Box 40
Jackson, MS 39205-0040

Dear Sir:

What a crass absurdity! In your editorial titled, "Gaming: Fordice's Appointment Criteria Flawed," you castigate Gov. Fordice when you should have written a panegyric. His criteria are not flawed! There should be no thought of diversity on a three member gaming commission, only quality!

The Gaming Commission has been the most praiseworthy of Fordice appointments. These three must deal with the most high powered financiers, lawyers, and entrepreneurs with hundreds of millions of dollars at stake. The commission must be above reproach, be steeped in the principles of business, be beyond intimidation, and be unbribable. Victor Smith absolutely meets these standards!

In addition, Victor is a principal supporter of Habitat for Humanity and Mission Mississippi. He also headed the Billy Graham Crusade in Jackson, is Vice President of the International Youth for Christ, organized the Christian Businessman's Association, and is active in numerous other Christian and civic organizations.

If you weren't so bent on toadying to your out of state Gannett bosses to enhance your career, you could discern that this appointment deserves accolades not criticism. You really stretched to condemn Victor's selection solely to satisfy your flawed idea of a "politically correct" choice.

With your monopoly, why must you always be negative about this community. Regardless of whatever is refracted through your prism, it always comes out pink! Lighten up! Don't contort reason to criticize when you should be praising!

Sincerely yours,
Signature
W. D. Mounger

WDM:pm

William D. Mounger
(Letterhead)

October 20, 1994

Letters to the Editor
The Clarion-Ledger
P. O. Box 40
Jackson, MS 39205-0040

Dear Sir:

Your biased editorials are bad enough without your writer, Mac Gordon, by omission, purposefully distorting an article! In his report titled, "Lott's Contributions Top $1.2 Million, Dwarf Opponent's," he stated that Trent Lott had collected $1000 each from 83 individuals and $197,722 from 150 Political Action Committees during the last three months. These facts are true, but why didn't he include the same detailed discussion of Ken Harper's subservient lackey by omitting the details because they were not favorable. An honest and fair reporter would have included the information about both candidates or have left it out altogether.

According to Harper's report, 15 individuals gave him $28,000 during the last quarter and PACS, nearly all Washington based labor unions, gave him $83,100 the last quarter, and $170,100 during this year. Trent's 83 donors gave 17 percent of his $488,336 for the last three months, and his PACS gave 40.5 percent. Harper's 15 donors gave 23 percent of his $123,810 for the last three months and his PACS gave 67 percent and, coincidentally, 67 percent of his money for the entire year.

Mac Gordon evidently did not show Harper's figures because they were detrimental in relationship to Lott's: 23 percent from 15 individual contributors versus 17 percent for Lott from 83; and PAC contributions, 67 percent for Harper versus 40.5 percent for Lott. Be fair! Tell the whole story or none at all. The egregious purposeful omission of unfavorable facts is just as bad as a deliberate lie!

Sincerely yours,
Signature
W. D. Mounger

WDM:pm

William D. Mounger
(Letterhead)

Focus! Focus on the only *real* issue in the campaign for Mississippi House District 66. That issue is which candidate represents your philosophy! In other words, which candidate supports and is in tune with those candidates for higher office whom you have previously supported.

Are you a conservative or a liberal? A Republican or a Democrat? Did you support Reagan over McGovern and Bush over Dukakis? Did you support Cochran and Lott for the U.S. Senate? This district supported all of the first choices listed above from 75 percent to 85 percent. The only candidate consistent with this record is Mike Gunn. A vote for Mike's opponent would be to undermine the demonstrated preferred direction of the voters of this district. Do not be fooled by the subterfuge of the independent label that Mike's opponent is professing. The liberals aren't fooled! All those liberals I can identify are supporting Mike's opponent.

Nationally this country is badly governed because voters continued to elect people to local office who do not represent their true beliefs. We cannot afford to repeat this error in District 66. Senators Thad Cochran and Trent Lott understand the importance of this election. Therefore, they are fervently supporting Mike Gunn. The other candidate is aligned with the party and individuals who have an agenda contrary to this district's demonstrated voting record.

Vote consistently with your beliefs! Vote consistently with your state and national votes! Vote for Mike Gunn on August 22.

William D. Mounger
(Letterhead)

May 30, 1996

Ms. Adriene Davis
Republican National Committee
310 1st Street, S. E.
Washington, D. C. 20003

Dear Adriene:

Enclosed is the information about the 1976 Mississippi delegation, sans my letter to Jules Witcover which I cannot locate. This material should be self-evident as to content.

At least six weeks prior to the convention, I informed David Keene and John Sears that Clarke was duplicitous and was going to double cross us. Sears and Keene vouched for Clarke as a gentleman and a man of honor and ignored my warning. Clarke had a greater debt to me than any other person and yet I knew that his desire to be on the winning side would overcome any such trite things as integrity, honor, and trustworthiness.

From these enclosures, it is obvious that David Keene and the Reagan staff continued to bypass me and were communicating with Clarke Reed until the Schweiker Monday. Then they pleaded with me to save the Mississippi delegation. Reagan phoned me Monday night and I told him that he had given me the world's greatest dose of ex-lax which had virtually eviscerated me. But I promised to do what I could in the face of such despicable tergiversation. After all that apostasy the delegation was barely lost 32 to 28. That count was a solid count. All of the 28 voted that way because they were for Reagan. We then split that vote to report 16 for Ford and 14 for Reagan. Personally, I would have preferred the unit rule to prevail so that the squirmy worm weaklings would be tarred and feathered when they returned to Mississippi.

As I said, you should read *Marathon* and obtain a copy of Harry Dent's book. And, I hope that the enclosed information will be helpful to you.

Sincerely yours,
Signature
W. D. Mounger

WDM:pm

Enclosures

John Ashcroft
(Stationary)

(Handwritten)

August 11, 1997

Dear Billy,

Thank you very much for hosting the get-together in Mississippi! It was a real privilege to meet with you and your hard-working fellow Republicans. We cannot give up on a *great* America. It was wonderful to know your mom (????). THANKS AGAIN!!

John

William D. Mounger
(Letterhead)

November 19, 1998

Letters to the Editor
The Clarion-Ledger
Box 40
Jackson, MS 39205-0040

In your Nation Roundup article titled, "Park Service Saves Civil War Battlefield," dated November 19, 1998, you egregiously and flagrantly misused the adjective "infamous" in describing General Stonewall Jackson's attack at the Battle of Chancellorsville. You stated thusly: "The spot where Civil War Gen. Stonewall Jackson launched his infamous flank attack against Union troops during the Battle of Chancellorsville has been preserved by the National Park Service."

If you desire to convey truth in your paper, I suggest that you invest in a good dictionary and a thesaurus. Of course, if it were your intention to distort the truth in your usual tendentious manner, then the proper use of words are of no concern to you. Among other definitions, infamous means: having a very bad reputation; notorious; in disgrace or dishonor. The successful attack at Chancellorsville in no way deserves such a description.

General Robert E. Lee's forces in front of Richmond, Virginia, were considerably outnumbered and outgunned; consequently, General Lee originated the extraordinary tactic of splitting his Army by ordering that General Jackson march on an extended and exposed route and attack the Union forces in their right flank. During his march General Jackson was extremely vulnerable to attack and Lee's whole army was also; but the northern forces did not avail themselves of the opportunity and thus were severely defeated. However, the North gained immeasurably because Jackson was accidentally killed by his own man.

In no way was this flank attack infamous! It was famous! Just because the Union forces were surprised and routed doesn't make it infamous. By your definition, General George Washington's successful surprise attack on the British/Hessian forces at Trenton, New Jersey, on Christmas Day, 1776, was infamous. An absurdity of the first order! The same as your description of General Jackson' attack!

The Japanese attack on Pearl Harbor was infamous because it was made as a sneak attack with no declaration of war. The Battle of Chancellorsville took place in the middle of a war! General Jackson was a devout Christian, whose battlefield conduct and Generalship, especially his Shenandoah Campaign and the Battle at Chancellorsville, have been among the most thoroughly studied, and admired, in all military history. No possible examination of any of his activities could possibly be described as infamous!

Whether you used the word infamous because of ignorance, or you used it for the tendentious purposes of demeaning General Jackson and the Southern forces, you have disgraced the cause of unbiased and fair reporting!

Signature
W. D. Mounger

"Park Service Saves Civil War Battlefield"
Clarion-Ledger, Roundup, November 19, 1998

SPOTSYLVANIA, VA.
The spot where Civil War Gen. Stonewall Jackson launched his infamous flank attack against Union troops during the Battle of Chancellorsville has been preserved by the National Park Service.

The Park Service paid $775,000 for 40 acres of private land off Route 3, to be included in the Fredericksburg-Spotsylvania National Military Park.

The ferocious battle that took place over four days in May 1863 resulted in nearly 30,000 deaths.

William D. Mounger
(Letterhead)

May 30, 2001

Mr. Bernard Goldberg
c/o *Wall Street Journal*
Editorial and Corporate Headquarters
200 Liberty Street
New York, N. Y. 10281

Dear Bernard:

Your column of 26th June, 2001, on the editorial page of the Wall Street Journal was revelatory, informative, poignant, and frankly expressed a viewpoint which I have held for a long time!

Bernard, I trust that you remember me from the imbroglio in the Mississippi delegation preceding and during the 1976 Republican Convention in Kansas City. My home is the same one where you camped out waiting for us to emerge from our supposedly secret meeting; and my nondescript office, where you interviewed me morning and afternoon for about a week, is in the same place, but is considerably better decorated and a little larger. My executive assistant, Peggy Mize, whom you got to know well, is still with me completing our 39th year working together.

Several times I have seen you giving special reports for CBS, and I wondered if the time might arise when I could make contact with you again. Not knowing what your philosophical inclinations were, but assuming they were in line with the anchor mentality of CBS, it did not occur to me that our world views might converge not diverge.

Lo and behold, your article! It is the best unveiling and rendering of how network journalists (?) do not understand their own biases. It answers why almost to a person each claims to being fair and impartial. They just don't comprehend that they are not pure and perfect and that they are not the fount of all wisdom and that their predilections are leftish.

Bernard, it is evident that I was captivated with your column. Also, if you are ever down this way, please give me a call. As a possible enticement, I am enclosing a brochure on the Majesty of Spain, the NO. ONE exhibition in the USA this year which I serve as Honorary Chairman.

Obviously, I hope that we can stay in contact and that you might even visit.

Sincerely yours,
(Signature) W. D. (Billy) Mounger
W. D. Mounger

WDM:pm, Enclosure

Statements Honoring William D. Mounger

People of Vision
May 9, 1995
Speech by Jim Furrh

I have the pleasure tonight of introducing you to the 1995 people of vision honorees, Jan and Billy Mounger.

Billy and Jan are dear friends of ours and a couple that Mary Leigh and I have come to admire for their contributions to our community, state and the nation. I have been associated with Billy in many business and political endeavors and as couples, we have travelled to many destinations.

Jan and Billy were married in 1956 and together, have become quite a couple. Jan in her quiet manner has endeared herself to many of us. And, Billy in his not-so-quiet manner has made a lasting impression on his community.

Before I spend a few minutes bringing to your attention many of Billy's accomplishments, I think it is accurate to say that for all of his contributions to Mississippi, to the nation's political affairs, Billy's success story begins with being a loving husband to Jan and a devoted father to their sons, Billy and Bobby.

Jan, the same can be said of you. We want to salute you and the boys for the support you have provided him over the years. Lord knows it hasn't been easy.

I had the pleasure of knowing Jan before she met Billy. She had just graduated from Newcomb College and I must admit that she was a New Deal liberal, but after getting hitched to Billy, in no time she became a strong conservative Republican.

Jan and I were reminiscing the other day about this occasion. I was asking her for some background information, some anecdote that would make my remarks a little more personal. We got on the subject of men losing their hair . . . with no one particularly in mind! I told Jan that it is said that men who are balding in the front are considered to be "great thinkers" . . . and I said that men that have lost some of their hair in back are considered "great lovers." Without hesitating, Jan said, "Yeah, and men who are balding in the *front and back* are men who *think* they are great lovers."

Again, we were thinking about no one in particular.

One remarkable thing we have learned about Billy Mounger is that he will say almost anything at almost anytime. It doesn't matter if he is in complete privacy or in a public setting. Billy has never been one for political correctness.

He once said of a local newspaper columnist, that if he took one more step to the left, he would be in Moscow. . . . This remark was made to a startled news conference at the Mississippi Republican Party headquarters in 1976. They remain close friends today.

As some of you know, Billy is quick to point out that he is a West Point graduate. He entered the Military Academy in 1944, having graduated from Central High School. Billy went to West Point to play football and serve his country . . . in that order. However, his football fortunes were short-lived. One day at practice, Colonel Red Blaik pulled Billy aside and told him he didn't have the size to compete at this level. (Incidentally, this team produced two Heisman trophy winners and nine All-Americans). That must have been humbling news for Billy who was a stellar athlete at Central High. Billy was left to ponder West Point without football.

He simply wouldn't consider quitting the service academy and heading back south to Jackson. Quitting was not an option and he most certainly did not want to face his dad with the news that he was returning after less than a semester. While at West Point, he compiled an outstanding record and was christened with the nickname "Curly." Now this is another story!

Billy did, of course, graduate from West Point. Some thirty years after leaving West Point, President Reagan appointed Billy to the academy's board of visitors in 1980. Certainly one of Billy's proudest moments must have been serving as chairman of the board of visitors at the Military Academy during his final two years on the board. After leaving West Point, Billy went on to serve his country in the air force as an aircraft commander. . . .

Can you imagine what it must have been like to have been in Billy's sights as the commander of a B-50 or atomic bomb airplane.

Billy served five years in the air force. And then earned a bachelor's and master's degree in petroleum engineering from the University of Oklahoma. And, along the way, he studied one semester of geology at Millsaps. In our business, that means he knows just enough geology to make him dangerous.

Billy's first experience in the oil business was as a petroleum engineer with Humble Oil Company in New Orleans. Fortunately for Billy, he received exceptional reservoir engineering training which has served him well in later years as an independent oil and gas producer.

After leaving Humble, he headed up the Deposit Guaranty Bank petroleum department for several years. Billy has been an independent oil and gas producer now for some twenty-five years. He had been successful in the business, but he has also labored to give something back to the industry.

He is a former chairman of the Mississippi/Alabama division of Mid-Continent Oil and Gas Association and remains a respected leader in the organization. Billy has also been active in the IPAA where he rose to the elected position of vice president of the executive committee and chairman of the finance committee.

And just last year, Billy received from Mid-Continent Oil and Gas Association, the association's Bill and Emmett Vaughey Wildcat Award . . . given annually to companies and individuals which have distinguished themselves in the industry.

Even as Billy was building a successful business in the 1960s, he was not completely fulfilled. He had a vision of something better than the political status quo. In his view, America was adrift during the politics of the 1960s, and Billy yearned to make a difference in helping this country become stronger and wiser.

Some thirty years after, the rest is history. As we all know, Billy is widely credited with helping build, from the ground up, the Republican Party in Mississippi and he has been active as well in national political affairs.

His elected or appointed positions in previous state and national campaigns are too numerous to mention tonight. They literally span thirty years and include serving last year as finance chairman for Trent Lott's campaign.

All of you know from personal experience that Billy is an adept fundraiser. He earned his spurs in this role in the 1960s. Some of you may recall that one of the watershed events of the Goldwater campaign in 1964 was the emergence of a fellow named Ronald Reagan. Perhaps the defining moment for Republicans in that campaign was Reagan's riveting speech in support of Goldwater. What you don't know is Reagan's speech was re-aired many times during the campaign thanks to the efforts of Billy and Wirt Yerger. Billy had far exceeded his fundraising goal from the Mississippi campaign and he and Wirt demanded that the Goldwater campaign spend this money to air the Reagan speech.

I agree with Billy on almost everything, but I recognize that not all of you agree with his political philosophy.

If you don't agree with Billy, you are in a lot of trouble. He is relentless. If you call him at the office and miss him, his recorded message is: "If you are a conservative Republican, I will return your call, if you are a moderate or liberal Republican, we'll see, and if you are a liberal Democrat, you probably don't have a chance.

Billy Mounger simply towers over the rest of the crowd who helped shape politics in the last twenty-five years. More than any one individual, he is responsible for the election to Congress of Thad Cochran and Trent Lott. Today, both these U.S. senators command as much respect as anyone in Washington, and I can tell you that both men credit Billy for much of their success.

Billy has never backed off from using his influence in Washington when it came to helping Mississippi. For instance, I recall that he pulled together the necessary connections with H.E.W. to land the major funding for the Methodist Rehabilitation Center.

In 1958 he was involved in the founding of Jackson Academy, which has become one of the outstanding schools in the state.

For all of my sincere comments about Billy, let's face it, he's not perfect. . . . As a couple, Billy is a bull in a china shop and Jan is the ultimate southern lady. There's an old saying "Never underestimate the power of a kind word or deed." Jan Mounger embraces this kind of thinking. Billy can be curt, indignant, and verbally abusive. He has taken out his wrath on governors, journalists, even presidents.

I want to share with you a portion of one such letter to president George Bush in 1990.

Dear Mr. President:

As you know, my Republican credentials are long term and impeccable. But, for the enlightenment of your toadies whose cordon sanitaire this letter must breach, the very succinct resume is included.

Delegate to Republican National conventions 1968, 72, 76, 80, & 84
Vice Chairman Mississippi Delegations 68–80
Southern Floor Leader Reagan-Bush 84
Nixon Finance Chairman 1968 & 1972
Mid-South Finance Chairman Reagan-Bush 1980
Mississippi Finance Chairman Reagan-Bush 1984
Recruited and Finance Chairman Thad Cochran
Finance Chairman Trent Lott for Senate 1988

Hopefully these credentials will circumvent whichever sycophant is designated to answer this letter. With circumvention assumed, here are my views.

Dispirited, disillusioned, disappointed, and disgusted—these words describe my reactions to the misguided apostasy of your "read my lips" pledge. Did you not understand the depth of the people's concern with taxes? Did you not understand or care about undermining the Republican Party?

To begin to make amends, you must terminate those pusillanimous prostitutes of pragmatism, John Sununu and Richard Darman. They have disserved you, the nation, and the Republican Party. Even if you don't understand how you were elected, at least your coterie should. Without such a drastic move, I fear you have squandered almost 30 years of effort, reducing the Republican and conservative causes to shambles. Next Tuesday, I fear, our Republican candidates will be routed.

Most of us loyal Republicans are:

Dejectedly, disquieted, and disemboweled,
Billy

Now, I don't know the meaning of all of these words . . . and I'm pretty damn sure George Bush didn't either. But the point is, Billy knew exactly what he wanted to say and how he wanted to say it. . . . He always has!

People of vision have many dimensions and one thing that characterizes all people of vision is that they do not rest on their laurels.

Just when we thought we had Billy figured out, he added yet another chapter to his record of service to the community.

In 1986, when the International Ballet was in dire need of a leader, city and state officials asked Billy to come to the rescue. Financial support for the upcoming competition had not been forthcoming from the state and the entire event appeared doomed to fail. Billy stepped in at the eleventh hour and raised the money necessary to put on a world-class competition.

Billy again was one of the leading fundraisers in 1990 and served as chairman of the board for the 1994 event which was also a resounding success. As is usually the case, Billy did far more than his share . . . and now the International Ballet has brought distinction to Jackson and put Mississippi in a light never before enjoyed by our state.

In recognition of his many years of service, Billy was the recipient of the 1995 Governor's Patron's Award for excellence in the arts.

More often than not, our wives do not get the recognition they deserve. Their identity is lost in our professions and our endeavors. Jan Mounger is an outstanding person in her own right and deserving of your recognition tonight. She has been an active member of First Presbyterian Church and the Kidney Foundation board. She is currently serving as president of the Friends of the International Ballet Competition. In addition, she has contributed her time to the Art Auxilliary, the Symphony League, the Salvation Army, Hinds County Republican Women and many other civic organizations.

Jan has been a steadfast supporter of Billy in his pursuits . . . and raised two fine sons. In my opinion, there is no higher calling or nothing more visionary than that of being involved in nurturing your children's character and their growth as individuals.

Your honorees tonight have spent a lifetime making a positive difference in the lives of people and in the affairs of their community.

I would like to quote from a letter written by a mutual friend who was unable to attend tonight. "You have given generously of your resources as well as so much of your time and leadership to truly *make a difference* for your city, state, and nation. You have truly exemplified MacArthur's words . . . *duty, honor, country.*" In summary, Billy is truly a modern renaissance man—he is interested in his family, church, oil business, tennis, arts, history, politics, West Point, and many other fields too numerous to mention.

I know Billy and Jan are honored to be in the distinguished company of the previous "People of Vision" honorees.

It is a distinct privilege to introduce to you at this time the 1995 People of Vision honorees, Jan and Billy Mounger . . . and you can guess which one will do the speaking.

NOTES

Chapter 1. 1976: The Political Storm Before the Calm

1. "Excerpt from Mr. Agnew's Dinner Speech," *Eagle, The Official Publication of the Mississippi Republican Party*, Vol. 7, No. 10, Oct. 1969.
2. *Marathon: The Pursuit of the Presidency, 1972–1976*, Jules Witcover, Viking Press, 1977, p. 447.
3. Witcover, 447.
4. Pickering retired in 2004 from his post as federal judge of the Fifth Circuit Court of Appeals after gaining a recess appointment following a long nomination battle waged by some liberal national Democrats to thwart President George W. Bush's nominees.
5. Witcover, 443–44.
6. Personal interview with the authors and Governor Haley Barbour.
7. Personal interview with the authors.
8. Personal interview with the authors.

Chapter 2. The 1930s: Big Bill and Little Billy

1. The best compilation of the Mounger name is found in the book *Monger-Mounger and Allied Families* compiled by Louise F. Wilcox, privately printed in the U.S.A. in 1991. That compilation is as follows:

The name Mounger is English and means "one who sells merchandise—a dealer." In Old Rome, a dealer in slaves was a mango. Long afterward, a mango came to be a mangiar (merchant); a mangiar became in time a monger. The surname is also used as a mounger of iron or ironmonger, and woolmonger, fishmonger, woodmonger. From England to America the name underwent many spellings, probably due to the pronunciation of the person who spoke the name, and the spelling ability of the person who wrote it in public records. Some of the variations are: Munger, Muniger, Mongo, Munga, Monger, Mongre, Manger, Mounger and, perhaps Mangum, Mangem and others.

The earliest reference so far uncovered is a relative by the name of a William Manger listed in the Hundreds Roll of County Wilshire, England, in 1255. There are many other references to the Manger name in the 13th and 14th centuries, but the Monger spelling has, to my knowledge, not been found prior to the 17th century. Nevertheless, my first ancestor to arrive in this country was JOHN MONGER (Munger) in 1638, however a WILLIAM UNGER (possibly WILL MUNGER), listed as a day laborer, came with Captain John Smith on the ship *Discovery* in 1607. Additionally, JAMES MONGER, a merchant of London, is listed on the second Charter of Jamestown, dated 13 May 1609, given by JAMES I and a CHARLES MAGNOR (MANGER?), a planter of Fowede Hundred, whose wife was Ellin, received a land grant for 650 acres of land on 1 December 1620. He sold this land on 8 February 1634 to William Hayward "gentleman of Crawsey Creeke" which indicates that Charles Magnor survived the Indian Massacre of 1622.

2. Personal interview with the authors and Leland Speed Jr.

3. When I returned to Mississippi after serving in the Air Force, this money became part of the kitty from which I began to invest in oil leases!

4. Unfortunately, very little is known about my mother's predecessors. She never talked about them, which leaves me with very little information. However, recently Tom McMillan of Alabama sent to me a copy of biographical memoirs written by Norvell Robertson, my great-great grandfather. This information is summarized as follows:

Jeffrey Robertson, Sr., was born in 1709, lived in Chesterfield County, Virginia, where he had a farm of 105 acres and several slaves. He sired eight children and died in 1784.

Jeffrey Robertson, Jr., was born in Chesterfield County, Virginia, on January 15, 1737, and lived there until his death in 1812. He married Sarah Norvell, daughter of George Norvell of Hanover County, Virginia. Jeffrey was enrolled in the Virginia State Militia in January 1781, and served three months. He had two sons, Norvell and Jeffrey.

Norvell Robertson was born May 22, 1765, in Buckingham County, Virginia. In 1791, in Georgia, he married Sarah Powell, who was born February 7, 1770, and died October 24, 1842. Norvell Robertson was enlisted in July 1781 in the Virginia State Militia, serving at Yorktown and helped to build the breast-works which protected the Continental army from the British. He was discharged at Yorktown on the day of Cornwallis' surrender of the British Army. He lived with his father until he was 21 years old; and he then left his native state for Georgia, arriving in Burke County, Georgia, on January 1, 1788, where he lived for three years, engaging in the contracting and building trade. He then moved to Rocky Comfort to teach school where he boarded with Martha Powell and met her daughter, Sarah, whom he married in 1791. He continued to live in Georgia until he migrated to Covington County, Mississippi, in 1818, settling on the west side of Leaf River at the junction of the Bowie. Here he lived for 15 years before he moved to about 15 miles north of Old Williamsburg, where he died and was buried in the Leaf River Baptist Cemetery on September 16, 1855.

Additionally, Norvell Robertson was a Baptist minister who pastored many churches including the Fellowship Church in Rocky Comfort, Georgia, and in Covington County, the Providence Church, and next, the Leaf River Baptist Church. Norvell Robertson had ten children with his tenth being my great grandfather, George Franklin Robertson, born circa 1812 at Rocky Comfort, Georgia. Unfortunately, I know nothing of him other than he sired eight children with the sixth being my grandfather, James Asaph Robertson, who was born on January, 20, 1861, in Covington County, Mississippi.

Nothing is known by me about my grandmother Stewart's kinsmen, but I do know that some recent members of the Robertson Clan have been successful. My mother's first cousin, Stokes Robertson Sr., was a successful lawyer and real estate investor in Jackson, and his son, Stokes Robertson Jr., was for many years a justice of the State of Mississippi Supreme Court. Otis Robertson, another first cousin, was a high official with Pepsi-Cola Company and thereby attained a position of prominence and wealth.

My mother was born in 1903 to Rosa Stewart and James Asaph Robertson. After my grandfather was killed, my uncles and aunts were forced to begin work at an early age to help support the family. This impecunious situation dictated that the only offspring who earned a college degree would be the eldest, Cecil Robertson, who became a doctor and practiced medicine in Wiggins, Mississippi. Unfortunately, he died in the early

1930s before he had attained a position of economic independence, leaving his family—three children and a widow—in dire straits economically.

Uncle Jessie migrated somehow to New Jersey and made a career as a postman. He had numerous children, whom I visited in the spring of 1948 while attending West Point—driving down in the 1947 Chrysler convertible which my father had given to me in anticipation of my graduation in June 1948. Uncle James moved to Los Angeles with my Aunt Jewel and the several members of his family. In the early thirties I spent a summer with them in Collins staying at the Gill house which was Aunt Jewel's family home. As a city boy, I first learned about the birds and the bees— and other informative things—in that small town environment, mostly from her brothers, Milton and Millard Gill. Uncle Denny never married, and consequently played with us much more than the other aunts and uncles. He was in the CCC during the Great Depression, and later worked as a lineman for the telephone company. He died in Jackson during the fifties. Uncle Dayton married Aunt Pearl who was part Italian and my favorite aunt. She was always friendly and hospitable and worked for years as a saleslady for the Emporium, from which she finally retired. Uncle Dayton was a very nice man we visited once in the North Arkansas mountains at a grape farm he co-owned with my Uncle Jack and Aunt Lana. Later he moved to Jackson and purchased a Sinclair gas station on North State Street where the Welty Library now is located; from his station I was able to obtain extra gasoline during the rationing of World War II. They had one daughter, Barbara, who was one class behind me in school. She graduated from Millsaps College and married John Christmas from Vicksburg whom I played in football in 1941 and 1942. John was the treasurer for Millsaps College from which he is now retired; they now live in Madison County, Mississippi.

Ross was my youngest uncle who, prior to retirement, was the editor of the newspaper in Muskogee, Oklahoma. We visited with them once when the family was in Oklahoma. He and Aunt Martha had two children: Ross, Jr., had a highly successful career as an attorney for Phillips Petroleum Company and retired at the Phillips headquarters town of Bartlesville, Oklahoma; Aunt Lena married a Yankee named Brady, from a supposedly prominent Indiana family; however, he died very young and left her with scant inheritance and a young daughter, Roseanna. The two of them lived with us intermittently and Roseanna attended Power Elementary School with me several years. She graduated from Millsaps College, married, moved to Dallas, and from there, I have lost all contact.

Aunt Lana, who loved to cook, married Uncle Jack Weaver who, eccentrically, would eat only ham and ham gravy with bread or grits. He was undereducated, but had a heart of gold and could fix anything. He had several opportunities to do well, but somehow never managed to succeed. At one time, he co-owned and ran a large ranch in Oklahoma where my mother and sisters spent several months; they moved to Jackson where he worked for the Kerr Tire and Rubber Company (a company partially owned by my father) in the Yazoo Mower division. My father also helped them obtain, at a substantial discount, a house with about twenty acres around it on Old Highway 80 west of Brandon. Later he sold it for a small profit when he could have made a great deal of money. They moved to Orlando, Florida, where he managed the Yazoo Mower operation in that city. Aunt Lana and Uncle Jack had no offspring but adopted a son, Don, who made a career as a sergeant in the U.S. Army and married a Japanese woman.

5. Personal interview with the authors and Nat Rogers.

6. My father had earned a law degree studying at night at the Jackson School of Law.

7. Personal interview with the authors.

8. Personal interview with the authors and Leland Speed Jr.

9. Personal interview with the authors.

10. Personal interview with the authors.

11. Personal interview with the authors.

12. The article continues:

Mr. Mounger, son of a Covington lawyer, was educated in the schools at Collins and at Mississippi State College, where he was graduated in the class of 1920. He was in the bank of Collins for three years after receiving his diploma, and studied law outside his duties, passing the state bar examination.

He came to Jackson in 1923 to become a teller in the old Merchants Bank and Trust company in the building across from the Old Capitol. In ten years of service with that institution he advanced to the position of assistant trust officer, and became trust officer with the Deposit Guaranty bank in 1933.

He was promoted to the vice-presidency in January of 1936, and has been very actively concerned with direction of the affairs of the bank for all these years, especially so during the protracted illness which recently claimed the life of President Donald.

A series of honors, distinctions and responsibilities have fallen to Mr. Mounger during his career in college and business life. He was a member of the select George Rifles at Miss. State, later Sigma Chi, social fraternity. He was an officer in the Reserve Officers Training Corps at Miss. State, and held several student offices of prominence and responsibility. Since graduation he has been a leader in Miss. State alumni affairs, being past president of the Hinds County chapter of the State association.

In Jackson, he has been identified with all progressive movements. He is a member of the board of directors of the Jackson Chamber of Commerce, past Potentate of Wahabi Temple of the Shrine, a leader in the Jackson Kiwanis Club, member of Galloway Memorial Methodist church [sic] and president of the Jackson Country Club.

Professionally, he is treasurer of the Mississippi Bankers association [sic] and active in banking councils in the state.

Mr. Mounger married Miss Veronica Robertson of Collins after his college graduation, and they have four lovely children in their happy home on St. Ann Street: Marjorie, 16, member of the graduating class of Central High, Billy, Junior, who is expected to make his dad a member of the Central High sideline quarterbacks' club next fall, Libby, 9, and Henry Hartfield, 6.

At 40 years of age, he is the youngest president of a major banking institution in the state, despite two decades of experience behind him. *

No other changes in executives were made at the Tuesday meeting.

13. Personal interview with the authors.

Chapter 3. The 1930s: A Father's Son

1. Personal interview with the authors.
2. Personal interview with the authors.
3. Personal interview with the authors with Fox Garraway.
4. Personal interview with the authors.
5. Personal interview with the authors.

* Editor's note: Bill Mounger actually was thirty-nine when he became president.

Chapter 4. The 1940s: Big 8 Football and West Point

1. Wikipedia, the free encyclopedia, "Fifteenth Amendment to the United States Constitution," June 28, 2005.

2. I spoke in later years with Strom Thurmond, who commented to me that "if I had been elected president, it would have been a different and better world." This is noteworthy because it was Mississippi U.S. Senator Trent Lott's reference of this often-stated comment by Thurmond, at a meal honoring the elderly South Carolina senator, that was blown out of proportion and led to accusations that Lott was a racist, causing his January 7, 2003, resignation as majority leader of the U.S. Senate. My first vote for president of the United States was for Senator Strom Thurmond on the Dixiecrat ticket in 1948.

3. That would be between $40,000 and $50,000 today.

Chapter 5. The 1950s and '60s: Finding Oil, a Wife, and a Life

1. Personal interview with the authors.

2. Personal interview with the authors and Herman Hines.

3. During my eight months in England I was paid per month $250 base pay, $125 flight pay, $45 quarters allowance, $40 rations allowance, plus $120 overseas duty pay. I received an unlimited amount of cigarettes at ten cents per pack, which I gave away since I did not smoke; and each officer was allocated a case of Seagrams liquor per month at two dollars per bottle. I lived like a king and saved a lot of money.

4. I never made much from that investment, but I got a brand-new Pontiac Catalina to drive yearly.

5. Years later in reminiscence, Nat Rogers wrote the following poem, entitled, "An All American Boss," about Bill Mounger:

> William Malcolm Mounger, Esquire
> Truly a man born to inspire
> A lawyer and an engineer
> Banker with vision—had no peer
> Deep loyalty always prevailed
> Family and friends he never failed
> No greed in his philosophy

Acted with generosity

Personal charm beyond compare

Ever ready to do or dare

A builder in the truest sense

Not inclined to straddle a fence

A proud Scot to the very core

The Mounger tartan did adore

Long hounded by disease and pain

Still courage followed in his train

He taught me so much not found in books

Never judge man or deal by looks

Instead find out what end is served

Maintain your poise, be steely nerved

Treat peers and staff with great respect

Forgive mistakes, next time correct

No finer man I ever knew

Stars in his crown are but just due.

6. This story was recounted by Nat Rogers during a personal interview with the authors.

7. Personal interview with the authors and Fred LaRue.

8. I have experienced many professors over seven and one-half years of university education while earning a B.S. in general education, a B.S. in petroleum engineering and a master's degree in petroleum engineering, and by far the best professor I ever had was Dr. Richard R. Priddy, my Millsaps College geology professor.

9. I had worked the summer of 1955 in Jackson for the Union Producing Company and had been involved with the unitization of the Soso Field in Jones and Jasper counties, where my father had several interests.

10. Personal interview with the authors and Herman Hines.

11. Personal interview with the authors.

12. Personal interview with the authors and Parham Bridges.

13. George Hunt, Doug Latimer, Dick Quin, among others, were joint owners in my lease. I eventually agreed to a proposition for three-eights of seven-eighths overriding royalty for a lease to Dorris Ballew and D. A. Biglane. I had been told that the deal would fall through if I did not sign. Later I discovered I could have drilled my interest on my own. Yet, as the youngest and least experienced, I did not want to sabotage that big deal.

14. In later years, President Reagan appointed me to serve on the West Point Board of Visitors (1984–1989), and I served as its chairman for two years, 1988 and 1989; and since 1994 I have continuously served as a trustee of the Association of Graduates, plus contributing substantially financially towards the needs of the academy. With time, I have begun to repay West Point, although its true worth to me is beyond any number of dollars.

15. The Petroleum Club of Jackson was founded in 1948 to offer a place of refuge for people involved in the booming oil-and-gas business in Mississippi to get with other interrelated businessmen. It was located in the King Edward Hotel where most members of the state legislature stayed, along with others of importance in state government. For many years, it was the premier private club in the state. The club put on dances featuring the big bands of the day including Harry James, Benny Goodman, and others. It also organized special trains and buses for such events as the Ole Miss-LSU game in Baton Rouge and the Sugar Bowl in New Orleans. In 1966 through 1967, the club elected me as its president and I felt deeply honored, not only because of its prestige, but also because my father was one of its organizers. I, unknown to the club membership, practiced a bit of unbridled individualism by exercising my power to appoint a secret membership committee to approve or disapprove applicants for membership. Since even the members of the committee would be unaware of each other, I decided that if only I knew who was on the committee, then I would name myself as a committee of one. For the two years of my presidency, I alone decided who could belong to the most prestigious private club in the state. During my tenure, Mississippi shut down liquor in all clubs in the state. The Mississippi Highway Patrol raided the Junior League of Jackson's Carnival Ball at the Country Club of Jackson where Warren Hood Sr. was King of the Ball. The governor, Paul Johnson Jr., had just vacated the club when the patrol pounced. From that time on, no private clubs could serve alcoholic beverages. Even though Mississippi collected a 10 percent tax on illegal liquor, it was still the last state in the nation to be classified as dry, and the police constantly ignored the flagrant breaches of the law. For instance, before they were to inspect the Petroleum Club, they would give the club an advance warning and all the liquid evidence would be safely secreted by the time the police arrived on the premises. As a consequence of this "drying up" of the state, Merill Harris, Jack Vaughn, and I divided all the liquor stash into lots and arranged for a

gala dance to auction off the lots, thereby disposing of all the alcoholic beverages in the club. From that time on, the club was dry until the next session of the legislature legalized whiskey, making Mississippi the last state to do so.

Chapter 6. The Early 1960s: Goldwater Rush!

1. Fred LaRue was involved in the initial group supporting Goldwater for president, having met Goldwater in Chicago once and having contributed $25,000 to the cause.

2. Personal interview with the authors.

3. Back in 1961, Goldwater had suggested that the United States would be better off if the Eastern Seaboard fell into the Atlantic and sank; that had riled liberals but it also raised the affections of many Mississippians. We had experienced liberal know-it-allism for too long. We felt that Republican northeasterners including Nelson Rockefeller had used Mississippians for too long. Goldwater's heart beat with ours. When northerners eschewed even visiting Mississippi for fear of being labeled racists, Goldwater had traveled to our state.

4. "Wirt Yerger Quits Post as GOP Chairman," *Jackson Daily News*, by William Peart, Feb. 7, 1966.

5. Peart.

6. "An Oral History with Mr. W. D. Mounger," The Mississippi Oral History Program of the University of Southern Mississippi; interview with Dr. Orley Caudill; Volume 311, 1977, p.43.

7. Personal interview with the authors and Clarke Reed.

8. "An Oral History with Mr. W. D. Mounger," The Mississippi Oral History Program of the University of Southern Mississippi; interview with Dr. Orley Caudill; Volume 311, 1977, p.43.

9. Personal interview with the authors.

10. *Marathon: The Pursuit of the Presidency, 1972–76*, Jules Witcover, Viking Press (New York, N.Y.), 1977, p. 442.

11. Witcover, p. 464.

12. Witcover, p. 450.

13. Witcover, p. 445.

14. Personal interview with the authors.

15. "Reader Says Person Can't Be Conservative By Proxy," *Clarion-Ledger*, Delmar Dennis, Nov. 3, 1966.

16. Walker in 1968 approached me at the Republican National Convention. He made the remark to me that the Republican Party had never done anything for him. Oh boy, did I straighten him out that time!

Chapter 7. The 1960s: Taking the Bull by the Horns

1. First, however, our state apparatus had to decide which presidential contender to support. To do so, local precincts throughout our state initially met in tiny rooms and towns around the state. Precinct gatherings amounted to a handful of people in a rural district or, in Hinds County, a meeting of hundreds of citizens who considered themselves Republican. Each precinct selected a chairman and elected delegates to vote at the county meeting, which then selected the county executive committee and representatives to the state convention. This was, in theory, a very representative form of GOP state party decision-making: The locals would in theory listen to their local constituents, then vote accordingly as they chose their delegates. Then, at the state convention, all the delegates in theory were to indicate whom they would support at the national convention. They also picked the state's GOP national committee man and committee woman, as well as the electors (one for each U.S. House District, and one for each senator to vote in the Electoral College) and the state executive committee, which then elected the state chairman and vice chairman.

2. "Alternate delegates" resembled honorable mention delegates in status; these folks enjoyed all the privileges of the actual delegates, down to meetings at the actual convention and key floor seats and banquets, etc. Their inclusion allowed party leaders to anoint and cultivate new workers and leaders throughout the state by including them in the convention process.

3. Personal interview with the authors.

4. "GOP Goes Conservative," *Clarion-Ledger-Jackson Daily News*, by Charles Overby, June 9, 1968.

5. Personal interview with the authors.

6. "Vote for Agnew, Head for Home," *Jackson Daily News*, by Charles Overby, Aug. 9, 1968.

7. "The City Seen," Charles Smith, *Clarion-Ledger*, Aug. 12, 1968.

8. Personal interview with the authors.

9. Personal interview with the authors.

10. Personal interview with the authors.

11. Personal interview with the authors.

12. Obviously, I like the limelight as does Clarke; being quoted on TV is interesting. And maybe I do like to be quoted over much. But on the other hand, I am convinced—and possibly in a self-serving way—that I am willing to subvert myself and my wishes to the other guys, and I did it for years with Clarke for the good of the cause.

13. In a column some time later, Mississippi political columnist Wayne Weidie assessed Jules Witcover's account of our Mississippi meltdown in his book, *Marathon—The Pursuit of the Presidency, 1972–76*. Weidie goes so far as to state, "The scenario can even be stretched that in 1968 Reed and Mounger gave us Richard Nixon, which then means they gave us Watergate in 1972." The logic is strained beyond real credulity, but nonetheless pains me!

Chapter 8. The Early 1970s: State Coffers, Candidates, and Hurricane Camille Explode

1. Personal interview with the authors.

2. Personal interview with the authors.

3. Personal interview with the authors with Billy Powell.

4. Personal interview with the authors.

5. Personal interview with the authors.

6. Personal interview with the authors.

7. AN ESOTERIC ANALYSIS OF THE PROS AND CONS OF RUNNING FOR CONGRESS IN THE 1968 AND 1970 ELECTIONS.

PRO

1. I believe I want to run!
    a. Enjoy making speeches.
    b. Like to influence people.
    c. Influence on national politics.

    d.   Want to attain the respect of the people.

    e.   Frustrated thespian—enjoy the limelight and recognition.

    f.   Another blow at the Democrats.

    g.   Easy way to leave the bank.

    h.   Not satisfied with what I have accomplished.

    i.   Fervent desire to lead.

    j.   Want to test campaign theories.

    k.   Know facts that need to be conveyed.

    l.   Be in the vortex of the action.

    m. If I lose—desire purged from my system.

    n.   If I don't run—may regret it for life.

2. Further the Republican Cause.

    a.   Principles are right.

    b.   I am dedicated to the cause.

    c.   Work for the future of my children.

    d.   Attain a breakthrough for the Mississippi GOP.

    e.   More influence in National Party.

    f.   Ask others to sacrifice—must do so too!

    g.   Influence the National Convention.

CON

1. Family Considerations.

    a.   Jan adamantly against.

    b.   Would have to move.

    c.   New school for children.

    d.   Less time with family.

    e.   Lose relationship with children.

    f.   Too many cocktail parties.

    g.   Washington—Ugh!

    h.   Away from family—parents.

    i.   Don't want to leave Jackson again.

    j.   Too much travel.

    k.   Constant work—too little free time.

    l.   Maintain two homes.

    m. Jan's father ill.

2. Bank—Other Activities.
   a. Disappoint Nat Rogers [President of Deposit Guaranty Bank] and Bill Vaughey [a close friend and national oil figure who helped set up the bank's Oil Department].
   b. Peggy [my secretary and assistant]—what would she do?
   c. Leave the Petroleum Department with excessive problems.
   d. Disloyal to bank customers.
   e. Only person conversant with Oil Department problems.
   f. Many pending transactions—bank and personal.
   g. Would terminate relationship with bank.
   h. Vice President of Independent Petroleum Association of America—needed by oil industry.
   i. Past President of Miss.-Ala. Mid-Continent Oil & Gas Association—needed for local oil affairs.
   j. Deeply complicated personal oil business.
   k. No replacement at the bank.

3. Personal Activities and Traits.
   a. Larger personal debt.
   b. Oil income down.
   c. Immeasurably complicated business affairs.
   d. Rise in interest rates—more money to service debts.
   e. Loss of approximately $40,000/year from bank.
   f. Would not be enough involved in oil business.
   g. I do not truly feel comfortable with strangers.
   h. May not have rapport with the people.
   i. Overweight.
   j. Not recovered totally from back operation.
   k. No campaign money—would probably have to raise all my own funds.
   l. No subsidy money—would be creating no new income while campaigning.
   m. Might lose humiliatingly!

8. During Nixon's 1968 campaign, we had convinced the national party that we should avoid spending a lot of money on Nixon advertising and state election efforts; we argued persuasively to the Nixon campaign leaders that Alabama governor George Wallace, a third-party candidate, was a shoe-in to take the Magnolia State no matter how much we spent,

so why not let us hold our monies and invest them into building for the future growth of the state machine? Wallace did, in fact, win 65 percent; Mississippi Republicans did not waste our money; and in 1972 and thereafter, the state party was that much stronger financially to support national and local candidates.

9. "The Mississippi Republican Party: One Candidate's Viewpoint," by Gilbert E. Carmichael; John C. Stennis Lecture; Mississippi State University; March 26, 1996, p. 4.

10. Personal interview with the authors and Thad Cochran.

11. Personal interview with the authors.

12. Personal interview with the authors.

13. It was at the home of Newton Dotson, who at the time was the Republican mayor of Clarksdale. He was elected in a special election but was beaten the next time because the black vote was about 70 or 80 percent in Clarksdale. He was the best mayor they ever had. We had obtained the largest Economic Development Authority appropriation in the United States of America that year to build a bridge for Clarksdale, solely because he was the Republican mayor. Then they kicked him out! They would never have had that bridge if he were not a Republican. I felt like dynamiting the bridge after they did that to him.

Chapter 9. Hinds County's Historic Shake-up

1. Palmer had become involved in Republican efforts as a good friend of Rubel Phillips, who was from his home town of Corinth. Ironically, Phillips at that time in 1972 sided with Breed and Moye. I was in Portugal in January of 2004, stayed at the ambassador's residence, and laughed again about using his office to undermine what Johnny himself supported.

2. "Mounger Unseats GOP Foe," *Clarion-Ledger/Jackson Daily News*, Charles Gordon, April 23, 1972, 1. An excerpt from the article follows:

William D. "Billy" Mounger, Jackson banker, unseated veteran Hinds County Republican Chairman Jack Breed Saturday in a Hinds County GOP Convention contest widely interpreted as a power fight between the state leadership and a contending faction.

The convention was held with close to 500 precinct delegates and spectators—including James Meredith, a black who is running as a sort of "independent" Republican for Democrat Jim Eastland's seat in the U.S. Senate—at Primos Northgate restaurant.

Following the successful race of Mounger against Breed for the chairmanship, the former's entire slate of executive committeemen and delegates and alternates to the May 20 state convention was also elected.

Observers read into the contest a battle between GOP Chairman Clarke Reed of Greenville and Dr. James Moye of Laurel, National Republican Committeeman from Mississippi, for the post long held by Reed.

In this version of events, Reed was the real central figure on the Mounger side, and Dr. Moye on that represented by Breed.

The convention included numerous testimonials to hard work done by Breed as county chairman for the past four years. But it also heard various speakers express dissatisfaction with the relationship between Breed and the state hierarchy headed by Reed.

Chapter 10. 1972: The Year of the Rising Republicans (Lott, Cochran, Carmichael)

1. *Wikipedia*, "James Meredith," June 28, 2005.
2. "The Mississippi Republican Party: One Candidate's Viewpoint," by Gilbert E. Carmichael; John C. Stennis Lecture; Mississippi State University; March 16, 1996, p. 4.
3. Carmichael, p. 5.
4. Carmichael, p. 5.
5. Carmichael, p. 5.
6. Wirt butted heads since the beginning with Carmichael and his Meridian Republicans and considered Gil considerably more liberal than the party as a whole; in 1964 Wirt kept Carmichael off of the state GOP executive committee for that reason.
7. Personal interview with the authors.
8. "The Mississippi Republican Party: One Candidate's Viewpoint," by Gilbert E. Carmichael; John C. Stennis Lecture; Mississippi State University; March 16, 1996, p. 5.

Chapter 11. 1972: Miami's Vice: The Nixon Renomination

1. Personal interview with the authors and Clarke Reed.
2. This same fear of bad press similarly stifled Chicago Mayor Daley's response at the 1968 Democratic National Convention in Chicago.

Chapter 12. 1972: Mississippi's Historic Statewide Elections

1. Personal interview with the authors.

2. Personal interview with the authors.

3. Personal interview with the authors.

4. Personal interview with the authors and Trent Lott.

5. "GOP's Top Post Changes," *Prentiss Headlight*, Wayne Weidie, April 27, 1977, p. 2

6. Nixon sent the following note to me, on White House stationary, dated November 29, 1972:

Dear Billy:

As I look back to our victory on November 7, I realize how much you and our other supporters from Mississippi contributed to one of the greatest landslides in American political history.

It would be impossible for me to repay you adequately for all the work you did for our cause during the campaign.

I can only assure you that over the next four years I shall do everything I possibly can to make a record which all Americans, regardless of party, will be proud of as we celebrate America's 200th Birthday in 1976.

With appreciation and best wishes,

Sincerely,

(Personal signature of "Richard Nixon")

Chapter 13. 1973: WLBT Station and I Make History

1. *Changing Channels: The Civil Rights Case that Transformed Television*, Kay Mills, University Press of Mississippi, 2004, 69–71.

2. Federal Communications Commission, FCC 73D-16, Initial Decision of Administrative Law Judge Lenore G. Ehrig, April 13, 1973, 214.

3. Federal Communications Commission, FCC 73D-16, Initial Decision of Administrative Law Judge Lenore G. Ehrig, April 13, 1973, 215.

4. FCC, Ehrig, 72.

5. FCC, Ehrig, 84–85.

6. FCC, Ehrig, 209.

Chapter 14. Carmichael's Debacle

1. "Mississippi Outlook," Paul Pittman, *The Tylertown Times*, Nov. 22, 1973. Pittman's article follows:

JACKSON—Make no mistake about two things. Gov. Ronald Reagan is a candidate for president in 1976, and regardless of the shock waves that have bothered the Republican Party both here in the state and nationally, the dynamic duo of Clarke Reed and W. D. (Billy) Mounger are in firm control.

Even a novice could have grasped this shortly after a twin-engined turbo-prop aircraft owned by Cappert Enterprises of Vicksburg touched down at the airport here shortly after 3:15 P.M. Friday.

The cargo aboard was Gov. Reagan, his wife, Nancy, and a retinue of aides and security men who took over ten rooms in the Downtowner Motel where they stayed the night of a $100-a-plate sell-out fundraising dinner in behalf of the rising Republican Party of Mississippi.

Reagan looks good. He gives the impression of a comer who is coming. And if he is taciturn about the Watergate affair and President Nixon's troubles, he can afford it.

Of all the states, Mississippi is probably firmer in wanting to support the President than any of them. At least, that's what a non-statistical poll being conducted by the two big Jackson newspapers indicates.

To appreciate the scene in this city Friday night, you need to go back . . . back to 1968 when the Mississippi delegation badly split on their choice and on the verge of a divisive eruption, caucused with Gov. Reagan at the national Republican convention in Miami, Fla.

This was late on a Sunday afternoon, and Gov. Reagan, just over a bout with a virus, was slightly uptight and trying to hide it.

Out of that caucus came the decision to stay with Nixon on the first two ballots, then poll the delegation under the unit rule and go for another candidate. The candidate was Reagan.

Ironically, it was Reed and Mounger who held the delegation together on that particular stance, much to the chagrin of Republicans like Dr. James Moye of Laurel and Dr. Ray Lee of Liberty.

Now the duo has dropped the other shoe. "His time has come," Reed told this reporter in an aside at the Jackson airport. "He's got the head, and he has the heart, plus name identification."

It is a fact, not overlooked by Gov. Reagan, that Reed speaks with authority when it comes to Dixie Republicans.

In a thinly-veiled move by Reed, the southern states GOP chairmen just happened to be called to a meeting in Greenville Saturday night. Oddly enough, Gov. Reagan dropped in for supper, before moving on to other appointments.

Also intriguing was a breakfast [sic] appointment with Reagan Saturday morning, which got fouled up by room service, but which was attended by former Governor John Bell Williams in the company of Mounger and Cong. [sic] Thad Cochran.

Reed has influence with Republican officials, a political commodity that he has carefully protected. He has not been able to penetrate the man, Nixon, an insular man at best, but he has managed to retain political connections, and hold his position, in spite of the GOP's problems.

None of this missed by [sic] Mounger. He is a good counterpoint to Reed. He's able to take the pragmatic approach and serve as a foil for Reed's political indiscretions.

Perhaps this explains the success of the GOP so far in the state. They've managed to fund their candidates' campaigns, extend their influence in the party and have enjoyed at least some modest success in getting their candidates elected.

After all, what more can you ask for?

2. Politics is the most expensive hobby known to man! If my wife ever knew how much money—not only time and effort but how much money, just directly out of my pocket—had gone into politics, I'm afraid she might leave me! *I* don't even want to know.

Chapter 16. The Republican Reed Begins to Bend

1. Ford had appointed to the Supreme Court John Paul Stevens, who turned out to be extremely liberal. And after Nixon's election in 1968, there were certain federal positions in the state to fill. Among them was head of the Federal Housing Administration, a highly desired position. Buford Yerger, Wirt's cousin, had been head of FHA under Eisenhower and was laterally transferred to Atlanta in 1960 after Kennedy was elected. Clarke and I brought him back to Mississippi to serve until retirement.

After three years, he retired and no one with proper qualifications who was also a loyal Republican was obvious to become his replacement. I then suggested my brother-in-law, Jimmy Roland, who was married to my sister Libby and was an assistant vice president at Deposit Guaranty in the real estate department. With Bill Wilkins's machinations, Jimmy was approved and appointed to the position. After Jimmy Carter was elected in 1976, Eastland would not let him be replaced because he was kin to me. When Reagan was elected, Trent Lott was disenamored with Jimmy because of his differences with a number of Gulf Coast building contractors. Trent desired to replace him and I did not attempt either to keep Jimmy on or to terminate him because at that time he and Libby were divorced. Ironically, Trent and Thad could not come to an agreement on who should be head of FHA and Jimmy was able to remain until he medically retired.

2. It bears repeating that in 1975 I had been with Clarke when we had picked up Ronald and Nancy Reagan at the Jackson airport to speak to a local fundraiser. At that point, Clarke had told Reagan in my presence that he needed to run for president in 1976, and that Clarke would support him all the way. That was always in my mind as the events I am about to relate played out. Still, I also understood Reed's stated desire to appear to be neutral at least early. He told me he felt that should be his role during the months leading to the 1976 Kansas City convention, but that he was all-out for Reagan.

3. Personal interview with the authors and Clarke Reed.

4. With regard to all the events leading up to the Mississippi Republican Party state convention in 1976, Reed offers another viewpoint. In a personal interview, he stated in an interview with the authors: "Here's the deal. I was always for Reagan, and I'm not denying that. But we had this rules thing [Rule 29] . . . where I was hanging in. See they [northern and midwestern Republicans] were going to come back [in 1976's national convention] with the whole argument about apportionment, the whole thing. See they didn't give up in '72. . . . The Rule 29 committee . . . [was] still meeting."

Reed says that, concerning the litany of events leading up to the 1976 national convention and during that convention, "I was definitely going to leave [the state party chairmanship] in '76. Hell, that would make ten years I was senior chairman of the United States. . . . So I said I'm going to see this rules thing through. . . . I said I'm going to see this thing through. . . . And so, I was for Reagan [in the summer of 1976], but the deal was in there, that I was to stay. . . . Dave Keene was hired on my behalf. But everybody understood what this rules thing was. You know, what we had to do. Okay, we elected the delegation that year, which is . . . on the basis [of] . . . unit rule. . . . So I assumed it would be an 80 percent Reagan delegation on that basis because that's kind of where we all were. And okay, things rocked along and there again, what can I do, it was understood?"

Reed says that, if he had not followed through as state chairman at the 1976 convention, Rule 29 may have come out poorly for small states like Mississippi, "and the party would still be dealing with that. . . . It would have hurt the party. It would have hurt the whole conservative structure, and Mississippi too. . . . Billy was saying, 'Well, you need to stay on because of this rules fight.' See, I went out as chairman or should have gone out at election time but I served through the convention and . . . that's the only reason I was there."

Regarding the back-and-forth pre-convention squabbles with Mounger concerning whether Mounger or Pickering should be vice chairman of the state delegation, Reed says Mounger's recollection seems correct. "There's a lot of stuff. I don't remember that. . . . I guess he's right. I guess I was that thoughtless."

5. "He Pays His Money and He Gits [sic] His Choice," *Reporter*, Editorial, Feb. 15, 1976. The editorial reads as follows:

Huey Long used to say he bought Louisiana legislators like sacks of potatoes. Evidently Billy Mounger, the Republican money man in Mississippi, deals in the market of GOP-candidate-on-the-hoof. When you're paid for by Billy Mounger, if you ever cross him, you can no longer stand under the Mounger Money Tree.

This is the message we got from the little flap that arose at the Republican state convention last weekend when Gil Carmichael had the temerity to allow his name to be considered for the vice-chairman of the national convention delegation, the job pre-empted by Mounger as Mr. Money-bags of the party.

It was not enough that Carmichael announced before the vote he would personally vote for Mounger. The fact that Carmichael nearly won even after that made him an "ingrate" in the Mounger book.

After all, Mounger had given his attributes for the vice-chairmanship:

that he was the single biggest contributor to the Carmichael campaign for governor last year, that he "personally raised" $200,000 and helped raise $400,000. What else does a man have to do to qualify himself for leadership in the Republican Party?

It was inevitable that a rift would finally erupt in the neat and proper pinstripe, button-down collar leadership of the Mississippi GOP between the progressive philosophy of Carmichael and the Neanderthal thinking of Mounger.

We got some indication of that last year when Clarke Reed, who plays the "Mr. Outside" to Mounger's "Mr. Inside" in the Republican One Two, remarked that he was amazed how popular Carmichael was when he didn't agree with half of what Gil said.

The fact that Carmichael came within three percentage points of becoming the first Republican governor of Mississippi since Reconstruction, and is the most attractive candidate the State GOP has developed, apparently doesn't give him a place in the Reed-Mounger palace guard.

What would have happened if Carmichael had been elected governor? Could he have won the vice-chairmanship of the delegation to Kansas City?

There is only one way for Mississippi to have a two-party state, and that is to have two viable, broad-based parties which are openly and democratically operated.

Obviously, the Democrats in Mississippi have gotten their act together and finally found an umbrella big enough to spread over the racial and philosophical differences of the past.

If the Republican party leadership remains held so tightly to the vest as was apparent in the state GOP convention, then Republicans will be back meeting in a telephone booth before long.

Perhaps that's the way Billy Mounger wants it. After all, he has all the dimes.

6. "GOP Factional Quarrel Deepens," Eyes on Mississippi, *Times-Picayune*, by W. F. Minor, April 18, 1976.

7. "GOP Split Developing?" *Jackson Daily News*, by Tom Eppes, April 12, 1976, p. 1

8. Delegates listed according to article, "Unit Rule OK," *Jackson Daily News*, Associated Press, April 12, 1976, 14.

9. "Unit Rule OK," *Jackson Daily News*, Associated Press, April 12, 1976, 1, 14.

10. "Unit Rule OK," *Jackson Daily News*, Associated Press, April 12, 1976, 1, 14.

Chapter 17. Summer 1976: Mississippi Skirmishes Grow Hot

1. "Why Reagan Chose Schweiker: An Insider's Account," by David Keene, *The Alternative: An American Spectator*, Nov. 1976, 13–15.

2. Keene, 13–14.

3. Keene, 15.

4. Keene, 15.

5. Goldberg has authored several books, two of which—*Bias* and *Arrogance*—address the liberal slant in the media.

Chapter 18. The Day the President Came to Town

1. Some delegates admirably stayed the Reagan course amid pressure. Malcolm Mabry, a member of the Mississippi House of Representatives, was solidly pro-Reagan and rejected all blandishments, staying with Reagan. Danny Jaber, an up-and-coming Republican from Natchez, had worked for Senator Howard Baker of Tennessee in Washington, D.C., and loved Baker. Ford's people told Jaber that Baker was going to be Ford's new running mate and that Jaber could make the nominating speech for Baker if Jaber would switch. Jaber stuck with Reagan. Also, Jim Egger of Caladonia remained loyal to Reagan as I knew he would, being a 1947 graduate of West Point.

2. I saw Richard Schweiker in Atlanta in 1977, and also in his Washington office. When I saw him in Atlanta I reminded him of that conversation, asking, "Do you remember that first conversation that we had?"

"I sure do," he replied.

I said, "I sure do appreciate your vote," because he voted with us; he was one of the people helping us carry our position in the Senate regarding deregulation of natural gas and the so-called "Carter tax" on crude oil.

He said, "Well, can't I see the light?"

I said, "Well, you have seen the light." A funny thing, somebody else called him a "born-again conservative."

He consulted me before every oil-and-gas vote for the rest of his time in the Senate.

Chapter 19. The 1976 Convention; Mid-Political Life Collapse at Kansas City

1. In a November 11, 1976, letter to David Keene, who by then had taken a post at Harvard's John Fitzgerald Kennedy School of Government, I wrote: "All of us must somehow co-ordinate our thinking so that we can build upon the Reagan base together with those who supported Ford in both the convention and general election. However, it is difficult for me to ascertain my most appropriate role. After being so deeply involved in building the Mississippi Republican Party, it is almost impossible for me to continue to work with the devious and duplicitous people with whom I have heretofore been associated. Any guidance or thoughts you have upon this matter will be greatly appreciated. . . . It was a great pleasure for me to have worked with someone as honorable as you during the fight for the nomination, and it was terrible that the effort had to be blighted by Clarke's flawed character."

2. Charles Gordon, a reporter for the *Jackson Daily News*, wrote an article making it sound as if I was aversive to the book *Marathon* and had tried to keep it from being read—on the contrary! His article ("Top-Ranking Writer Tells of Mississippi and the GOP," the *Jackson Daily News*, Aug. 21, 1977, G-3) follows, along with my letter disabusing it:

> Perhaps the major contribution of an important new book on the heated chase of the presidency in 1976 is its account of the attitudes and activities of the Mississippi Republican Party as the great campaign developed.
>
> Jules Witcover, author of *Marathon: The Pursuit of the Presidency*, is presently coauthor of a column of political and other types of comment appearing several times weekly in the *Jackson Daily News*.
>
> His associate is Jack Germond, another veteran of covering politics and politicians and writing about them. Witcover worked many years for the *Washington Post*, Germond for the *Washington Star*.
>
> The two make a formidable team. And Witcover, writing of one of the most stirring of recent American presidential campaigns in *Marathon*, does an incredible job of recreating the details of the fantastic 1975-76 imbroglio.
>
> One could spend a lot of time and newspaper space recalling to memory some of the byblows of that campaign that had been occupying time and attention prior to and embracing the Republican National Convention which convened in Kansas City a year ago last Tuesday. . . .

The Mississippi segment deals to large extent with Clarke Reed, Billy Mounger, Gil Carmichael, Doug Shanks, Charles Pickering, David Keene (Reagan's Southern Coordinator), Harry Dent (former Nixon advisor who was pulled out of private law practice into the Ford assembly line), Haley Barbour, Tommy Giordano, the battle over "16-C," John Connally, John Sears, and various and sundry lesser figures and artifacts. . . .

Consider a few quotations from the Mississippi sections of *Marathon:*

—"Charles Pickering, a young state senator with his eye on the governorship . . ."

—"Reagan's campaign in Mississippi, led rather casually at the beginning by Billy Mounger, an ace fund-raiser for the party, went along . . ."

—"Douglas Shanks, a 29-year-old Jackson city commissioner, who was head of what passed for a Ford campaign in the state. . . ."

—"(Gil) Carmichael, who was very pro-Ford . . ."

—"Dent started calling him (Clarke Reed) 'the reluctant kingmaker' . . ."

—"Cheney (Richard, Ford chief of staff) dined with Dent and some Ford delegates at (name deleted by business editor), which passes for a good restaurant in Jackson."

—"But Billy (Mounger) told me," Witcover quotes Reed at one point as saying (when Reed wanted Mounger to help combat some Carmichael claims) " 'Well, I got a tennis tournament this week.' So help me." Then Witcover wrote: "Reed as delegation and state chairman was trying to stay neutral, but he was so outraged by Carmichael . . . and so frustrated, that he moved in'" . . .

—"Politics used to be fun. Not now."—Clarke Reed

Some of that may have something to do with the rumor that somebody (Mounger?) (Reed?) is going around Jackson and buying up all the copies of *Marathon* available, so's to keep uncouth reporters or other readers from getting hold of them.

I wrote the following reply to Charles Gordon that was printed in toto by the *Clarion-Ledger/Jackson Daily News:*

Mr. Charles B. Gordon
Jackson Daily News
311 East Pearl Street
Jackson, Mississippi 39201

Dear Charles:

Your article in the Sunday paper titled "Top-Ranking Writer Tells of Mississippi and the GOP" was an example of deficient reporting. You parroted Witcover from his book *Marathon* with no attempt on your part to ascertain the accuracy of his statements. Additionally, you obviously did not read the entire section of the book which concerned Mississippi—pages 442 through 510; for if you had, you would have gotten a much truer perspective than scanning two short chapters in order to fill a column with sensationalism.

Yes! I am buying copies of the book; however, to disabuse you, not as you imply to get them off the market, but to see that they get the widest dissemination. If you had shown elementary reportorial ability, you would have known that the book is relatively complimentary to me and that the excerpts you printed did not depict my true role in the imbroglio.

Jules Witcover never contacted me about our schismatic delegation. I intend to communicate to him his inaccuracies and improper conclusions. Since you are personally acquainted with me, it is incomprehensible that you would be as negligent as Witcover. Your statement, "I have no idea how specifically accurate all Witcover has written about the GOP's struggles in this state might be," in no way excuses your lack of effort in discerning the truth.

For your edification, the approximately 68 pages (not just the two chapters you refer to) concerning the tribulations of the Mississippi delegation are reasonably correct. However, it galls me that I am so prominently mentioned but was never questioned as to my activities in the campaign. It is inexcusable for a so-called "Ace" reporter to avoid checking with people such as myself.

Assuredly, it is true that I could, and should, be criticized for a casual Reagan Campaign in the beginning. Nevertheless, no one (neither Ford nor Reagan) thought that the Mississippi delegation would be important. Everyone believed that one candidate would have the nomination clinched by convention time and that our delegate selection process should be aimed at building the party, not torn by schismatic competition. It was assumed that the delegates could represent a cross section of the party and that under the "unit rule" the wishes of the majority would prevail without the necessity of excluding the minority. The process worked as designed with approximately 80% of the delegates pro-Reagan as reflected by Reagan's popular support among the party and the people. Also, Clarke Reed was committed to

Reagan, along with Tommy Giordano, and others. I assumed (improperly so) that they were people of integrity and honor who could be trusted. Reed, in particular, had given his pledge to Reagan in the spring of 1975 when the three of us were privately together. He also suggested that we work as a team (as we had for 11 years) on behalf of Reagan with my being the avowed chairman and his being the silent but effective covert operative. He accompanied me to Washington to accept the Reagan chairmanship. Additionally, Reed recommended David Keene to be Reagan's Southern Coordinator and gave his personal pledge to Keene to support Reagan unless he was totally out as a candidate by convention time. Up until the choice of Schweiker (a convenient smokescreen for Reed's apostasy), David Keene, in Reagan's headquarters, was communicating with Reed, not me. Most assuredly, I am open to castigation, but not for the selection of delegates but for my naïveté in trusting such dishonorable people.

In the end, the Mississippi delegation was lost, not because of the delegate selection process but by the duplicity of certain individuals and more properly the "quadriplicity" of Reed and Giordano. The final count was 32 to 28 and no one contends that we could have lost the delegation without the blatantly crass sellout tactics of Reed, et al for their own vain-glorious, egocentric benefits.

The most disturbing inadequacy of your reporting concerns the quote, "But Billy told me, 'Well I got a tennis tournament this week.' So help me." The implication is that I was either playing in or handling some pleasureful local tournament which I would not deign to quit for the sake of the campaign. If you had even bothered to ask your fellow, very capable, reporter, Bernard Fernandez, he could have informed you that I was Tournament Chairman of the National Boys 16 Clay Court Championships. The only two times that Mississippi has ever hosted National Championship Tennis Tournaments were those that I held in 1975 and 1976. It was not held in Mississippi in 1977 because I would not agree to expend the substantial effort required because of the dearth of appreciation from those who should have been cognizant of its importance, such as yourself. I had committed to run the tournament two years in advance and boys from several foreign countries and the fifty states were competing. Clarke, the Reagan Campaign, the party, and many others knew that I would be working twenty hour days for two weeks on that tournament and that I might as well have been comatose relative to anything else. The reason this tennis incident received so much notoriety was because it served Reed's purposes to depict me as a shirker. Clarke had to surface momentarily to counteract Carmichael's devious misleading maneuvers and he was grossly uncomfortable in being openly exposed in opposition to the Ford campaign. Actually, I worked every spare minute telephoning during the tournament from Wednesday on, and several hours every night beginning Wednesday with Wirt and Swan Yerger. With a modicum of effort, you could have ascertained the truth.

The beneficence of your article is that it has brought attention to *Marathon*. I want everyone to read it in order to appreciate what went on during the most traumatic times of my life and certainly of other's too. There are other areas where Witcover is incorrect, but overall the book is as accurate as could be expected from a writer who did not diligently contact all of the main participants. After reading the 68 pages on Mississippi a person will have a perspective of how the shallowness and lack of character of so many people could affect the destiny of our country so adversely.

Sincerely Yours,
W. D. Mounger

WDM: pm
CC—Mr. Jimmy Ward, Editor, *Jackson Daily News*
CC—Mr. Charles Smith, State Editor, *Clarion Ledger*

3. On December 9, 1976, after Jimmy Carter won over Gerald Ford, a small group of Reagan supporters from Mississippi met with Ronald Reagan at a suite at the Jackson Hilton. I organized the meeting. Amid an informal, relaxed atmosphere, we urged Reagan to stay active in politics, as I reported to the *Clarion-Ledger* in a December 9, 1976, article entitled "Reagan Urged to Remain Spokesman for GOP." The article quoted me thusly: "We told him we want him to stay active and contribute all he can to the party. He's the best spokesman there is for expressing the conservative philosophy."

Chapter 20. Giving the Shank to Shanks

1. "GOP's Top Post Changes," *Prentiss Headlight*, Wayne Weidie, April 27, 1977, p. 2
2. "Outlook," *Tylertown Times*, Paul Pittman, 1977.

Chapter 21. Jumbled Alliances: The GOP Swarms Eastland

1. "GOP's Top Post Changes," *Prentiss Headlight*, Wayne Weidie, April 27, 1977, p. 2

2. This comment came from a personal interview with Charles Pickering concerning Mounger.

Chapter 22. Jon Hinson

1. I wrote the following list of thoughts on Hinson's electability after he won the GOP primary:

HINSON—ELECTABILITY

1. Open seat previously held by Thad Cochran, a three term very popular Republican—78 percent of vote 1976.
2. Experience—5 years as Administrative Assistant to Charles Griffin (Cochran's Democrat predecessor) and 4 years as Cochran's A. A.
3. Strong support from large and well respected family from rural, southern part of District—19,000 total votes in District with 69 percent Primary vote against 3 other candidates. (2/3 of vote in home county with 7 Democrats and 4 Republicans competing.)
4. Most effective TV candidate in history of Mississippi politics.
5. Strong Republican organization in Hinds County (50 percent of vote in District).
6. Two black independents and one white woman independent also in race—nine out of ten of their votes will come from the Democrat.
7. Historically, the District has never elected a liberal and Hinson is well founded in his philosophical conservatism. Hinson is supported by the three living ex-holders of the office (2 Democrats and 1 Republican).
8. Top priority by Congressional Campaign Committee—maximum help allowed by law from National Party.
9. Strong coattail effect from Thad Cochran's Senate Race—Cochran will carry District at least 3 to 1.

OPPONENT

1. John Hampton Stennis—the only plus he has is his father's name.
2. Personally Stennis is the most unattractive candidate a major party has nominated in Mississippi.
3. Stennis is campaigning as a Jimmy Carter liberal with the idea of currying favor with Tip O'Neal before he is elected.
4. No friend of the Oil Industry while serving in Mississippi House.
5. Strong endorsement of AFL-CIO.
6. Lost or broke even with unattractive Democrat opponent in every county in District except Hinds. Polled only 36,000 votes in runoff after outspending opponent more than 2 to 1 and got only 57 percent of primary vote.
7. The Democrat primary vote was askew due to judgeship votes and to thousands of "anti" votes against the present unpopular Governor who was running for Senator.

2. In hindsight, I have often thought about how convincing Hinson was. Closet homosexuals are extremely good campaigners because their whole life is a lie, making them very clever liars. Bill Clinton's life was also a lie, but he wasn't lying because he was a homosexual; he was lying because he had the other sexual problems. They can lie so well that they can look a TV camera directly in the lens, and be convincing. They are great candidates because they can make you feel that everything they are saying is totally true and that they believe it.

3. Typical of Wirt, I had carried the whole campaign on my back. Yerger and I, to this very day, play tennis with regularity, dine out with our wives, and banter about dissonant recollections of who should carry the blame regarding parts of the Hinson days. We also argue about who should get the credit for various episodes of fame or potential shame. In reality, we often were both involved like smoke and fire, thunder and lightening.

4. I received many letters from Hinson, who was highly diligent in maintaining contact. An example is the following letter, dated February 25, 1980, on official stationary of the House of Representatives:

Mr. W. D. "Billy" Mounger
Deposit Guaranty National Bank Building
Jackson, Mississippi 39205

Dear Billy:

I want to thank you for giving me the book, *Restoring the American Dream*. I found it to be most inspiring and reflective of the values we hold dear.

It was good to spend some time with you while I was in Jackson, and I look forward to seeing you again soon.

Best wishes.

Sincerely,

Signature

Jon

JH:ps

5. "Jon Hinson Dies at 53," Associated Press, Jackson, Miss., July 25, 1995.

6. "Jon Hinson Dies at 53," Associated Press, Jackson, Miss., July 25, 1995.

7. On August 8, 1980, Jon Hinson issued the following "Statement of Congressman Jon Hinson" to the public and media:

There are few who would find it easy to engage in a public discussion of that within us which strips bare our human frailty. Frankly, I would much prefer to share personal circumstances within the confidence of family and friends in a setting that permits the comfort of understanding; or to share these circumstances within the confidence of religious counsel that permits the reaffirmation of strength and direction—both of which I have done with some frequency. However, with great regret I must risk affronting the sensibilities of many who would also prefer to leave the discussion of past personal problems and difficulties within the privacy of close relationships, and share with you a difficulty of mine from several years ago.

As a preface, let me offer a few insights involving the period during which I underwent a personal crisis. It is well known that I chose public service as a career early in life and it is also well known that my largest ambition within this career I chose was to be the United States Representative for this district. However, early in 1976, I came to believe that this ambition would never be a reality. For one thing, I was working for a man holding the 4th District Congressional Seat for whom I had the very highest admiration and who was serving this district with great competence and distinction. In addition, other political factors within the state seemed to disallow any hope for the realization of my ambition.

To be quite honest, I had to that point lived a life amazingly free of disappointment and adversity, but during this 12-month period I was visited with every fear and self-doubt ever conceived. It seemed that all my aspirations, my hopes, and my efforts began to evaporate. This confrontation with self-doubt and fear took a regrettable toll on my professional and personal life. I realize that it is hard to have others understand one's fears. Problems that seem awesome to oneself can seem minimal to others. Nevertheless, my reactions during these months reflected completely my great sense of disappointment and subsequent sense of purposelessness and isolation with which I wrestled unsuccessfully for this time.

In September 1976 I was accused of a misdemeanor of committing an obscene act in Arlington, Virginia. This accusation was never brought to trial. For a number of personal reasons I determined it was best with the matter of paying a $100 fine for creating a public nuisance.

In October, 1977, slightly over one year later, a fire occurred in a Washington, D. C., theatre which showed X-rated films. Although I was not seriously injured, nine people lost their lives. I was one of the four survivors of that fire. Subsequently, civil suits were filed in the District of Columbia by the survivors or by the families of those who died. I am not a party to those suits, but I was asked to provide a deposition relating to my knowledge of the event. I did so in June, 1980, voluntarily and without subpoena.

I must be totally frank and tell you that both of these incidents were in areas frequented by some of Washington's homosexual community.

In all personal crises the reasons are difficult for even the individual to perceive and are convoluted and deeply hidden requiring great personal introspection and thought. Needless to say, I have invested a considerable amount of time in struggling to understand what happened to me.

What I would like you to know is that from this period of such great stress, I have discovered strength, resolve, and a renewed, strong sense of purpose. I have learned one of the greatest lessons life has to offer—that disappointments are not irreversible, and that, without question, the good Lord does indeed work in mysterious and miraculous ways. There is one piece of advice that I would emphasize time and time again to others who find themselves facing their own crisis. Seek the advice and counsel of one's minister as I did.

I will also tell you that this was not accomplished alone. Blessedly, I rediscovered my basic religious values, and thankfully, I had Cynthia who has been, through it all, my confidant, my friend, and now my wife. She was there through this entire spiritual crisis and to my great good fortune she was there when it ended. The most positive recollection I have were her words after the fire. She said to me, "Today we start putting it all back together." The other solid recognition I had is that I survived. I believe I lived for a reason.

As you might imagine, Cynthia and I engaged in a considerable amount of discussion at the time of these circumstances. Frankly, it was our mutual determination to put this period firmly and irrevocably behind us. We resolved to ourselves and to each other to make every day count from that point forward. At the same time, we did not place these matters behind us to be buried and wrapped in secrecy. We have shared this information with a good number of our family, friends, and members of my staff. We were always prepared to deal with these matters publicly. It would have been useless and destructive to allow these occasions to paralyze us and prevent us from pursuing our mutual interests and goals and fulfilling our obligations. We never considered hiding, but decided instead to live with courage and commitment to achieve a meaningful and highly productive life together.

In a sense, this press conference offers both of us some relief, and I think you will understand that we find comfort in being able in a complete sense to put these incidents behind us—frankly. We both still feel a deep sense of commitment to that new beginning upon which we embarked. While we still seek our privacy in this personal matter, we have embraced enthusiastically our convictions and our desire to share ourselves and our blessings. It is the highest privilege of my life to represent this district in Congress. I shall continue to offer my services, and my service will continue to reflect the genuine love and regard I feel for this district and its people.

Inasmuch as this personal matter is wholly unrelated to my record and service in the Congress, I am going to respectfully decline to answer any questions. I do wish to thank you for your attention.

8. "Mississippian Gains Despite Sex Issue," by Wendell Rawls Jr., *New York Times*, October 4, 1980.

9. Wendell Rawls Jr.

10. Mike Allred, a Jackson lawyer and Republican, called for Hinson's resignation in this March 9, 1981 letter. "PERSONAL AND CONFIDEN-TIAL . . . Honorable Jon Hinson . . .

Dear Jon:

As one of your earliest and closest supporters, I feel a deep and personal loss at your moral failure which has had such a devastating effect on your personal life and, through its effect on you, a most detrimental effect upon the high principles that led so many of us here in Mississippi to support you. I do not pretend to understand the compulsion which led you to such unspeakable behavior. However, in making a decision about the course nec-essary to be followed hence forward, it matters little whether you were driven by illness or by the Devil. In any event, your paramount consider-ation, having allowed yourself a reasonable time for reflection and recupera-tion, must be to live up to, at this your last and final point of decision as a public servant, the sacred trust that you have been given through the efforts and support of so many people whose only motive in helping you was love of our Country.

Unfortunately, you do not have available to you any alternatives that are positive or that offer you any future reward. You cannot under any circum-stances continue to hold the office. You cannot possibly take any satisfaction in the act of resigning. After resigning, your return to private life will not be easy for you.

Calling upon the gifts of loyalty, support, guidance, friendship and help that I have given you in the past, I respectfully ask that you forthwith resign in the interest of the people of the Country and in the interest of your con-stituents. You have no alternative. You deserve none.

If you will resign and in this final act live up to the public trust that you have accepted, I, for one, will not understand or condone, but I will forgive what you have done through human weakness and lack of moral strength. If you, having violated your sacred trust in so many ways heretofore, refuse to resign through selfish motives, I shall take all available actions to recall your election or otherwise remove you from office. In this event—and here I speak only for myself—there shall be no end to which I will not go through avail-able legal and political means to see you out of the office and in jail if at all possible.

For an honorable man who has sinned through weakness, however terrible and beyond understanding, one can have compassion. For a man without honor who will not accept the consequences of his own actions and who would crassly, callously and selfishly prostitute the public trust of a high office, no compassion and no forgiveness can be had.

We have the legal ramifications of your case under study. You must make, declare and carry out your decision to resign without delay or the decision will not be left in your hands.

Very truly yours,
Signature
Michael S. Allred

11. Senator Thad Cochran once jokingly called the sticker-laden door "obscene."

12. "Jon Hinson Dies at 53," Associated Press, Jackson, Miss., July 25, 1995.

13. When Jon Hinson resigned, he left a vacancy in the Fourth Congressional District. The Republican Party had held the seat for more than eight years and very much desired to keep it, but I did not want a large number of Republicans vying for the seat. I worried it might fragment the electorate and dissipate the Republican finances leaving only two weeks before the final election to reorganize. It was suggested that the party put on a primary and then a runoff, if necessary, to narrow the choice to one candidate. I opposed this option, arguing logistical and expense problems. Others, such as Senator Thad Cochran, supported a primary.

I convinced the party apparatus that a caucus should choose the nominee. The caucus was composed of those delegates chosen from the Fourth District who had attended the 1980 Republican State Convention. It is believed that this is the only time in Mississippi that such a process has happened. Among those in competition: Liles Williams, Andy Taggart, Bob Everett, Arnold Dyer, and Delbert Hoseman. All were strong candidates but I favored Williams because he worked for Stuart C. Irby, Jr. (my very good friend and Mississippi's number-one philanthropist). Liles was a rock-rib conservative, he had come up the hard way, and he appeared to be an overall very good choice. Ironically, when the caucus occurred, I was traveling in China and could not attend; but with Wirt Yerger, Jim Furrh, and others there and with me letting certain strategic people know my wishes, Liles Williams received the nomination. Additionally, those who had participated as candidates were pledged not to oppose the winner in the special election. Since Liles lost, in hindsight I should have let the system operate normally.

With me serving on Liles's executive committee and raising a large portion of his funds, Liles received 25,000 votes, or 45 percent, with the main Democrat Wayne Dowdy receiving 15,000 or 22.5 percent of the votes. It was conceived that Liles could pick up the 10,000 votes of a defeated Democrat to win the two-week runoff. When the final votes were counted, Liles had gotten the 10,000 extra votes, but Dowdy had turned out 25,000 new black votes that had not voted two weeks before to win by a razor thin 912 vote margin. Democrat Governor William Winter had set the election for the Tuesday after the Fourth of July; some Republicans figure this date was chosen so that many Republicans would still be out of town at the beach or skiing, etc. I said, "There were enough Republican votes sunning on the beaches of Destin to have won the election for Liles."

Two years later, Williams ran against Dowdy again. The Mississippi tradition of backing incumbents demonstrated its efficacy. When that second campaign was looking bleak, Liles's Executive Committee came up with an issue that I thought was a game breaker, but Liles presented it to the media in a completely ineffective way. I had given not only my money and fund-raising support to Williams, but also had provided Williams with an issue that I thought would help break the congressional race open in Williams's favor. But Williams lost again. As a result, I told Williams: "Liles, I could give you the sword Excalibur and you would turn it into a wet piece of macaroni."

Chapter 23. Political Years of Joy in the 1980s

1. The deflowering message on the machine happened to be from a Democrat congressman from Texas, who stated, "Billy, you do not know me, but I am Greg Laughlin, a congressman from Texas, who has just been appointed to the Board of Visitors of West Point, and I wanted to talk about the upcoming meeting. I am a conservative Democrat, a Texas A&M graduate, a Lieutenant Colonel in the reserves. I have been the prosecuting attorney for Houston, Texas, and was the West Point liaison officer for Houston. I think that qualifies me to have my telephone call returned." Greg was laughing when he made this spiel and I concluded that if a Dem-

ocrat congressman thought the message was funny, I would just leave it on. It remains there today. And regardless of effort, I cannot design a superior message.

2. "Ronald Reagan Enjoyed Strong Miss. Support."

I first met Ronald Reagan in 1967 in his governor's office in Sacramento, Calif. We had flown there for him to shoot a television spot for Rubel Phillips for governor. His presence was so exhilarating that it gave me goose bumps. No one else has ever caused that sensation in me.

Afterwards, I was with him at least 40 times. The second was in New Orleans in 1968, in his suite in the Roosevelt Hotel. The third was in Miami where he then was running against Richard Nixon and Nelson Rockefeller. Reagan was much preferred. Nevertheless, I helped the Mississippi delegation go for Nixon as I feared if Nixon were defeated, Rockefeller would win.

Uniting state Republicans

The next was in Jackson in 1973 in the Heidelberg at a Republican fundraiser, over which I presided. He came several others times, and during one of these visits, I asked, "Governor, how do you get along so well with the press when they are almost universally against you?" He answered thusly: "Well, Billy, my mother always told me not to anger the mother alligator until I had crossed the stream."

In 1975, he spoke to a crowd of 1,600 people in the coliseum. I introduced him with the line: "Here is our Moses, Ronald Reagan, to lead the Republican Party, this state, and nation out of the political wilderness."

When I rode to the Walthall Hotel with him and Nancy, he held her hand the whole time, evidencing a truly loving relationship.

He spiced his speeches with jokes such as: "A father had two sons—a pessimist and an optimist. The father gave the pessimist a roomful of toys. Afterwards, he heard the boy crying. The father asked why. 'I am afraid I will break or lose some of the toys and that makes me unhappy,' the boy said. The optimist son received a room full of horse manure and proceeded to happily shovel the manure. The father asked why. 'With a pile of manure this large, there must be a pony in here somewhere,' the boy said." This joke demonstrated his attitude toward the problems of the country, which created a new positive attitude making us proud of America again.

A beneficial relationship

In November of 1975, I became Reagan chairman in Mississippi for the Republican nomination for president in Kansas City. He came to see the delegation in June of 1976 with some movie star friends—Jimmy Stewart, Ephraim Zimbalist Jr., Festus and others—and came again in July after several delegates began apostatizing to Gerald Ford.

The upshot of all the weakness and wavering in the delegation was that Mississippi finally voted 32 to 28 for Ford. This result was devastating to the average Republicans in Mississippi who were overwhelmingly for Reagan.

From 1976-80, I belonged to the Citizens for the Republic (Reagan), then Reagan overwhelmed everyone at the 1980 Republican National Convention in Detroit, where the Mississippi chairman of the delegation was Trent Lott and I was the vice chairman. Reagan named me Mid-South finance chairman and together with Trent Lott, we helped him carry the state handily.

The state enjoyed an extremely close and beneficial relationship with the Reagan administration.

Those who played roles in electing Reagan president, including large majorities in Mississippi, can be proud to have helped elect someone of the friendliness and stature of Ronald Reagan, the man who restored our self-confidence and our faltering economy, and caused the downfall of communism.

William D. "Billy" Mounger, a Jackson oilman, was former President Ronald Reagan's Mid-South finance chairman in 1980 and state finance chairman in 1984.

3. "When a Convention Mattered," *Wall Street Journal*, Al Hunt, July 27, 2000, A23.

4. "Candidates' Big-money Supporters Cannot Sit Back During Campaigns," *Clarion-Ledger*, Judy Putnam, June 5, 1981.

5. Judy Putnam.

6. In an interview in 2004 with the authors, Trent Lott recalled some of the thinking that went into his taking the state chairman's post in 1980: "We had lost Mississippi in '76 by 10,000 votes to Carter, but we were close. And [in 1976] I kept telling the Ford people, who did not want to come to Mississippi, if you would just let him come, and . . . let me bring him to the Fifth District, because in order to win Mississippi at that time, statewide, you had to carry my district by a 50,000 vote margin. So finally,

but belatedly, they said 'Okay' and he [Ford] came to the coast. He rode down the Mississippi on a boat with three past Democrat congressmen, . . . with Bill Colmer, Tom Abernathy, and John Bell Williams. They got on the boat I think at Vicksburg, and they stopped along the way, came to New Orleans and got off and then Ford came over and he made stops in Bay St. Louis, Gulfport, Biloxi, Ocean Springs, and Pascagoula. By the way, his chief of staff at the time was Dick Cheney, who was on that trip with him. And we carried the district by over 40,000 votes. But that was not enough. We came up 10,000 short in 1976."

7. I like to joke that when I walk up Capitol Street and start climbing the hill, people peel off in echelons in front of me and I'll have just an empty sidewalk while walking up the hill. Frankly, mostly due to politics, I get headaches and misery. Jan gets extremely unhappy by things that are written in the paper and things that come out on TV. I just cannot sit back and not be involved and not try to make the world move in a direction that I feel is right. There's something in me that will not allow me to sit back.

8. Memo to Wirt Yerger and W. D. Mounger from T. Calvin Wells, Wells, Downey & Wicker. Re: Investigation of Election Violations in Washington and LeFlore Counties and Presentation of Cases to the Credentials Committee of the Republican State Convention. Date: May 20, 1980.

I was retained to investigate election violations in Leflore and Washington counties, which occurred in connection with the Republican Precinct Caucuses held on April 26, 1980. The results of my investigation and subsequent presentation of facts to the Credentials Committee of the Republican State Convention on May 9, 1980, are outlined below.

On April 8, 1980, the Leflore County Republican Party Executive Committee passed a motion to use an apportionment system in allotting each precinct delegate to the Leflore County Convention. The system they used provided for one delegate for each precinct casting up to 500 votes for Gerald Ford in the 1976 Presidential Election and one additional delegate for every 100 votes above 500. In other words, *one* (original emphasis) delegate was awarded for the first 500 votes and *five* (original emphasis) delegates were awarded for the next 500 votes. Such a system of allotting delegates is inconsistent with the laws of Mississippi as well as the Call of the Republican

Party which requires apportionment according to the *number* (original emphasis) of votes received in the various precincts by Gerald Ford.

The North Greenwood Precinct cast only 39.55 percent of the Ford vote in Leflore County and yet, under that system, the North Greenwood Precinct received 54.29 percent of the delegates allotted to the County Convention. (The total Ford vote in Leflore County was 5,872 votes, using highest elector, of which the North Greenwood Precinct cast 2,322. The North Greenwood Precinct was allotted 19 delegates while the other 16 precincts were allotted only one each.) No attempt was made to properly apportion delegates but instead, a system was implemented which diluted the votes from the other 16 precincts and gave total control to the precinct which cast only 39.54 percent of the Ford vote.

It is my opinion that such a system is *illegal* (original emphasis) and would be declared invalid by a court of law. Although the Credentials Committee ruled that there was substantial compliance, it is obvious that after viewing the system and the vote totals that an illegal system was used.

There were numerous violations which occurred in Washington County and there is no doubt that these irregularities affected the outcome of the County Convention.

I obtained a sworn affidavit from Mrs. Virginia F. Morris which stated that she was at her usual voting place from 9:55 a.m. to 10:15 a.m. and that no caucus was ever held. A black woman, who was at the voting place to decorate for a wedding reception, was a witness and she confirmed Mrs. Morris's story. Before I could get her to sign a sworn affidavit, she and her husband were contacted by someone who advised them that they would cause a lot of trouble for themselves if they said anything. She was also told that they would be required to retain a lawyer and appear in court and based on that, she refused to say anything further. Four delegates showed up at the County Convention representing this precinct and despite the objections of Mrs. Morris, they were seated.

Three delegates (two of which were Reagan delegates) elected at the precinct caucuses were unseated because of the Residency/Registration laws. I have several sworn affidavits stating that the Chairman of the Credentials Committee, Frank Powers, advised them that the law required that you be registered in that precinct thirty (30) days prior to the caucus and furthermore that you must reside in the precinct in which you voted.

The law states that domicile continues until removal to another locality with intent to remain there and abandonment of the old domicile without intent to return (Hubbard vs. McKey, 193 So.2d 129, Miss. 1966). I have a sworn affidavit from Ann Tolbert stating that she owned property in the precinct in which she voted and intended to build on and return to that property in the near future. She also stated that Mike Retzer, Chairman of the Republican Party, attempted to get her to sign a statement of support and after her refusal, he challenged her credentials.

Ironically, Mr. Retzer, under the rules used at the Washington County Convention, was not qualified to participate. He registered in the precinct in which he voted on April 11, 1980 (less than 30 days prior to the caucus). His wife registered on April 21, 1980, and one of the delegates seated from the precinct in which no caucus was held also registered less than 30 days prior to the election.

It was also stated that the report of the Credentials Committee was unanimously accepted by the County Convention. I have sworn affidavit to the contrary.

The minutes of the County Convention show no method for choosing alternates for the State Convention in the event a delegate was unable to attend. At the Credentials Committee meeting on May 9, Mr. Retzer said they would advance based on the order they appeared in the minutes. I have a sworn affidavit from Charles H. Burton, minister of the Leland United Methodist Church, that the suggestion was made by Mr. Retzer and accepted by the convention that the alternate delegate receiving the most votes would be the number one alternate. Reverend Burton also stated that he counted the votes and that Dr. Simmons received 24 votes to lead the ballot for alternate delegates. However, Dr. Simmons was not listed as first alternate.

Finally, I was told by the Credentials Committee that I would need to show that these irregularities affected the outcome. They advised me to obtain the tally sheets used in totaling the votes for delegates and alternates. Dr. Tommy Simmons called the Convention Chairman who referred him to Joan Carr. Mrs. Carr agreed to make him a copy but before doing so, she was advised by Mike Retzer to destroy the tally sheets. I have sworn affidavits from Dr. Simmons and Reverend Ted Land which state that Mrs. Carr advised them that Mike Retzer instructed her to destroy the tally sheets.

This is only a short summary of my investigation, but as you can see, the events that occurred in Washington and Leflore counties are quite serious. The Call of the Mississippi Republican Party which provides that all qualified electors may participate in the selection of delegates was totally ignored and in both counties the laws of the State of Mississippi were violated."

9. In June of 2005, Mike Retzer was named by President George W. Bush as the United States Ambassador to Tanzania.

10. "GOP: Babies in Bath-water," *Capital Reporter*, Bill Minor, Dec. 11, 1980, 3. Minor's column follows:

Will success spoil the Mississippi Republicans? From the amount of bickering, factionalism and distrust that seems evident in the State GOP ranks, you wouldn't think their candidate carried Mississippi and won the Presidency.

Sounds like the good ole Mississippi Democrats, doesn't it?

And if the Republicans go down the same road as the Democrats, squabbling and fighting, they will see their effectiveness as a political entity greatly diminished.

Although the Mississippi Republicans don't want to admit it, a major factional split obviously is building, with the camps divided between followings of the party's two highest elected public officials—U.S. Sen. Thad Cochran and U.S. Rep. Trent Lott.

The irony is that only a short time ago, the biggest problem the Mississippi Republican party had was how to survive as a political organization without any elected officials. Now the problem is how to co-exist with two GOP office-holders with national standing who represent different Republican philosophies.

Hatchet buried?

Here the other day, at the special meeting of the GOP State Executive Committee, called by State Chairman Mike Retzer to force a showdown with Lott backers who wanted him removed, when the ouster move failed, everybody tried to bury the hatchet.

But there was a strong underlying feeling afterwards that the hatchet won't stay buried for long.

The next test seems to be coming in the inaugural activities for Ronald Reagan next month and how the oldtime Mississippi Reaganites fare in the arrangements, which are pretty much being directed by their nemesis, Retzer.

There was talk in advance of the meeting to unseat Retzer that those behind the ouster were making veiled threats to some committee members to line up against Retzer or the school band from their home town wouldn't march in the inaugural parade. Evidently none of thos (sic) threats surfaced in the closed door session that ended with Retzer getting a shaky 15-10 vote of confidence.

Those behind the effort to dump moderate Retzer, such as Dr. James Moye of Laurel, an original Reaganite, staunchly contend that Lott did not orchestrate the ouster move, or seek to give it impetus.

Retzer and his followers, including former State Chairman Clarke Reed, the silver-haired former chairman who is the best known Mississippian in national GOP circles, evidently are willing to concede that Lott did not mastermind the ouster move, but they are convinced he could have stopped it if he wanted.

There's no question that Lott is the rallying point for the hard-line Reagan forces in the state GOP, as was evident at Detroit when he was made chairman of the delegation, an obvious snub of Retzer, since the State GOP chairman has traditionally headed the delegation.

Lott had been state chairman for Reagan during the campaign for the presidential nomination and, of course, became state chairman for Reagan in the fall presidential campaign.

"Never knows who I am"

Ironically, when Reagan came to Columbus in late October to speak for the second time in Mississippi, as he alightened from the airplane, the first Mississippi GOP leader he recognized among the group to greet him was Reed, rather than Lott, his state chairman. Lott was said to have remarked to some that Reagan "never seems to know who I am."

Perhaps now that Lott has won the House Republican Whip post, proving he is a rather persuasive campaigner even among Republicans from throughout the nation, Reagan won't need a cue card to remember Lott.

While Lott's stock is rising in the GOP nationally, political fate has also played into the hands of Cochran, who now under a Republican-controlled Senate emerges in a position of major influence as chairman of sub-committees in both the powerful Appropriations Committee, and the Agriculture Committee, that is of vital Mississippi interest.

Cool on Cochran

The patriarchs of Mississippi hardcore conservative Republicans, Billy Mounger and Wirt Yerger, consider that Cochran went off and left them to join forces with the moderate wing of the Republican Party.

So, now, Lott, who is very much in tune with their thinking is their philosophical leader. Since the election of Reagan, they perceive Cochran as being isolated from the central forces which will direct patronage and other emoluments they expect to flow from the White House.

The natural consequence is that Cochran, whose position in the Senate will make it impossible for Reagan to circumvent, becomes the leader of the Retzer-Reed forces in the sate party organization.

What direction the intra-party struggle in the GOP takes will depend heavily on what attitude Reagan takes on matters about which his oldtime loyalists down here seem to be taking liberties in interpreting to their advantage.

Perhaps it will take Reagan himself to step in and do some headknocking to bring the Mississippi GOP forces together.

11. Idi Amin was the oppressive dictator of the African country of Uganda.

12. "Dixie Democrats Dilemma: Black Apathy, White Resistance in Ol' Miss," by Adrian Lee, *Philadelphia Daily News*, Nov. 13, 1984.

13. Back in 1976, when Bush's name was being tossed around along with Howard Baker's to be named Gerald Ford's vice presidential running mate, I offered a quote to a member of the national press: "If you've got Gerald Ford you've got blah! If you put George Bush on there you've got blah! Do you want blah, blah?"

14. W. D. Mounger, *Clarion-Ledger*, March 18, 1983.

15. I say "30 percent" because the "plebes" plus the First Class "Beast" detail amounted to about 30 percent of the Corps of Cadets.

16. Personal interview with the authors.

17. Personal interview with the authors.

Chapter 24. Bill Allain

1. "Mississippi Outlook," Paul Pittman, *The Tylertown Times*, May 24, 1979.

2. Leon Bramlett, a wonderful guy from Clarksdale, had lost in the Republican primary in his first attempt at governor in 1979.

3. The state GOP party learned a lesson from that. It taught that if you

don't have a campaigner who, more or less, has a fire in his belly to win, then you ought not be backing him or he ought not to be running.

4. Personal interview with the authors and Spell.

5. "Homosexuality allegations rock Mississippi race," *The Miami Herald*, by Fred Grimm, November 6, 1983.

6. Personal interview with the authors and Trent Lott.

7. "Homosexuality allegations rock Mississippi race," *The Miami Herald*, by Fred Grimm, November 6, 1983. The entire article follows:

JACKSON, Miss.—Mill Street, rough and rundown but only six blocks from the capitol, has long been the heart of Jackson's sexual commerce. Prostitutes linger at the curbs. Lately, it's also the home address of probably the muddiest, most scandalous personal accusations ever slung in Mississippi politics.

The campaign for governor—a real yawner two weeks ago with Democrat Bill Allain anywhere from 17 to 30 points ahead in the polls—has turned bizarre.

Issues of education, employment and regulation of industry have given way to talk of drag queens and sexual liaisons. It's no longer politics, but polygraphs that count.

The campaign for Tuesday's election has dissolved to a single question: Is Bill Allain homosexual?

"I've never seen a campaign like this in Mississippi. I've never seen a campaign like this anywhere," said Bill Minor, a University of Mississippi political science teacher and a political reporter in the state for 36 years.

For the past two weeks, backers of Republican Leon Bramlett have been firing off accusations that Allain has regularly paid for sex with male transvestites he's picked up along Mill Street, a forbidding neighborhood of slum housing, a few warehouses and some coarsely adorned beer joints.

Allain, 55, serving out a term as state attorney general, has spent most of his time since then denying "these disgusting lies."

Last month, before the campaign underwent its scandalous metamorphosis, Bramlett fired his campaign coordinator rather than wage a "negative campaign." Bramlett, 60, a tall, wealthy Delta farmer, a one-time All-America football player, was upset over a television commercial that asked, "Can you trust Bill Allain?"

How times have changed.

Bramlett now talks of little else but the accusations against Allain. "This has overshadowed all the other issues," Bramlett said Thursday. "This is bigger than any of us. This is bigger than I am. This is bigger than Bill Allain. The Democratic Party. The Republican Party."

"I'm just trying to stay out of this mess," said black independent gubernatorial candidate Charles Evers, former mayor of Fayette and, according to his autobiography, a onetime Chicago pimp. "I'm the only left for the people to vote for," he said.

"It's dirty politics, but I'm afraid there might be something to it," said Shelly Sullivan, a Jackson secretary. "It looks like we don't have much of a choice."

Former Gov. Ross Barnett said, "I've always voted Democratic, but I can't say who I'm voting for Tuesday. This is bad."

Bramlett offered to drop out of the election if Allain took three independently administered lie-detector tests—providing, of course, that the results cleared the Democrat.

Allain's accusers weren't satisfied with the test his lawyer arranged for him to take Wednesday in New Orleans. Allain distributed results that said, "There is nothing in the examination to indicate Mr. Allain is a homosexual or has been involved in homosexual activities."

Allain declared there would be no more tests.

"I said I would take one test. I took one test. That's it," he said, rather angrily.

Allain's problems evolved from rumors of his alleged homosexuality circulating in Jackson since at least before he upset Evelyn Gandy in the Democratic primary runoff. But in mid-September, three wealthy Jackson oil brokers, Neal Clement, Victor Smith, and Billy Mounger, all Bramlett backers, asked prominent Jackson attorney William Spell to investigate.

Mounger said he didn't want Mississippi to repeat the embarrassment suffered in 1980 when U.S. Rep. Jon Hinson, after denying allegations of homosexuality, was arrested on sodomy charges in a Washington men's room and was forced to resign. Mounger had been one of Hinson's major financial backers.

Spell, a former administrative assistant to U.S. Sen. John Stennis, said, "I didn't think there would be anything to it," but he agreed to look into the rumors. On Sept. 27, Spell said, he hired detective Robert Pendleton to investigate. Less than a week later, Spell claimed, Pendleton returned with confirmation.

Spell and Pendleton compiled a report, bound in blue and, in a small box printed on the front like a Surgeon's General's warning: "Notice. The enclosed contains sexually explicit material concerning Attorney General Bill Allain. If such material is objectionable to you for moral, religious or personal reasons, please do not read the contents."

Inside were depositions and lie detector confirmations from three black transvestites: David Holliday (known as Devia Ross), Donald (Donna) Johnson and Grady Arrington (Nicole Toy). The Mill Street trio offered very graphic descriptions of sexual encounters with Allain. And there were statements from a pair of maintenance men who claimed they saw stacks of "queer magazines" by the water heater in Allain's apartment.

On Oct. 14, Spell took his blue book to the media. Jackson's largest newspaper, *The Clarion-Ledger*, brought in the three drag queens and hired its own polygraph expert. They passed, said executive editor Charles Overby. "But I didn't think the newspaper's role was to expose sex habits."

The Clarion-Ledger and other newspapers and television stations held the story. Rumors burned across the state like wildfire, but it wasn't until Oct. 25 that Spell held a press conference, forcing the issue into the open.

Democrats were aghast and angry. Gov. William Winter called it a "vicious attempted character assassination." Both he and state Democratic Party Chairman Danny Cupit have held fast in their support of Allain. But a few other prominent Democrats have allowed qualifiers to creep into their statements backing Allain.

Allain countered first with his ex-wife, Doris Rush, who went on television to abhore [sic] the allegations. Spell came back with the divorce complaint Rush filed in 1970, claiming Allain stopped having sexual relations with her a few weeks after their 1964 marriage.

Then Spell came up with three Jackson policemen who swore they had noticed Allain on a number of occasions circling the block and cruising slowly down Mill Street, stopping to talk to male prostitutes. "Trolling," Detective William R. Gardner called it.

Last week, Bettye F. Johnson, mother of Donald (Donna) Johnson, signed an affidavit saying her 23-year-old was a junkie. "He will do anything for money and I know that he will lie at every opportunity," she said. Her husband made a similar statement.

"We did that of our own free will," she said Thursday. "Nobody pressured us."

Meanwhile, Johnson, Holliday and Arrington are being kept "out of town" at some secret location, paid $50 each a day to make up for some lost income, plus $12 expenses, Spell said.

"I don't know what's going to happen to them when they come back," said Shawanda Smith, 27, a Mill Street transvestite. "Donna was stupid, anyway. Allain was good for $50 and $60 every time he came down there, and now that's ruined."

Smith sat in the Watergate Beer Garden, a dank little pub at the corner of Mill and Monument streets. He said the revelations that shocked the rest of the state were no surprise on Mill Street. "We all know about Allain. He's been coming down here for years."

Even members of Bramlett [sic] staff doubt that the scandal will do much more than narrow Allain's winning margin. One poll showed Evers picking up a few points, from nine to 12 percent.

But if Allain fails to win an outright majority Tuesday, the election, according to the Mississippi Constitution, must then be decided in the House of Representatives, where Democrats hold a huge majority. It doesn't meet until January.

There's a theory circulating in Republican camps that the Democratic leaders fully expect more damaging revelations but that they are maintaining their support of Allain to keep the GOP from winning the its [sic] first Mississippi governor's race since reconstruction.

"They think Allain will win, be forced to resign and [Democratic lieutenant governor candidate] Brad Dye will take over," said one Republican.

Spell said the whole campaign had hurt him. His son, William Spell Jr., resigned from his father's firm in protest, announcing he was voting for Allain. "This could destroy me," Spell said. "But I felt like the people of Mississippi should know."

"I'm not sure about anything in this whole mess," said Bennie Day, a mechanic. "But I guess Mississippi is going to look bad. I don't think I'm . . . going to vote for anybody Tuesday. I think I'll just go fishing."

8. Personal interview with the authors and Bill Spell.

9. In the summer of 2004, Dick Morris spoke to a Republican gathering in Mississippi. I had the opportunity to talk with him, and I mentioned to Morris that *O'Reilly* interview. Morris replied, as if to affirm my hunch was right, "Oh yes, we had a really hard time in that situation."

10. On September 1, 1987, after withdrawing from the race for the Republican Party presidential nomination, Paul Laxalt wrote me the following letter:

Dear Billy:

When I needed you, you were there, even though you knew it was a "long shot" situation.

What that translates to me is that you committed to a belief without first putting your finger to the "political wind."

In this rather difficult business of politics, I've come to value your type of person more and more.

Whatever lies ahead, I will always consider you to be a true friend.

Sincerely,

(Personal Signature of "Paul")

11. "Mounger Talks about Election Allegations," Melissa Lambert, *Daily Mississippian*, February 22, 1985, Vol. 75, No. 105.

12. "Former Gov. Bill Allain's Pre-Election Sex Scandal Revisited," Fabayo Ajanaku, *Jackson Advocate—The Voice of Black Mississippians*, May 24–30, 1990, Vol. 52, No. 35

Chapter 25. Two Decades of Electoral Success: Fordice, Parker, Tuck, and Barbour

1. Jim and Mary Leigh Furrh, Charlie and Vivian Williams, Leslie and Dorothy Lee Lampton (my eighth and ninth grade girlfriend), Ruth and Ed Kendrick, and Jan and I once traveled to Pisa in Northern Italy. Jim straightened the Tower of Pisa by tilting his camera—unintentionally! Our thirty-some-odd bags (a few very heavy) were stored at the train station. We lavishly tipped two Italian porters to move our luggage and to make certain that we were boarding the proper car on the correct train for Nice, France. When the train arrived, they tossed our bags onto the end of a car and vamoosed. Upon entering the car, we saw that the compartments were reserved for "Fernando." We inquired of the conductor whether we were in our correct seats and he said "yes," and told us to ignore the signs. Next he stated that we had to move our bags and align them along the aisle outside the compartments. When the train stopped at Genoa, a large number of Spanish students boarded the train with their escort being Fernando! He berated us profusely, ordering us to evacuate his compartments,

and we were adamant in not doing so, for the conductor had told us to be seated there. We were later informed that Fernando had called us every bad word in the Spanish language. A new conductor who had boarded in Genoa appeared and ordered us to move. (Our previous conductor was drunk and therefore unreliable.) We then moved into the adjoining car until being told that our actual seats were five or six cars farther back. We had to retrieve our inordinate number of bags—some of great heft—and lug them all back through aisles clogged by Spanish students. To exacerbate the situation, Fernando and his cohorts had moved a number of bags several cars forward. With much effort we miraculously retrieved all our luggage. Another person had joined us during this *opéra bouffe*, and I sat by him when we finally settled in the car where the lavishly tipped Italian porters should have deposited us. As is my wont, I garrulously and openly talked to him. He told me he was from Massachusetts and Hawaii and was a writer. I immediately assumed (improperly so) that he wrote travel tracts for magazines. Among other things, I stated that he must be a liberal, which he did not dispute, and I told him about many of my conservative Republican activities. That person turned out to be Paul Theroux, who was writing a book about his travels titled *The Pillars of Hercules*. He became very concerned that the train was not going to stop long enough at Nice for us to unload our gross amount of baggage; consequently, he diligently assisted our unloading efforts. Some months after returning home, Talmadge Rutledge from Lafayette, Louisiana, called and stated that I was the darndest person he ever saw because my name was always showing up in print, even in a travel book. With that notification, I purchased *The Pillars of Hercules* and, lo and behold, the following is what Theroux wrote about us, with me being the only one identified and with much embellishment of my southern style of speaking:

There were six older American couples in the train, bewildered by the weather, burdened by seventeen heavy suitcases. They were from Jackson, Mississippi, and they soon became embroiled with some Spanish students in a fuss about seats. The blustering turned to abuse. It was a blessing that these gentle people were not aware of what was being said to them in Spanish. They were the sort of patient Americans whom I had seen being taken advantage of and overcharged all over the Mediterranean. It did not matter that they said Antibes as though it rhymed with "rib-eyes," and pressed their faces to the window and chanted "Monny Carla." After all, no one else here could have pronounced the grand Mississippi name Yoknapatawpha.

"You're a yella-dog Democrat," Billy Mounger said to me, concluding—correctly—that I would vote for a yellow dog before I'd vote for a Republican.

I said, "I think I'd vote for a yellow dog before I'd vote for a Democrat, too."

He laughed at that. He said, "We're yella-dog Republicans. We're probably the most right-wing people you probably ever met."

"Go on then, shock me, Billy," I said.

"I'm chairman of the Phil Gramm for President Committee."

"That is pretty shocking." Mr. Gramm claimed to be the most conservative candidate of all the Republicans.

"That ain't the story," Mounger said. "One of our guys back there is against Phil Gramm. Says to me, 'I don't want no oriental damn woman as the First Lady in the White House.'"

Mrs. Gramm, born and raised in Hawaii, was of Korean descent.

"You said it, Billy, he's one of your guys." [Source: *The Pillars of Hercules: A Grand Tour of the Mediterranean*, by Paul Theroux, Cape Cod Scriveners Company, 1995, 484–485.]

2. Personal interview with the authors and Trent Lott.

3. Steve Guyton switched to Republican on my recommendation and both congressmen Roger Wicker and Chip Pickering put him on their staffs to coordinate Academy appointments. Consequently, I work very closely with Guyton, especially about West Point prospects and cadets.

Chapter 26. Saving the U.S.A. International Ballet Competition

1. An international ballet competition had been held in Tokyo, Japan, in 1977, but it predominately featured Japanese dancers, mainly judged by Japanese jurors, and did not continue to exist.

2. Other international political incidents have occurred at the USA IBC. In 1986 the Communist Chinese *danseur*, Lin Jianwei, disappeared the night before the third and crucial round of the pairs competition, leaving his partner to dance for herself alone in an unpracticed routine. He defected and eventually danced for the Houston Ballet. In 1986, a Taiwanese competitor marched in on opening night with his Taiwanese flag, and

in protest the Communist Chinese international juror walked off the stage; in 1990, when the USA IBC displayed the Taiwanese flag among the represented nations, the Chinese Communist government protested through our department of state, which forced us to remove the Taiwanese flag.

3. I have devoured the Russian history of all the czars and the Communist leaders and have read everything Alexander Solzhenitsyn has written that has been translated into English, including all three volumes of the *Gulag Archipelgo.*

4. While in Moscow, some interesting experiences occurred, one when Flo and Howard Stover, Elaine and Manny Crystal, and Jan and I were utterly lost and blundering around Moscow, attempting to locate the Praga Restaurant. Seeking directions, Flo and Manny knocked on the door of an imposing building, which unknown to them was the Moscow Communist Party headquarters. I yelled at them, but it was too late and an armed guard chased them away. We could have been imprisoned in the Gulag Achipelago. After we finally located the restaurant and were returning to the hotel in a taxi, Jan and I, along with the Crystals, were passing the notorious Lubyanka Prison (the headquarters of the KGB, with the huge Dzerzhinsky statue in front) where untold political prisoners were tortured, executed, or just plain disappeared. When Manny yelled, "Stop the car! Billy wants his picture taken before the Lubyanka," the taxi driver panicked and protested, *"N'yet! N'yet!"* He was petrified with fear that if we stopped, the KGB would grab us, never to be seen again. After passing the Lubyanka, he turned to me and blurted, "Who are you? James Bond?" Later, while in the orchestra section of the Bolshoi Theatre for the gala International Ballet Performance, I identified Boris Yeltsin, the then-recalcitrant-mayor of Moscow, who moments later emerged into the theatre with the Moscovites going wild as we would in this country for a celebrity. That was the moment that I knew a new day had dawned and that the people of Russia had lost their fear of repercussions from the KGB.

Another near–Gulag, Archipelago–event occurred on Arbat Street, a pedestrian shopping area in Moscow, when I brazenly bargained to pay dollars for a lacquered box, which the vendor agreed to sell for "forty cash." He took Shirley Gussio of Vicksburg and me through a fifty-yard-long Sally Port and turned right through a long courtyard, left through an alley, then through a small courtyard, yet another alley, and finally left again where he halted behind a small building. I deathly feared that the KGB would apprehend us and that we would disappear to Siberia, never to be heard from again! I asked the vendor why all the secrecy when I had offered dollars out loud for the box. He retorted: "I did not agree to 'dollars.' I agreed to accept cash, and the authorities do not understand what the word 'cash' means." He left us stranded within the depths of the buildings. When we finally wended our way back and emerged through that Sally Port, Manny Crystal exclaimed, "I thought I would never see you again!"

Chapter 27. Exhibiting for Mississippi

1. The Knights Hospitaller of St. John of Jerusalem who hailed from Mississippi included: Pat Fordice—who was also given the title "Grand Dame"; W. L. "Buck" Stevens; Dr. Brent Harrison; Dr. Robert Smith; William D. Mounger. We each were presented the following magnificent proclamation:

Sovereign Orthodox Order

Of

The Knights Hospitaller of St. John of Jerusalem

Former Russian Grand Priory in St. Petersburg

high Imperial Protector his highness

Prince Michael of Russia

Jerusalem 1090-1291, Cyprus 1292-1310, Rhodes 1311-1523,

Malta 1530-1798,

St. Petersburg 1798-1917, France 1928, United States 1977

In nomine Patris, et Filii, et Spiritus Sancti, Amen

Remembering that his Imperial Majesty, Paul I, Emperor and Autocrat of All

Russias,

Elected Grand Master, proclaimed the Autonomy of our order by decree and

through treaties,

Proclamations and decrees of January 15, November 29, 1797,

August 26, October 27, November 5, 13, 29, 1798; February 1, 1799; etc, etc,

and ,

Remembering that his Imperial highness Grand Duke Alexander of Russia

and

Grand Duke Andrew of Russia together with the hereditary commanders of

our

Order continued to promulgate the venerable traditions and history of the
Sovereign Order of Saint John of Jerusalem;
And now therefore, in accordance to the vows solemnly sworn, and upon the
recommendation or our Council, who have hereby recognized the
qualifications of
WILLIAM DONALD MOUNGER
To whom we extend our greeting and confer upon him or her the rank and
title of
KNIGHT OF HONOR
of the Sovereign Orthodox Order of the Knights Hospitaller of
St. John of Jerusalem, former Russian Grand Priory in St. Petersburg
Pro fide, Pro utilitate hominum
Whereby, all privileges, rights and duties appurtenant to this rank are hereby
Acknowledged; and
Whereby We have caused this WARRANT to be issued.
Done this 9th day of November
The year 1997 of the Lord
At the Grand Magistracy of our order
On behalf of the Council

2. I wrote the following poem in celebration of our dinner at the Governor's Mansion:

Grande Dame Pat and Her Knights

Here's to Grande Dame Pat of Fordice,
She's full of virtue with no vice.
Her Knights are commendable, mostly tens,
First, the Illustious, Sir Buck of Stevens;
Then there's the valorous, Sir Brent of Harrison,
The radiological chief of her garrison;
Next, the redoubtable, Sir Robert of Smith;
One who's accomplishments are like a myth;
Last, the heroic, Sir William of Mounger,
The one who's the elder not the younger.
Through these Knights, much has been done,
But hopefully their tasks have just begun.

First, was the matter of medical supplies,
On which St. Petersburg much relies;
The total was more than twenty-five million,
So, sick children may still see the sun.
Next, the Exhibit, the magnificent Palaces,
For which they are proud, with no malices;
Five-hundred-fifty-four-thousand saw this event,
Their compliments for Jackson were most fervent.
They've accomplished much this Knightly Crew,
However, there's plenty they still can do.
Yes! Grande Dame Pat commands her Knights!
To do good deeds, they'll avoid no fights!

Sir William Donald Mounger K.S.J.
Governor's Mansion
Jackson, Mississippi
December 12, 1997

3. Henry Holman of Jitney Jungle arrived with a Baptist group and paid full price. He would have had apoplexy if he had known we had paid only thirty dollars per night!

4. These two rooms contain brass plates crediting their refurbishment to the Mississippi Commission for International Cultural Exchange.

5. We visited the duke's apartment in Madrid, where he showed us the bullet holes in his private chapel from the Spanish Civil War in the 1930s. His apartment also contained many invaluable antiques including the lanterns from the stern of the command ship of his ancestor, Admiral Santa Cruz, who won the historic naval battle of the Gulf of Lepanto on October 7, 1571, forever halting the further western expansion of the Ottoman Turk empire.

6. This is an old West Point saying. When plebes were asked to request additional food for upper classmen from the kitchen, our black waiters would often reply, "There ain't no mo' in the kitchen."

Chapter 28. A Life: Enjoying Family and Friends

1. A significant and controversial religious-political event was engendered through a granddaughter of Edwin Mounger—Ann Leonora

Mounger, daughter of Edwin's son, Thomas. Ann Leonora married a very prominent Georgian, who was a large landowner and possessor of many slaves. Thomas Greenwood died in 1825, leaving Leonora with the land and slaves. In 1844 she married James Osgood Andrew, a bishop in the Methodist Episcopal Church. In 1845 a Methodist annual conference of bishops in Philadelphia, Pennsylvania, directed Andrew to manumit the slaves or resign as bishop. He protested that his wife was the slave owner, not he, with the consequence that in 1845 the Southern Methodist Church was severed from the North and was not reunited until 1940.

2. The Jasper Grays were famous for signing up early in the Civil War and for fighting in many battles, and almost all of them were killed.

INDEX